HISTORY OF WARE COUNTY

BLOCK HOUSES OF THE OKEFINOKEE SWAMP

HISTORY
OF
WARE COUNTY
GEORGIA

By

LAURA SINGLETON WALKER

Sponsored by
The Waycross Woman's Club,
Mrs. Ellen Goodrich Townsend, President

1934
MACON, GA.
THE J. W. BURKE CO.
PUBLISHERS

This volume was reproduced from
An 1934 edition located in the
Publisher's private library,
Greenville, South Carolina

All rights reserved. No part of this publication
may be reproduced, stored in a retrieval system,
transmitted in any form, posted on to the web
in any form or by any means without the
prior written permission of the publisher.

Please direct all correspondence and orders to:

www.southernhistoricalpress.com or
SOUTHERN HISTORICAL PRESS, Inc.
PO BOX 1267
375 West Broad Street
Greenville, SC   29601
southernhistoricalpress@gmail.com

Originally published: Macon, GA. 1934
Reprinted by:
Southern Historical Press, Inc.
Greenville, SC
ISBN #0-89308-034-9
All rights Reserved.
Printed in the United States of America

DEDICATION

"The history of a country is its life which should never die but be handed down through all generations."
Our work has been a labor of love. We therefore affectionately dedicate this book to the Founders of Waycross, Dr. Daniel Lott, Dr. Benjamin Williams, Mr. William S. Bailey and Capt. Cuyler W. Hilliard, who unselfishly created this city and whose memories must be preserved as long as this municipality shall live.
"A country without ruins is a country without memories, and a country without memories is a country without history."

FOREWORD

Looking backward to the time of the early settling of Georgia one finds that inherent hunger for land and room drove the immigrant out toward the unoccupied spaces. For various advantages it was natural to discover that the nearness to one another of several families in particular regions was the normal condition of organizing themselves into a civic body for common defense. Each community thus created was of necessity, vitally related to the colony in which it existed while it continued to utilize its resources and develop toward maturity.

The history of a town concerns, on the one hand, a record of the outward manifestations of its progress through accumulated years, and on the other hand, an analysis and interpretation of its hidden forces, its motives, purposes and character.

During periods of war, from years when Indian savages menaced the infant settlement to the period when the civilization of the world was menaced by foe even more unscrupulous and fiendish, Ware County has made unstinted offerings of her manhood and her treasures for the defense and maintenance of the public welfare. Heroes on many martial fields, and officers who have reached positions of exalted rank and efficient service have shed glorious lustre upon our town escutcheon.

The social life of Waycross has been distinctively democratic—class division and prejudices being commonly ignored in a spirit of kindly fellowship. Family ties are so strong and affection for the home region is so deep and durable that those, who from time to time, have found occasion to transfer their residence elsewhere, never lose sight of kinship with the place of their childhood.

In undertaking the compiling of this book it has been my desire to make it a publication that would be pleasing, not only to the present generation, but to the generations to come as well. We believe we have placed before the people of Ware county an interesting book, faithfully recording in photos and words all the familiar places of years ago, also the scenes of our boys and girls of today, and as years roll on bearing with it the many changes of time and destiny, this work will be of priceless value to those who have sentiment for the town, and the many other familiar landmarks so dear to all Waycross and Ware county people.

In placing this history before the public, we desire to express our gratitude for the kindly encouragement and the more than liberal support we received from the people of Waycross and Ware County. A work of such magnitude as this, involving such a great amount of detail labor, could not well have been prepared without the generous assistance, the hearty co-operation of a large portion of the community; and that such aid has been given us, together with a generally expressed approval of our undertaking, we gladly put upon record.

The author is indebted to Mr. John Greer and Mr. Folks Huxford for valuable information furnished liberally for this History of Ware County; also to Mr. and Mrs. John Lott, Mr. Jack Williams, Mr. Ralph Newton, Mrs. T. B. Folsom, Dr. B. H. Minchew, Mr. Liston Elkins, Miss Dorothy Blythe, and Mrs. Mattie Thigpen Williams who have assisted in this work in an untiring way. Especially am I endebted to Dr. A. H. Wright of Cornell University for the maps that appear in this book, also for pictures of the Okefinokee Swamp, where he spent many months pursuing intensive Biological Reconnaissance of this Wonderland of Southern Georgia.

CONTENTS

Page

CHAPTER I ------------------------------------- 1

Spanish Explorers—Hernando De Soto—Osceola, A Citizen of Ware—Billy Bowlegs of Billy's Island—The Wilde's Massacre—The Treaty—Indian Trading Houses—Seminole Indians—Two Indian Girls Captured in Ware—Memories of Indian Days—Forts and Block Houses.

CHAPTER II ------------------------------------ 19

County Creation—Appling Before Ware Was Cut from that County—Ware County—Nicholas Ware—Early Settlers—Georgia Land Lottery, Showing Some of the Homes of the Early Settlers—Land Lots of Ware—Racepond—Naming Kettle Creek.

CHAPTER III ----------------------------------- 37

Churchyard Record—Kettle Creek Cemetery—Mount Pleasant Cemetery.

CHAPTER IV—*Rivers of Ware* -------------------- 44

Satilla River—Suwanee River.

CHAPTER V ------------------------------------- 50

Okefinokee Swamp—Okefinokee, the Beautiful—Looking Backward Over a Century.

CHAPTER VI—*Trails and Roads* ------------------ 58

To Old County Road—Trails, Roads and Highways—The Old Train Road—Kennard Settlement and Trail—Blackshear's Trail—Columbus or Market Road—Barnard's Trail—Okefinokee Swamp Trails—Dixie Highway South of Waycross.

CONTENTS

Page

CHAPTER VII ------ 80

 Georgia Taverns—Tebeauville—Tebeauville Tablet Unveiled—Waycross—How Waycross Received Her Name—Waresboro—Waresboro Lodge Number 217—Trees of Ware County—Trees of Waresboro—Soil of Ware County—Memories of Long Ago and Some of the Men Who Gave Character to Waycross.

CHAPTER VIII ------ 109

 Some of the Oldest Churches of Ware—Trinity Methodist—Love Feasts at Waycross—First Methodist—First Presbyterian—First Baptist—Grace Episcopal—Catholic—Central Baptist—First Christian.

CHAPTER IX ------ 128

 Ware County's First Schools—Waycross Schools—Waresboro Schools and Other Ware County Schools—Record of the Members of the Board of Education—School Chronology.

CHAPTER X ------ 144

 Happenings in Waycross.

CHAPTER XI ------ 150

 Utilities—Gas and Coke Company—Ware's First Board of Health—Waycross Water Works—Waycross Fair Association—Waycross Concert Band—Waycross Rifles.

CHAPTER XII ------ 159

 First Merchants of Waycross—Glimpse Into Past Activities.

CHAPTER XIII ------ 162

 Politics—Prohibition—Loving Cup.

CONTENTS

Page

CHAPTER XIV—*Waycross Newspapers* ------------------167

    Waycross Headlight—Waycross Reporter—Waycross Evening Herald—Waycross Journal—Journal-Herald—The Millwood Advance.

CHAPTER XV—*Co-operative Extension Work* -------------174

    4-H Clubs of Ware County—Pure Bred Pigs—First Canning Clubs of Ware.

CHAPTER XVI—*Social and Civic Organizations* ----------181

    Waycross Clubs—Lyman Hall Chapter D. A. R.—Jonathan Bryan Chapter D. A. R.—Francis S. Barton Chapter U. D. C.—The Children of the Confederacy—Hospital Association—Kings Daughters and Sons.

CHAPTER XVII—*Military* -----------------------------197

    Revolutionary Soldiers of Ware—Ware's Unknown Soldier—Captain North's Militia Company—Captain J. J. North—Miscellaneous—Indian War Troops of 1838—Ware Heroes of 1838—War Between the States—War Records—Marked Confederate Graves—Reminiscences of War Life—Joel Sweat's War Reminiscences—Stories of the War of 1861—History of South Georgia Camp U. C. V.—Cannon in Phoenix Park—Going Away—Flanders Field—Ware County Men Who Died in Service during the World War—Red Cross—Canteen.

CHAPTER XVIII—*County Officers* ---------------------297

    Ordinaries of Ware—Sheriffs of Ware—Treasurers of Ware—Justices of the Inferior Court—Clerks of the Inferior Court—Justices of Peace, Waresboro—Justices of Peace, Waycross—County Officer's Bonds—District and County Senators — Congressional Districts — Solicitor — Brunswick Circuit.

CONTENTS

Page

CHAPTER XIX—*Story of a Tragic Death* ---------------316

　　In Memoriam—An Old Southern Mammy, The Last of Her Race.

CHAPTER XX --320

　　The Negroes of Ware—Evelina Hilliard—King Scarlett—Stiles Scarlett—Floyd Swelson—Adella Dawson—

CHAPTER XXI—*Hundredth Anniversary of Ware County* --325

BIOGRAPHIES ---------------------------------------329

ILLUSTRATIONS

	Page
Block Houses of the Okefinokee Swamp	Frontispiece
An Old Southern Mammy, the Last of Her Race	319
Atwell, Mrs., and one of Her Canning Club Girls	177
Bailey, William	90
Bailey, Mrs. William	90
Bennett, Hon. John W.	341
Billy Bowlegs	5
Bradshaw, Mrs. Herbert M.	196
Cox, John M.	61
Debatable Land, Which is Situated Between the Altamaha River and the Satilla River	45
Dimmock, Mrs. Edith	196
Dixie Highway	63
Entrance to Suwanee River	48
Fort Jackson, Where the Treaty of 1814 was Made With the Creek Indians	10
Goodrich, Mr. Walter	387
Goodrich, Mrs. Walter	387
Hilliard, Cuyler	91
Hilliard, Mrs. Cuyler	91
Hilliard, Joe and Evelina	321
Hinson, W. L.	401
In the Heart of the Okefinokee	51
Jenkins, Mrs. Lucius	408
Lott, Dr. Daniel	88
Lott, Mrs. Daniel	88
Lott, Mrs. Walter	422
Lott, Walter	422
Lott, Judge and Mrs. Warren	425
Lott, Mr. John	427

ILLUSTRATIONS

Lott, Mrs. John	427
Mattox, Charles	60
Mitchell, Joseph	60
McDonald, Col. William	432
Murphy, Mr. and Mrs. Herbert	445
Officers and Board Members Waycross Womans Club	194
One of the Markers Along the Dixie Highway	77
Parker, Mrs. W. F.	457
Parker, William	463
Parker, Mrs. William	463
Pastors Who Have Served Trinity Methodist Church	112
Perham, Judge Alexander P.	465
Quarterman, Rev. and Mrs. John Way	470
Red Bay (Gordonia Lasianthus) Edge of Pine Barren Near Starling Branch on Chesser Island Road	53
Rivers of Ware County	47
Rollison, Mrs. J. A.	196
Sharp, Mrs. Fannie Lott	423
Showing New Road Leading to Fort Jackson	8
Stanton, Valentine	495
Sweat, Brig. General J. L.	505
Sweat, Carey M.	509
Thomas, Hon. Banner H.	513
Thomas, Rev. W. H. (Uncle)	515
Townsend, Mrs. William G.	196
Unveiling a Tablet That Marks Old Tebeauville	86
Walker, Mrs. Laura Singleton	Facing Page 15
Ware County as Cut From the Tallassee Country	11
Waresboro High School Pupils and Trustees	96
Wilson Highway to Washington, D. C.	62
Williams, Mrs. Benjamin	89
Williams, Dr. Benjamin	89
Williams, Jack	522
Woodward, Dawson W.	61

MRS. LAURA SINGLETON WALKER

THE AUTHOR, MRS. J. L. WALKER

By John W. Greer

By right of achievement as well as fitness, Mrs. John L. Walker of Waycross was selected by the authorities of Ware to write the history of the county.

Since a history of Ware county, without mention of Mrs. Walker would be as a flower without its fragrance, it must needs that one of her numerous friends have the honor to contribute this brief sketch, and owing to my long acquaintance with her and family, the privilege has been granted me. I glory in paying this tribute to her, the author of this work, a free service to her beloved home and people, perhaps the last public service, she says, she will attempt—the crowning glory of her life.

By temperament Mrs. Walker is a natural born writer and by self-determination she has achieved a reputation and fame that extends not only over the State of Georgia, but over the South where her ancestors have been prominent since the inception of the nation.

Especially has she won great favor over South Georgia where her radiant personality has been so identified and her historical work, so valuable in bringing to life the dead records of this section, that her name will live throughout the ages as a brilliant and charming part of this territory, much of whose history lay dormant and forgotten until her supreme devotion and untiring energy began to unearth the dead cities and overgrown trails of the early part of this nation.

A large part of the population of this territory little dreamed how rich in history is this coastal plain section of the state, and only those who have followed her throughout the rehabilitation of its annals know her real worth to this country and how the future will look upon her as a pioneer of our best selves—the things our children will most prize when we have ceased to strive for the common elements of life.

Mrs. Walker is a born aristocrat as well as a born writer, although that is the last thing she would have wished me to insert in these annals. Her greatest ambition is to be known and remembered as a herald of real democracy—a member of society who loved and worked with the masses.

When I asked her who her ancestors were, she replied without apologies or further explanation, "I was a victim of the reconstruction days along with others of Milledgeville."

That was all she volunteered to say until I asked her about her father and his work. "He was my teacher," she said, " and a man of rare intelligence and education." And then I got the key to her rich mind and her predilection as a writer.

Mrs. Walker's paternal ancestors were the Singletons of South Carolina and her mother's people the Christians of Virginia and the Wests of Maryland, either side of which would establish her blue blood, while her nobility of heart, the rich quality of mind and her gentleness of manner fixes her true claim to aristocracy.

Her disposition is so quiet and smooth one would never suspect that beneath it all is a burning enthusiasm that carries her through long periods of persistent effort and nervous strain. And at times, I have seen the flash of that burning energy that completely captivated her hearers either with humor or sarcasm. She knows how to use both with success. It required close association with her to know what a vast store of knowledge she carries with her concerning people and events. She is so modest in the use of her richly stored mind that her friends learned more from her by direction than she would dare profess, unless the situation appealed to her benevolence, to use it for the good of others. She loves her friends without reservation and her greatest joy is to let them know that she loves them and appreciates the best that is in them.

Mrs. Walker has written promiscuously on historical subjects, mostly in relation to the Southern section of Georgia. She is the author of "Dead Towns of Georgia," "Story of John Floyd," "Georgia's Trails and Roads," "Stories of Some Old Church Yards in Georgia," and a pamphlet entitled "Frederica."

Her husband, Dr. John L. Walker, deceased, was one of the leading physicians of Georgia and practically his whole professional career was spent in Waycross where he was honored and loved as few men. Their union was honored by three fine sons and one beautiful daughter. Doctor Robert Walker is the natural successor of his honored sire, and is almost his image in appearance and manner.

It is fortunate for Ware county that she has among her own citizens one so well qualified to do this work which the other counties of the state are doing—preserving the records of people and achievement. Georgians probably have started too late to preserve all the elements that go to make up a full report, but Ware, at least, can rest in the assurance that hers is first or among the first in quality and completeness.

CHAPTER I

INDIAN AND SPANISH HISTORY

SPANISH EXPLORERS

COLUMBUS—PONCE DE LEON

THE great Admiral Viceroy, Christopher Columbus, once remarked: "I have established all that I supposed—the existence of land in the West. I have opened the gate and others may enter at their pleasure, as indeed they do, arrogating to themselves the title of discoverers to which they can have little claim, following as they do in my tracks!"

Columbus little dreamed that the ingratitude of mankind would eventually sanction the claims of these adventurers so far as to confer the name of one of them on that world which his genius had revealed.

PONCE DE LEON

Ponce de Leon was with Columbus on his second voyage to the "New World" sojourning for a while in Porto Rico.

Florida doubtlessly owes her entry into European history to this dreamy adventurous navigator. She unquestionably deserves her name which afterwards displaced all previous appelations—La tierra de la Pascne Florida —the land of the flowery feast. Ponce de Leon, after traveling along the coast seemingly for many miles on the eastern and western sides of Florida, part of which became Georgia, returned to Porto Rico, but later became Governor of Cuba and while serving in that office made his home there. In 1521 he made another landing on the shores of the beautiful peninsular of Florida. Often the weather-beaten adventurer and companion of Columbus imagined he heard the voice of a siren ever calling him to the land where "none grows old"—the land of the Fountain of Eternal Youth. He heard the song that never fails to lure the heart of the old—the song of joyous youth, of fresh love and alluring hopes. "Gold and Silver, Fame and Honor! What paltry baubles in comparison with Eternal Youth!"

Ponce de Leon hastened to secure the conquest of the picturesque land of "Bimina", marched forth with men and arms. "His efflorescence, his own resurrection, was the festival he had in mind" when he named the land now known as Florida. While at Apalachee Bay he was wounded by an Indian, returned to Cuba and in a short while died from his wound.[1]

Hernando de Soto

It has generally been an accepted piece of information that De Soto passed through the lands where Irwin (and Ware County) are now located, and some historians think that he probably passed out of Florida through a part of the Okefinokee Swamp; anyway, historic pages tell us that in 1539 Hernando de Soto, a Cavalier of Spain landed in Florida with an army of six hundred select soldiers and proceeded north into the lands of the Cherokees. He encountered on the march dangers and endured difficulties which have no parallel, save in the annals of Mexican and Peruvian conquests. They marched from Osachile through the Apalachee country, passing through a "swamp of such dimensions, so vast, so impenetrable that the Spaniards ever afterwards called it the "Great Swamp".[2] A treacherous Indian guide piloted this adventurous army down a trail leading through this land of cypress and tangled grape vines. The trail was barely wide enough for two men abreast to

---

1. Hernando de Soto and His men in the Land of Florida, by Grace King. 2. By some authorities supposed to be the Okefinokee Swamp; by others the Ohahichee Swamp.

pass in any degree of comfort. It wound like a serpent between the huge trunks of cypress trees, wedging one against another in the dark watery soil; no lights or signs of day, nothing visible overhead but a canopy of grey moss, decorated with coils and loops of gaunt black vines. The path at the bottom was like a trail through a chasm.

The detachment of the army had gone but a short distance into the swamp, when they saw ahead, Indians prepared like stoics awaiting their coming. The hostile army that De Soto found stationed there was composed of native dwellers from surrounding forests to the number of several thousand, painted, plumed, and armed according to their customs. They were soon engaged in a deadly battle. For hours they fought hand to hand with all the fury of demons. The Indians held their own, creeping from tree to tree, hiding behind bushes, crawling on the ground with the noiselessness and quickness of serpents. They picked off the Spaniards, one by one, wounding them by scores, with the sudden storm of arrows, surprising them on all sides. The Spaniards, jaded for want of sleep, were unrelentingly teased into ill temper, accusing the trees of turning themselves into warriors and the sky raining down arrows against them.

The few open spaces where the horses might have formed chances of escape, the Indians had blocked with felled trees, making a barricade of timber and branches tied from tree to tree with vines. Though the Indians planned many devices for impeding the travel of the Spaniards through the swamp, they advanced slowly, finally reaching the open country, leaving many riderless horses behind, and the descendants of these Spanish animals, at this late day, are found in the marsh ponies,[1] that are frequently seen on the islands along the coast of Georgia.

OSCEOLA ONCE A CITIZEN OF WARE

Osceola was a Georgian by birth, he first saw the light of day in 1800 in the northwestern part of the state. His

---
1. Garcilaso de la Vega's History of Florida.

Indian home was located on lands now known as a part of Muscogee county.

Osceola's mother belonged to the Red Stick Tribe, a branch of the Creek Indians. She married William Powell, who was an English trader; he remained with the Creeks for over twenty years. Osceola had the appearance of a full blood Indian and in a lordly way represented his brave race. He was sometimes called Powell, instead of Osceola, but he preferred his Indian name.

In 1808 a quarrel occurred among the Lower Creek Indians; the mother took her young son, Osceola, and left their home on the Tallapoosa river and sought the fastness of the Okefinokee Swamp. Osceola and his mother remained there nine years. Powell and his two daughters continued to live in Georgia for a short time, but later emigrated to the west.

Osceola had many tragic adversities to come into his life after leaving the Okefinokee Swamp, for he found a spirit of insurrection in Florida. While in the Southern part of Ware, they often heard that General Charles Floyd or General Thompson would soon be among them to drive them out under the lash. Osceola met General Thompson on one of his visits to Fort King and was insolent to him, for which offense he was imprisoned. Osceola soon was released but continued his defiant spirit toward General Thompson. Many times he lay in ambush near Fort King, waiting for his opportunity. One afternoon when General Thompson and Lieutenant Smith, not suspecting danger, were walking out some distance from the fort, the opportunity came. Osceola and his comrades fired, killed both the general and the lieutenant. Then, after killing the emloyees at the settler's store, continued their depredations by burning the building. They set off to join their comrades in the Big Wahoo Swamp on the With-la-coo-chee. It was there that Osceola was captured and imprisoned.

Osceola, although only thirty-six years of age, had become worn and frail from active warfare. He spent only a short while as a prisoner at Fort Moultrie, near Charleston, South Carolina, before his death. He was buried on Sullivans Island and a simple marker has been put above his resting place by the Seminole Clan of Indians from Florida.

To Osceola, a Georgian by birth, living in Ware county for nine years, Florida has placed monuments and tablets to his memory and on May 12, 1887, a county in Florida was named in honor of the silver tongued Osceola of Georgia.

Billy Bowlegs of Ware

During the War of 1812-14 and through the entire War of 1834, Secoffee (father of Bowlegs) was quite active in the interest of his race, for he was a respected chief among the Seminole Tribe. He was probably the chief known to the English as the "Cowkeeper," mentioned in the quotations in Bartram's and in the G e o r g i a Colonial Documents, as living well toward the south and spending most of his time in warfare with the Spaniards.[1]

The Oconee chief who participated in O g l e- thorpe's first general Indian Council, was "Oneekachumpa" called by the English "Long King." It does not appear whether Secoffee was his successor or merely the leader of those Oconees who went into Florida. I do not know on what authority Bartram Brinton places the in-

BILLY BOWLEGS

---
1. Information from Georgia Colonial Documents. Page 626.

vasions of Florida by Secoffee in 1750 but the date appears to be approximately correct, and is important as to establishing the beginnings of the Seminole as a distinct people.[1] Secoffee's two sons were King Pain and Bowlegs, and they were the principal chiefs of the Seminoles. The Americans marched on to within a few miles of the Indian's stronghold when the Indian Chieftain with the warriors began the attack from a thick hummock. At first, the Indians could not be seen, but Colonel Newman ordered his men to pretend flight and this pretense drew them out. There was a fierce fight and King Pain was mortally wounded, but the invaders were forced to retreat under the cover of night. King Pain was succeeded by his brother Bowlegs, whose Indian name is given by Cohen as Islapaoya (meaning "far away"), Cohen says that the Alachua settlements were broken up in 1814 by General Jackson and Bowlegs was killed. I feel that the killing of Bowlegs was a mistake, for as late as 1840 Bowlegs was living on an island in the Okefinokee Swamp, and even years since 1840, an island in the Swamp has been called Billy's Island. It was my great pleasure years ago to hear a very interesting gentleman, Captain Burrell Sweat (often called "Uncle Burrell") stop on the street and tell of the Indians that he had known when Waycross had been a small village. He was especially interesting in telling of having bought fish and swamp animals from Bowlegs and that he had often seen him peddling along the sidewalks of Waresboro. Capt. Burrell Sweat often visited the great old Indian Chief at his Island home.

There are three other Billy Bowlegs of the Seminole Tribe, whose history can be found in the Bureau of American Ethnology, but I think this is Ware county's Billy Bowlegs.

THE WILDES MASSACRE

During the stormy period of our country's history, when tragic enormities and cruel massacres occurred frequently along our frontiers, Ware county came in for her

---
1. Information from Fairbanks History of Florida.

share of death from the tomahawk and deadly rifles in the hands of the Creek Indians. This first tragedy of Ware took place in July, 1832, in the Wildes settlement, which is located between what is now Washington Avenue in Gilchrist Park, a subdivision on the south side of Waycross and Du Buss Bay.

Mr. Wildes, an English settler, came to Ware seeking cheap lands which he secured for a mere pittance building a home near where Waycross was later located. At this time United States troops were engaged in driving the Indians out of the Okefinokee Swamp and the surrounding districts, and the settlers grew careless, feeling secure with a soldier's camp on the banks of Kettle Creek, only a few miles away. One day while collecting ash wood in the bay Mr. Wildes saw signs of Indians in the swamp and he came to the house and told his wife of impending danger. Mrs. Wildes besought him to get what things they needed together and leave for the Wilkinson settlement, but Mr. Wildes thought this unnecessary. That night Mrs. Wildes went into the yard where they cooked on open fire and heard the Indians coming. She quickly returned to the house and again asked her husband to pack and leave. All night they heard the Indians but no attack came until daylight Sunday morning when Mr. Wildes stepped from his house. Thirty rifles "spoke" together, but not until after Mr. Wildes returned to what he then thought was safety. He loaded his rifle and opened fire. The Indians killed seven, six of the Wildes family and the twelve-year-old Wilkinson girl. The Wildes' baby was brutally murdered with a lightwood knot which they buried in its head. Four of the Wildes' children and the Wilkinson boy escaped, making their way to the Post House kept by Mr. Stancil, two miles away. The house once stood on the ground later owned by Mr. Dan Williams situated on the road to Blackshear. The Indians burned the Wildes home after having secured all they wanted of the household goods.

Late in the afternoon the soldiers reached the annihilated home of the Wildes family and buried them near where Ben Collins later lived. A large tree is all that marks the graves of murdered pioneer family of Ware county.[1]

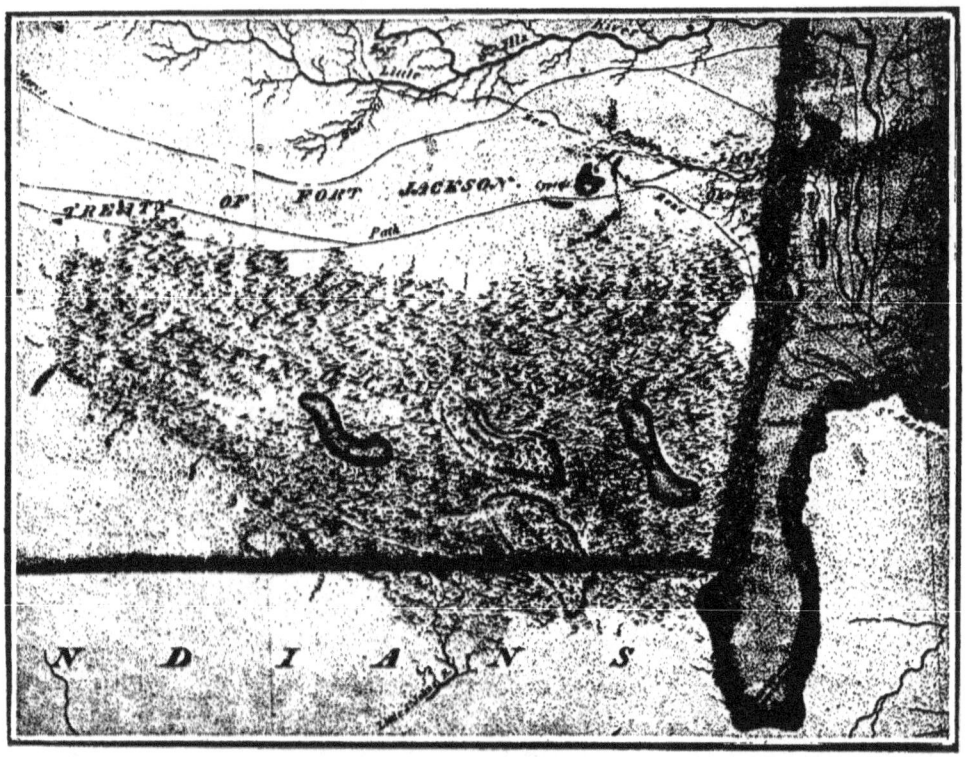

SHOWING NEW ROAD LEADING TO FORT JACKSON

Indian Treaties

Indian treaties that gave to Ware County the Tallassee Country was within the boundaries of Georgia, and were fixed by the original charter. There were four great tribes of Indians: viz: the Creeks, the Cherokees, Choctaws and Chickasaws. These last two were so far away to the westward that they never came into contact with the whites during the colonial period. The Cherokee country was more than two hundred miles from the first settlement on the Savannah River and it was several years be-

---

1. Facts obtained from Mr. J. L. Wildes, the story was told him by his father and Uncle Rube, both of whom escaped at the time of the attack by the Indians.

fore any relations were either sought or established with them.

The first treaties were, therefore, with the Creeks, who inhabited all the southern, central and eastern portions of the province.

On May 21, 1733, General Oglethorpe met the head men of the Creek nation at Savannah and entered into an agreement with them by which the whites were to sell certain goods to the Indians at fixed prices, and to make restitution to them for any injuries that might be inflicted by the settlers. On the other hand the Indians agreed that the trustees of the Colony should have the privilege of settling upon and using the lands which the nation did not want for its own use; pledged themselves to give no encouragement to any other white men to settle there; not to rob or molest the settlers sent by the trustees, and to "keep the talk in their heads as long as the sun shines and the water runs."

The treaties made with the Creeks in 1785 ceded to the white settlers the land known as the Tallassee Country, lying south of the Altamaha River.

In 1790 in reference to George Washington's invitation, McGillivray, the head man of the Creeks, concluded a treaty with Henry Knox, then secretary of war, as the sole commissioner for the United States. This treaty combined with the one made August 9, 1814 with Andrew Jackson at Fort Jackson, Georgia (later Alabama), confirmed the two treaties to give South Georgia the Tallassee County, lying south of the Altamaha River.

TREATY

"August 9, 1814 a treaty was made between Andrew Jackson on the part of the United States and a number of the Creek chiefs at Fort Jackson. By its provisions the Indians ceded all of the southern portion of the state."[1] The Indians, who signed the treaty at Fort

---
1. Indian Treaties of Georgia Colonial Records.

Jackson, acknowledged having violated their treaties and ceded a tract equivalent for expenses of the war. "This treaty was signed by Andrew Jackson and a number of

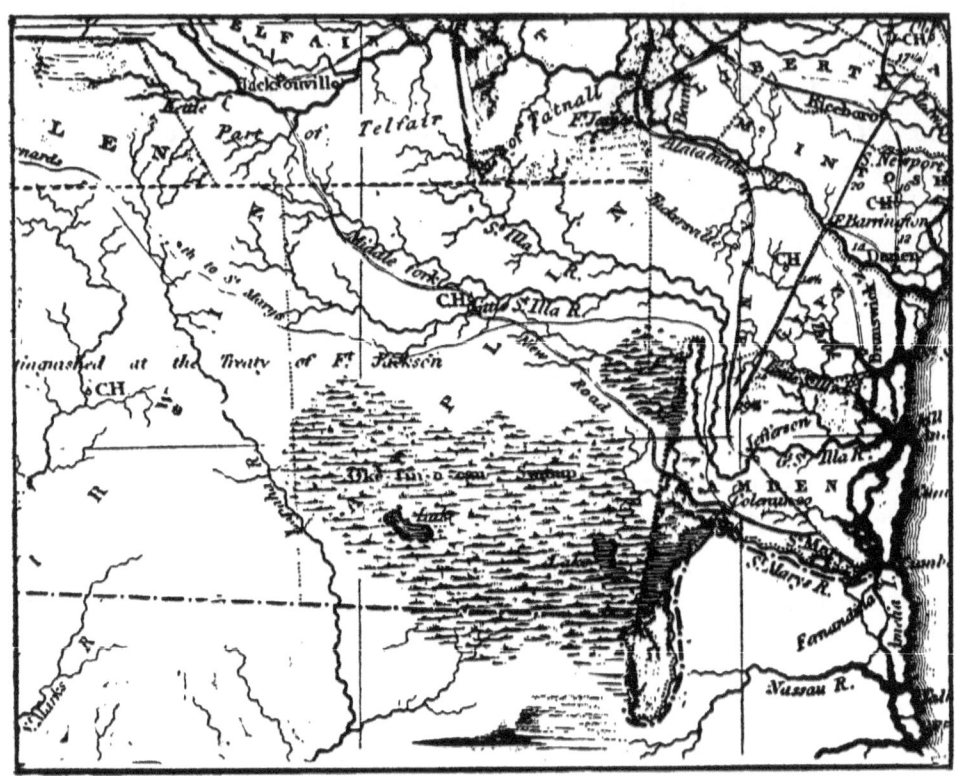

FORT JACKSON, WHERE THE TREATY OF 1814 WAS MADE WITH THE CREEK INDIANS

Creek chiefs, deputies and warriors. The strip of territory lay between the Creek Indians on the north and the Seminole Indians in Florida on the south."[1] This strip of land had been, since the coming of the settlers, a bone of contention between the two races. The treaty at Coleraine confirmed this land as the Tallassee strip.[2] This much coveted section in southern Georgia was a vantage ground between the Indians and the white settlers; both sides contending for their rights. Later a penalty was meted out to the Indians for becoming British sympathizers in the War of 1812, and the Indians

---

1 and 2. White's Historical Collections of Georgia.

were forced to relinquish their claims to the land and it became the property of the white settlers. Ware County was cut from a part of the Tallassee strip.

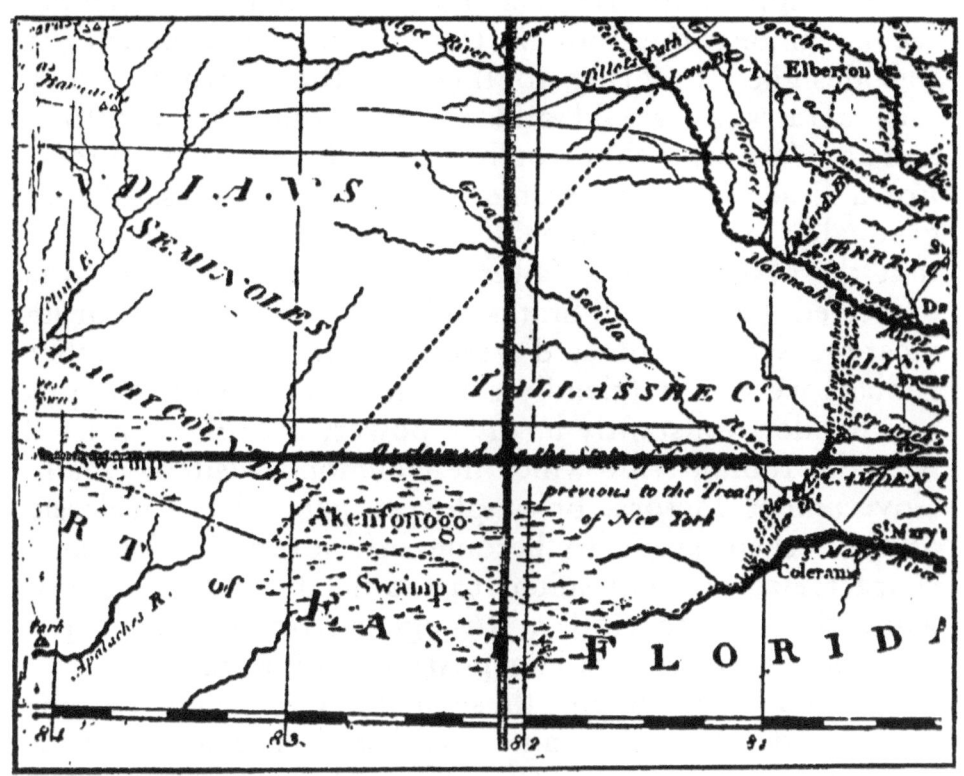

WARE COUNTY AS CUT FROM THE TALLASSEE COUNTRY

Indian Trading Houses

By Act of Congress April 18, 1875, the establishment of Government trading houses was authorized. Soon there were established fourteen trading posts among various tribes of Indians, which were as follows: Coleraine, on the St. Marys river, Georgia, 1795; Jellico, blockhouse on the Hiwassee, Tennessee, 1795; Fort St. Stephens, Alabama, 1802; Chickasaw Bluff, now Memphis, Tenn. 1795; Detroit, Michigan, 1805; Arkansas, 1805, and others.

The post at Coleraine only lasted two years, and was

moved to Fort Wilkinson, and in 1806 was removed to Fort Hawkins.

The United States hoped by the establishment of these trading houses to create a more satisfied and friendly feeling among the Indians toward the Government. It was designed to bring to them in their own territory such affairs as would add to their domestic comfort, and at a fair price that would undersell the private trader. For a time the policy seemed to be most successful, but gradually the Government came more and more to see that the system was a failure. Every trading house was protected by United States soldiers, and the factor in most cases thus protected were indifferent as to whether Indians were in a friendly attitude or not, while the private trader, constantly in their power, became identified with the Indian tribe which he commonly visited. Again, Government factors, or employees generally, carelessly allowed their stock to become inferior and of such a character as was not suited to the needs of the Indians, while the private trader, through adroit measures, put the United States' trading posts out of business.

All the posts except those in Georgia have become towns and cities. Coleraine was considered at the time the Government established the trading post there one of the most important Indian settlements, and Chickasaw, now Memphis, Tenn., one of the most doubtful. The settlers in the early days of Ware county traded at Coleraine.

Seminole Indians

In the autumn of 1838 the Seminole Indians, who were still carrying on their warfare against the United States, made an irruption from the fastness of the Okefinokee Swamp upon the southern frontier of Georgia. The Governor of the state, as soon as he received information of the fact, ordered a portion of the militia to repair to the scene of action, to render assistance and protection to the south Georgia citizens. He selected General

Charles Floyd of Camden County for the command. With his accustomed promptness he met the call. The object of this campaign was to drive the invading Indians from the state and expell them from the Okefinokee Swamp. The service was one of no ordinary character. It required all the fortitude and patient endurance of man to meet the privation and difficulties of the attempt to penetrate this region of solitude. In the language of General Charles Floyd:—"The foot of the white man had there never left its impress; the crawling reptile there basked in warm sunshine upon the miry banks of its turbid pools; the wild beasts there held their court; the savage there retreated as to a fortress, fear of which he might bid defiance to his pursuers." Later the time came when this dark and desolate spot could no longer offer a safe asylum to the Indians. General Floyd pursued the retreating foe to the borders of the swamp, and then began an arduous and toilsome march, such as seldom falls to the lot of the soldier. The swamp was entered, and the whole body of the troops penetrated and passed and repassed through it. General Floyd placed himself at their head and carrying his own knapsack upon his back, he played the part of the common soldier in all things save authority—thus encouraging his men and stimulating them by his example. General Floyd and his soldiers passed from one side of the swamp to a central crossing of the Suwanee river on the opposite side without an encounter with the Indians. They had recently deserted their former abode on a large island, later known as Floyd's Island, in the heart of the swamp where were found many things that had been used by them. Emerging from the border of the Okefinokee, General Floyd and his men had an encounter with the Indians and the Indians were routed.[1]

---
1. Information obtained from the Floyd family records, in possession of General John Floyd's great granddaughters, Misses Zoe and Isabella Blackshear.

Two Indian Girls Captured in Ware

"Think you a little din can daunt my ears?
Have I not in my time heard lions roar?"

Captain Miller must have entertained such thoughts when, in a magnanimous way, he took care of the poor little screeching, screaming, kicking Indian girls that General Floyd and General Hilliard's men had captured near the Okefinokee Swamp in the tall grass that bordered this place.

It was indeed a problem to the men to know what should be done with these two girls who appeared to be fifteen or sixteen years old. The gallant Captain Miller relieved the tense situation by offering to take them home to Mrs. Miller, hoping that she could improve their wild cat tendencies. Alas! the taming of the shrew was nothing compared to Mrs. Miller's great undertaking. These maids of the forest remained with the Miller family for three months and all that they were ever able to teach them was to bring in the wood. They were often locked in a room to keep them from running away.

Captain Miller's family decided that the best place for these girls were with the Indians and, like Hortensio, he felt "From all such devils good Lord deliver us!"

He held a family conference and no objection was made to his suggestion that they be sent to a Seminole tribe of Indians who were located at St. Augustine, Fla. Billy Bowlegs was the chief over this tribe and to his care these girls were to be assigned.

Captain Miller and some of his recruits went to Waresboro and hired Jim Cobb to take the girls back to their own race of people.

Memories of Indian Days

A story was told to Mr. Manning Thigpen by his grandfather, Mr. Stafford Davis, a centenarian, who once lived in that part of Ware that later was incorporated into the forming of the county of Coffee. This is the story, "Indian Days in Ware."

"I well remember the day when our tents were first pitched on this almost unlimited space of wild lands in southern Georgia. Here all was fresh and nature was then primeval and revelled in space. The devouring hand of progress had not then stamped the country with a network of steel, nor had the marks of trade and commerce blackened the skies of blue. The promiscuous hymns of nature, the clarion echoes of our bugles, the baying of our dogs, and all the glad domestic sounds of animals seemed to join partnership with man, and sometimes I feel that I again hear the hearty blows of the woodcutter's axe, the crash of falling trees, and the reckless wood notes of the first songs which these solitudes had heard since the creation. How often I look back upon the pleasures and fond remembrances as a green spot in the almost illimitable garden of the past, for in those beautiful days of the long ago, we not only had our happy days but many anxious days and nights of apprehensive disturbances. We consecrated our cabin in this forest with the affecting and tender name of home, and I have seen many a spot since where nature is picturesque in privacy and seclusion, but none more Eden-like than the little home in the wiregrass settlement of Ware.

"One day I had a vague feeling that we were approaching a cataclasm, and as night came on the feeling of depression increased, but being always friendly with the Ware County Indians—we often exchanged corn with them for venison—I could not feel apprehensive that I would be molested by them. However, there was a spirit of unrest among these poor children of the forest, for they had been notified by the government that the lands upon which they lived were no longer theirs and an army was on the way to drive them beyond the waters of the Mississippi. I soon found that there was no doubt that we in a short while would be apprehended by the Indians, for we heard their war cry a far way off. Knowing of the great disturbance among the Indians and some of the white settlers I had in a way prepared for the safety of my family by cutting a block out of the puncheon floor of our cabin, making a secret passage leading out from beneath the house to the cornfield beyond. The war whoop was rapidly sounding nearer each minute, and the yells of the savages and the sharp reports from their flint and steel rifles rang clearly out on the night air. I hastily barred the doors of the house, for we had no locks in those days, and soon had my children out of bed together with my wife and our infant fled to the cornfield. The startled hares, deers, and other wild animals of the woods bounded away from our path and we soon found a safe retreat in the cornfield some distance from the cabin. The children realizing that danger lurked near did not make a sound, not even a whimper from our baby. They seemed to feel that an impending disaster was lurking close by that endangered their lives. While my family was out of sight of the Indians, they were not out of the sound of their voices and hatchets. They cut down the door, and entered our home, and finding no one there, they seized an axe, butcher knife, some lead and gun powder, leaving the house unharmed. They entered the smokehouse and took all of the dried beef and other commodities and left, singing a chattering song that meant peace. The next day I put my family in the settlement fort, and secured at the Camp on Kettle Creek a squad of soldiers and chased the Indians to the Okefinokee Swamp, where they disappeared among the dense trees and tangled vines. That was our last encounter with the Indians for General Charles Floyd and his soldiers had marched into the heart of the Okefinokee, and gradually drove these men of the forest out on their westward journey."

Indian Encampment

According to Mr. Alex. Eunice, a large body of Indians made camp some three miles southeast of Waycross in 1862. They were of the Creek tribe and were trying to make their way into the Okefinokee Swamp. Mr. Eunice went into their camp where he found them cooking terrapins which they had caught in the vicinity. Mr. Eunice offered them salt and such other supplies that he thought they needed, but they refused. They did inquire of him, however, the direction into the swamp and the following morning they broke camp and moved south.

Forts and Block Houses

There are four old forts in Ware county, located near the southern division of the Dixie Highway. The first on the road is Fort Mudge, a temporary fortification built during the Florida war. It was abandoned when peace was restored. A few miles beyond Fort Mudge is Fort Dearborn. It was also a temporary structure and was about 13 miles south of Fort Floyd, (named for General John Floyd). It is located near the northeast corner of the Ware county side of the swamp. This fort was erected by the United States government and was occupied from Nov. 15, 1838, to Sept. 25, 1839, when it was abandoned. Fort Gilmer, named for Governor George Gilmer, is situated in a bend in the Suwanee river, just where it forks into Suwanuchee creek. Floyd's Trail leads out from this fort and ends on the opposite side of the swamp, at the entrance to Fort Dearborn.

The names of the blockhouses that once stood on the Ware county side of the swamp are: Fort Barnam, Fort Muse, Fort McClain, Fort Mills, Fort Smith and Fort Walker.

Now one hundred years have passed since Ware county was created. The wilderness, the village, the town, have long since changed into a city! A new volume of life and activity have taken their places. Farm lands are stretching out into broader enterprises, in competition with other towns and cities, whose communities come rumbling back in prosperous exchange. The county site, like a great leader, is ever going forward, and is often called by the euphonious name of the Magic City of the Wiregrass.

CHAPTER II

COUNTY CREATION

SOME EARLY SETTLERS OF APPLING COUNTY BEFORE WARE WAS CUT FROM THAT COUNTY

THE first settlers were Nathan Dean, John Taylor, Henry Taylor, Silas O'Quinn, Moses Vickers, John Johnson, John Hawkins, John Smith, D. Redish, D. Summerall, R. Strickland, Samuel Selliars, John Pervis, A. Eason, G. Moody, John Robertson, Jesse Carter, Samuel Carter, Thomas Woods, R. and S. Swilley, B. George, and some of the most prominent families were the Mobleys, Halls, Overstreets and Wilcox.

Those who drew land during the year 1838 and prior to that date were Eric Josnson, Allen McDonald, John Rigdon, Smith Deen, Franklin P. Hall, Louis Williams, William Williams, Wilson Tanner (soldier of the War Between the States), Viney Chancy (dumb), Sarah Legget (widow), Wyton Clary, James Fiveash, Anderson Sanderfords (orphans), Daniel M. G. Wilkerson, Andrew Boyd, Allen Strickland, Elizabeth Sanford, W. Morgan, Solomen Sellers (Revolutionary soldier), William Hurst (soldier War 1861), Ezekiel Cothron, James Fiveash, Jesse Cummey, William Brooker, John Graham, John Williamson, Mary Bennet (widow Revolutionary soldier), Neil Wilkinson, Ivey Smith, (Revolutionary soldier), Lorenzo D. Bowen, John J. North, Evin Asbel, Archibald Davis, George Nelson, Elijah Graham.

APPLING COUNTY

Four years after the treaty made at Fort Jackson, (later known as Fort Oglethorpe, two miles from the city of Savannah), was consummated, Appling County was created by an act of the Legislature which was approved on December 15, 1818. The following counties were taken from Appling: Irwin in 1818, Telfair laid out in 1807, later had a part of Appling added to it during the year of 1819, Clinch in 1850, Coffee in 1854, Charlton in 1854 was cut from Wayne and Appling, Echols on December 13, 1858, and Ware on December 15, 1824. On July 27, 1914, an act was approved creating by Constitutional amendment the county of Bacon. This county was created out of lands embraced[1] within the present limits of Appling, Pierce and Ware Counties.

Appling County was named in memory of Daniel Appling, who was born in Columbia County, Georgia, on August 27, 1787. His father was John Appling, a native of Virginia and on coming to Georgia, settled in what is now Richmond,[2] but later Columbia County. His mother was Rebecca Cater Appling.

WARE COUNTY

Ware County was created by a legislative enactment December 15, 1824, and was named in honor of Nicholas Ware, of Richmond County.

Ware was created out of lands situated in Appling County, and early in the year of 1825 an election was held in the new county for Justices of the Inferior Court, which at that time had charge of all county matters. The following justices were elected and were commissioned March 2, 1825: William Smith, Solomon Hall, John S. Stewart, Jr.; Philemon Bryan and Absalom Thomas. The election for county officers was not held until the next year, when the following were elected: William G. Henderson, Sheriff; Joseph Bryan, Clerk of the Superior and Inferior Courts; Zachariah Davis, Surveyor; and Joshua Sharp, Coroner. At the same time that the justices of the Inferior Court were elected in 1825, Philemon Bryan was elected the first State Sena-

---

1. White's Historical Collections of Georgia.   2. Bernard Suttle's Life of Appling.

tor from Ware County, while John S. Stewart was elected the first representative.[1]

As early as 1818 home seekers began to drift in and settle on land near Kettle Creek. Quite a number came over into what is now Ware from Appling and Irwin Counties. Wherever they formed a settlement they were obliged to build block houses and fortified places called "stands" for the protection of the people who lived in the sparsely settled localities of southern Georgia.

The Indians from Florida often made incursions into the counties of Camden and Ware, who after murdering some of the families, stealing, and destroying their farms, and burning their dwellings, would disappear into the fastness of the Okefinokee Swamp.[2]

In 1840 while Charles McDonald was serving as Governor of Georgia, he was called upon by the pioneers of this part of the state for protection against murderous attacks from the Indians in Florida. Governor McDonald promptly communicated information to the Secretary of War, and at the same time authorized a sufficient force to be raised at once composed of volunteers, to pursue the enemy and capture and drive him from his hiding place. In the meantime he took all necessary steps for the security of the white settlers, deeming it his sacred duty not to shrink from any responsibility when the property and lives of the frontier inhabitants were in danger of being destroyed.

The signing of the fourteenth treaty fixed the territorial lines in which about twenty counties in southern Georgia have since been made, Ware County being among the number. Ware was cut from the Tallassee Country.

NICHOLAS WARE

Nicholas Ware, for whom Ware County was named, was born in Caroline County, Virginia, son of Capt. Robert Ware, who was an officer in the Revolutionary War.

---

1. Huxford's History of Clinch County. 2. White's Historical Collections of Georgia.

There is a difference of opinion as to the date of his birth. One record shows that it was 1769 and another one February 16, 1776. The Georgia Roster of The Revolution shows that he petitioned for 250 acres of land in Washington county Feb. 2, 1784, and also shows that his name appears among the "Certified lists of Georgia Troops". Such being the case, Mr. Ware was probably born in 1769. After the Revolutionary War his father was one of that large number of Virginians who came to Georgia to live. Nicholas was placed in the Academy of Dr. Springer, where he received a thorough English education, studied law in the city of Augusta and attended law lectures in the famous school Gould and Reeve at Litchfield, Conn, Admitted to the bar, he began the practice of the profession in Augusta, and rapidly acquired a lucrative practice. He was several times a representative to the General Assembly of Georgia from Richmond County, and was a capable member of the Legislature, and was much esteemed by his constituents.

In 1819 John Forsyth, then Senator from Georgia, resigned, and the vacancy was filled by the election of Freeman Walker, at that time Mayor of Augusta. Mr. Ware was appointed Mayor to serve out the unexpired term of Freeman Walker, and when Mr. Walker resigned from the United States Senate in August, 1821, Mr. Ware was elected to fill out Mr. Walker's term in the United States Senate. He served as Senator from 1821 to 1824, and in September of that year was in New York at the time of Lafayette's visit to the United States, which was being celebrated in that city. Mr. Ware was taken ill and died there on September 7, 1824. He was considered to be a man of great ability and unimpeachable honor. That he was highly esteemed in Georgia is proved by the fact that in 1824 when the County of Ware was cut from Appling, it was named in his honor.

Early Settlers

No county in Georgia ever had a better class of settlers than those who came to Ware from adjoining counties. Few of them were people of large means, but they were industrious, pious and thrifty.

Life in this primitive settlement was very simple. The farmer raised about all that was needed in the way of provision for family use, such as rice, corn, potatoes, sugar cane, cows and hogs.

Many of the first families lived on large land lots, remote from one another, and made no other effort than to live comfortably, and in an independent way. For years they only raised family supplies, spun, and wove their clothing, handling but little currency. In those days it was difficult to go to market, on account of bad roads, and not daring to leave their families unprotected at home, for fear of an Indian raid. They went once a year to Trader Hill, Center Village, or Coleraine, finding little trouble in securing all needful clothing, some salt, calico, cotton and woolen cards and nails. This was about the extent of their purchases. They always had something to sell. The hides, beeswax, tallow, syrup, chickens, bacon and eggs kept them from ever discussing "hard times".

They sold at the Trading Posts, fat hens for $1.50 per dozen, eggs for 10c and 12 1-2c a dozen, fine beef was furnished at 3c a pound, and fresh pork and bacon at 6c per pound.[1]

The woods and fields at that time abounded with quail and doves, and during the fall and winter, rabbits, raccoons, o'possums and squirrels were plentiful.

The houses were of logs, built by the home seekers themselves, while not very attractive they were comfortable.

Among the first settlers may be included: William Smith, A. Jernigan William Dryden, James Fulwood, John Williams, James Sweat, John Moor, Thomas Allman, Joseph Dyall, Philemon Bryan, Joseph Bryan, W. M. King, M. J. Miller, Thomas Newborn, L. Walker, James Jones, General Thomas Hilliard and M. Addison, John Spikes, George McClellan, Abner Jones,

Hopkins Howell, John Stewart, David J. Miller, William Fowler, Samuel T. Henderson, Hugh Booth, John Inman, Sr.; William Bennett, Daniel J. Blackburn, Stephen Hooker and David Bryan.[1]

GEORGIA LAND LOTTERY
SHOWING SOME OF THE EARLY SETTLERS OF WARE

An Act

An act was passed the ninth of June, eighteen hundred and twenty-five, to dispose of and distribute the lands lately acquired by the United States for the use of Georgia, from the Creek nation of Indians by a treaty (made) and concluded at the Indian Springs on the twelfth day of February, eighteen hundred and twenty-five.

"The section of the state including these lands was ceded by the Indian Spring Treaty of February 12, 1825, which was not ratified and on account of which Gen. McIntosh was put to death by a delegation of his own nation, at his home in the present Carroll County, May 1, 1825. The transfer of this territory to the state was officially consummated by the treaty made at Washington City, January 24, 1826, when an agreement was made that the Creek should vacate on or before January 1, 1827. This treaty was not recognized by Gov. Troup, and he ordered the survey into districts by terms of the Indian Springs agreement. The Federal government and the state became involved in a serious controversy which was not amicably adjusted until the holding of the conference at Fort Mitchell (once in Georgia, later in Alabama) November 15, 1827, when the United States agreed to pay the Creek Indians $28,000 for the territory."

Muscogee, Troup, Coweta, Lee, and Carroll counties were then created to embody the newly-acquired territory,

---
1. Court House Records of Early Settlers—from 1821 to 1828.

and other counties are subdivisions of the original five, 1, Lee; 2, Muscogee; 3, Troup; 4, Coweta; 5 Carroll.

In what is now Ware County the lands were surveyed out into squares 490 acres each and which later were granted by the State under the lottery system. It was sold on an average of five dollars per lot and could be paid for by the installment plan if so desired. Those entitled to draw in the Land Lottery were every free white male twenty-one years of age and upward, a citizen of the United States, and inhabitant of Georgia three years immediately preceding the passage of this act, and who had paid tax, entitled to one draw; every free white male of like description having a wife and legitimate child or children under twenty-one years of age, entitled to two draws; all widows with like residence, all free white females, all families of orphans, under twenty-one years of age whose fathers were dead, one draw; those having neither father nor mother living, two draws, provided the person did not draw a prize in the last lottery.

WARE COUNTY

GEORGIA LAND LOTTERY REGISTER NO. 1

This State Register shows that David Sutton and Winnie R. Henderson were the first to draw in the Land Lottery for lands in Ware County. Jabez L. Dowling and Wiley O'Steen were the next fortunate drawers of land, as were the following early settlers: Juniper Griffice, John Branham, John W. Smith, J. A. M., and Mary Walker, Dread Newburn, James Drawdy, John Dryden, Nathaniel Permenter, Joshua Sharp, R. S. Bryans, John Hawthorne, Zion Davis, Rachel and James Lee, Joseph Bryan, Burwell Jones, Thomas Hilliard, Joseph Wilkerson, William G. Henderson, Moses Prescutt, Benjamin Hollond, William R. Wright, N. V. and M. Pennington, James O'Steen, George Tatum, John L. Stuart, L. A. and H. Douglass, John Lee, Moses Prescutt, Marrian Wilkerson, William Edmunds, Mark Lott's orphans, Elizabeth Stalbry, David Henderson, William Carver, John Williams, Levi Lee (soldier), Allen O'Steen, Jeremiah Underhill, Claton Jones, Samuel Gutery, Theophelus Keen, Obediah O'Steen, Annie Wigins, Arthur Pitman, Seaborn Goodwin, Lewis Green, James Gillstrap, Deiruis Dowling, John McClain, Jeremiah Underhill, Thomas Newburn, Sampson Hall, James McDaniel, George Jennings, John Guttery, Sampson Carver, William G. Henderson, Mary Thomas, made application for land previous to 1839. Lawrence Smith, Arnold B. Fussell, Jeremiah Walker, Daniel Green, John Fulwood, David Hunter, Lear Tillett, Winiford Dyess, Thomas Simmons, Wiloughby Cason, Robert Dickerson, Elias Waldron, Peter and Nancy Smith, Berryan Henderson, Joel Dryden, John Tillet, William Denason, David Hickox, John McClain, David J. Miller, Nathan Beesley, William Thompson, Specey Rusheon (widow Revolutionary soldier), Ezekiel, S. Miller, Josiah Williams, Benjamin Milton, Edward Mansell, Ezekiel S. Miller, Henry Stone, Willis Cason, William Levins, Hester Beverly, William King (Revolutionary soldier), John Smith, John J. North, William Basley, Allison Cason, Hester Beverly, William Levins, David Sears, Willis Cason, William Guy and Elijah Mattox, who settled in Waresboro in 1830, going there from Tatnall County where he was born in 1798. His dealing in land was extensive, and he served on the staff of Governor Charles J. McDonald as his aide-de-camp.

Georgia Land Lottery No. 3

William Carver, soldier (Motes)	John Gatland .... (Motes)
John Williams .... (Motes)	Thomas Newburn .... (Green)
Seaborn Goodwin .... (Green)	Lawson Hall .... (Motes)
Lewis Green, soldier .... (Lees)	David Sutton, R. S. .... (Motes)
Dennis Dowling	Murray R. Henderson .. (Bryan)
James Gillstrap	John W. Smith ....
John McLain .... (Bryan)	J. A. M. and Mary Walker ....
James Candis .... (Rebecca)	Dread Newburn ....
Jeremiah Underhill .... (Dowling)	James Drawdy, soldier (Bryan)
John Stally (Stalvy) .... (Motes)	John Dryden .... (Bryan)

Nathaniel Permenter .... (Motes)
Joshua Sharp, Revo-
 lutionary Soldier ....
John Hawthorn .... (Motes)
Zion Davis, Revo-
 lutionary Soldier .... (Motes)
Richard Carver .... (Motes)
James O'Steen ....
Joseph Bryan .... (Bryan)
Burwell Jones .... (Dowling)
Thomas Hilliard .... (Bryan)
Joseph Wilkerson .... (Greens)
William Vinzant .... (Bryans)
John Peterson's
 Orphans .... (Motes)
Richard Godwin ....
Sarah Gatland, widow .. (Bryan)
Josiah Sirmans .... (Motes)
John R. Stone ....
Moses Prescott .... (Motes)
Benjamin Hollon ....
Isbin Giddens .... (Bryans)
William Edmunds .... (Motes)
Mark Lott's Orphans .... (Motes)
Elizabeth Stalvy .... (Motes)
Joel Lott .... (Motes)
Lewis Davis .... (Motes)
David A. Henderson .....·(Bryan)
James McDaniel .... (Greens)
George Jennings .... (Bryans)
Sampson Carver .... (Motes)
Annie Wiggins, widow (Greens)
William Miller, Revolution-
 ary Soldier, living in Bul-
 lock, when he drew lands
 in Ware for services in the
 Revolutionary War.
William G. Henderson (Bryans)
Theophhiln Keen .... (Greens)
Obediah O'Steen's
 Orphans .... (Motes)
Arthur Pittman .... (Greens)
Levi Lee, soldier .... (Lees)
Allen O'Steen .... (Bryan)
Clayton Jones .... (Bryan)
Samuel Guttery .... (Motes)
Berryan Henderson .... (Sweats)
James Jones .... (Ware)
Abraham Register .... (Thomas)
Edward Mansell .... (Williams)

Land Lots of Ware County

A little light is thrown on some of the earlier settlers of Ware, by the following extracts from the deed records, relative to Lots 155, 154 and 157 of the 8th district.

Lot 157

This lot is now situated within the corporate limits of Waycross, and embraces most of "Riverside" subdivision. The Lott Cemetery almost touches the southwest corner while the A. C. L. railroad runs inside the southeast corner.

1. Granted by the State to Thomas Newmans of Tatnall county, but can find no deed from him.

2. Deed to one-half of the lot from John Spikes to George McClellan, both of Ware county, dated Sept 15,

1826. Witnessed by Thomas Hawkins and Philemon Bryan, Justice Inferior Court. Conveys "one-half of said lot or so as to include the improvements of the said John Spikes."

3. Deed to same half from George McClellan to Abner Jones, both of Ware county. Witnessed by Hopkins Howell and John L. Stewart, Justice of Inferior Court. Dated Jan 15, 1827.

4. Deed to same half dated Nov. 12, 1827 from Abner Jones to Silas Hilliard. Witnessed by David J. Miller and John Jones, Justice of Inferior Court.

5. Deed to same half dated Aug. 30, 1848 from Silas Hilliard to William R. Wilkinson, both of Ware county. Witnessed by Cuyler W. Hilliard and Austin Smith, Justice of the Inferior Court.

6. Deed to same half dated Sept. 1, 1848 from William R. Wilkinson to Thomas Riggins, both of Ware county. Witnessed by R. G. Dickerson and John E. Dickerson, and probated before John T. Clough, J. P.

7. Deed to same half dated Nov. 1, 1852 from Thomas Riggins to John B. Riggins. Witnessed by William G. Riggins and James Fulwood, Justice of the Inferior Court.

8. Deed to same half dated Jan. 2, 1855 from John B. Riggins to John T. Clough, both of Charlton county.

Thus it will be seen that this lot had improvements on it, probably a home, as early as 1826, as John Spikes mentions in his deed to George McClellan that he conveys all his improvements upon the lot. It is probable that all the parties named to the foregoing deeds, lived upon this land in the order given. All the parties including witnesses lived in this county.

Lot 155

This lot was granted to James Harper of Newton county June 10, 1826, and by him conveyed to James Cobb of Tatnall county two days later. The lot is situated mostly within the corporate limits of Waycross, the B. & W. (now A. C. L.) railroad running the southwest corner of the lot. Most of Deenwood subdivision is on this lot, as is "Winona Park".

James Cobb of Tattnall county deeded this lot to Andrew Boyd of Ware County July 11, 1826. Witnessed by John Jones, Sr., and Thomas Newborn, J. P.

Andrew Boyd of Ware county deeded it to Jeremiah Walker Sept. 4, 1827. Witnessed by John Jones and Wm. P. Fowler, J. P.

No deed found from Jeremiah Walker.

Later, this lot was sold by Richard Bourn, Sheriff of Ware county, to Elijah Mattox, as property of James Cobb of Ware county. Deed dated Jan. 4, 1840. Sold under an execution issued from Ware Superior Court in favor of Abr. Hargraves.

Lot 154

This lot was deeded by William Lord to John Moore, both of Wilkinson county, Dec. 4, 1826. Deed signed in Wilkinson county. This lot lies immediately west of lot 155, and the B. & W. branch railroad runs through it, as also does Kettle Creek.

John Moore seems to immediately have moved to Ware county, as in his deed to this lot, dated Sept. 13, 1827, he says he is "of Ware county". He sold it to Absalom Cassy of Ware county. Deed witnessed by James Bryan and William R. Fowler, J. P.

No deed found of record from Absalom Cassy.

The next deed seems to be that of Salena Taylor of Wayne county to Jeremiah Underhill of Ware county, dated July 29, 1831. Witnessed by Jabez L. Dowling and Mark Addison, Justice of Inferior Court.

Deeded by Jeremiah Underhill to Thomas Newborn Sept. 15, 1831. Witnessed by Jacob Godwin and D. J. Blackburn, J. P.

Deeded by Thomas Newborn to James Gillan Oct. 3, 1832. Conveys all northwest of Kettle Creek of this lot. Witnessed by Elijah Mattox and D. J. Blackburn, J. P.

All of the lot southeast of Kettle Creek deeded by Thomas Newborn to John Rowell Aug. 22, 1832. Witnessed by Elijah Mattox and D. J. Blackburn, J. P.

John Rowell conveys his part to James Gillan Aug. 5, 1833. Witnessed by Elijah Mattox and Thomas Newborn, J. P.

James Gillan conveys the entire lot to Hugh Booth Feb. 9, 1837. Witnessed by James Cobb and G. B. Williamson.

Hugh Booth conveys the entire lot to Mark Addison March 2, 1838. Witnessed by Martin T. Miller and Thomas Hilliard, Justice of Inferior Court.

Elizabeth Addison (presumably the widow of Mark Addison) conveys the entire lot to Abraham Hargraves Nov. 12, 1839, for $225.00. Witnessed by Silas Hilliard and R. McDonald, Justice of Inferior Court.

Lot 156

This lot is located in northern part of Waycross and embraces most of Riverside Park, Northside and College Park subdivisions.

Deeded by L. Berry Watts of Campbell county, to John Newborn of Ware county, April 4, 1838. Deed signed in Campbell county.

Deeded by John Newborn to Silas Hilliard Jan. 21, 1840. Witnessed by Onslow G. Keith and Banner Thomas, J. P.

Deeded by Silas Hilliard to David Cason Mar. 29, 1841. Consideration $150. Witnessed by Eurydice Jeffords and Harmon V. Jeffords, Justice of Inferior Court.

Deeded by David Cason to Hillery Cason April 30, 1847. Witnessed by Cuyler W. Hilliard and John T. Clough, J. I. C.

Deeded by Hillery W. Cason to Josiah Peeples of Ware county Nov. 4, 1852. Witnessed by Berry Walker and W. B. Folks, J. I. C.

Deeded by Josiah Peeples to William S. Bailey Nov. 3, 1857. Consideration $450. Witnessed by David Rowell and Banner Thomas, J. P.

Racepond
By Alexander McQueen

What is now known as Racepond, a station on the A. C. L. Ry., near the Ware county line, derives its name from old Race Pond. Old Race Pond, as its name implies, is a peculiarly round cypress pond, which lies about two miles from the present station and postoffice of Racepond and between the present Racepond and the Okefinokee Swamp.

When we sought to obtain data about this old pond and the still plainly evident race track around it, we could find no old citizen who knew anything about it. We finally sought information from Mrs. Lydia A. Stone, owner of old Race Pond and principal owner of the village of Racepond, and she gave us a rather interesting history of this old race track around the cypress pond.

She tells that her father joined a company of soldiers, who enlisted in the war against the Seminole Indians about 1836, and that her father came as a young man from Coffee county and joined his command encamped at this old pond.

Her father's name was William Smith and in later years, after he became an old man, he told her the story of this camp and how the spot happened to get the name of Race Pond.

It seems that this particular company of soldiers was at this spot for the purpose of capturing as many of the Indians as possible and sending them to the Western Reservation. The Seminoles had retreated to the then almost impenetrable fastness of the great Okefinokee Swamp and these soldiers were encamped on the outskirts for the purpose of catching those who happened to venture out to the mainland.

This gave them a great deal of leisure, as only a few soldiers were on patrol duty at one time, and to while away their leisure hours this race track was constructed and the horse racing was engaged in as exciting past-time, all the soldiers being mounted. It was at a time in our history when there was as much pride in the saddle horse as is now evidenced in the automobile and airplane. In a wilderness country horseback riding was the only means of transportation, and at that time there were a great many excellent saddle horses.

This encampment of soldiers remained at this spot for several months and the race track was frequently used, as is evident to this day. The track today is plainly discernable, the sand around the pond being still slightly packed showing that it was used a great deal.

This company of soldiers remained at this camp until General Floyd, with this company and others, finally penetrated the swamp and drove the Indians out, most of them escaping, going out of the swamp near Moniac and making their way to the Florida Everglades. It was this remnant that escaped deportation and their descendants are yet to be found in the Everglades of Florida.

After this expedition, William Smith and several other soldiers decided to settle in the section near the great swamp. Mrs. Stone states that her father carried her to this old camp and race track and pointed out several things connected with their camp life. Among the things pointed out to her when she was a girl was a grave near the race track of a soldier who was wounded by the Indians and died in the camp. His grave was marked by lightwood markers, but these have long since rotted down.

Mrs. Stone says that she remembers the exact spot where this unknown Indian fighter lies peacefully sleeping. He is unknown and his grave is unmarked, but it was such adventurous spirits that finally wrested this country from the Indians and made it a safe place for the pioneer white settlers.

It was shortly after this expulsion of the Indians that several families—the Carters, Crews and others—came to settle in the section around Racepond, and descendants of these hardy pioneers are still prominent citizens of that community.

MILITIA DISTRICTS

The oldest district in the county of Ware is the Waresboro or the 451st district. It was originally called Hookers District, although this was a local name and not the official designation. Districts were, and are numbered consecutively, the first district, was in Savannah, the oldest one in the state. The 451st was created about 1821, as the first justices of the peace in this district were elected that year and commissioned March 12, 1821. They were Joseph Dyall and David Bryan. Four years later James Fulwood and Samuel T. Henderson were elected and commissioned July 6. 1825.

The old name of Hooker's District was probably connected with William Hooker who was elected sheriff in 1828, and it is very probable that he was captain of this militia district about that time. Each district had a captain for the militia of that district, and for a long time it was the custom to call the districts by the name of the district captain. Each district, when created, was supposed to contain one hundred white men subject to military duty, and each district had two justices of the peace. The state relied upon the militia for its military protection and the Governor was commander-in-chief, and could order them out at any time for the purpose of quelling riots, insurrections, or Indian troubles at any point in the state. They could not be ordered out of the state for service. Thus came the districts to be called militia districts, and while primarily for militia purposes they were in a sense a justice district and still in another sense an election precinct. Georgia is the only state that now designates her justice districts as militia districts.

On certain days of the year each district had its muster day; generally all the districts in a county meeting the same day at the county site. Here they went through the usual military drilling and training for two or three days. Such occasions, of course, drew all or nearly all of the inhabitants of the county and many athletic contests and other attractions were provided. Incidentally, there were generally many drunks and fights, although the people as a whole enjoyed the occasion. However, of late years the militia aspect of each district has disappeared, and while the districts are still known and officially designated as "Militia Districts", it is primarily for the purpose of indicating a justice district or election precinct.

Next to the 451st district, the 584th was the oldest. This district was created in 1825, and the first justices were Elisha Green commissioned July 6, 1825; and on Sept 24, 1825 Thomas Newborn was elected to the other justice. Daniel J. Blackburn was commissioned justice on April 16, 1827, and Jacob Godwin on March 19, 1828. This district was locally known as Holland's District. This district is no longer in Ware.

The 586th district was also created in 1825, and the first justices commissioned were Archibald Miller and Shadrach Sutton. This district is now wholly in Clinch County, known as the Mud Creek district, but will shortly be in the county of Lanier. In those days it comprised a big stretch of territory with only a few settlers in it, extending into the present counties of Coffee, Atkinson and Echols. From the "History of Clinch County", it is observed that the first settlers in what is now Clinch were located in this district in 1822. These pioneers were Josiah Sirmans (born in 1767) and his sons, Benjamin, Abner and Jonathan Sirmans, and John Tomlinson, William Tomlinson, Moses Tomlinson and David Johnson. William Smith settled on Red Bluff Creek the next year. He was a Primitive Baptist preacher, and died in 1841. This district was locally known as Griffis District. The following Griffis lived in this district about this time: Charles Griffis, Sr.; Joel Griffis, Berry and Samuel Griffis, Sr.

The 590th district was also created in 1825, and Jeremiah Johns and William Dowling were commissioned justices in this district August 10, 1825. This district is probably now in Pierce County.

The 719th district was created in 1828, and is now in Echols County. It took in the eastern part of Echols and the present Fargo district of Clinch County. Dempsey Dougherty and Stephen E. Tucker were commissioned justices in this district on Nov 11, 1828. Absalom E. Thomas and Joseph L. Rodgers were their successors and were elected in 1830.

The 970th district was created in 1839 and is now wholly in Clinch County. It is known as the Magnolia District, it being in the district that Magnolia, the first county seat of Clinch was located. The county site was later moved to Homerville in 1860. David Register and Benjamin Cornelius were elected justices in this district and commissioned on Nov. 18, 1839. Two years later both men were re-elected.

The above embraces all the older districts of original Ware county and the reader can get a fair idea of the growth of the county by noting the creation of these districts. Of course, the original districts have been altered several times since their creation, but they retain their numerical designation.[1]

FIFTH MILITARY DISTRICT

WARE COUNTY

First Company	Date of Commission
Captain, John Lee	March 2, 1864
First Lieut., Wm. Wilson	March 2, 1864
Second Lieut., W. T. James	March 2, 1864
Third Lieut., L. T. Taylor	March 2, 1864
Fourth Lieut., Wm. Bailey	March 2, 1864

Copied from Archives of History, Atlanta, Georgia.

---

[1] Information of Militia Districts obtained from Mr. Folks Huxford of Homerville, Ga.

The Naming of Kettle Creek

Immediately after the Wildes Massacre by the Indians the Secretary of War authorized a sufficient force to be raised at once, composed of volunteers of Ware county to pursue the enemy, and advised that they capture as many as possible and drive them from their hiding places. This squad of soldiers were camped on the banks of a creek three miles west of Waycross, and while they had adequate supply of camp fire utensils, they were sadly in need of a suitable vessel in which to make coffee. It was their good fortune to find a well preserved iron kettle embedded in the sands of the creek near their camping place. In the nomenclature of Georgia such names as Suwanoochee, Chickasawhatchee, Colewahee, Muchatoochee, Kinchafoonee, testified that the Indians gave each stream a name from their musical vocabulary. However, the Spaniards, French and English changed some of them. Kettle Creek may once have had a soft rhythmic Indian name, but through the desire on the part of the soldiers to memorialize the kettle found in this limpid stream of Ware, they named it Kettle Creek.

Captain David J. Miller of Ware county served as an officer in this camp, and this story was told by Mr. David Miller, to his son, an honored citizen of Ware.

CHAPTER III

CHURCHYARD RECORDS

KETTLE CREEK CEMETERY

HE oldest cemetery in Ware county is the Kettle Creek Church Cemetery. It was here that many of the early settlers are buried. In 1833 the first interment took place when one of the citizens of Ware, a Mr. Jones, was buried there. The first marble tomb placed in this cemetery was above the grave of Captain William Henry Miller, a soldier of the Revolutionary War. In this place also rests the remains of one of the founders of Waycross, Captain Cuyler Hilliard. This place was once a "show spot" of the early settlers, the moss covered trees were magnificent, and the isles between the lots were wide and green. Here among the graves of a generation that had joined the "silent majority", the boys and girls, the young men and women strolled, and talked of love, and dreamed of life too young and too happy to end.

Each year the citizens who have loved ones sleeping there are called together to put the cemetery in order, and not a foot of space in this "God's Acres" is neglected.

KETTLE CREEK CEMETERY RECORDS

A. E. Blackburn, born March 15, 1811; Died April 21, 1904.

Jesse Deen, born Aug. 12, 1810; died Dec. 17, 1872.

Elias D. Waldron, born Dec. 22, 1856; died Oct. 5, 1885. This man's father, Elias D. Waldron, born June 7, 1811, died Oct 20, 1894. Ramah Church Cemetery Clinch County.

Winifred, wife of G. B. Williamson, born Jan. 1, 1824; died Sept 12, 1874.

George B. Williamson, born July 1, 1811; died Sept. 6, 1880.
Catherine Watson, born 1814; died March 3, 1910.
Ezekiel S. Miller, born June 15, 1812; died March 4, 1863. Son of William Miller.
Martin T. Miller, son of William Miller, born March 12, 1797; died May 2, 1883.
Nancy, wife of Martin T. Miller, born April 7, 1805; died Dec. 7, 1890.
Cuyler W. Hilliard, born Nov. 25, 1825, son of Thomas Hilliard; died April 12, 1903.
James Inman, born Dec. 10, 1814; died Aug. 4, 1897.
Cyrene M., wife of James Inman, born Feb. 16, 1821; died May 24, 1875.
John A. T. Inman, born March 15, 1819; died Dec. 16, 1881.
Pheby Cason, born Jan 26, 1827; died June 15, 1894.
Delila Wilkinson, died June 22, 1887.
Mrs. Nancy Brewton, born August 3, 1804; died Oct, 1846.
Ellen (Dyas) Miller, born 1819; died May 31, 1896.
Nancy Barber, wife of Obidiah Barber, born Feb. 19, 1829; died Nov. 6, 1874.
Matilda, wife of Obediah Barber, born Sept. 9, 1848; died August 11, 1898.
Rosa, daughter of Obadiah Barber, and wife of J. R. Youmans, born Aug. 15, 1877; died 1900.
Mollie Beverly, died June 19, 1906; age 35 years.
Banner J. Waldron, born March 25, 1834; died April 1, 1899.
Samantha Waldron, born Jan 1, 1839; died Jan. 22, 1925.
Harriet Isaac, born August 11, 1820; died Aug 3, 1900.
Carrie Land, born Aug. 4, 1834; died Feb. 9, 1913.
Jerry M. Jefford, died June 19, 1908, age 64 years.
Martha McDonald, consort of Donald J. McDonald, and daughter of Solomon and Elizabeth Mobley; died July 8, 1861, age 25 years.
Miriam, wife of M. A. Thigpen, born Mar. 12, 1857; died Aug. 13, 1909.

Maggie Thigpen, born Sept. 3, 1861; died Jan. 1, 1867.
Travis T. Thigpen, born July 30, 1863; died Dec. 4, 1900.
Mary Thigpen, daughter of T. T. and Mary Thigpen, born Sept. 7, 1848; died Apr. 6, 1906.
T. T. Thigpen, born Aug. 13, 1824; died March 6, 1896.
Mary, wife of T. T. Thigpen, born May 7, 1826; died Sept. 17, 1899.
Barbara Thigpen, born April 8, 1846; died Aug. 16, 1924.
Joseph R. Thigpen, born March 14, 1867; died Dec. 15, 1918.
Elizabeth Blackburn, born June 22, 1849; died March 3, 1925.
Mary Blackburn, born Aug. 7, 1826; died Feb. 9, 1900.
Frederick Blackburn, born Oct. 16, 1862; died Nov. 20, 1895.
Daniel J. Blackburn, born Aug. 16, 1851; died Sept. 25, 1924.
Cynthia A. E. Blackburn, born March 16, 1811; died April 21, 1904.
Mary M. Bailey, daughter of Wm. S. and Mary E. Bailey, born Apr. 9, 1852; died Oct. 8, 1870.
M. J. Inman, born Dec. 19, 1851; died Oct. 1887.
Sarah Inman, born June 3, 1853; died Nov. 23, 1917.
John Bachlott, died Aug. 24, 1873, age 79 years.
Martin T. Clough, son of Jno. T. and Serena Clough, died Dec. 25, 1862, age 14 years.
Col. John T. Clough, died Jan. 14, 1859, age 41 years.
Serena C. Sweat, daughter of Martin and Nancy Miller, died Oct. 3, 1883.
Jane Sweat, born Feb. 12, 1838; died Mar. 24, 1899.
Newton Sweat, born Jan. 10, 1837; died Nov. 23, 1913.
Amy, wife of James Lynn, born July 5, 1823; died June 11, 1893.
Barbara, wife of E. Taylor, born Feb. 28, 1839; died Dec. 17, 1902.
E. Taylor, born April 12, 1834; died Jan 31, 1906.
Matthew Tatum, Sr., born Apr. 14, 1853; died Mar. 21, 1921.

James I. Barber, son of Obadiah Barber, born Mar. 28, 1852; died Oct. 22, 1926.
James Lynn, born Dec. 9, 1818; died July 7, 1906.
A. J. Blitch, born Feb. 13, 1863; died Dec. 23, 1926.
Margaret Lucelle Sweat, born Aug 27, 1862; died April 24, 1913.
Chestine D. Tripp, born June 1837; died Sept. 11, 1900.
James Tripp, born April 5, 1837; died Sept. 1, 1900.
Abraham Hargraves, died May 15, 1870, age 33 years.
Leon A. Hargraves, died Oct. 23, 1882, age 21 years.
Warren J. Sweat, born March 22, 1862; died Sept 14, 1884.
Dr. Randal McDonald, born in Scotland Isle of Skie immigrated to America with parents at age of eight, born April 24, 1797; died Dec. 21, 1864.
Georgia McDonald, wife of James McDonald, born Jan. 22, 1853; died Oct. 5, 1875.
Donald James McDonald, born June 28, 1825; died April 7, 1871.
Minnie M. Jeffords, wife of Dr. G. R. Thigpen, born Dec. 28, 1875, died April 7, 1899.
David J. Jeffords, born Feb. 1, 1853; died Dec. 30, 1893.
Ellen Miller Jeffords, wife of David J. Jeffords, born Aug. 15, 1854; died March 1, 1925.
Minnie M. Jeffords, wife of Dr. G. R. Thigpen, born Dec. 28, 1875; died April 7, 1899.
S. P. Jeffords, born June 27, 1847; died May 29, 1900.
Annie (Jeffords) Walker, born Sept. 10, 1849; died Nov. 6, 1916.
Chas. Oliver Jeffords, born June 16, 1873; died June 19, 1899.
Martin C. Jeffords, born Feb. 12, 1871; died July 29, 1896.
Nancy Purdon, daughter of Nathan and Nancy Brewton, born Aug 12, 1840; died Oct. 8, 1901.
Lilla J., wife of Gordan G. Parker, died Nov. 11, 1883, age 28 years.
Cyrene C., wife of H. Morgan, died Jan. 7, 1867, age 19 years.

Tobitha McDonald, wife of Wm. A. McDonald, died Nov. 7, 1859, age 33 years.

Randal J. McDonald, died Oct. 13, 1885, age 34 years.

Rev. Wm. A. McDonald, died June 4, 1896, age 79 years.

Rebecca McDonald, wife of Rev. Wm. A. McDonald, born Oct. 4, 1841; died March 7, 1907.

Elizabeth, wife of Donald J. McDonald, and eldest daughter of Abraham and Rhoda Hargraves, who departed this life Oct. 17, 1850, age 20 years. Around this grave is a fence, made of the heart of the pine, and put together with wooden pegs (for nails were scarce in those days) any way the pegs were more durable. This fence is truly a relic of the past, for after standing there for 80 years it is still in perfect condition.

Obediah Barber, born July 15, 1825; died Dec. 28, 1909.

William Miller, who served his country in the Revolutionary War, died Nov. 27, 1837, age 78 years.

Amy Barker Miller, died Oct. 23, 1931.

Records collected by Mrs. Mattie Thigpen Williams, assisted by Miss Carrie Perham.

Providence Church Yard

William Combs, born Aug. 25, died March 23, 1911, buried in Providence Church Yard, Ware County.

Wilson Godwin, born July 8, 1815; died Dec. 6, 1894.

Daniel Corbit, born Dec. 13, 1854; died June 15, 1880.

D. E. Geiger, born April 16, 1832; died March 15, 1885, buried in Providence churchyard, Ware County.

Richard R. Corbit, born 1833; died Feb. 13, 1903, buried at Providence Church Cemetery, Ware County, son of Daniel Corbit.

Col. John T. Clough, born Feb. 5, 1817, in New Hampshire, died Jan 4, 1859.

John O'Steen, born in 1832; died May 20, 188_, Providence Church Cemetery.

Records Secured From Markers in Mount Pleasant Cemetery

Name	Birth	Death
George H. Tatum, Sr.	April 15, 1859	Oct. 29, 1928
R. Elizabeth Tatum, wife of Geo. H. Tatum, Sr.	June 30, 1867	June 23, 1917
George W. Edenfield	Aug. 2, 1842	April 2, 1917
Bill W. Wildes	Aug. 26, 1857	June 20, 1922
Eliza Wildes	Aug. 16, 1855	June 21, 1921
Sarah J. Wildes	Sept. 30, 1830	Aug., 1909
John Wildes	1826	March 30, 1881
Laura J. Wildes	Nov. 14, 1868	Jan. 14, 1919
George Martin Wildes	Dec. 7, 1857	April 22, 1887
Priscilla Woodard, wife of M. M. Woodard	Oct. 17, 1846	Oct. 12, 1916
Mollie Stone	May 1, 1856	May 31, 1912
Jasper Beverly,	April 15, 1851	March 9, 1923
Martha E. Beverly	March 23, 1851	Oct. 23, 1928
Ardelia Thrift	May 2, 1848	April 14, 1891
Emily Belle Harrell	March 4, 1820	Jan. 2, 1907
Taylor Harrell	1847	1924
Rebecca Harrell	1870	1914
Bettie Harrell	1852	1930
John Williams	May 11, 1832	Feb. 17, 1894
Nancy Williams	May 24, 1838	Jan. 29, 1928
Neil Aldridge	March 22, 1824	Oct. 13, 1901
Lewisinda Aldridge	Birth unknown	June 28, 1896
Elizabeth Mullis	Aug. 4, 1861	July 29, 1902
Chas. H. Musgrove	Aug. 15, 1849	March 20, 1915
D. G. Eunez	March 18, 1837	Feb. 8, 1897
Mrs. L. A. Welch	Apr. 22, 1847	Oct. 27, 1917
John Harrell	Age 71 yrs.	Nov. 11, 1919
Robert Justice	1860	1920
E. S. Aycock	1840	1924
L. A. Rogers	Jan. 31, 1859	Dec. 4, 1916
Susan E. Scott, wife of L. E. Stewart	Sept. 3, 1857	Feb. 16, 1904
E. A. Martin	Jan. 7, 1866	Feb. 20, 1920
Francis M. Martin	Aug. 10, 1872	Feb. 7, 1920
Winnie Jeffers	Feb. 23, 1835	March 13, 1910
Jacob Summerlin	Nov. 28, 1849	Dec. 22, 1907
Martha Elizabeth Summerlin	Sept. 4, 1851	March 27, 1923
Sarah, wife of D. A. Eunez	May 23, 1813	Aug. 18, 1837

Name	Birth	Death
J. H. Strickland	March 3, 1847	Jan. 28, 1931

"A friend to his Country and a believer in Christ."

Nancy, wife of J. H. Strickland	Oct. 21, 1841	Dec. 23, 1917
Ambrose Woodard	July 14, 1829	Dec. 2, 1895
Ardelia Woodard	Nov. 28, 1838	Nov. 11, 1907
Sarah, wife of Geo. Tatum and Geo. Dunham	1827	Nov. 26, 1906
Lawrence Anthony	Dec. 8, 1818	Sept. 7, 1878
Sarah Ann, wife of Lawrence Anthony	Feb. 17, 1818	July 6, 1897
Lewis J. Henderson	April 15, 1828	Nov. 21, 1868
Bettie E., wife of J. D. Henderson	Age 43 yrs.	Nov. 16, 1837
J. F. Hendrix	Aug. 3, 1818	Nov. 13, 1907
Harriet E., wife of J. F. Hendrix	Mar. 12, 1818	March 14, 1891
Taylor Hendrix	March 25, 1849	July 5, 1925
B. A. Godwin	Sept. 15, 1850	Dec. 9, 1923
Susana Godwin	Age 104 yrs.	Dec. 7, 1897

Tombstone Records Copied by Mrs. J. E. W. Smith and Mrs. Vesta Smith Brown.

CHAPTER IV
RIVERS OF WARE

Satilla River

CAPTAIN JEAN Ribault, while sailing along the coast of Florida, gave French names to the rivers for the rivers in France. He named one "Riviere Somme." Le Moyne later made another innovation by substituting the name Aine (Aisne) for Ile de la Somme. The Spanish invaders renamed the beautiful river that flows through Ware county St. Illa in honor of Capt St. Illa, a captain in the King's Army, but by common usage it is now universally called Satilla.

The Satilla river rises in Irwin county, flows through the northern part of Ware, forming an eastern boundary line of Charlton between Pierce and Brantley, flowing through the southeastern part of Brantley, passing through the entire center of Camden county and empties into St. Andrews Sound in its onward course to the Atlanic Ocean.

All the tributaries of Satilla River rise within the Tifton upland or the coastal terraces. They are apparently sluggish streams with sandy banks and bottoms. Near Waycross the Satilla River is about 150 feet between banks. Little Satilla River, (Alabaha, Hurricane Creek), and Seventeen mile Creek are the principal tributaries. The area drained by the Satilla River and its branches is approximately 3,500 square miles.

Historic Places on the Satilla

Gaspard de Coligni, high-admiral of France and one of the leaders of the Protestant or Huguenot party, in seeking for a place to settle, visited lands near the mouth of the Satilla River. Here they cast anchor and pitched their tents. They were graciously received by the Indian Chief of the country. On the 30th day of June, 1564, at the break of day the Frenchmen assembled themselves at the sound of the trumpet, that they might praise God for their favorable and happy arrival.

On the banks of the Satilla River is located Burnt Fort;

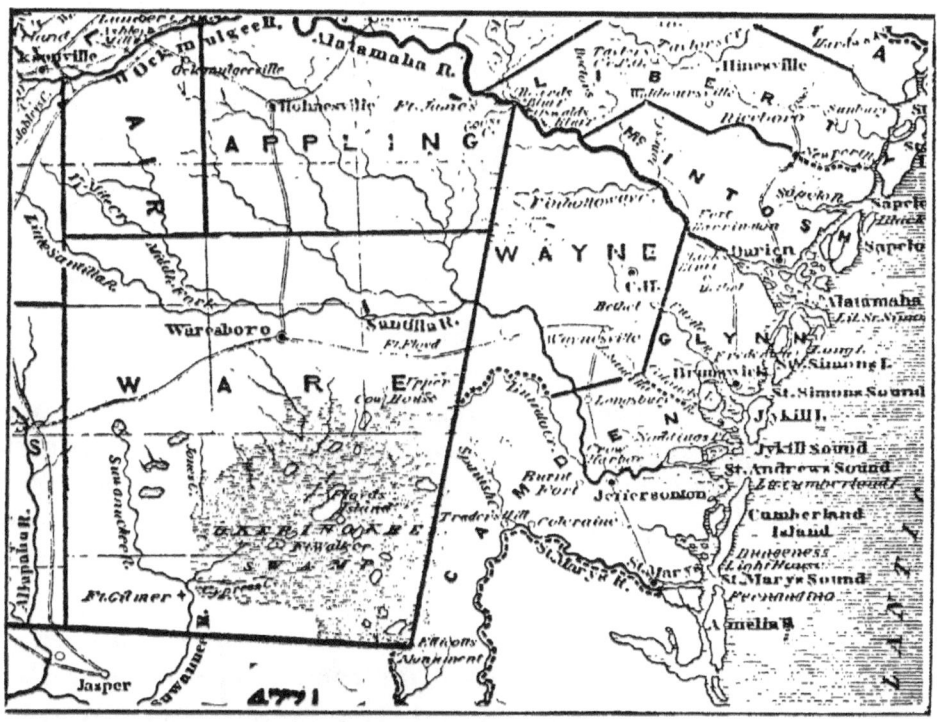

1842-1845—MORSE, S. E. AND SAMUEL BREEZE MORRIS, N. A. ATLAS, MAP 18, GEORGIA, N. Y. 1842, SHOWING THE DEBATABLE LAND, WHICH IS SITUATED BETWEEN THE ALTAMAHA RIVER AND THE SATILLA RIVER

the history of this fort is shrouded in mystery. The founder of the colony may have built it to protect the frontier, or it may have been built by the Spanish as an outpost against Indian invasion. One of the early settlers said it was used before the war to put the "run away negroes in", and it may have been built by the early settlers of South Carolina for the protection of their colony against the invasion of the Spanish settlers in Florida.

During the early years of the colonial settling of Georgia, the land south of the Altamaha River, reaching across an uninhabited tract of country to the Satilla River, was a region known as the Debatable Land. It was deserted and unbuilt (see map). Legally, nothing was settled as to the ownership of this land by the War.

After Edmund Grey was driven from Brandon in the northern part of the state, he and his followers settled on the Satilla River, not far from the present Village of Bailey's Mill. The settlement was named New Hanover. Here outlaws, fugitives from justice, etc., always found a welcome and in time the surrounding territory was peopled with that class of inhabitants. Desperadoes had no valid title to the lands and acknowledged allegiance to no civilized government. The people of Georgia and South Carolina entertained fears that this lawless settlement might cause trouble with the Spanish of Florida or the Creek Indians, and petitioned the Crown for their removal. Commissioners from the two colonies were affronted by order of Mr. Pitt; these commissioners succeeded in inducing the outlaws to remove from the territory and New Hanover on the Satilla River ceased to exist.

This ground along the Satilla River was made historic owing to the unruly frontier men crossing the Altamaha without permission. At the time when Spain's friendship was most important, it was threatened by a violation of the Neutral Ground Law. The northern part of Ware County and a huge part of Appling, Irwin, Wayne, Glenn and a small corner of Camden Counties compose the section of what was called Neutral Ground which was commonly called the "Debatable" Land.

General John Floyd's home, located at Fairfield, was on the Satilla River; it was here that the first boat race in Georgia took place.

Jefferson Town, the original county-seat of Camden, stood on a high bluff of the Satilla River. This town at one time was quite a cotton market, but is now one of Georgia's Dead Towns.

Fort McIntosh, a Revolutionary stronghold, was built in 1776, on the northeast side of the Satilla River, some distance inland to protect the exposed frontier from the attack of the British.

This river abounds in game, fish, trout, pike, pickerel, commonly called jack, several varieties of perch, red breast, brim and mammoth perch.

A ridge runs through the county upon which the town of Waycross is located. All streams to the east of it flow into the Atlantic, and those west into the Gulf of Mexico.

SUWANEE RIVER

The Suwanee river forms the great drain of the Okefinokee Swamp, and rises in the pine lands of Ware County, a little to the north of the swamp. It runs nearly through the center of it, receiving creeks of considerable size during its passage. It flows out toward Florida from the southwest corner of the Okefinokee. This river usually has a width of forty yards and a depth of three feet, with a current of great rapidity, contrasting strongly with the ordinarily diminutive stream of the north branch of the St. Marys. The Suwanee Basin in Georgia contains about 5,520 square miles in the southern part of the State, and includes most of the Okefinokee Swamp. Only the headwaters of Suwanee River, short streams flowing southeastward into Okefinokee Swamp, lie wholly

Granite Shaft to Stephen Collins Foster on the bank of the Suwanee River at Fargo, Ga., unveiled October 27, 1928.
(Gift of Charles J. Haden, of Atlanta)

RIVERS OF WARE COUNTY

within the State of Georgia. Alapaha and Withlacoochee Rivers, much larger streams, enter the Suwanee beyond the State line.

ENTRANCE TO SUWANEE RIVER

A granite shaft, weighing more than three tons, is standing near the headwaters of the Suwanee river, at Fargo, placed there as a memorial to Stephens Collins Foster, whose lilting melody "Suwanee River" made the stream famous in song throughout many sections of the world. The shaft was given by the Hon Charles J. Haden, a patriotic citizen of Atlanta, Georgia, and bears the following inscription:

"Erected in Memory of
Stephens Collins Foster
At the Source of the Stream
Which he made Immortal in Song
Suwanee River."

Mr. Haden, who originated the idea of paying lasting tribute to Foster's name and memory, made this impressive statement on the occasion of the unveiling at Fargo. "Let us never forget that the Suwanee River is a Georgia river, Georgia gave it to the world, and Stephens Collins Foster made it famous".

Dr. R. H. Powell, president of the Georgia State Woman's College in Valdosta, delivered the principal address, calling attention to the world-wide popularity of Suwanee River and others of Foster's heart songs. He said that "Foster occupies a place unique in the song history of the world, and he has written songs that appeal to the hearts of men, and their appeal has been more widespread than that of any songs ever penned. The pioneers who went West in the days of the trek toward the Pacific were led in their covered wagons by the strains of Foster's 'Oh, Susanna'. We cannot help but think somehow, that no home on earth is quite so sweet as a Kentucky home, all because of the magic of Foster's 'My Old Kentucky Home'. We should always remember out of respect to Foster, that the Suwanee River did not make Foster famous, it was Foster who made Suwanee famous."

CHAPTER V

OKEFINOKEE SWAMP

NO PLACE in Georgia is looked upon with a deeper interest than the Okefinokee Swamp, that covers a large portion of Ware county. This place is seldom without visitors who go there for scientific research work pertaining to a variety of subjects. A considerable area in the swamp is covered with small islands of which Floyd's, Billy's, Honey and Black Jack are the largest. On the borders of these islands there is present low hummock land which sustains vigorous growths of many kinds of trees. In numerous places on the different islands are dense growths of small shrubs, almost impenetrable, except where wild cats, bears and deer have made their trails. Beyond these thickets one often finds existing a complete mat of bamboo briars as much as ten feet high and many of them an inch in diameter and armed with thorns which are the real daggers of the swamp. The open march often affords the only support for the feet in wading through the soft springy mud, which yields to the weight of a man, so that sometimes victims have been known to sink to their shoulders in the marsh. Many of the small islands and clumps of trees dot the "prairies", as they are called, and these are generally surrounded by a floor of moss which is sometimes firm enough to hold one's weight and again forms a floating island or surface over the water. In many instances fresh water marsh or saw grass springs from this mass and makes it appear as though it were solid ground. In stepping upon one of these floating islands it will seldom break through, but it will rise and sink for some twenty feet around. Because of this, the great swamp derived its name—Okefinokee or trembling earth.

The Yaupon, holly and magnolia trees add great beauty to the islands of the swamp.

In the prairies are many open holes, free from vegetation and several feet in depth, and in these are found alligators sometimes ten to twelve feet in length, though

IN THE HEART OF THE OKEFINOKEE

otters are more numerous along the streams which connect the main open prairies with Billy's Lake and the Suwanee River. Billy's Lake is about four miles in length, from 100 to 300 feet in width and its greatest depth in places has never been definitely determined. This lake is perfectly clear and abounds in the finest trout and jack fish, which frequently have been known to spring into a boat at night when a light is carried. In summer hundreds of alligators may be seen sporting their unwieldy forms along the banks of the streams, while ducks and other water fowls are found in the greatest numbers.

Just at dusk white herons may be seen settling in the

trees on the banks of the small islands until they look like a solid white wall. Occasionally a goose is heard, uttering his melancholy croak as he flaps his broad wings, ever on the outlook for the hunter's shot. Squirrels are seen more often in the woods on the islands and owls, whip-poor-wills and wildcats keep their respective noises throughout the night time in this great wonder land.

The real beauties of the Okefinokee have been seen by some but few articles and books have been written where its actual charms has been sufficiently described. The moving picture people from time to time have taken scenes of the wild life and naturalists from all parts of the country have visited there often with their cameras, hoping to gain snapshots of some of the wonders which they know exist in our great swamp.

Okefinokee the Beautiful

Few pens have been able to describe the beauty of the Okefinokee Swamp, this wonderland in Southern Georgia, and no brush has been able to reproduce the varied colors of the woods, for the exquisite blending of shades has been touched by a Master hand into one brilliant glow that is inimitable. It matters not how dull one's imagination is, or how dead one's enthusiasm may be, the natural beauty of the Okefinokee will stir every inanimate sensibility into life.

Old trees are there, like grey dusty warriors, that have battled with the elements and have withstood storms of the centuries. Flowers bloom there the year round that are found in no other place this side of the Atlantic, and no ferns are found elsewhere with such feathery fronds that are ever waving on the banks above the limpid streams.

"Big Water" stretches for miles through a labyrinth of moss-draped cypress which is mirrored in a maze of loveliness on the bosom of the stream. Water-lilies are sprinkled everywhere and pitcher plants are there with receptacles full of insects.

Dr. Francis Harper refers to the beauty of this place in his "Okefinokee Swamp as a Reservation". To behold the marvelous array of natural scenery in the Okefinokee wilderness is something apart from all ordinary experiences. It is all but impossible to convey in words an

RED BAY (GORDONIA LASIANTHUS) EDGE OF PINE BARREN NEAR STARLING BRANCH ON CHESSER ISLAND ROAD.

adequate idea of its exquisite primeval beauty, or the emotion it inspires. Practically every piece of literature on the swamp, from William Bartram's account of this "Most Blissful Spot of the Earth" to Will Henry Thompson's fine appreciation, reveals something of the singular fascination that the place holds for those who have been so fortunate as to gain acquaintance with it.

Bear and deer hold high carnival there and birds of rare plumage often stop over in their migratory flights to southern climes. Okefinokee is a refuge for such rare and splendid birds as the wary-billed and pileated woodpeckers, the wood ibis, the sand-hill crane and the American egret. Seven species of ducks are found wintering here; hooded merganser, mallard, black duck, green winged teal, pintail, wood duck and ring-necked duck. In the somber depths of the bays, about the first of June, we may find the nest of the Acadian fly-catcher which delights in the solitude of the moss-draped trees above the clear, brown water. In the Okefinokee is the only place in Georgia where one may find the sand-hill crane and the limpkin.

It is the only place in the United States that still has the Indian trails just as they were when the red men were the kings of the forest. Many of these trails are followed today by cattle which have been instrumental in their preservation. The Indians were poor road makers, had few tools and never built bridges, so their trails lead to the lines of least resistance, crossing always at shallow fords.

The islands of the swamp are connected by those trails of long ago. Old strongholds are there, morose and sullen, giving out little of their defense and departed glory.

Legends cluster about this place that cannot be vouched for and yet why not believe them, since no doubt they pale beside the reality of tragic warfare that took place there in the passing of De Soto and his army.

The Spaniards accused the trees of turning themselves into warriors and the sky of raining down arrows.

On Oct. 29, 1889, an act was passed by the legislature authorizing the sale of the Swamp to the Suwanee Canal Company, which was organized for the purpose of draining the swamp in order to get the valuable yellow pine and cypress timber that grows on the islands. The swamp was sold for about 26 cents an acre and the company attempted to open a canal to the St. Mary's river. However, the scheme proved impracticable.

A large part of the big swamp is in Ware county and is now owned by Mr. Daniel Hebard of Coleraine and Penn.

Looking Backward Over a Century

*"Do you ever dream Carita,
Of a twilight long ago
When the stars rained silver splendor
From the sky of Okefino?"*

The Enchanted Island

Years have almost grown dim in number since the red man inhabited the lands of Southern Georgia. The smoke from their wigwams and the fires from their Councils went out nearly a century ago when they passed down the trail, leaving behind them only the graves of their forefathers and comprehensive traditions of their peaceful, and later, feudal days.

Situated in the lower section of Ware County is a wonderland of great beauty, rich in romance and history, and was once the "Happy Hunting" ground of the Lower Creek and Seminole Indians. The Indians gave this place its name, E-cun-fi-no-can or Okefinokee (Quivering Earth). This swamp is about forty-five (45) miles long and has an average breadth of thirty-five (35) miles, and was once quite a rendezvous for the Indians, as the place abounds in game and fish of many kinds. Bears are numerous there, as well as deer and great droves of other wild animals.

Deep into the swamp the blazed trees tell of camps of the Indians. Splashes of sunlight steal through the dark green branches of immense trees, whose gnarled and twisted trunks assure one that they have seen centuries come and go. The soil is soft and spongy with mold of numberless summers and the trails that lead through the woods are carpeted with centuries of dead leaves. A certain horrified gloom possesses one while passing through this land, and none can fail to grasp the imminent suitability of the Swamp's Indian name, "Quivering Earth".

Long time ago when our state was young and the

years trailed by unnoted except by the notches on a post or tree, some Indians were lost in the depths of the Swamp. The further they penetrated the dark jungle the more intricate became the way. The Suwanee River passed by them as it had hours before, but they saw nothing familiar in the stream that now had taken on a blue hue like a turquoise sunk in the folds of green velvet. Over the river a sheen of light and romance lay, and the hunters saw in the distance an island that to them, appeared to advance toward the opposite side of the river, then recede and deliberately fade into mist. The Indians with deft hands peculiar to their race, constructed a boat that served the purpose of conveying them to the spot where the island appeared to be. The nearer they approached the island the more convinced they became that the place was enchanted. Birds dipped, swayed, advanced and retreated, but never crossed the river that divided them from the mainland. Sometimes music as weird and beautiful as that of the Siren would be heard sinking almost to a sob, and then dying out on the air with soft lute-like tones of an Aeolian Harp. Wafted on the breeze from this mysterious island was the most exquisite perfume of many colored flowers that grew along the river bank. Gardenias and Magnolia trees were seen on every side. As the Indians drew near the bank of the river that washed the shore of the strange island, they were hailed by an elfish-looking being that fled at their approach, but soon returned, accompanied by several beautiful women. They displayed fear instead of surprise at seeing the strangers so near their home. The Indians told them they had lost their way in the forest and were in danger of perishing. The women supplied them with food and warned them to depart to escape the cruelty of their husbands. The Indians saw castles in the distance, the homes of these strange people, and said they were of Spanish architecture. The women urged them to hasten away as soon as possible, and told them that their lives were in danger. They said that the men of the island were warriors and pirates of the most cruel type, and allowed no one to escape who landed there. The hunters after wandering about in the forest for days, at last found the trail that led to their camp. They told the story to their tribe of the Enchanted Island and of the beautiful women whom they called "Daughters of the Sun". Some of the young warriors were in favor of invading the mysterious island but when they returned to the place the island no longer receded as they approached, but was as still and beautiful as a "Midsummer Night's Dream". Not a human being could be seen and the castles were reduced to a pile of Coquina rock. Great clouds of butterflies filled the air, and the cry of the bittern was softened by the music of the Suwanee river flowing merrily on towards the "Land of Flowers".

THE OLD COUNTRY ROAD

Where did it come from, where did it go?
That was the question that puzzled us so
As we waded the dust of the highway that flowed
By the farm, like a river—the old country road.

We stood with our hair sticking up thro' the crown
Of our hats, as the people went up and went down
And we wished in our hearts, as our eyes fairly glowed,
We could find where it came from—the old country road.

We remembered the peddler who came with his pack
Adown the old highway, and never went back;
And we wondered what things he had seen as he strode
From some fabulous place up the old country road.

We remember the stage-driver's look of delight,
And the crack of his whip as he whirled into sight,
And we thought we could read in a glance he bestowed
A tale of strange life up the old country road.

The movers came by like a ship in full sail,
With a rudder behind in the shape of a pail—
With a rollicking crew, and a cow that was towed
With a rope on her horns, down the old country road.

And the gypsies—how well we remember the week
They camped by the old covered bridge, on the creek—
How the neighbors quit work, and the crops were unhoed,
Till the wagons drove off down the old country road.

Oh, the top of the hill was the rim of the world,
And the dust of the summer that o'er it curled,
Was the curtain that hid from our sight the abode
Of the fairies that lived up the old country road.

The old country road! I can see it still flow
Down the hill of my dreams, as it did long ago;
And I wish even now I could lay off my load
And rest by the side of the old country road.

CHAPTER VI

TRAILS AND ROADS

JOSEPH MITCHELL, CHARLES MATTOX AND D. A. WOODWARD, ROAD BUILDERS

WARE COUNTY COMMISSIONERS

THE AGE of the Ware County Commissioners would preclude their names from appearing in the Biographical section of the history of Ware County, for only the lives of the early settlers are included in this volume. This history, however would not be complete without a record and the names of the wonderful paved road builders of the county of Ware. A record of men who build roads must be kept, not like the history of Indian Trails and pioneer road builders were kept, for we must have imperishable records of the progressive men who so unselfishly have built the county roads.

Joseph D. Mitchell, Charles L. Maddox and Dawson A. Woodward built the first paved roads in Ware County. They had to forge their way through the siege of non-progressive voters to accomplish their improved road building and they lived to realize that there is no case on record where any community has ever regretted the improvement of highways. So intimately are the public highways connected with every phase of community life that almost any method devised, to measure the benefits of good roads, is incomplete. It is doubtless true, however, that it is easy for good road advocates to underestimate the difficulties of bringing about a reform in their condition.

The form of good road building in Ware passed through many improved methods and some of the roads

CHARLES MATTOX   JOSEPH MITCHELL

built by the county commissioners will hold up for some years to come; for they are constructed of the most enduring and best selected road building materials.

One of the most conspicuous pieces of work accomplished by Napoleon was the building in France roads and bridges. When asked what was his greatest achievement, he did not tell of the great battles that he had won but exclaimed, "Behold the Roads and bridges of France."

No county in the state has more enduring and more artistic bridges than those that span the different streams of Ware. The outstanding constructive projections put forward by Joseph Mitchell, Charles Mattox and Dawson Woodward for the upbuilding of the municipality they have served, are the bonds for county improvements that have been issued: $700,000 for schools; $630,000 for roads, and $150,000 for a county hospital.

They have ably assisted in eliminating the old one-room community school house and consolidated schools

DAWSON W. WOODWARD   JOHN M. COX SUCCEEDED MR. MATTOX IN OFFICE

are now in many localities of the county. Through their constructive efforts a community club house has been provided for the convenience of the 4-H Club girls and the farmer boys. They also have beautified the county park and grounds around the court house and the extensive grounds about the new hospital.

Although the county commissioners have continually engaged in constructive activities their names are irrevocably connected with the building of county roads, ones which thousands of people ride over daily.

Mr. Mattox has recently passed into the Great Beyond, and it can be truthfully said of him, "Well done, thou good and faithful servant". He did on earth the best that he was fitted to do.

Trails, Roads and Highways

When we travel over crooked roads and even crooked streets, we rarely stop to think that we are passing over some of the roads blazed by Indians or trodden down by cattle. Old roads and trails of our first settlers did not come about by accident for many of them were marked out by Indians, always in a direct route and along the best line of transportation.

The first paths through the state were scarcely two feet wide, and were made by the soft moccasined feet of the tawny savages as they walked silently, Indian file, through the forest. These paths later were deepened and worn bare by the heavy cowhide shoes of the white settlers, while others were formed by the slow tread of domestic animals—the best of all path makers.

A part of the Dixie Highway came down an old Indian trading path, known as Barnard's Trail. It passed through the central part of Ware and passed out of Waresboro on the Old Kennard Trail.

Captain Elijah Blackshear with a detachment of militia opened up a military road, probably used later as a stage road, from the Big Bend of the Ocmulgee River, presumably where Jacksonville stood or now is, in Telfair county, to Camp Pinckney on the St. Mary's River, in 1814. This road was later known as Blackshear's Trail or Road; it is thought that it crossed the Satilla river a few miles from Waycross, at a point where a ferry was operated for many years. It ran through the lot of land

whereon the A. C. L. shops are now situated. It also passes through lot No. 213 in Gilchrist Park.

The old Columbus road extends through Ware on its way to Traders Hill. The Troupville road is blazed over the Old Train road, while a part of the recently-built highway from Valdosta to Waycross is built over a part of both these pioneer roads. The old Columbus road passed through Ware on its way to Trader's Hill. The Wilson Highway, named in memory of Woodrow Wilson, and the Nancy Hart Highway, named for a North Georgia woman who stood her ground with the Tories, passes through Waycross.

A howl of disapproval went up from all old stage

drivers when the railroads became the most popular line of travel, for the trains soon gained a firm hold on the people. Accidents on the railroads frequently occurred, and as often happens exaggerated accounts were made the most of by those who opposed the new mode of transportation.

The first railroad was an experiment, built to carry stone to Bunker Hill Monument. Oliver Evans in 1772 began to experiment upon the construction of a steam carriage to run upon the ground, but it remained for John Stevens to combine the steam carriage and railway. The first rail cars or coaches were run by horse power. It is interesting to read Mr. Evan's prediction, which is as follows:

"I do verily believe that the time will come when carriages propelled by steam will be in general use, as well for the transportation of passengers and goods, traveling at the rate of fifteen miles an hour, or three hundred miles per day." In 1813 he predicted that the time would come when a traveler could leave Washington in the morning, breakfast at Baltimore, dinner at Philadelphia and have supper at New York, all in the same day's traveling. Almost as fast as birds fly, fifteen to twenty-five miles an hour."[1]

Evans' and Stevens' predictions came true. The coming of the airplane prophesied by Tennyson in his Locksley Hall some eighty years ago has been fulfilled.

THE OLD TRAIN ROAD

*"We yearn beyond the skyline
Where strange roads go down."*

Few who daily travel along Gilmore Street in Waycross realize that they are passing over one of Georgia's historic highways. It has ever been a much-used road, being first used as an Indian Trail, followed by a Spanish Bridle Path, next the Train Road and now in

---
1. Excerpts from an article by Miss Clara Patterson, Easton, Md.

some parts the Dixie Highway. It became a thoroughfare from the time it was blazed through the pioneer country, because it was the most direct route that led to four noted trading posts in Southern Georgia.

The Train Road (as it was known) passed over Suwanee Creek, formerly known as Cox's Hammock. After leaving that part of the road that led out from Gilmore Street this wagon trail crossed at Blunt's Ferry and there the road forked, the main crossing at Cypress Creek passed through a corner of the Okefinokee Swamp, not far from Fort Gilmer, on by Fort Moniac going over Pine Log Crossing Place, (named by the Indians) to Trader's Hill through Uptonville, by Bethel Church, Sardis School, Prospect Church, by Coleraine, down a part of King's Road and ended at St. Marys. The other branch of the Train Road extended to Live Oak, Florida.

The families who settled along the road that skirted the Okefinokee Swamp were the Stones, the Griffins, the Smiths, the Lees, the Blunts, the Craverns, the Yarboroughs and the wonderful hunters—the Obediah Barber family.

Massacres and robberies often occurred along the way, but the sturdy pioneers knew little of fear, especially when banded together with their long train of wagons.

However, the white settlers had many difficulties to overcome before leaving home. Saturday was their market day and the women and children had to go along with the men to escape being scalped by the Indians. It was the stealthy step or the startling cry that caused their existence to be anything but peaceful. When at home, the women guarded every inch of ground around their settlements while the men worked in the fields. Tragedies were common; the trusty rifles were often taken from above the door to bag a wild cat, a bear or an Indian.

The train of many wagons loaded with men, women and children carried with them to market the finest of corn, potatoes, sugar cane, the fattest of the flocks and herds, together with hides, skins of otter, wild cats and coons, beeswax and tallow. Noisy chickens and dogs announced their arrival at the trading posts of Coleraine, Traders Hill, Centerville and St. Marys—all at that time situated in Camden county.

Disastrous happenings took place along the old train road in the spring of 1836, and from Pickett's History of Alabama the following account is obtained.

"The Indian sky still remained darkened by scenes of murder and robbery. The Chehaws and Creeks, instigated by William Burgess, a trader in the Spanish interest, plundered the store of Robert Seagrove, at Traders Hill upon the St. Marys river, killing Fleming, the clerk, and two travelers named Moffet and Upton. They most cruelly beat with sticks a woman residing there named Anne Grey.

"Six miles further on they killed families of men, women and children moving in wagons.

"Another murder took place at Fence Pond. This place was twelve miles below Traders Hill. A train of wagons stopped there for the night, and the next morning when the travelers were ready to continue their journey, the Indians made a raid on them, killing one of the men, robbing the wagons and taking all that they could carry with them."

The following letter, dated March 9, 1838, from one of the settlers along the old train road, shows that hectic times existed down in Camden.

"It is my painful duty to inform you of another horrible Indian massacre in this county. On the night of the 16th of March a party of Indians most inhumanely butchered Mr. George Gillette, his wife and two children, and a lad of one of his neighbors who was there that fatal night; in all five. As soon as the information of the deed reached us, we repaired forthwith to the place of slaughter, and I, with a small party of citizens, took the trail and followed it until we became satisfied that they had full time to reach the Okefinokee Swamp; here we abandoned the pursuit as hopeless, for so few men can be secured for the purpose of scouring the swamp."[1]

Another letter received by a St. Marys citizen, dated Nov. 24, 1838:

"It is again my painful duty to inform you of a most shocking Indian massacre—I mean the murder of Mr. John Tippins and family. Mr. Tippins was bringing his wife and children out of Florida to see her parents, and when within a few miles of her father's house, was fallen in with about seven Indians, between 10 o'clock A. M., and 12 o'clock M. Mr. Tippins was shot from his horse, the Indians then made an easy capture of his helpless family and vented their savage spleen by beating them on the heads with their tomahawks. Mrs. Tippins lived (senseless) about forty hours, but did not speak; her skull was smashed in many places by the tomahawk. She died in the arms of her father, Mr. David Mizell. Her children are not yet dead, although the skull of each is fractured in many places by the tomahawks. This melancholy occasion took place in this county last Monday not far from Ocean Pond.

"We are most critically situated. The Indians on the North of us close to the Okefinokee Swamp, on the South in the Nation our market road leading from here to any market accessible to us passes through their gateway. We are here exposed on the border of the Okefinokee down both sides of the Indian gangways to the Nation and no protection whatsoever from the army."

A notice of an assassination that occurred March 28, 1839, near the Old Train Road down in Camden, appeared in the "Recorder"—a paper published at the old capital at Milledgeville.

"On Saturday night, March 11 instant, a party of Indians made an attack on Mr. David Lang's house, situated on the South ferry about thirty miles from St. Marys, and killed Mr. John A. O'Steen while he was sitting at supper. The Indians then made a rush upon the house,

---
1. Information from Pickett's History of Alabama, Mr. Dave Miller, and from some of the old settlers along the road.

which was checked by Mr. Lang's son, a mere lad, shooting one of the Indians who was entering the door.

"The family of Mr. Lang immediately closed the door, which the Indians attempted to force open, but failing retired taking off Mr. O'Steen's horse. These Indians caught and scalped the young negro but it is thought the boy will survive his wounds."

The names included in these letters are often found among people living in Camden, Charlton, and Ware.

The Old Train Road has followed rather faithfully the Indian Trail, Bridle Path, and Post Road. Only now and then an old terminus has been dropped or a detour made to shorten distances or to include a new point of interest. However, the main route remains the same. In years gone by, we as a people were slow to realize how closely these paths, hewn out by our sturdy pioneers through the trackless forest of our state, were interwoven with our real history. An imperishable marker should be placed on every historic road in memory of our military highways, stage coach and covered wagon days.

Kennard Settlement and Trail

Kennard Settlement is located in what is now part of Dougherty county. The founder of this noted Indian Trading post was Jack Kennard (half blood, Scotch and Indian). A part of this settlement lies between Tut-tal-lo-see and Hil-cha-too-chee creeks, and the name only appears on old maps of "Indian Land Cessions of Georgia" published in 1733-1835, while a record of the trail and settlement exists in some of General David Blackshear's letters written in 1812.

Jack Kennard carried on a lucrative commerce that extended to important Indian towns on the Chattahoochee river, also among the white settlers in the Tallassee country.

During the war of 1812 Jack Kennard served as a guide for General Floyd's and General Blackshear's armies, protecting them through the wilderness and fastness of the river swamps. He assisted these soldiers in building block houses for the protection of the white settlers in Southern Georgia. Several years before the war of 1812 he blazed a trail out from his trading post to different Indian towns. The trade which he so much desired was carried on in the Barnard Settlement, a little to the North, now Montezuma. This path soon became an important post road, extending through white settlements and Indian towns of Southern Georgia. It led out from Hitch-e-ee creek in what is now Chattahoochee county, passing through the southern corner of Worth, central part of Colquitt, northeastern part of Brooks, northern part of Lowndes, through Clinch, central part of Ware, skirting the Okefinokee Swamp, passing Coleraine, Traders Hill, and ending at St. Marys.

Information from "Old maps and Old Letters of General David Blackshear."

OLD BLACKSHEAR'S TRAIL

Many interesting facts in the history of our country are being unearthed in the bringing from obscure places the old topographic maps of Georgia. The early surveys show the contour lines of the old trading paths and roads and many of these roads form boundaries of lands in different sections of the country.

The Blackshear trail has the distinction of forming several boundaries in its routing to McIntosh county. This military road is found on several old maps, winding a circuitous route in and out of the once thickly forested lands of Southern Georgia. It passes many miles along the banks of the Ocmulgee and Flint rivers, opening an avenue of protection for the struggling colonies along the coast. Part of the road that was opened for the passing of General Blackshear and his army was followed exclusively in many places, and when asked why he diverted his route he replied: "I like to travel along the banks of the rivers owing to the convenience of receiving supplies for my army." He also had to blaze the road for many miles out of the way on account of the river swamps, and the only direct line of travel that followed to Darien was after the road merged into the old Barnard path in Pierce county.

Blackshear's military road had its beginning from Big Bend of the Ocmulgee river near Hartford, once the county seat of Pulaski. It was cut through the entire county on to what is now Dooly county, passing along the banks of the Flint river in what is now Crisp county.

Here the army camped and built Fort Early. General Blackshear describes the building of this fort by his men, in a letter sent to Governor Mitchell, on Aug. 13, 1813.

The road passed out of Crisp into Lee county, where General Blackshear and his men spent the night at Chehaw village at the lower part of Wilcox, passing directly through the entire length of Telfair. Dr. B. M. Kennon's pharmacy at McRae is located in the middle of the old road, which passes along through old Jacksonville in that county.

It crosses little Ocmulgee into Coffee, through Appling, and here it passes in the Barnard Path, crossing Hurricane Creek into Pierce where Gen. Blackshear, with 5,000 Indian prisoners, together with his men, camped, the ground later being selected for the county site of Pierce county and named Blackshear.

The road after passing into Ware county is designated in the Ordinary's office as passing through lot 212, Gilchrist Park. This road, after leaving Gilchrist Park, passed down the old Train Road that leads out along the borders of the Okefinokee Swamp; here two miles of the military road was corduroyed and the logs are serving today the same purpose for which they were put there over a hundred years ago, making a causeway over the marshy place. It passes Braganza, crossing Spanish Creek at Uptonville, through Bethel Church, Sardis School, Prospect Church, South across Cowhouse just below Starland Branch, comes in then diagonally westward toward the swamp border to the Saint Marys River.

It then traverses a corner of Camden, and cuts through Glynn to McIntosh county.

The soldiers often had to swim swollen streams and raft over their army supplies. No obstacles were so great that they were not surmounted by General Blackshear's intrepid soldiers.

Columbus or Market Road

Columbus road must have crossed many old trails and wagon roads, for in the long ago all trails led to Coweta Town, and to Autosee, the most important settlements of the Creek nation. Tookabatcha, the capital of the Creek Confederacy, was just beyond. When Muscogee county was a wilderness and Coweta and Autosee were the only villages in that locality, many famous trails led up to these towns. The one from Uchee Town, twenty-five miles from Ebenezer, was three hundred miles long, and led through a primeval forest and was the one traveled by General Oglethorpe on his way to the great Peace Council held at Coweta Town.

December 26, 1831, an Act of the Georgia Legislature, signed by William Lumpkin, Governor, appointed a committee of two, Isaac Bailey and William G. Henderson, to mark out and survey a road through the State from Columbus to St. Marys. Eight hundred and fifty dollars were set aside for that purpose. Messrs. Bailey and Henderson were urged to build the road with "Pineheart timber that would last," and the Indians especially advocated the road of wood be used in the construction of the "Market Road". Whether the committee looked upon the small appropriation as some did the amount called for in the Shackleford Bill ("Not enough to scarcely cut the weeds along the road during the year"), history does not say. Three years later, however, an Act of the Legislature, signed by Governor Lumpkin, set aside $7,500 for cutting, clearing, and putting in good order the Market Road, previously surveyed and marked out, from Columbus to St. Marys. The Columbus road was the Highway to the sea, passing the important trading post of Traders Hill, in Charlton county, at that time one of the most active commercial places in Georgia. It led through Center Village in Camden county, missing Coleraine about a mile, although traders who passed along the Columbus road frequently turned into the King's Highway to barter and to sell at Coleraine. The Market, or Columbus road, was one of the longest in the State, and branched out to several trading posts on its frontiers. The "movers" into Georgia, the gypsies and the peddlers, sought this road, for people were living close to the roadside, just as they do today wherever there is a well-built road running through a county. The country people have always claimed that the old Columbus road was cut and cleared by the troops who were annihilating the Creek Indians. It is possible that General Blackshear and his troops assisted in the work.

Through a great many counties, which included Ware, the historic Columbus road is passing today, but times have changed and few ever stop to ask the question why is this old road called by that name, or why has it a name at all.

"Where did it come from, where did it go?
That was the question that puzzled them so
As they waded the dust of the highway that flowed
By the farm, like a river—the old country road."

It's glory is in the vanished years for the old Market Road lost its importance when the railroad came.

Story of Barnard Trail

Among the trading paths that did much toward the developing of Georgia was Barnard's Path. It linked Indian villages in the western part of the State to the Spanish settlements on the southeastern coast. It became a constantly-used path by both Indians and white settlers and each year brought pioneers seeking suitable lands for farms and homes. This path developed into a great thoroughfare—heavy carts creaking with merchandise were a common sight along this path that led to important trading posts at Traders Hill, Coleraine, Centerville and St. Marys.

Barnard's Path was named for Timothy Barnard and it was he who blazed this trail. He was a Scotchman and his wife was an Uchee Indian. He was a well known mail rider during the years of 1796-1805 and often passed through this part of the county—frequently stopping for the night at Traders Hill on his way to St. Marys. He was often the only human in this vast wilderness, traveling for days with no wigwam nor house in sight. In cold weather flint and steel to make a fire, a blanket on the ground for a bed, a bit of provision for himself, corn for his horse and the mail that he carried—this was his equipment.

Timothy Barnard was an early settler in the Indian country and Barnard's store, about oue hundred and twenty-five years ago was an important trading place. Barnard's Trading Post is now the beautiful little town of Montezuma. His son, Tompoochee Barnard, was in the battle of Callabee, serving under General John Floyd. He was cited for bravery as a soldier in the War of 1812, also during that war he acted as an interpreter of the Indian language for General Floyd. Timothy Barnard's half-blood Indian children were noted for their beauty and intellect. They settled near him on the Flint river. It was through the lands of William Barnard near the line between Macon and Sumter counties that the main Barnard Path led.

Early maps in "Cary and Lea's Complete Historical and Geographical Atlas of 1823" show this Trading Path and it is also marked in "Tanner's New American Atlas", also on Sherwood's Map published in 1818. At that period there was no Ware county, it being included in Appling county and was not laid out until 1824. However, Barnard's Path was used by early settlers on their journeys to the Trading Post in the southern part of the State, passing through the central part of Ware county. Burr's Map of Georgia, 1839, shows that the trail passed a short distance east of Waresboro where it must have merged with a trail leading out from Darien to the southeast on to that part of the Darien trail lying south of the Satilla river. The Barnard Path passed over the post road as far as Waresboro—this the early maps of Georgia show.

The Barnard Path forked, one line extending from Barnard Settlement and ending at Beard's Bluff on the Altamaha river in Wayne county. The other path led out from Uchee creek in Alabama, passing Ft. Mitchell, crossing the Georgia line a few miles from Columbus, passing parallel for twenty miles the ancient Horse Path, running out through the following counties: the lower part of Muscogee, central part of Chattahoochee, lower part of Marion, through Schley and Macon counties, passing over the Flint river near the cross road where Barnard's store once stood, following south along the banks of the Flint river, through Dooly, Crisp, and the corner of Turner down through the central part of Daugherty, crossing Ocmulgee Town Path, passing through Worth, Tift, and Berrien, crossing the Alapaha river, passing through the northern part of Clinch, the central part of Ware, crossing Hurricane creek in Pierce county, down through the southern part of Wayne, crossing the St. Marys river, passing over two sections of Charlton county, crossing through a corner of Glynn, down the western part of Camden, then crossing the Satilla river ending at St. Marys.

From the very beginning Ware county was destined to be at the crossing of the way, for before there was a county, four important roads passed along this route and later one of the stage lines was in daily use. Barnard Path, Kennard Path, Old Train Road and Blackshear Military Road are the names of some of Ware county's old highways. There is nothing complex about the name of the county seat of Ware for the name became logical through situation. Waycross is not only a railroad crossing but a place where trails meet.

Okefinokee Swamp Trails

Hunter's Trail

This old trail in the Okefinokee Swamp was blazed by Colonel R. L. Hunter, of Milledgeville, Georgia, who was appointed on Dec. 3, 1856 to make a survey of the swamp to ascertain the practicability of its drainage, and while in this place blazed a trail through the swamp to Soldier's Camp, it passed by one of the Ellicott Mounds, and ended at Trader's Hill.

Floyd's Trail

Floyd's Trail was blazed by General John Floyd and his soldiers. This trail had its beginning at Old Hartford in Pulaski County in 1814, when the company of soldiers were ordered to St. Marys and other sections of Georgia to quell the Indians. General Floyd found after blazing his way through the wilderness of Southern Georgia that the nearest route to St. Mary's was through the Okefinokee Swamp. They entered this place at Fort Gilmer, crossing the Alapaha river, where they took a boat route to Fort Walker, crossing the northern corner of Floyd's Island (named by Gen. Charles Floyd in honor of his father, Gen. John Floyd) passing Fort Dearborn (now Folkston) on to Coleraine, traveling down the Barnard Trail to St. Marys.

Indian Trails and Mounds in the Okefinokee Swamp

The Islands in the swamp are connected by Indian trails extending over the land that surrounds the Islands. One leads out from Soldier's Camp; north of one of the Ellicotts Mounds and winds on to Tehill, and ends at Black Jack Island. From Honey Island a trail goes across a nameless body of land and ends on the banks of the Suwanee river.[1] Craven and Hickory Hammock are connected by a trail.

One trail from the Pocket to Honey Island, from Pocket to Jones Island on to Billy Island, a trail from Billy Island to Minnie Lake Island on to Craven Island, also a trail goes from Billy Island to Honey Island [2]"All these except the last one are primarily through a typical bay forest, tangled and almost impassable. Most of these courses are over old Indian trails which are now little used. Whenever the bay goes between two islands or between an island and the outside mainland, e. g., Chesser Island and the mainland or Jones Island and the Pocket, it is called a "dreen", and the trail is called a "causeway" or "Crossing" in the "dreen". A "dreen", therefore, is usually a narrow strip of bay formation. The trails were difficult in old days and are too difficult for the present. In 1912 we came over Gen. Floyd's corduroy road (70 years or more old) the present trail from the Pocket to Billy Island. In 1912 we tried three trails from different points before we could reach Minnie Lake Islands through the dense cypress bay tangles. The surveyors for the cypress lumber company always find their most useful tool a Cuban machete to cut the liances or cat briars, or "bamboos", (Smilax) which thwart their progress."

Indian Mounds

Indian mounds exist on the following islands: one on Black Jack, two on Billy's Island, one on Jones, three on Floyd, one on Minnie, one on Mixon Hammock and one on Cravens Hammock.

Several years ago while Mr. Hebard's (owner of practically all of the Okefinokee) employees were cut-

---
1. Mr. John Hopkin's map of the Okefinokee Swamp. 2. From "The Habitats and Composition of The Vegetation of Okefinokee Swamp" By Dr. A. H. Wright and A. A. Wright.

ting a road from the boat landing to his hunting lodge on Floyd's Island, they had to excavate through a part of an Indian mound. They unearthed a skeleton, some pottery and beads. The bones of the skeleton were large and in a perfect state of preservation.

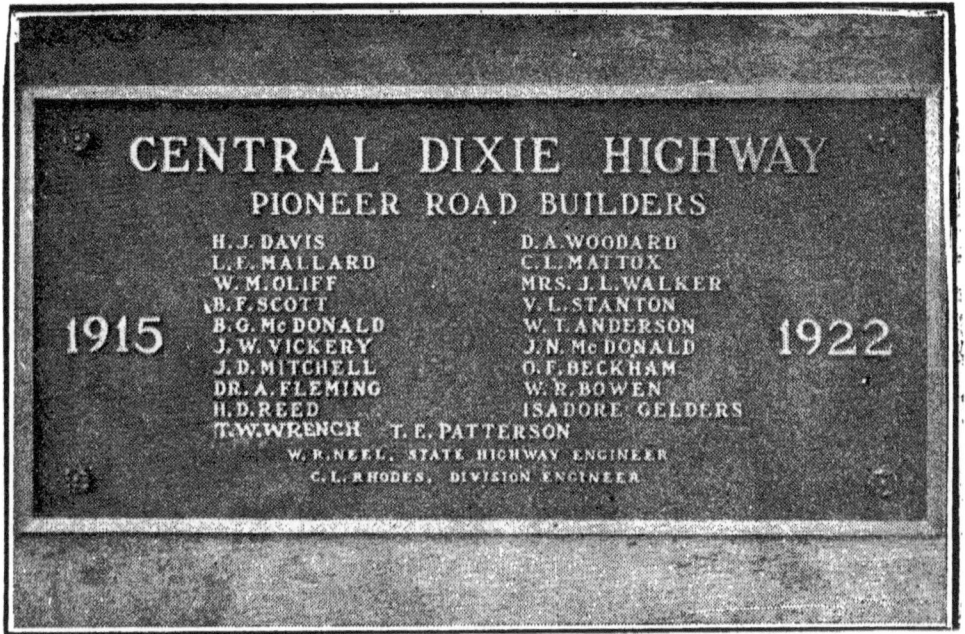

ONE OF THE MARKERS ALONG THE DIXIE HIGHWAY

Dixie Highway South of Waycross

There is no joy in life like the joy of the trail; for on the paved highways "days trip off like a gypsy tune", with the call of the road ever mysteriously beckoning on and on. Dreams of far-off times in a mystical way come, and questions are often in the mind of the thoughtful traveler. Who blazed this path? Was it done by Indians, wild beasts and cattle, or was it cut through the wilderness by the early settlers?

A part of the southern division of the Dixie Highway was cut through the primeval pine forests by soldiers who served in the Seminole War, and a part was blazed by the early settlers living near and along the border of the Okefinokee Swamp. The Highway after entering Pierce county crosses the historic Blackshear military road. Down this old road traveled Gen. Blackshear and his men, who cut the road from Pulaski through Camden and McIntosh counties for the purpose of protecting the southern frontiers from the depredations of the Indians. A letter from Gov. Mitchell to Gen. Blackshear, dated at Milledgeville, Aug. 4, 1813, shows the gravity of the situation and why the road was cut:

"Dear Sir:—From the representations I have received of the fears of our people on the frontier, under the present state of hostility, I have to request that you will proceed to that part of the frontier within your brigade, and adopt such measures as will afford some security to the inhabitants, until the troops now ordered to be got in readiness are marched to the attack of the Indians.

"I have thought since I saw you, that the best mode of securing the whole of our lower frontier will be to erect a fort and blockhouse on the middle ridge over the river, between that and the Ekau-fo-no-ko (Okefinokee) Swamp and occupy it with a suitable garrison. This would save us the trouble and expense of garrisons for all the forts along our frontier and would hold the Indians in complete check."

The Dixie Highway passes a few of the block-houses that were built by some of Generals Floyd and Blackshear's men. The first fort reached is Fort Mudge, a temporary fortification built during the Florida War and a few miles to the north of this fort is Fort Floyd. Fort Dearborn is passed a few miles down the road. These places can be easily located, although built with wood and mud over one hundred years ago, the foundations are still there.

During the Seminole War some of the soldiers under Capt. Miller camped on lands known later as Race Pond. The Indians named it that because the soldiers raced their horses up and down the road. The Dixie Highway now passes over this primitive race track.

The highway crosses the old historic Kings Road at Folkston; but when the new route to Jacksonville was made the circuitous Kings Road was passed over only now and then. This road was once a Spanish trail winding its way mainly by the Indian Villages and the homes of the white settlers. Gov. Grant, the first English Governor of Florida rebuilt the road, extending it from St. Augustine to Savannah. It passed the trading posts at Coleraine and Traders' Hill. These places were a mecca for the Indians, the French, and the Spanish, and on trading days they often paid their full toll in blood for the possession of a vantage point.

Kings Road, ten miles this side of Jacksonville, is paved in brick and passes through a labyrinth of magnificent live oak trees festooned in veils of gray moss. One cannot help linking this old Spanish trail with El Camino Real, and some day it may be traced to the gates of the historic Alamo in Texas.

Thus the Dixie Highway passes out of Georgia down the beautiful road of dreams, with lingering visions of quaint people of other days, into the land of ever-blooming flowers, and the land that leads to the "Fountain of Eternal Youth," the land where none grow old.

CHAPTER VII

LOOKING BACKWARD

Georgia Taverns

One of Note Existed in Ware County

THE FIRST taverns were not built for the exclusive use of the stage travelers, for a part of each building was reserved for the comfort of the townspeople and held as a meeting place for the interchanging of news and opinions. The sale of solacing liquors brought about incidental sociability and the importance of the tavern to some towns was far greater than to the traveler. The places were a mecca for the old men and idlers of the village.

One of the first taverns of note in Georgia whose history and location are being well preserved is Tondee's tavern in Savannah. It was there the citizens of Savannah assembled in response to the first bugle call of patriotism and there the "council of safety" held weekly meetings, and there, on July 4, 1775, assembled the provincial congress, which formally severed the tie of allegiance between the colony and the crown.

George Washington, while in Savannah in 1771, "was conducted by the mayor and wardens to a very good lodging and partook of a good dinner at the coffee house. Dined with members of the Cincinnati at a public dinner given at the same place."

Lafayette, while in Savannah, stopped at a house kept by Mrs. Maxwell. This house is still standing, and is owned by a private citizen of that city.

Among other taverns of less note in Georgia was one in Augusta, situated on the corner of Ellis and Center streets. It was here public sales and auctions of various kinds took place. The "Tory Fox Tavern" was later converted into the Virginia House.

In 1784 Billup's tavern was the popular place for travelers. It was situated on the old Lexington road in what was then Jackson county, but now Clarke. It was in this tavern that a committee met to decide the question of a logical site upon which to build the state university. The committee which was appointed to make the decision consisted of John Milledge, Abraham Baldwin, George Walton, John Twiggs and Hugh Lawson.

Milledgeville being the capital when the tavern was the popular hostelry, had several that were well patronized, among which was Lafayette Hall, the most spacious, fronting on both Jefferson and Hancock streets, Eagle Tavern on Wayne street and Captain Jarrett's on the north end of the same street, near Jarrett's spring. Mrs. Scott's tavern, on the road that ran from Milledgeville to Nickajack, was a place of great comfort and convenience. It was situated thirty-four miles from Cowsewatte Town and eighteen miles from "Daniel Ross' Place" on the Tennessee line, and proved a necessity and benediction for the weary stage coach travelers who were often delayed on account of the deep-rutted roads.

There was a tavern at Cross Keys in Bibb county; also one in Macon that is noted in the annals of the past as having sheltered Lafayette during his visit to that city in 1825. At Indian Springs was the celebrated Varner House. The taverns at Travelers' Rest and at Madison were popular places, both situated on the stage road.

Micajah Williams kept a licensed tavern in the town of Washington. On record we find that he sold, with meals, drinks as follows: "Good Jamaica spirits, per gill, 1d; good Maderia wine, per bottle, 4s8d; all white wine, per bottle, 2s6d.," etc. In front of the tavern was a large picture of General Washington hanging as a swinging sign. John Clarke used to come to town and like most men of his day got drunk. They all did not "cut up", however, as he did on such occasions. He went into stores and smashed things generally, as tradition says, but he always came back and paid for them like a gentleman. Once he came into town intoxicated and galloped down Court street and fired through the picture of Gen. Washington before the tavern door. This was brought up against him later when he was a candidate for governor, but his friends denied it.

John Lamar kept a relay station in Putnam county. His place of "entertainment" was situated on one of the oldest stage lines in the state, which ran from Milledgeville to "Rock Mountain" (now Stone Mt.)

On the old Capital road half way between Eatonton and Madison, the Thompkins Inn had its being and is still standing where it formerly was, a center of life and affairs. It was once the resort for judges, lawyers, the clergy and the laity, politicians and merchants. Men from Putnam and Morgan counties met there to talk over the happenings of counties and state. Like all places of its kind, it served as news disperser, for there were few newspapers in those days.

The old Waresboro relay station was kept by Peter Bedford and was situated at Waresboro (then the county site of Ware), where three stage coach lines crossed. It was a stopping place for travelers going to Troupville (dead town) in Lowndes county; also for those going to Trader's Hill and St. Marys. The noted Barnard horse path, with its single file of travelers, led up to this old inn in order to exchange horses for the journey on to Coleraine and St. Marys.

Many an old tavern is still standing that witnessed scenes of the Revolutionary days and some could once again furnish comfort and cheer for the tourists of today if only reclaimed and put in order. It has been many a day since good cheer was dispensed within these doors, but a renewal of their quaint customs would be popular and many who are seeking new thrills would welcome the return of the inns that once registered a day's journey. The old coach has passed out of existence, the old-fashioned travelers have gone on a longer journey, but the roads are still here and the old-fashioned tavern is still standing where:

> "Long ago, at the end of the route,
> The stage pulled up, and the folks stepped out.
> They have all passed under the tavern door—
> The youth and his bride and the gray three-score,
> Their eyes were weary with dust and gleam,
> The days have gone like an empty dream.
> Soft may they slumber, and trouble no more
> For their eager journey, its jolt and roar,
> In the old coach over the mountain."

TEBEAUVILLE

One can hardly call Tebeauville a dead town, for the lights have never gone out in the village, although her people have moved a mile farther, taking the railroad station with them. On the deserted site an up-to-date railroad shop, which probably cost more than it would have taken to buy the whole of Ware in pioneer days, keeps this old town from being silent, while railroad tracks now cover the level plain of wiregrass. Tebeauville, though not a village of much size, at the outbreak of the war of 1861, nevertheless furnished several recruits to Colquitt's brigade, among which numbered the gallant Major Philip Coleman Pendleton. He participated in several Virginia campaigns and was in the thick of the fight at the Second Battle of Manassas. Lewis Beauregard Pendleton, a writer of distinction and a son of Major Pendleton, was born at Tebeauville. From the pen of this gifted author have come a number of popular books for young people, including: "Blind Tom", "In the Wiregrass", "Carila", "Bewitched", "In the Okefinokee", "The Sons of Ham", "In the Camp of the Creeks", and many others, into which he has woven the scenery of his boyhood home in south Georgia. He has also written an excellent biography of Alexander Stephens. The Hon. Charles R. Pendleton, of Macon, who was perhaps the strongest individual Georgian in journalism, is another son of the distinguished pioneer. Colonel Pendleton spent five years of his early life at Tebeauville and from his son, Charles R. Pendleton, the following facts have been obtained:

"Philip C. Pendleton settled in that portion of Waycross known as 'Old Nine', later as Tebeauville, in 1857. At that time a Savannah company headed by James Screven, father of the late John Screven, was building a railroad from Savannah to Thomasville. The western terminus was then at a point some ten or eleven miles west of Blackshear. The old stage road between Thomasville and Brunswick passed here, with a fork running to Burnt Fort on the Satilla River. Mr. Screven named the station Pendleton. However, the man thus honored took the first train to Savannah and caused the name to be changed to Tebeauville in honor of his father-in-law, Capt. F. E. Tebeau, a member of one of the old Savannah families. Perhaps a year or so later a civil engineer came along surveying the route for the old Brunswick and Albany railroad. When he arrived at Tebeauville he made a side proposition to Mr. Pendleton to run the prospective city off in lots and to give him each alternate lot. Mr. Pendleton did not think that the man was authorized thus to approach him, and suggested that he tell the president of the road to see him in regard to the matter. Miffed at this rebuke, the engineer went back three or four miles, pulling up the stakes as he went, and made a curve to miss Mr. Pendleton's land. If one will stand at the crossing near Tebeau Creek, in the heart of Waycross, and look toward Brunswick, he can see the curve in the road, caused by this effort of the engineer to make something on the side. Thus Waycross was born and Tebeauville died. Mr. Pendleton moved to Lowndes County in 1864. Tebeauville was called 'Number Nine', because it was the custom of the railroad company in those days to number the stations.

"One of the local traditions to which some of the old residents point with great pride is that, when in command of the coast defenses, at the beginning of the war, General Robert E. Lee stopped for a short while in Tebeauville. Many of the people who lived here then remember to have seen this "Man of the Hour" who still lives in the hearts of the people today. Among the citizens who resided here then were the Tebeaus, the Reppards, the Remsharts, the Parkers, the Grovenstines, the Millers, the Bachlotts, the Sweats, the Smiths, and Cottinghams."

A mile from Tebeauville is a network of railroads around which a city grew almost in a night. Her lights are shining over miles of territory, beautiful homes are dotted here and there, and progression is seen on every side. The many roads crossing this way suggested the name of this town—Waycross—the capital of the wonderful slash pine, and the Magic City of Southern Georgia.

Tebeauville Tablet Unveiled May 10, 1917

On the above date the tablet, marking the site of old Tebeauville, was erected and donated by the Lyman Hall chapter of the Daughters of the American Revolution, of which Mrs. J. L. Walker was regent.

The principal address of the occasion was delivered by Hon. Otis Ashmore, of Savannah, who was introduced by Professor A. G. Miller. Mr. Ashmore's address was an eloquent and interesting one, calling attention to the importance and value of recording history. He said we have all been too content to make history rather than record it. He referred to some of the historic spots of Georgia and his address was interspersed with historical references highly interesting and valuable.

In presenting the tablet, Mrs. Walker said:

"This is a cold and critical age, an age of progress and development. Progression brings us to the danger line of forgetting the love and gratitude we should feel for those who have made history for us. This modest tablet, draped in our nation's flag with its burning stripes and

UNVEILING A TABLET THAT MARKS OLD TEBEAUVILLE

ever multiplying stars, rests upon the ground of Ware county's dead town, Tebeauville, whose citizens helped to make Waycross.

"To you, Mr. Mayor, the honored chief magistrate of our city, it is my privilege and pleasure to present to your charge this simple stone. As it passes from our hands to yours we hope it will impress our citizens with more reverence for the picturesque and romantic history of our early days and inspire them to further perpetuation of our old landmarks."

Mayor Scott T. Beaton accepted the tablet for the

city. In doing so he highly commended the Lyman Hall chapter for their patriotic services, and said:

"On behalf of the City of Waycross, as its official head, I desire to express to the ladies of this organization the city's appreciation of the unselfish and patriotic action upon their part that made possible this celebration today. In my opinion marks of the highest and best citizenship are to be found in the people who would preserve records of the past with the same enthusiasm as they embrace opportunities of today. This is true because one would not care to have written upon the pages of history a past not radiant with good. The good ladies of the Lyman Hall chapter of the Daughters of the American Revolution, together with our entire population, rejoice in our city's past, and proudly preserves for future generations the beginning, and the early days of Waycross when it was not 'a crossing of ways', but Tebeauville.

"What Waycross has done since the days of Tebeauville is well worth recording, not alone for what the past holds for us, but more as an inspiration to the present and future generations. When Waycross was Tebeauville some of its inhabitants were blind to any chance for development and progress in this particular section of Georgia, but there were others who were filled with faith in their section, and could see the Waycross of today, and it is the spirit of these men that this tablet is dedicated. There are those among us today who are too dull to feel the throbbing pulse of an intensely industrial life, but there are others of us who are sensative to our opportunities and who are dreaming big things for the future of Waycross, and it is in behalf of this latter class that I accept with thanks, in the name of the city, this tablet that is to mark for centuries the beginning of Waycross, "The Magic City of South Georgia!"

The tablet was unveiled by Mrs. Mary Parker and Mrs. J. A. Lott. The occasion was one of the most interesting in the history of the city, and was attended by a number of out-of-town people who as former residents and descendants of residents of what was the beginning of Waycross took a deep interest in the event. Music was rendered during the afternoon by the Waycross concert band.

DR. DANIEL LOTT

MRS. DANIEL LOTT

WAYCROSS

Waycross was created in 1872, but was not incorporated until March 3, 1874. This was done by a special act of the General Assembly. The founders of this town were: Dr. Daniel Lott, Dr. Benjamin Williams, Mr. William Bailey and Captain Cuyler Hilliard.

Dr. Daniel Lott settled first in Waresboro. He was originally from Bullock county, and in 1871 came to what is now known as "Old Waycross". Dr. Benjamin Williams settled in the same locality, also coming here the same year that Dr. Lott did. He was formerly from

North Carolina, but came to Ware county from Burnt Fort in Camden. Mr. William Bailey's native home was in the state of Maine, and when coming to Georgia settled first in Telfair county, later lived at Burnt Fort, and in 1870 came, together with his family to Ware county. Captain Cuyler Hilliard lived during the early

MRS. BENJAMIN WILLIAMS   DR. BENJAMIN WILLIAMS

part of his life in Camden county, but later was prominently known as one of the first settlers of Ware county.

Days of activity followed the settling of this little town in the Wire Grass. "Daylight Saving" was unknown to these industrious people but they gauged their activities by the rising and setting of the sun. They cut some of their finest timber from the lands southwest of the line of travel, now known as "Plant Avenue". The logs were loaded on small rafts, which were floated, in charge of a pilot, down the Satilla river to Burnt Fort, where they were transported to a barge and sent to Savannah and other ports.

The stopping place on the railroad near this settlement, for the convenience of travelers, was nothing more than a shed, situated just across from where Wilson's corner is now located. This place was known as the Junction.

Mr. William Bailey settled a camp, composed of a

WILLIAM BAILEY   MRS. WILLIAM BAILEY

number of families in tents, on what is now Williams Heights, just below the land formerly owned by the late Major McGee. This place acquired the name of "Yankee Town", supposedly named because Mr. Bailey's former home was once "Beyond the Mason and Dixon Line". This settlement was made for the purpose of cutting the timber on the surrounding lands in that section.

There was once a saw mill near Yankee Town, just across the railroad in front of where the Sims' residence is and some of the other homes along the way toward the Satilla river. The mill was owned by Mr. George

Grant, who later sold it to Dr. Daniel Lott and he moved it to Waresboro.

When Dr. Lott and Susan, his wife, came to Waycross, they brought with them a large family, and the small "Saw Mill" house was not adequate for their comfort, and they found it necessary to occupy five of the houses.

MRS. CUYLER HILLIARD   CUYLER HILLIARD

As early as possible Dr. Lott erected a large and commodious home where later his son Joel Lott lived. The house is standing at the present time well preserved on Plant Avenue.

Dr. Lott made a standing proposition, that he would give a lot of land to any white person who would promise to erect a nice house upon it. A number of people accepted this proposition and consequently he gave away many lots on Butler Street, also Plant Avenue. Many of the homes that now exist on Plant Avenue were secured in that way.

Dr. Daniel Lott built the first warehouse, which was situated in the "V" formed by the intersection of the Brunswick, Albany, Atlantic & Gulf, afterward the A. C. L. The first telegraph station in the town was opened in this warehouse, Mr. O. D. Parker being among the first to serve as telegraph operator. Colonel Cary W. Styles, Mr. Clough and Mr. John Lott built the first brick stores in Waycross. From Tebeau Creek towards Quarterman Street school is known as "Old Waycross" and it was in this section that the stores were built, now designated as Lower Plant Avenue. Mr. William Parkers' brick building was completed soon after that of Mr. John Lott's.[1]

The founders of this city were most active in speculating in wild lands which brought them wealth and prominence. Circumstances conspired to make this projection not only feasible but profitable.

Before the War Between the States, a railroad from Brunswick to Albany had been put under way. It had been graded from Brunswick to Waresboro; then the county seat of Ware. The projectors intended it as an offset to the railroad from Savannah to Thomasville, and the two were shown to cross each other about three or four hundred yards west of the old mill site. The war coming on, it was abandoned and a few miles of rail, that had been laid, were torn up and used for war purposes. This railroad was completed soon after the Civil War.

Busy years swept over this section, the bridle path through the woods soon changed into a well-worn road, on which buggies, carriages and wagons often rolled down the shady aisles of pines. There was no idleness in this place, everyone worked. This little village was throbbing freely with life and influence of a fast-growing community, a city gradually being hewn out of a wilderness.

---
1. Information obtained from Mr. and Mrs. John Lott.

How Waycross Got Its Name

Dr. Lott, ever on the alert, sought frequent conferences with Major Harry Haines, Superintendent of the Savannah Railroad. It was Dr. Lott's great desire to enlist Major Haines' co-operation in the scheme of building a city. There being ample hotel accommodations in Blackshear, they often held their conferences there. It was during one of these meetings that the editor of "The Georgian", Mr. B. F. Allen, was called in to assist the two men in selecting a name suitable for the new town.

A complete map of the future city was spread before them and the word "cross" seemed to have been fixed in the minds of all three as a part of the name. The puzzle was a "prefix" or "suffix", one that would always be appropriate. Mr. Allen suggested that there be a place in North Georgia called "Norcross", connection of "North" and "Cross", he did not know then, nor did they, that the place was named in memory of Old Jonathan Norcross. The names "Westcross", "Eastcross" and "Southcross" were brought forward, but neither nor any contraction sounded suitable. "Newcross" was suggested, then "Crossways" and finally "Waycross", which was accepted. The name of "Newcross" came near being accepted, but the certainty of the city growing old and the name being unsuited, settled its fate. The men decided that Waycross would be suitable so long as the world lasts[1].

"Uncle Thomas" (Rev. W. H. Thomas) always contended that it was providentially named as the "Way of the Cross" and that here was the center of the world.

Waycross a Religious Town

In the early days of Waycross it was considered to be one of the most religious towns in the state, nearly everyone was deeply interested in some kind of sacred belief. Frank Stanton, the poet, who was often a visitor

---
1. Information given by Editor B. F. Allen, Pearson, Georgia.

to the town had the following to say in The Smithville News of which he was editor during the year of 1888.

"We have just returned from a very pleasant trip over the B. & W. railroad as far as Waycross and naturally feel like saying a few lines about it.

"Did you ever stop in Waycross? It is a very pretty town, or rather city; and is growing every day. It is a clear case of a town coming to the railroad—which has fostered it and made it grow.

"But for those who are of the World, Worldly, Waycross is a very solemn place on Sunday—perhaps "quiet" would be a better word. The people go to church there six days out of the week, and go six times on Sunday. They are enlisted for The War, and they mean business. Nearly everybody in the town is identified with the church.

"As the train rolled up to the B. & W. depot, a solitary policeman was pacing the platform and singing in an undertone:

> *'If you get there before I do,*
> *I'm bound for the promised land.*
> *Just tell the rest I'm coming too—*
> *I'm bound for the promised land!*

"Can you show me where the hotel is?' I asked him.

> *'If you get there before I do,*
> *I'm bound for the promised land.'*

"By slow degrees he sung me towards it, where I met and shook hands with the hotel porter, who immediately handed me a card whereon was printed:

"Are you ready to die? Sinner! *This* night may be your last!

"I told him *that* three dollars was all I had, but *to* take that and spare my *life*. He seemed surprised, and *said* he would *furnish* me with a few tracts for breakfast and a good *sermon* for dinner.

"I then intimated that I would like to register, and on

being informed that the night clerk was holding a prayer meeting down at Blackshear, I ventured in and having scrawled my autograph on a page bearing the inscription, 'Make Us Wise Unto Salvation', I followed the porter up the legended stairs and was shown into a room which contained two Testaments and some instructions about blowing out the lamp.

"I had scarcely closed my eyes for a much-needed nap, when I was awakened by someone singing 'Arise, my soul, arise!' and thinking this was a warning that breakfast was ready, I arose, and found the daylight was two hours ahead of me.

"Shortly afterward my brother, Valentine Stanton, came around and informed me that church was ready, and I was forthwith ushered into the presence of an old-time Methodist love-feast[1].

"You must go to church if you go to Waycross. There is no doubt about that. But it's good to go that way sometimes and helps a man's faith wonderfully.

"I only spent half dozen hours in town, but even in that short space I saw a good deal, and heard more. I saw the vision of a great city, hovering mirage-like over a wiregrass sea; I saw a happy and prosperous people painting their future beautiful; and the *sound I heard* as that vision faded from my view, was a song of thanksgiving from the people to the people's God."

WARESBORO

Waresboro was named the county site the same year in which the county was created, and the territory around this place is said to be the oldest in the country. The people who lived at Waresboro in the first years of its existence, had very little communication with the outside world. Railroads and telegraph wires were unknown. An occasional mail coach made its appearance at this isolated town, sometimes monthly and sometimes yearly, depending upon the amount of mail matter that accu-

---

1. Soon after this meeting here, he wrote "The Love-Feast at Waycross".

mulated at Camp Pinckney, then the distributing office for this section.

All the marketable produce in the surrounding country was hauled either to Traders' Hill, Center Village or Camp Pinckney. These "Trading Posts" were over fifty miles away. The settlers always purchasing a year's

WARESBORO HIGH SCHOOL PUPILS AND TRUSTEES

Standing, left to right—1, Ed Jeffords; 2, C. Wilson; 3, ————; 4, Hilly Spence; 5, Jim Thomas; 6, ————; 7. S. P. Settle Sr., Teacher; 8, J. D. Smith; 9, ————; 10, ————; 11, ————; 12, Mr. Mullis. Middle row, left to right—9, Mrs. S. P. Jeffords; 10, Myram Spence. Bottom row, left to right—1, ————; 2, Bill Strickland; 3, Ob Giddins; 4, ————; 5, Gaines Thigpen; 6, ————; 7, Martin Jeffords; 8, Jim Caswell; 9, John O'Quinn.

supply of everything needed when they sold their produce, rarely visiting these markets more than once a year.

Waresboro was considered a remarkably healthful place. An old record states that during the period of twenty-five years only four people died; one from old age of ninety-two years, another killed in a horse race by being thrown against a tree; another killed in a drunken brawl, and another died of pneumonia contracted while bear hunting in the Okefinokee Swamp. The bear hunter was the only one to die a natural death in all that time; so it is readily seen that a physician's life there was one of inactivity.

Waresboro was for some years the only town or village in the county. It being the county site was sufficient reason for its importance. Here the affairs of the county was administered until 1872, when Waycross became the county site. The courthouse at Waresboro was a large one-story log building with two small side rooms, used for offices, and often during court the jury serving on a case would retire to the woods merely in charge of a bailiff and make up their verdict.[1]

In May, 1872, an election was held in the county to vote on the proposition of removing the county site from Waresboro to Waycross. The canvass proved a bitter political battle which engendered much feeling on both sides. Waycross finally carried the day and the county site was accordingly moved.

Dr. Williams, Dr. Lott and Mr. Bailey built a small court house but soon after it was completed it was burned by the hand of an incendiary, and practically all records, data and other information pertaining to the early settlers was destroyed. This was not only a loss to historians but to the lawyers as well.

The old court house at Waresboro, no longer in use, was dismantled and removed at night to Waycross while the "Rude forefathers of the hamlet slept". Those who braved danger of being molested in their daring undertaking were Jack and Marion Mock, William Webb, Ran Cason, Edward Cottingham, William McClure, William Green, John and Warren Lott.

Dr. Daniel Lott paid for the rebuilding of the court house and became the Ordinary, but soon resigned, being unwilling to take the infamous and long-to-be-remem-

---
1. Information from Folks Huxford.

bered iron-clad oath then required of every office-holder in the Southern States.[1]

WARESBORO MASONIC LODGE NO. 217, WARESBORO, GA.

This lodge was established by dispensation in 1857 with the following members and officers showed in its first return made that year Under Dispensation:

Randal McDonald, W. M.
Charles L. Walker, S. W.
John Lee, J. W.
Daniel Lott, William B. Folks, P. B. Bedford, David Davidson, members. The Grand Lodge that year (1857) allowed the dispensation to stand until the next year before granting a charter, probably deeming that wisest in view of the few members. The foregoing members were named in the dispensation as charter members.

The return made next year, 1858, under charter, showed:

Randall McDonald, W. M.
Chas. L. Walker, S. W.
John Lee, J. W.
David Davidson, Treas.
William B. Folks, Secy.
P. B. Bedford, S. D.
Daniel Lott, J. D.
William D. Smith, Tyler.
John C. Nicholls
William W. Smith
D. J. McDonald
B. H. Tanner
Daniel E. Knowles
George Geotte
W. J. Rivers
B. D. Brantley
William Rennie
L. R. Thompson
J. B. Cason
James Inman
Rev. James Stewart
Joseph McQuaig
Thomas Byrd
Dr. L. C. Mattox
J. A. Harper
Early Davis
E. G. Brewton
J. D. Smith
A. J. Miller
D. P. Levine
W. B. McLendon, f. c.
John H. Mattox, f. c.
L. W. H. Pittman, f. c.
Joseph Hillman, e. a

---
1. Information from Mr. John Lott.

At that time, 1858, regular meeting nights were on 2nd and 4th Friday nights in each month, 27 initiations, 26 passings and 23 raisings were reported that year, which constituted a good report.

The return made next year, 1859, showed that the lodge was meeting on 2nd and 4th Saturday nights in each month, and had had 10 initiations, 11 passings, 13 raisings, and two members had resigned.

The following membership was reported:

Chas. L. Walker, W. M.
Dr. Wm. B. Folks, S. W.
John Lee, J. W.
D. J. McDonald, Secy.
Thomas Hilliard, Treas.
Daniel E. Knowles, S. D.
Daniel Lott, J. D.
Wm. D. Smith, Tyler
Randal McDonald, P. M.
P. D. Bedford
David Davidson
John C. Nicholls
William W. Smith
B. H. Tanner
George Geotte
W. J. Rivers
L. W. H. Pittman
B. D. Brantley
William Rennie
L. R. Thompson
John B. Cason
James Inman

Rev. James Stewart
Joseph McQuaig
Thomas Byrd
John H. Mattox
Dr. L. C. Mattox
Jos. A. Harper
Early Davis
E. G. Brewton
J. D. Smith
A. J. Miller
D. P. Levine
W. B. McLendon
Joseph Hillman
James Douglas
Allen Strickland
J. W Stephens
C. S. Youmans
John A. Thompson
W. G. Stewart
Talbot Little
W. H. Myers
Daniel Rentz

No report after 1865.

TREES OF WARE COUNTY

Few towns in Georgia can boast of more beautiful or finer shade trees than Waycross. This is especially true of that part of the city known as Old Waycross, which was settled first, and oaks in that part of town were planted with the laying off of the first streets. These first trees were planted by Mr. John Lott and "Uncle Thomas"—the Rev. W. H. Thomas Other streets in town were originally planted by property owners who lived along the different sidewalks. Now the Park and Tree Commission have taken over the tree planting work. A number of memorial trees have been planted and give promise of shading many generations who will pass beneath them.

The oldest living things in Georgia are some of the trees in the Okefinokee Swamp. These trees had their beginning when a race alien to ours roved at will beneath them; for it was under the canopy of these moss-covered trees that the Seminole and Creek Indians roamed daily, led by Billy Bowlegs and followed by the boy, Oceola. Beneath these trees the Confederate deserters found shelter, making there a safe retreat during troublous times of war. It was the trees that sheltered the black cattle driven into the swamp by the Indians then fortifying themselves against the invasions of the whites during the Seminole War. These cattle were numerous in South Georgia and were found in great numbers by the early settlers. Some of the trees in the swamp were cut years ago and if rings in the body of them reveal their age, they were growing when Columbus discovered America.

Trees at Waresboro

Long years ago when Ware county was young and Waresboro was its county site, quite a little colony of men from other settlements cast their lot there. Among the number were some real tree planters who had a vision of a city beautiful, with shady streets. They wrought in a magnanimous spirit of rivalry with nature—or rather they worked in full fellowship with her. When they planted they selected, to shade the streets of their little town, the live oak, a tree long-lived and perpetual in its verdure. It is interesting to realize that already three generations of people have walked beneath the beautiful oaks planted so wisely over a half a century ago. The patriotic citizens who did the unselfish work of planting these trees were General Hilliard, Dr. Daniel Lott, Captain James McDonald, Colonel William McDonald, Mr. Austin Smith and later Captain Crawley and Major Spence. These men may later have put forward more effectual work in the interest of their fellowmen but their tree-planting will continue to bless mankind for ages yet to come.

SOIL OF WARE COUNTY

There are three well marked and characteristic soils in this section: (1) a light, sandy, thin, poor soil, covered with saw palmetto and full of roots; (2) the loose, dark, sandy soil, containing a large amount of vegetable matter; and (3) the reddish, clay soil. The first is adapted to the production of potatoes and ground peas; cotton is successfully cultivated in the second; while the third excells in the sugar-cane. Corn yields a prolific crop on the darkest soils, especially when fertilized by the black swamp muck, which is found in inexhaustible quantities in the ponds and small swamps scattered here and there throughout this section. Along the banks of the Satilla river, there crops out a pure white marl, almost entirely consisting of carbonate of lime, which readily decomposes this muck and fits it for plant food.

Near Waycross experiments have been made showing that the soils of this section are admirably adapted to the culture of fruits, figs, grapes and watermelons.

This section of country was formerly looked upon as utterly worthless, so that when the citizens of Savannah projected a road through it to the Gulf, the name of "Cuyler's Desert" was applied to it.

Dr. Thomas Janes, Commissioner of Agriculture of

the State of Georgia, in his report on Georgia soils mentions Ware county in this manner: "I have seen no section in which the people seem to secure a comfortable supply of food with less effort and can see no reason why the whole country may not be made equal, if not superior to that section of Prussia where Frederick the Great founded the city of Berlin. There is the greatest similarity in the soil and topography of the two sections.

In the continuation of this sandy belt toward the west, near Thomasville, a German, Mr. John Stark, has made in one year 1,800 gallons of wine, which to my taste, equals the finest vintage of 1857 on the Rhine, and his sparkling wines will bear favorable comparison with Longworth's Catawba from the vineclad hills of Ohio.

Nowhere in Louisiana have I seen the sugarcane grow more luxuriantly or yield a greater amount of saccharine juice than in this section of the country."

For sheep farms, the grazing is naturally supplied, little shelter is needed in winter. Nature is responsible here and yields readily to the intelligent and industrious efforts of mankind. The climate and soil is such that intensive and scientific agriculture brings wealth, for it is here that flowers are ever blooming, and herds feed in pastures that never wither.

Ware can produce a money crop the year round, while the climate permits roses to bloom in all seasons. It's always rose time in Ware.

B. F. ALLEN'S MEMORIES OF THE LONG AGO

SOME OF THE MEN WHO GAVE CHARACTER TO WAYCROSS

Among the leading spirits, besides Dr. Daniel Lott, in the upbuilding of Waycross were Drs. W. B. Folks and B. F. Williams, Judge W. B. Williamson and Messrs. Herbert Murphy and James Knox.

Dr. W. B. Folks, besides doing a general practice

was the railroad physician and surgeon. He was the friend and confidant of Maj. Henry S. Haines, the superintendent of the Atlantic & Gulf railroad, and was a potent factor in securing the right-of-way for the branch line to Jacksonville, Fla., and it was in his honor that the little city of Folkston was named. He was the father of Drs. Frank and Gus Folks, and W. B. Folks. In these gentlemen he left a goodly heritage to the city of Waycross.

Dr. Williams was a quiet gentleman, he owned all the land on which Waycross is located lying south of the Savannah railroad and east of the Brunswick railroad, a very small portion of which he had sold at the time of his death. His residence was located south of the railroad just off the right-of-way. He had a most interesting family of children—sons and daughters—among them Judge J. S. Williams. His descendents ranked perhaps second among the people who made Waycross the thriving city it is. One of his daughters intermarried with Mr. Warren Lott and is the mother of Maj. Warren Lott, of the American army of occupation in Germany, and who is a West Pointer. He went to West Point by appointment of Hon. W. G. Brantley.

Judge Williamson was the only resident attorney when I arrived at Waycross; he had practically retired from the practice because of age. His residence was a short distance north of the court house on the public road, now known as Albany avenue. He was too feeble to take any active part in public affairs, but his advice was frequently sought in shaping the future of the city.

Mr. James Knox was the leading merchant. His store was located on the east side of the street in front of the court house, across from the triangular block. He did a thriving business. He and his descendants did much to shape the destiny of the city.

Herbert Murphy was a contractor and builder. He came as the leader of a colony from New Jersey. Some of the colony settled at Waycross and some at Glenmore—notably J. M. Stiger, J. G. Steffis, and others. Mr. Murphy was attached to Waycross by the splendid opportunities in his line of business, and had a splendid crew of employees who came with him from New Jersey. He, at the time, owned the little triangular block in front of the court house and on which he had erected a two-story wooden structure and occupied for mercantile purposes. This passed away with the purchase by the county.

The business section was located near the court house along Albany avenue, the triangular block across the street east. The merchants were Knox, Highsmith, Casons, Hohenstein and Lovenstein. There were two or three others but their names have gone from my memory.

Among the names of prominent families not already mentioned were the Baileys, Millers, McQuaigs, "Father" Thomas, Prof. Chas J. Jenkins. The influence of these people is still perceptible in the life of the city.

The first young man I met after going to Waycross was in the home of Prof. Jenkins, where I had secured board, a young man raised in the territory of the present Atkinson county—E. M. Pafford by name. His father, Hon. Rowan Pafford, had carried him there to go to school, and secured board for him at the home of Prof. Jenkins, the two were friends until his death last year.

I next met V. L. Stanton, the youthful agent of the Brunswick & Albany railroad, as it was known then, and the acquaintance ripened into a friendship that has been lasting. Stanton was a man, he loved his adopted home, and the impress of his personality has been stamped on Waycross at every step of her growth.

My next acquaintances were two young barristers, who had just graduated in law at Savannah from the offices of Rufus E. Lester and Julian Hartridge. These young men, John C. McDonald and Leon A. Wilson were reared at and near Waresboro and had come back to their native hearth to win fame and fortune in the practice. They stand at the head of the Waycross legal fraternity, and are in comfortable circumstances. Waycross owes much of her success to the wisdom and guidance of these young men.

I remained in Waycross until after the Spring Term 1881, of Ware superior court. It had become current that I was an attorney and it led to my accepting fees in several small matters.

One of my clients was Capt. N. Dixon. He had, like many good men of that day, homesteaded his property to save something from the capricious maw of his creditors, and wanted an order to sell a tract of real estate for re-investment.

Another client was a negro man. He had gone into Lovenstein's store and bought some small article and tendered the merchant a $20 gold piece from which to get his pay. Lovenstein treated the $20 gold piece as a $1 in silver and gave change accordingly. No power of persuasion could be brought to bear by the Negro to get Lovenstein to make correction. A warrant was sworn out for the merchant, and it finally resulted in Lovenstein paying back the $20 gold piece, my fee and the court costs. The negro had his employer there ready to swear he had paid him the $20 gold piece only a few minutes before and it was all the money he had when he went into the store and there could be no mistake about the matter. Hon. John C. Nicholls represented the defendant.

The court was presided over by Judge Martin L. Mershon in an efficient and painstaking manner. This reminds me to say that Judge Mershon was reared in Clinch county, at or near Magnolia the old county seat. My research leads me to the opinion that Judge Mershon had little or no opportunity as a young man for cultivating his mind. His surroundings were also unpropitious, and his environment was the father of his future dissipation. He was a rare genius, a perfect gentleman, with a most remarkable memory. He had read Shakespeare's plays and it was his delight to repeat page after page of them from memory. I am not sure where he received his legal training if, indeed, he received any at all. My best information is he caught the inspiration to become a lawyer from attendance upon the semi-annual visitations of "big" (superior) court, and the monthly sessions of the justices' courts at Magnolia; that he borrowed books and read law at home and at the same time he acquired his knowledge of Shakespeare, and that he became an attorney and advocate despite himself.

The State's interest in the court was looked after by another Clinch county boy— Simon W. Hitch—who read law in the office of Hon. John C. Nicholls. Like Judge Mershon, Mr. Hitch secured what he knew of the law by native ability and a dogged determination to succeed. And they did succeed.

My recollection is that Lieutenant-Colonel Atkinson, an uncle of Judge Spencer R. and Sam Atkinson, was the foreman of the grand jury at that term of the court. At that time there was not such a strenuous effort to make people good by law and hence the grand jury did not remain in session but three days and not exceeding a dozen bills of indictment were sent up to the court for attention. The solicitor-general's office was not the bonanza of recent years.

There was not a very large array of attorneys at the court, but among those who were there was one, Nathan P. Bedford, who sought prominence in the political world as a scalawag; a republican for the spoils of office. However, his efforts to secure office under the republican administration was very disappointing to him, as it was not forthcoming. Bedford, I think, was a resident of Ware county and a man of some learning. He was at Ware superior court trying to get a Republican line-up that would send him to congress from the old first district. The Savannah republicans would have none of Bedford.

Leaving Blackshear in the early part of 1874, I became a partner with C. R. Pendleton in the publication of the "Times" at Valdosta. The partnership lasted two years.

In 1876 I began the study of law and was admitted to the practice in May, 1877, in Lowndes superior court. Began the practice at Valdosta; found that there was plenty of room at the top, but I didn't have the means to tide me over until I could climb to the top. I had spent all I had and could earn preparing myself for admission.

I became discouraged for once in my life, after a legal career of eighteen months, I was easily persuaded to join a partnership in the newspaper business at Quitman as associate editor of the "Reporter", owned by Joseph Tillman.

In October, 1880, Mr. Tillman persuaded me and my younger brother, W. A. Allen, to move the plant to Waycross and join him in the publication of the "Waycross Reporter".

The move was a very unfavorable one and W. A. Allen at the end of the year severed his connections with the business, and myself and a young man by the name of Butler Jones undertook the job of issuing the paper. I remained about two or more months longer.

Waycross, although it had captured the county seat of Ware county from Waresboro, was a most insignificant place. The Savannah railroad maintained its station at "Tebeauville", or "Old Nine", but would let passengers off at Waycross. Of course it had to stop before crossing the Brunswick railroad's track. The Brunswick railroad maintained its station at the crossing. It was a most crude affair, built out of rough lumber and mounted on high stilt-like pillars. A young man by the name of J. D. DeLoach was agent of the Savannah road and another young man by the name of V. L. Stanton was agent of the Brunswick road, and he was not very proud of his quarters. It was told whether as a joke I know not, that a train from Brunswick jumped the track and knocked Stanton's chicken coop off the pillars into the depths below.

There were two hotels. The King House was kept by Mr. William King who came from St. Marys. It was also built of rough lumber and located about a hundred feet southeast of the crossing. The Satilla House was located northeast of the crossing. It was a splendid wooden building and kept by two maiden ladies—the Misses Shine.

The only church building was Methodist, built by Dr. Daniel Lott out of wood and was located on the site of the present Trinity Methodist church.

The school house was also a small affair, just about large enough to accommodate fifty pupils and the school was taught by Prof. C. J. Jenkins. It was built by Dr. Lott.

He also erected a county court house of wood on the site of the present building. It was a two-story structure and very well arranged for a court house.

All the buildings in the place were rough, the "Reporter" was located on the second floor of a storehouse owned by Mr. James Knox, and unceiled. It was an uncomfortable and unfit place for a printing office, especially during the extreme cold winter that had passed.

The half dozen stores were dingy wooden structures and not very inviting. But there was a promise of better things in the future.

CHAPTER VIII
CHURCHES

SOME OF THE OLDEST CHURCHES IN WARE COUNTY

HE OLDEST church in this county is Kettle Creek Church, although the first building has been replaced by one of more modern type, and the next oldest is the Waresboro Mission Church, then follows the log church at Tebeauville, while the oldest church in Waycross is Trinity, and a small Methodist Church at Old Nine. The following are some of the names of the oldest rural churches in the County: Pine Valley, Mount Green, organized by Rev. William McDonald, Booth, Friendship, Wesley Chapel, Salem, Philadelphia and Ezekiel, Providence or Camp Branch Church, Glenmore Congregational Church, Wayfare or Cow Creek Church. This church was organized in Ware, when a part of Ware was set aside for the forming of Clinch County, this church was left on the land contributed toward Clinch and later when Echols was organized, the people of that county fell heir to this church. It was never moved but had the distinction of having existed in three different counties.

PROVIDENCE, OR CAMP BRANCH CHURCH

Providence Church is of the Primitive Baptist denomination, and although located about a mile across the line in Ware County, has always been closely associated with Clinch County, therefore the history of this church will not be amiss.

A small band of Primitive Baptists met at this point and organized themselves into a church on the third day of February, 1844. They were constituted as a church on the first Sunday in March (March 2nd), 1884. The following is the covenant of the original members, copied from the church minutes:

COVENANT: For as much as Almighty God by His Grace has been pleased to call us whose names underneath subscribed out of darkness into His marvelous light and all of us have been regularly baptized upon a profession of our faith in Christ Jesus and have given up ourselves to the Lord and to one another in a Gospel church-way to be governed and guided by a proper discipline agreeable to the Word of God, we do therefore in the name of our Lord Jesus and by His assistance, covenant and agree to keep up the discipline of the church members in a most brotherly affection toward each other while we endeavor to punctually observe the following rules, viz: in brotherly love to pray for each other, to watch over one another and if need be in the most tender and affectionate manner to reprove one another that is if we discover anything amiss to go and tell him his faults according to the direction given in our Lord's Gospel, and not be whispering and back-biting. We also agree with God's assistance to attend to our church meetings, observe the Lord's day and not absent ourselves from the communion of the Lord's Supper without lawful excuse, to be ready to communicate to the defraying of the church expense.

These things we do covenant and agree to observe and keep sacred in the name and by the assistance of the Holy Trinity. Signed by the mutual consent of the members whose names are underneath subscribed. March 2, 1844. John Minshew, Rachel Minshew, James J. Thomas, Duncan Henderson, Belinda Henderson, Richard A. Bennett, Tobitha Bennett, William S. Bennett, Nancy Bennett.

After the organization was perfected, Rev. Isham Peacock was called as the first pastor of the church which call he accepted. Duncan Henderson was then selected as clerk, and regular meeting days were fixed for both monthly and annual meetings.

The following is a list of the pastors since the organization of the church, barring two periods when the list was not obtainable:

Isham Peacock, 1844-1845; Rubin Crawford, 1846-1848; John Dryden, 1849-1854; Rubin Crawford, 1855-1860; H. Cowart, 1861; John Dryden, 1862; Rubin Crawford, 1863; Daniel Palerson, 1863; James M. Mullis, 1863; Reubin Crawford, 1864; Daniel Palerson, 1864; James M. Mullis, 1871-1880; Jas. C. Williams, 1881-1882; R. H. Bennett, 1890; E. W. Dilbern, 1891; James A. O'Steen, 1892; D. B. Sheffield, 1894; James A. O'Steen, 1895-1901; W. H. Tomlinson, 1902-1905; H. J. J. Markey, 1906-1908; J. C. Hewett, 1909; Richard A. James, 1915-1916.

From about 1910 to 1915 the church had no regular pastor, while the minutes do not disclose anything relative to the period of 1864-1871 and 1882-1890. The following is a list of the church clerks since 1844, with the exception of 1882-1890:

Duncan Henderson, 1844-49; Richard A. Bennett, 1849-59; Asa Geiger, 1860-1861; William T. James, 1861-1873; W. P. Nunez, 1873-1880; J. H. Miller, 1881; J. R. Dickerson, 1890-1915; B. M. James, 1915-1916.

Duncan Henderson, who was the first clerk, was born about 1800 and was a brother to John S., and Daniel Henderson. He married Miss Belinda Stafford, a daughter of Josiah Stafford. To them were born four children, viz: Andrew J., Jack, David and Mary Henderson. His membership was with Providence Church until his death in 1863. He was for many years a trustee for the church property.

Note: Information obtained from the History of Clinch County, By Folks Huxford.

Trinity Methodist

"The groves were God's first temples" and while for a very short time, trees with leafy branches formed a roof above the worshipers who first settled in Ware. Soon, however, arbors took the place of the trees and stately structures for divine worship soon followed. Now no city in Georgia can claim more benign influence of the spirit of churches or be more profoundly felt than in Waycross and Ware county.

First row, standing—Rev. C. L. B. Davis, Rev. J. M. Glenn, Rev. E. M. Whiting, Rev. R. A. Brown, Rev. J. C. Gillespie. Second row—Rev. T. M. Christian, Rev. W. H. Thomas, Rev. W. T. McMichael, Rev. W. H. Scruggs.

The first church building erected in Waycross was an old wooden structure that stood in the street known then as Parallel and Racetrack, where these streets came together, and where Trinity church now stands. Dr. Daniel Lott practically gave all the lumber, and with the help of others, a place of worship was established. Rev. Howard W. Key, the son of Bishop Key, was the first pastor, and the Methodists, Baptists and Presbyterians worshiped there together. Indeed it was a beautiful illustration of the Psalm, "Behold how good and pleasant it is for brethren to dwell together in unity." This church was built in 1872 and served for some time as Union church.

After the building of the First Methodist church, Trinity was reorganized and in 1895 had less than fifty members. This church was made into a mission and for two years received an appropriation from the Mission Board to aid in its support. The charter members and those who soon rallied to their assistance, were called upon to make many sacrifices to keep the work moving. Soon the official board of the church requested the Board of Missions to make this church a self-sustaining station, applying the usual appropriation to the more needy churches. Trinity the first year paid the assessments in full and raised for all purposes over $5,000, a portion of which was set aside to aid in building on the site where their church is now located, a handsome new brick structure. The plucky Trinity members paid as bills fell due, and by the time that the new church was completed, they were ready for their dedication services. The work of building the new church was done under the direction of the following committee:

Rev. J. M. Glenn, Chairman; D. B. Sweat, Secretary; B. H. Thomas, Treasurer; C. C. Buchanan, R. P. Byrd, E. M. Cason, and Joel Lott. J. B. Strickland was the contractor. Every morning during the progress of this work of building this temple of worship, Mr. Strickland opened the day's labor with prayer.

The first official board of the new church were: Stewards—Rev. W. H. Thomas, Chairman; R. P. Byrd, Secretary; B. H. Thomas, Treas.; C. C. Buchanan, J. W. Adams, D. B. Sweat, E. M. Cason, W. H. Bradley, Henry Agarthen and Daniel Lott.

Sunday School Superintendent, D. B. Sweat; Assistant Superintendent, B. H. Thomas.

This church in "Old Waycross" was much beloved by the early settlers who built the first place of worship there. Some are living who formerly held their membership there who still cherish hallowed memories of happy days that are gone when they sought and found the Savior within its sacred walls. The following ministers have served the church:

1901 J. M. Glenn
1902 J. H. Mather
1903 J. M. Foster
1904 J. W. Arnold
1905 J. W. Arnold
1906-07 B. E. Whittington
1908-09 H. C. Brewton
1910-13 J. B. Thrasher
1914-15 J. C. Flanders
1916 W. F. Quillian
1917 J. C. G. Brooks
1918 W. E. Arnold
1919-20 C. M. Ledbetter
1921-24 Jas. R. Webb
1925-28 J. E. Sampley
1929 J. H. Allen
1930-31 W. A. Kelley

LOVE FEAST AT WAYCROSS HELD AT TRINITY CHURCH

Its History and Origin

(The history and origin of the poem, "Love Feast at Waycross", was written by a former beloved citizen of Waycross, the Rev. D. B. Sweat, who now lives in Lakeland, Fla.)

Waycross was a very religious town back in the early eighties. I do not know whether the old town has lived up to the standard set thirty years ago, but it made a fine start at that time and was known far and wide as the most religious town in the South.

I was reminded of the old days by a request I had the other day for a copy of Frank Stanton's poem, "The Love Feast at Waycross". Mr. Stanton spent several days in Waycross, the guest of his brother, V. L. Stanton, after which he went to Smithville and started a little weekly paper. It was there that the Atlanta Constitution discovered him and he remained on the staff of that big daily until his passing away in the early part of 1927.

While in Waycross he dropped in at the love feast, which was a regular feature of the Sunday service at the Methodist church which stood in the street immediately west of the present Trinity church. First church was not built at that time. Mr. Stanton was deeply impressed with the service, as his poem indicates. His brother read it in the love feast the following Sunday. I asked the privilege of printing it in the Waycross Reporter, on which I was employed, and set it up by hand. That was before the typesetting machines were invented.

The poem is as follows:

*It was in the town of Waycross, not many weeks ago,
They had a big revival thar, as like enough you know;
An' though many was converted an' for pardon made to call,
Yet the Sunday mornin' love feast was the happiest time of all!*

*'Twas a great experience meetin' and it done me good to hear
The brotherin and sisterin that talked religion there;
You didn't have to ax them, nor coax them with a song,
Them people had religion, an' they told it right along!*

*Thar was one—a hard old sinner—'pears like I knowed his name,
But I reckon I've forgot it—who to the altar came;
An' he took the leader by the hand, with beamin' face and bright,
An' said, "I'm comin' home, dear fren's, I'm comin' home tonight."*

*Then a woman rose an' axed to be remembered in their prayers;
"My husband's comin' home," she a-sheddin' thankful tears;
"I want you all to pray for him he's lived in sin's control,
But I think the love of Jesus is breakin' on his soul!"*

*Then a young man rose an' told 'em he had wandered
 far away,*
But felt like comin' home ag'in, an' axed 'em all to pray;
*An' such a pra'r they made for him! I'll hear the like
 no more*
Till I hear the sweeter music on the bright celestial shore.

*Any shoutin'? Well, I reckon so! One brother gave a
 shout;*
Said he had so much religion he was 'bliged to let it out!
*An' the preacher joined the chorus sayin'; "Brotherin' let
 'er roll!*
A man can't keep from shoutin' with religion in his soul!

I tell you, 'twas a happy time; I wished 'twould never end;
Each sinner in the church that day had Jesus for a friend;
*But a good old deacon said to 'em, while tears stood in
 his eyes!*
*"There's a better time than this, my frien's, a-comin' bye
 and bye."*

*I hope some day those brethern'll meet with one accord
In that higher, holier love feast whose leader is the Lord;
An' when this life is over, with its sorrows and its sighs,
May the little church at Waycross join the great church
 in the skies!*

The "good old deacon" referred to was the venerable old saint Rev. W. H. Thomas, and in the original poem it read, "But Uncle Thomas said to 'em," etc. The preacher who is referred to as "joining the chorus", was Rev. E. J. Burch, pastor of the church at that time. I think the one who said he had "so much religion he was 'bliged to let it out", was Mr. William Parker.

First Methodist Church

In 1893 the First Methodist Church was built, Trinity no longer being adequate to hold the large membership of this fast-growing city.

A handsome brick structure was erected on Gilmore Street at a cost of $20,000. Early in September, 1892, the committee appointed for the building of the First Methodist Church organized itself for work. This committee consisted of T. E. Lanier, H. Murphy, William Parker, W. J. Smith, Lemuel Johnson, Leon A. Wilson and S. W. Hitch, T. E. Lanier was selected Chairman; L. A. Wilson, Secretary; and W. J. Smith, Treasurer. Mr. H. Murphy was requested to act as general overseer in the arrangements for beginning the work. On October 27, 1892, the plans were presented by Rev. George W. Matthews, being an exact model of a new church edifice at New Haven, Conn., whence that gentleman had gone to see this modern church structure, and brought back photographs of its interior. The plans were adopted and Mr. George Feltham, Architect, was engaged as superintendent of construction. On Jan. 1, 1893, ground was broken, and the work begun, and in a year the edifice was completed.

The building was erected upon ground that had been sanctified by one of the greatest revivals Waycross has ever known, when a tent was spread upon the lot afterwards purchased from Dr. B. F. Williams. Rev. William Waller conducted the revival services, in which scores were converted and added to the church. Upon this plot of ground several tent meetings of glorious power were held by Rev. J. P. Culpepper, David Tasker, and other prominent evangelists. The sainted Miller Willis was often in attendance during the revivals.

The church was dedicated by Bishop J. C. Granberry, of Virginia during Dr. C. C. Dowman's Presiding Eldership.

The names of pastors serving the church are: G. W. Matthews, A. M. Wynn, J. W. Domingoes, G. G. B. MacDonell, T. M. Christian, A. M. Williams, J. B. Johnstone, J. A. Harmon, Charlie Jenkins, J. P. Wardlaw, Osgood Cook, L. J. Ballard, C. M. Jackson, J. H. Scruggs, Loy Warwick, E. F. Morgan, O. B. Chester, J N. Peacock and J. M. Outler.

The first Superintendent of the Sunday School was V. L. Stanton, assisted by W. W. McCulley.

The first board of Stewards was composed of H. Murphy, Chairman; E. P. Peabody, Secretary; Miss Georgia Wright, Treasurer; John A. Lott, Oscar Lott, S. D. Pittman, M. D. Blackshear, R. H. Murphy, S. W. Hitch, W. W. McCulley, L. A. Wilson, J. N. Horne, E. A. Pound, L. Johnson and V. L. Stanton.

First Presbyterian Church

A regular meeting of the Savannah Presbytery convened Nov., 1886, the following committee was appointed to organize a Presbyterian church at Waycross:

Rev. J. W. Rogan, Rev. Paul F. Brown, Rev. J. W. Quarterman, and Elder John Patterson. Two of this committee met in Waycross and organized this church on March 4, 1887, with thirteen members, viz;

Mrs. Sarah Williams, Miss Rosa Screven, Mrs. Leila Mitchell, Mrs. Spottswood, Mrs. Laura Quarterman, Miss Bell Knox, Miss Mattie Williams, Miss Lena Quarterman, Miss Winnie Quarterman, Mr. William Williams and Mr. William Screven.

For the first year the faithful servant of God, Rev. J. W. Quarterman, was the spiritual leader of the people constituting the session of the church.

On January 1, 1889, Mr. W. P. Williams was elected, ordained and installed ruling elder, and was the first lay member to represent the church in an ecclesiastical court, the Synod of Georgia, at Thomasville. Rev. I. B. Davis supplied the church from 1889 to Feb., 1892. Rev. W. S. Porter was called to the pastorate March 31, 1892, and was pastor for two years. Rev. E. D. Viser was stated supply from March, 1895, to Nov., 1895. On July 12, 1896, the Rev. R. A. Brown was called. He served the church 22 years. Following Dr. Brown was Dr. J. S. Sibley, who served until 1923. After Dr. Sibley came Rev. T. J. Ponder and the present minister is Rev. Louis C. LaMotte.

First Baptist Church

The First Baptist Church of Waycross, Georgia, was organized and instituted on the 22nd day of March, 1882, the exercises taking place in the Methodist Church of Waycross, which stood at that time on the same site now occupied by Trinity Methodist Church.

There were seven original members who constituted the First Baptist Church of Waycross, as follows: Mr. and Mrs. J. R. Knight; Mr. and Mrs. E. D. Wilson; Mrs. Palmyra Johnson; Miss Mary E. Shine and Miss Emma Shine. The first pastor of the church was W. E. Perryclear.

It was during Mr. Cross' pastorate that a house of worship was built. This house was located on Albany Avenue, at or near the point where the Hereford Filling Station and sales stable are now located. The building committee of this house of worship was composed of H. P. Brewer, Alexander O'Quinn, J. R. Knight and Rev. G. M. Cross.

On November 17, 1886, after accepting the resignation of Rev. Mr. Cross which had been tendered on October 13, 1886, the Church unanimously called as its pastor Rev. W. H. Scruggs, at a salary of $200 per annum, and shortly thereafter Rev. Mr. Scruggs began his service as pastor. The Church grew rapidly under his pastorate. The congregations greatly increased and many new members were added to the church, and as early as 1890, within less than four years after the pastorate of Dr. Scruggs began, the house was entirely too small and the members of the Church decided to build a larger house of worship.

At that time the portion of Waycross now known as "New Waycross" has just begun to grow and develop, and after some considerable confusion, disagreement and discussion, it was finally decided by the Church membership to undertake the erection of a new building on the site on which we are now located, and on which a splendid house of worship has recently been constructed, the Church having acquired this location by gift from Mr. W. B. Plant after a personal interview with him by the pastor, Rev. W. H. Scruggs. A building committee was created, consisting of the following members: J. R. Knight, H. P. Brewer, Thomas L. Brown, Alexander O'Quinn and Rev. W. H. Scruggs, and the erection of the house began either in the latter part of 1891 or the early part of 1892.

This building committee found a great deal of trouble, and had considerable worry in their efforts to raise the money with which to erect the house of worship, and it has been said that but for the efforts of Miles Albertson, J. W. Johnson and F. C. Owens, the committee could not have succeeded.

Rev. W. H. Scruggs served the Church continually from 1886 until the spring of 1908, when he voluntarily resigned. His work during these years in behalf of Christianity, generally, and the Baptist cause particularly, will never be forgotten. The Church was then without a pastor for more than a year, and finally Rev. A. M. Bennett began his pastorate in the fall of 1909, and served the Church for two years, and the Church was again without a pastor for nearly a year, when Rev. W. P. Price began his pastorate which lasted for seven years—he leaving us in 1919. We were again without a pastor for nearly a year when Rev. J. M. Haymore took up his pastorate with us and served until November, 1921. We then called to the pastorate of the Church Dr. W. H. Rich, our present pastor, and he began his pastorate with us on May 1, 1922.

At the time Dr. Rich came to us we were considering the erection of a new house of worship, the old frame building erected in 1892-1893 being too small for the congregation, and out-of-date.

Soon after Dr. Rich's pastorate began the Church definitely decided to undertake the erection of a new house of worship, and finally in the spring of 1926, the congregation moved out of the old house and it was razed.

After much discussion the members of the Church voted to rebuild on their original site and the members soon got together under the leadership of the pastor, Dr. Rich, in unity and determination to build a house of worship that would be a credit and ornament to our city. And the present building in which we are today worshiping in the main auditorium for the first time, is the result of a great united church, full of love, I hope, for the cause and for each other.

I may state that the First Baptist Church of Waycross is a corporation, duly incorporated under the laws of the State of Georgia in 1926, controlled by a board of trustees. The board that has labored so zealously as a building committee in conjunction with the pastor in the building of this house are: W. C. Parker, Chairman; C. E. Gibson, H. C. Bunn, I. W. Odum, W. G. King, B. G. Parks and G. R. King.

About the time work began, the Church suffered a very great loss in the death of one of said board, to wit, our much-beloved brother, G. R. King, familiarly known to us all as Russell. May I pause to pay a tribute to his memory. He was one of our most loyal members and, I believe, the most devoted Christian, and the entire Church membership felt very deeply and keenly his loss as one of our members, and as one of our trustees. David M. Parker was elected to succeed him on the board.

As a result of the efforts of these trustees in connection with out beloved pastor Dr. W. H. Rich, we have completed the splendid building in which we are now worshiping.

Information furnished by Col. John W. Bennett.

Grace Episcopal Church

The first Episcopal service ever held in Waycross was in the Ware County Court House, and the preacher was the first Bishop of Georgia, the brilliant John Watrus

Beckwith—said to have been the greatest pulpit orator of his day.

At this time Waycross could only boast one place of worship, Trinity Methodist Church, a small frame building. Grace Episcopal Church, built in the Fall of 1884, followed. For a long time this congregation worshiped in Mrs. Oleman's school house ministered to by Mr. A. G. P. Dodge of St. Simon's Island.

Mr. Dodge was a man of wonderful spiritual force, and had planted the church and built schools in several out-of-the-way places in his native land and in India.

With his sympathetic assistance, the little handfull of Episcopalians built Grace Church, the second place of worship of Almighty God in the growing city of Waycross, a little frame chapel, small and unpretentious but surmounted by the cross, the emblem of its faith, and an object of loving pride to the few who worshiped there.

Soon the congregation grew until the monthly service given by Mr. Dodge was insufficient, and a regular clergyman was called.

Thus there came to Grace Church as its first regular Rector a man beloved of all who knew him no matter of what religious faith, one of the sweetest characters the world has ever known, the Rev. D. Watson Winn, of Richmond, Virginia. After a few years Mr. Winn was called to St. Mark's Church, Brunswick, Georgia, and following him came a man of fine character and ability, a man who made few friends, but who was ardently loved by that small coterie, an East Indian by birth and a man of wonderful culture and mental attainments, Rev. Stuart Martin. He in turn was followed by Rev. Jesse Bicknell, a man loved by all who knew him, and one who had a wonderful influence for good among the young, and especially the boys of the community.

Those who followed Mr. Bicknell as rectors of Grace Episcopal Church, were the Rev. J. W. Turner, Rev. W. W. Kimball, Rev. F. F. Milbank, Rev. Thomas

Stafford, Rev. M. Campbell Stryker, Rev. R. A. Russell, Rev. S. J. French, Rev. Carl Corbun, and Dr. H. N. Turner.

The charter members and builders of Grace Church were:

Mr. and Mrs. U. J. Williams
Mrs. Mary Remshart Parker
Mrs. Elizabeth Oleman
Mr. and Mrs. Star
Mrs. Dixon

The little chapel with its only adornment the cross, has long since been replaced by a beautiful church of Spanish architecture.

CATHOLIC CHURCH—ST. JOSEPH'S CHURCH

Mrs. H. B. Plant deeded in 1884 to Bishop Gross of Savannah, one city block in Waycross to be held until such time as the Catholics of this city saw fit to erect a church upon it. The construction of the church took place during the year of 1889, the building of which was due largely to the efforts of the late Miss Hannah De Vanny and Mr. Jeremiah Cronin of Savannah. Their zeal and continual activities in behalf of the church were soon crowned with success and St. Joseph's church became an assured reality. The following year it was dedicated, which ceremony was performed by the late Bishop Becker of Savannah. The little church was filled, and on this occasion, the learned prelate's masterly discourse interested not only those of his faith but the many non-Catholics who attended the ceremonies. This church at that time ranked as a mission, owing to the limited number of resident Catholics, and was supplied at monthly intervals by a priest from the Brunswick church. Owing to faulty construction, the edifice did not prove worthy, and it was almost demolished in an autumn gale a few years after being built.

In the summer of 1898 the erection of the present church was begun on the same spot and was completed the next year. It is a neat and substantial structure, occupying the corner of the block intersecting Tebeau and Elizabeth Streets. Its simplicity of outline is given a pleasing effect by the artistic stained glass windows on the front and sides. The interior is finished in plaster and natural yellow pine with exposed beams and ceiling. On the wall space behind the altar is hung a large painting of the Madonna, a Raphael copy, which formerly adorned the old Cathedral in Savannah.

Mrs. William Cason was as largely responsible for the building of the present church as Mr. Cronin was for the erection of the original church, She, too, was untiring in her zeal and devotion in enlisting aid, and never became discouraged, although sometimes it was indeed hard to meet the payroll of the builders. Father Luckie so often admonished her to be brave, especially against obstacles. He once said, "That church shall surely be your monument, at least God has chosen you as His instrument to push on the work."

The people of Waycross, irrespective of creed, contributed in a generous way to the construction of the Catholic Church. Some of the most honored and beloved citizens of this city still commune there, while others have passed to a higher realm.

Central Baptist Tabernacle

It was during the early spring of 1909, the mammoth shops of the Atlantic Coast Line Railroad Company had been opened, the progress of the city was going by leaps and bounds, strangers were to be seen in every direction, houses were in such great demand that small cottages were in many instances occupied by two families. What shall we do with all of these new people? This was the question being asked by many of the older citizens. At Scruggs Pharmacy, in the Phoenix Hotel Block, Messrs. John W. McGee and Calvin Parker were standing at the soda fountain and Mr. McGee said to Mr.

Parker, "It seems to me we ought to get a large tent and place it in a central portion of the city, where we could have a convenient place of worship for this great influx of population." This remark so impressed Mr. Parker that as they walked from the building he said, "It is the thing to do." They at once got with C. H. Lowther, T. S. Paschal and W. F. Eaton and repaired to Mr. Parker's office in LaGrange hotel building, where they planned for the buying of a large tent. Later they arranged with Mr. R. G. Scruggs to allow the tent to be placed on a beautiful lot he owned at the corner of Brunel and Reed streets. Within a few days the project was thoroughly agitated, meeting with enthusiastic favor in every quarter of the city.

The tent came and was erected. Mr. B. B. Gray, of Leliaton, Ga., very kindly donated a carload of flooring, which was used to floor the entire tent space and build an attractive platform large enough for a hundred singers. This, with a piano placed upon the platform, gave a very attractive place of worship.

On May 30, 1909, the first service was held with an overflowing congregation. The text used on that occasion by Pastor W. H. Scruggs was: "Come unto me all ye that labor and are heavy laden and I will give you rest."—Matt. 11:28. The invitation was graciously received by several in the congregation.

The work thus begun created such interest that the entire congregation felt impressed to organize a church, buy the lot, and build a permanent house of worship. On Sunday morning, June 13, 1909, the congregation met with the view of organizing. Letters were called for and 109 were presented. Then Pastor Scruggs and Rev. G. S. Baxter, acting as Presbytery, duly organized Central Baptist Tabernacle under a tent on the beautiful lot corner of Brunel and Reed Streets. The Church adopted the Articles of Faith and Church Covenant held by the Piedmont Association.

Later realizing the great need of a permanent building free-will offerings were made by many, the offerings varying in amounts from five cents to five hundred dollars. Bro. T. W. Morrison then kindly offered to loan the church enough additional money to put the building where it could be used. His kind offer was accepted and on June 20, 1910, a large and representative congregation from the city met on the lot where the building was to be erected, tent having been removed, and engaged in a most delightful song and prayer service, followed by addresses from the pastor and Rev. T. S. Herbert, of Douglas, Ga., after which dirt was broken—the beginning of the basement for the brick structure, 55 x 105 feet, with three towers, through which the winding stairways a roof garden of the same dimensions would be reached.

On December 9, 1910, the cornerstone of the building was placed by Dr. W. L. Pickard, Pastor of the First Baptist Church of Savannah, Ga. The address was beautiful and impressive. The prayer, made as he placed the stone, was a benediction.

The work continued until March 19, 1911, when the building was opened and the first service was held, conducted by Pastor, assisted by Rev. R. Y. Walden, Rev. J. F. Harbin and Rev. B. A. Pafford. It was a great service. God in the person of the Holy Spirit was with us.

By A. P. Perham,
Church Historian.

First Christian Church

This church was organized during the month of June, 1917. The congregation was composed of eleven members, and for a short while worshiped under a tent. The pastor in charge was Rev. A. J. Mize. He served one year.

The second pastor, Rev. I. S. Bussing, served two years and in 1920 he, together with the members of his congregation, built a chapel. The church has steadily increased in membership and the little chapel has now been replaced by an attractive stucco house of worship.

Rev. W. J. Mott was untiring in his efforts to build a larger church and during the six years of his pastorate here worked in an efficient way for the erection of the First Christian Church which was completed in 1924.

Rev. W. A. Everhart served this church two years and was followed by the Rev. Charles S. VanWinkle, who has served as pastor four years.

CHAPTER IX

WARE COUNTY'S SCHOOLS

HE FIRST academy opened for educational purposes in Ware was located in Waresboro. The children of the different settlements attended the school, and some of Ware's most useful men and women were taught to read and write at this once primative seat of learning.

The academy was organized in 1829 and although the teachers were poorly compensated during these early years for their work, the school continued, and has never gone backward. However, it at one time had a year of reverses. The state's appropriation, called "The Poor Fund", of $236.67 was misapplied and converted to speculation.

Wildsville and Kettle Creek Schools.

These two schools were organized in 1830.

The Kettle Creek settlement was located not far from Kettle Creek Church and Cemetery, and the Wildsville School was located not far from Dubuss Bay, southwest of Waycross. The following report made by Mr. David J. Miller to Governor Lumpkin shows about all of the existing history of these two schools of the early days of Ware.

To His Excellency The Governor.

Ga.

Sir.

Ware Co.

Annexed you have a correct return of Kettle Creek and Wildsville Schools in the County of Ware for the Political year, 1831.

Name and Place of School	Name of Teacher	Male Scholars	Female Scholars	What Taught	Money Year	Received Month
Kettle Creek	Daniel I. Blackburn	17	20	Spelling Reading Writing	1831 $991.61	April
Wildsville	Samuel Sweat	8	7	Spelling Reading Writing		

Money Disbursed

	Year		Month
Kettle Creek	1831	$79.50	June
Wildsville	1831	$45.00	June

Certified per

David J. Miller, Trustee of
Poor School Fund, Oct. 1, 1831.

THE FIRST SCHOOL IN WAYCROSS

The first school taught in Waycross was in a log house donated by Mrs. Benjamin Williams, but as new settlers came in an appropriation was voted "for supporting an Academy" by which not only education but piety, religion, and morality should be promoted."

The academy was built on a plot of ground where the residence of Col. Leon A. Wilson now stands. Mr. George S. Roach was the first school master, and following Mr. Roach was Mr. Charles Jenkins.

Other schools were opened during the following years. One taught by Misses Emma and Mamie Shine, one by Mr. Preston Settle, and one by Mrs. Oleman.

In April, 1882, a mass meeting was called to discuss the feasibility of establishing a local school system. The necessity was keenly felt and the people were equal to the emergency. A building committee, composed of Dr. Wm. B. Folks, N. Dixon, T. H. Morton, H. Murphy, and H. W. Reed were appointed.

At the first meeting Dr. Folks was elected chairman; H. W. Reed, Secretary; T. H. Morton, Treasurer; and H. Murphy, Superintendent of Construction. A site was secured from the S. F. & W. Railway Company for the erection of a wooden building to be known as the Plant Institute, in honor of Mr. H. B. Plant, President of the Plant System Railroad (now A. C. L.). Rev. W. H. Thomas (Uncle Thomas) was collector for the committee, one thousand and eleven dollars being subscribed. Work was started and the foundation completed early in 1883. It was then discovered that it would be impossible to collect a sufficient fund to complete the building and start the school. Work was suspended for a while, and the untimely death of Dr. Folks put a temporary check to the construction of the schoolhouse.

In 1886 another mass meeting was called and the following committee was appointed: T. H. Morton, Alexander O'Quinn, E. B. Crawley, H. P. Brewer, and A. R. Bennett. Later a board of Trustees was elected to complete the building and carry on the school. The Board consisted of C. H. Crawley, A. R. Bennett, T. H. Morton, H. W. Reed, B. Sirmans, W. J. Smith and H. Murphy. The school was opened Sept., 1887, with Mr. J. D. Groff as principal, Miss L. M. Ingram, and Miss Mamie E. Shine as teachers. Mr. Groff served the school from 1887 to 1890. Mr. R. M. Bridges succeeded Mr. Groff, serving from 1890 to 1894. The first graduating class of this school took place during the superintendency of Mr. Bridges. At that time there were ten grades in the school. The names of graduates were: Mary Hitch, Minnie Knight, Lula Knoff and Joe Brewer.

Standing on the corner of Isabella and Lott street, occupied as a boarding house, is this old schoolhouse. It was removed from the lot to give a place for the Central High School.

In 1887 the legislature passed a bill providing for a public school system in Waycross. It provided for an ad valorem assessment which many citizens paid promptly; a few resisted on the grounds of the constitution, and succeeded in restraining its collection. Another bill was passed Dec. 26, 1888, approved by the Governor, and adopted by the people with only four dissenting votes. A system of education was permanently established upon an enduring basis.

The rapid growth of the city soon rendered the institution too small for the seating capacity was limited to three hundred. Something more modern and commodious was found necessary, and plans were made to erect a structure in keeping with the increasing importance of the city. In the Spring of 1893 an election was held to decide the question of "bonds or no bonds". Bonds were carried by a large majority. The city was bonded for $25,000 for school purposes; of this sum $22,000 was expended in the erection of the present High School edifice which was completed in 1895. This school building for white children accommodates from six hundred to seven hundred pupils; the attendance increasing from 380 in 1895-6 to 540 in 1898-99. The grounds comprise an entire block in the heart of the city.

Prof. McDonald from 1894, and part of '95, as superintendent, and the Board of Education who presided then were: H. P. Brewer, Pres.; W. J. Carswell, Secty.; Warren Lott, Treas.; A. M. Knight, J. M. Wells, L. Johnson and W. M. Toomer.

In the fall of 1895 Prof. A. E. Pound filled the position of Superintendent of the public schools and served until 1912, resigning to enter other fields of labor. It was through his untiring interest that Morton Avenue School was built in 1907.

Prof. A. G. Miller became superintendent of the public schools in the fall of 1912 and resigned in 1928. Waycross had the first High School in 1913 during Mr. Miller's term of office.

Isabella and Quarterman Street Schools were opened in well equipped brick buildings in 1913.

Mr. Ralph Newton succeeded Mr. Miller as superintendent of Waycross schools; and it has been through his untiring interest that Waycross High School has been made a member of the Southern Association of Colleges and Secondary Schools, Class A.

Administration of Schools—City

The agencies involved and controlling the city schools are a city board of Education and a city superintendent of schools. The City Board of Education consists of eight members who are elected at the regular general election. These members receive no salary but give freely of their time to all school interests. The city superintendent is chosen secretary to the board of Education for a term of one year. The law provides for no special qualifications for this office, but great care is taken to secure a man whose education and experience fit him for the position. Number of members of Board of Education, seven; City Manager makes eight. They are elected every two years for a term of four years; three members elected in 1931; four members to be elected in 1933.

Superintendents and Principals of Waycross Schools

SUPERINTENDENTS

J. D. Goff	1887-1890
R. M. Bridges	1890-1894
.... McDonald	1894-April 1, 1895
E. A. Pound	1895-1812
A. G. Miller	1912-1928
Ralph Newton	1928-

Apparently the superintendents were also principals until 1905 when D. C. Colson, the first man other than the superintendent was elected.

HISTORY OF WARE COUNTY, GEORGIA 133

PRINCIPALS

1905	1906	1907	1908
D. C. Colson	....	Nolan A. Goodyear	Calhoun Mays

Mrs. R. M. Bridges, Howe Street ....
Miss Willie R. Beck, Quarterman St.......................
R. R. Holmes, Colored School ....

1909	1910	1911	1912
	Knox Starling	J. K. Starling	Q. L. Garrett
	Mrs. R. M. Bridges, Howe		Mrs. T. J. Gurr, Howe
R. R. Holmes	Mrs. T. J. Gurr, Quarterman		Mrs. Bridges, Quarterman

1913	1914	1915	1916
Q. L. Garrett		J. W. Bagby	

Miss L. Middlemas, Jr. H.
Miss W. R. Beck, Isabella
Mrs. T. J. Gurr, Howe
Mrs. A. Findlay, Quarterman
Miss Lena Phillips, Gilchrist
R. R. Holmes, Negro

1917
J. W. Bagby
Middlemas
Beck
Gurr
Findlay
Phillips
Holmes

1918
T. M. Purcell

1919
C. H. Tinsley
Carrie Shropshire
Holmes

1920

1921
Tinsley
Middlemas
Beck
Bessie Middlemas
Findlay
Vera Floyd
Holmes

1922
E. S. Barney
L. Middlemas
Beck
B. Middlemas
Findlay
Bessie Dunn
Holmes

1923
W. D. Miller
W. S. Lester

1924

1925

1926
Ruby Meeks
Mary Letford, Crawford

1927
W. D. Miller
L. Middlemas
Beck
B. Middlemas—Lily Jelks
Findlay
Meeks
Letford
J. D. Gaither

1928
S. H. Sherman
Jelks
Mary Sue Cannon

1929

1930
A. R. Walton

1931

L. L. Ison
Geo. King

Record of Members of the City Board of Education

A review of the history of the City Board of Education reveals some very interesting facts, connected with it as the following records of the officers show not only members but Charter members:

H. W. Reed, charter member, Jan., 1889, resigned Jan., 1894. John M. Marshall, Jan. 1889, died while in office Jan., 1892. He was a charter member. W. J. Carswell, Charter member, Jan., 1889, died while holding office in 1912. S. W. Hitch, charter member, Jan., 1889, resigned March, 1898. A. O'Quinn, charter member Jan., 1889, term expired March, 1890. H. Murphy, charter member, 1889, resigned 1891. Dr. J. L. Walker, elected by board, 1890, resigned March 1898. H. P. Brewer, elected Jan. 1891, resigned Dec., 1903. Lemuel Johnson, elected Jan., 1891, resigned Dec., 1905. A. M. Knight, elected Jan., 1894, term expired Dec., 1909. J. C. W. Smith, elected 1894, resigned June, 1895. S. S. Fitzsimmons, elected Jan., 1895, resigned July, 1897. J. M. Wells elected Jan., 1897, declined. W. M. Toomer, elected July, 1897, resigned Nov., 1905. Warren Lott, elected June, 1898, died 1907. L. F. Henning, elected June, 1900, resigned June, 1901. J. C. Humphreys, elected June, 1901, term expired 1909. V. L. Stanton, elected 1903, term expired Dec., 1914. D. F. Kirkland, elected June, 1905, resigned Sept., 1906. Dr. J. L. Walker, elected Sept., 1906, term expired Dec., 1914. C. E. Murphy, elected Jan., 1908, term expired Dec., 1913. B. G. Parks, elected Jan., 1910, term expired Dec., 1915. E. J. Berry, elected Jan., 1910, term expired Dec., 1915. A. M. Knight, elected Oct., 1912, resigned Dec., 1912, and Mrs. J. R. Whitman appointed to his unexpired term. W. W. Lamdin, Jan., 1913, term expired, 1915. Mrs. W. W. Sharpe, Mrs. J. R. Whitman and Mrs. Jack Williams, elected 1922, terms expired 1924.

Officers of the Board

H. W. Reed, President, 1880-1894. Dr. J. L. Walker, President, 1894-1898. A. M. Knight, President, 1898-1899. H. P. Brewer, President, 1899-1903. W. M. Toomer, President, 1903-1905. W. J. Carswell, President, 1905-1912, V. L. Stanton, 1912. J. M. Marshall, Secretary, 1889-1892. W. J. Carswell, Secretary, 1892-1905. E. A. Pound, Secretary, 1905-1912. A. G. Miller, Secretary, 1912.

School Chronology

County School Commissioners

B. Sweat	1876
J. D. Smith	1888-1913
J. R. Bourne	1914-1916
John Lee	1916-1917
C. W. Pittman	1917-1925
R. C. Cavender	1925-1931
T. L. Everette	1931

School bond issue of 1912 for $25,000.

Illiteracy in Ware.

Illiterates among children of school age in Ware County, according to 1923 census, 45, according to 1928 census, 22.

Census of school age in Waycross of 1923, shows 30 illiterates, 1928 census shows only 1.

In 1930 night schools for white adult illiterates were held. Between 30 and 40 were registered.

In 1928 a negro night school was taught at Center City High School building by Cora Reddick. The oldest pupil was 60 years old and the youngest thirty-five. This school ably did its part toward helping the negroes whose chances had been limited on educational lines to learn to read and write[1].

---
1. Information incorporated in the history of the schools of Ware County, was furnished by Mrs. F. B. Folsom.

ORGANIZED WAYCROSS SCHOOLS—(White)

School	Location	Organized	No. Teachers	No. Grades	No. Pupils	School Year
Central High	Mary St.	1887	12 and Librarian	3	299	9 months
Jr. High	Mary St.	1913	10	2	352	9 months
Isabella	Isabella St.	1913	11	6	344	9 months
Morton Ave.	Morton Ave.	1907	12	6	396	9 months
Quarterman	Quarterman St.	1907	9	6	293	9 months
Crawford	Crawford St.	1926	7	6	175	9 months
Gilchrist Park	Gilchrist Park	1913	5	5	130	9 months

WHITE SCHOOLS IN WARE COUNTY—(Continued)

School	Location	Consolidated From	No. Teachers	No. Grades	No. Pupils	Principal	School Year
Ruskin	Ruskin	Thrift, Griffin Ruskin	3	8	45	Miss Mae Wilson	7 months
Camp Branch	3½ Miles Northeast of Manor	No Consolidation	2	7	46		6 months
Cason	8 Miles North of Waycross	No Consolidation	1	7	17		6 months
Riverside	3 Miles Northeast of Waycross	No Consolidation	1	7	16		6 months
Jordan	15 Miles North of Waycross	No Consolidation	1	7	19		6 months
Tatum	11 Miles South of Waycross	No Consolidation	1	7	26		6 months
17 Mile Post	17 Miles South of Waycross	No Consolidation	1	7	10		6 months
Emerson Park	2 Miles West of Waycross	Emerson Park Kettle Creek	3	10	64	Mrs. E. K. Balcomb	8 months
Davis-Edenfield	20 Miles Northwest of Waycross	No Consolidation	1	7	20		6 months
Community Consolidated	7 Miles South of Waycross	Strickland, Braganza, Ft. Mudge, Crews	3	7	64	Miss Mary Paschall	7 months
Millwood	Millwood	No Consolidation	4	9	79		8 months
Suwanee	12 Miles South of Manor	No Consolidation	1	7	24		9 months

WHITE SCHOOLS IN WARE COUNTY—(Continued)

School	Location	Consolidation of	No. Teachers	No. Grades	No. Pupils	Accredited	Principal	School Year
Wacona	Hebardville	Pine View, Jamestown	13	11	554	Yes	Omer Jones	9 months
Waresboro	Waresboro	Waresboro, Stampede, Friendship, Pine Valley, Fairfax	1 music teacher 12 teachers	11	444	Yes	T. L. Everett	9 months
Dixie Union	11 Miles North of Waycross	Bennett, Lynn, Bolen	5	8	210		Mrs. S. B. Hargraves	6 months
Bickley	18 Miles North of Waycross	Beach, Lee, Moore, Bickley	5	8	147		C. H. Parker, Jr.	6 months
Woodward-Godwin	6 Miles East of Waycross	Woodward-Godwin	2	8	57		Mrs. E. B. Calhoun	6 months
Mt. Green-Sycamore	3½ Miles Southeast of Millwood	Mt. Green, Sycamore	2	7	45		Miss Catherine Pittman	6 months
Coleman	15 Miles Northwest of Waycross	Not Consolidated	2	7	41		E. S. McCarthy, 1930-31	6 months
Melton	8 Miles South of Waycross	Not Consolidated	1	7	22			6 months
Inman	3½ Miles North of Manor	Not Consolidated	2	7	45			6 months
Manor	Manor	Sedgwick, Mixon, Pittman	4	8	74		O. M. Palmer	8 months

COLORED SCHOOLS — WAYCROSS

School	Location	Year Completed	No. Teachers	No. Grades	Aver. Yearly Attendance	Accredited
Center City High School	Butler and McDonald	1926	9	6-11	242	Yes
Reidsville	Snelson St.		5	1-5	212	
North Side	Bokum St.		8	1-5	393	
Hazzard Hill	Sycamore St.		6	1-5	199	

The negro school in Reidsville was constructed in 1895 at a cost of $3,000.00, Prof. Floyd Snelson was the first principal of the high school. Mrs. Annie B. Johnson was in charge of the intermediate, and Miss L. J. Stoney, the primary department. Crawford, Center City, annexed to Central High, 1926.

COLORED SCHOOLS IN WARE COUNTY

School	Location	Consolidated From	No. Teachers	No. Grades	No. Pupils	Principal	School Year
Glenmore-Manor	1½ mi. East of Manor	Manor Glenmore	2	7	42	Theodosia Hoover Gray	6 months
Beach	Beach	No.	1	7	20		6 months
Deenwood	Deenwood	No.	1	7	24		6 months
Jamestown-Grant	2 mi. Northwest of Waycross	No.	1	7	18		6 months
Telmore	Telmore	No.	1	7	37		6 months
Ruskin	Ruskin	No.	1	7	16		6 months
Green Swamp	3 mi. West of Waycross	No.	1	7	19		6 months
Waresboro	Waresboro	No.	1	7	23		6 months
Fairfax	Fairfax	No.	1	7	29		6 months
Haywood	Haywood	No.	1	7	18		6 months
Cross Roads	Crawley	No.	1	7	33		6 months
Millwood	Millwood	No.	1	7	12		6 months
Hasty	Hasty	No.	1	7	17		6 months
Boonstill	4 mi. Sou. of Millwood	No.	1	7	16		6 months
Ft. Mudge	Ft. Mudge	No.	1	7	14		6 months
Crews	Crews	No.	1	7	13		6 months

Piedmont Institute

In 1901 the Baptists in this section began debating the advisability of establishing an institution for Southeast Georgia.

Piedmont Institute was chartered by the Superior Court of Ware County under the title of Bunn-Bell Institute in 1907 with authority to confer college degrees. The institution was open to students in the fall of 1909. In 1914 its name was changed from Bunn-Bell Institute to Piedmont, because of the name of the Association in which it was established. It has been the ward of Piedmont, New Sunbury, Consolidation and Smyrna Associations from its beginning. Piedmont Institute was adopted into the Mercer University System in 1919.

On April 13, 1926, a dormitory for boys was begun. One year later this building was dedicated and named the T. A. Parker Memorial Hall.

For many years Piedmont was the only school of its kind in Southeast Georgia. Boys and girls desiring more than an elementary education became students in this institution.

In recent years the State of Georgia realizing that too little was being done for its youth in an educational way began to formulate plans to meet this need. State schools, branches of the State Universities were established in many districts, the counties consolidated their schools. Thus it was that the boys and girls near their own homes could receive a high school education, having trained teachers and comfortable modern buildings.

The state and consolidated schools with state money could give the boys and girls a higher education at a low cost, while Piedmont had to depend on students and friends for its maintenance. The friends of the Institute realized that Piedmont together with other schools of its kind in the State had long filled an educational need, but with changed conditions the usefulness of these schools seemed to be at an end. In view of these things those in charge of Piedmont deemed it advisable to close the doors of this institution in May, 1928[1].

E. G. Hall, B. S., of Knoxville, Tenn., was elected as the first president and served one year, 1909-1910.

E. L. Ray, A. B., was the second president and served two years, 1910-1912.

W. S. Peterson, A. B., was elected as third president and served two years, 1912-1914.

M. O. Carpenter, A. B., was the fourth president and served four years, 1914-1918. He was vice-president one year under President Ray and two years under President Peterson.

J. F. Watson, A. B., was elected fifth president and served one year, 1918-1919.

W. C. Carlton, A. B., A. M., was elected sixth president and served nine years, 1919- 1920.

---
1. Information on Piedmont Institute furnished by Miss Lela Somerall.

CHAPTER X
HAPPENINGS IN WAYCROSS

IN 1872 Dr. Daniel Lott sold all the tract of land west of the A. & G. Railroad to J. W. Remshart, and with Mr. Remshart and William Parker (his son-in-law), there lived in Tebeauville some five or six families. All told the population of this little settlement at Tebeauville would not have numbered more than one hundred souls.

Drs. Daniel Lott and William B. Folks obtained a charter for a railroad from Waycross southward to St. Marys river and ultimately to Jacksonville, and it was through the influence of these men that Colonel H. S. Haines was prevailed upon to accept the charter, and when the Plant millions were brought into account the line that made Waycross and gave her the possibilities of a quick inland city was constructed and advertised all over the world as "The Waycross Short Line to Florida". This flaming legend hung in the steamship offices and on the piers of North river and fluttered in the breeze at Plymouth Rock and invited the tourist from the old world as it spelled out orange blossoms and perpetual sunshine to the befogged Scotchman on the banks of the Clyde or the gloom-wearied denizens of London town. And so, on June 21, 1880, Dr. William B. Folks, in company with Colonel Haines and other railway men, and the municipal body of Waycross, lifted with his own hands (holding the shovel) out of the earth, immediately in front of the Joe McQuaig house, where now is the Union station, the first shovelful of soil that was to set in motion the enterprise of building the Waycross Short Line to Florida[1].

---
1. Excerpts from an article by V. L. Stanton, deposited in the Y. M. C. A., later the municipal corner stone.

In 1868 Mrs. Grovenstine was postmistress. The postoffice at that time was located in Old Nine, the station was then known as Tebeauville, located near the A. & G. road (later the S. F. & W.)

The first street to be paved in Waycross was Plant Avenue, then followed Gilmore, Gulf and Albany.

It doubtless will be of interest to many Ware county people to know that the block upon which Judge Warren Lott, Charles E. Murphy, H. Murphy, R. H. Murphy and D. B. Sweat once resided was Dr. Daniel Lott's cornfield, and on that piece of ground he raised the finest yield of corn ever realized in Ware county. He came within a few bushels of making one hundred to the acre.

Mr. William Wilson gave the following facts: "There was a street railway in operation in Waycross almost half a century ago. I have a picture of the first conveyance on this street railway system, a horse car which served 'courthouse, hotels and depot' as is revealed in a sign on the old car. The picture was taken in front of the Grand Central Hotel which was located where the Phoenix now stands. The Grand Central was a three-story brick structure owned by H. Murphy. The mule-drawn street car is shown with its conductor, Turner Brewer, at the reins. The photograph was taken forty-seven years ago." This street car was sold to the manager of the hotel on St. Simons, and for years carried passengers arriving on boat at St. Simons.[1]

The Atlantic and Gulf Railroad was the first railroad through Ware County and was from Savannah to Thomasville. It was about the year 1869, the station in Ware was named Number 9, but later became Tebeauville.

In early days of railroading the stations were numbered. Later when the country began to settle up, and towns were located between the regular numbers, to avoid fractional numbers for stations the number system was abandoned.

In 1868 Tebeauville boasted of only four families:

---
1. Information furnished by Mrs. L. G. Jenkins.

Mr. John Baschlot, Postmaster, his daughter, Mrs. M. M. Grovenstein and her children, John, Lizzie, Kate, Rosa, Farley and Joe; and the Rev. Lewis C. Tebeau and his wife and children, Emma, Eddie, Minnie and Charley. In the fall of 1868, Rev. W. Remshart, his wife and daughter, Isabella and his son-in-law, Capt. William Foster Parker, his wife and children, Orville D., Geo. Foster, Sumter B., Lucy M., Maggie M., moved to Tebeauville.

Mr. John Remshart was the first railroad agent. George Rollings the first telegraph operator. Orville D. Parker became the telegraph operator at Tebeauville in 1872.

The first railroad from Savannah was called Atlantic & Gulf, then changed to Savannah, Florida & Western Railway, then the Plant System and later the Atlantic Coast Line. The Waycross-Jacksonville short line was built about 1881.

Some years after the Atlantic & Gulf was completed to Thomasville, the Brunswick & Albany Railroad was started, but was stopped at Waresboro, or a short distance west of that place. The War coming on, owing to need of rails, the rails on the Brunswick & Albany road were taken up and used elsewhere by the Confederate government for use on more important roads to move troops. The Brunswick & Albany was rebuilt after the war, about 1869. Capt. W. F. Parker was appointed their agent at Tebeauville. The B. & A., using the A. & G. tracks from the railroad crossing at the old part of Waycross to No. 9 to connect with the A. & G.

The little church schoolhouse at old 9 was built by Mrs. B. F. Williams, who then lived at Sunny Side on the Satilla River. Mrs. Jane Remshart, Mrs. Grovenstein, Miss Isabella Remshart (Mrs. J. H. Redding) Mrs. Mary E. Parker and others, were leaders in the Sunday School.

The church was served by a circuit rider as pastor.

Tebeauville was abandoned as a station in 1881 with

the opening of the new part of Waycross and the station was moved to its present location in Waycross.

In 1870 there were five dwellings, one boarding house, one store, the warehouse, and the water tank in what was then Tebeauville.

Mr. John Lucius Clary was an engineer and Mr. Dave McGee was a conductor on a construction train on the Atlantic & Gulf Railroad. Mr. Clary was a brother of Mrs. Susie Burnett.

This is partly the way Waycross obtained an artesian well.

"Mr. Leopold Weise informs us that he will give a festival for the benefit of the artesian well at Oleman's hall on Thursday night, June 17th. He proposes to go into this matter unaided, bearing the full expense himself, and with a view of helping our town in the needed boon and will ask only the patronage of the people. Everybody here knows Mr. Weise and the people are assured of an affair full of enjoyment and a rare treat. Mr. Weise is the right man to get behind the great project of drilling for better water." (Copied from The Waycross Headlight, dated 1886.)

Captain Edward Crawley was also an important projector in this progressive movement for the benefit of public welfare.

A notice appeared in the paper urging that all citizens attend the festival given by the "progressive and liberal-hearted Mr. Weise". This notice was signed by T. E. Lanier, Warren Lott and L. A. Wilson, Com.

A general progressive awakening overspread Waycross during June, 1886, for the paper called attention to the fact that Waycross needed electric lights, and the editor admonished the citizens that electric lights could be furnished at about the cost of kerosene light now in use. That year they not only worked for an artesian well, but put forward a projection for a lighting system.

The first state senator from Ware County was Philemon Bryan who served from 1825 to 1827 and John L. Stewart was elected the first representative. The original line between Irwin and Appling counties, extended along the line between dividing the Seventh and the Eleventh Land District of Irwin county. This caused most of the present Mud Creek to be in Irwin county.

THE TRAIN WRECK AND THE DESTRUCTION OF THE OLD A. C. L. STATION

One Sunday morning in 1883 while Mr. V. L. Stanton was busy at his desk in the railway station, and Wilbur Beaton was in the office selling tickets, there was a rustle and puff of engines, and in another minute the Western Fast Mail on the Plant System had plunged into the B. & W. passenger train, which was crossing at that time. Engineer Bill Divine's attention was attracted by some commotion near the old Satilla House and in the brief moment that he looked away with his hand on the throttle of his engine it plunged into the baggage car of the B. & W. passenger train, raising this car almost bodily and thrusting it over on the depot. Mr. Stanton and Mr. Beaton, with the passengers were entrapped in the demolished building. No one was hurt seriously; even the little negro office boy, for whose safety great apprehenson was entertained, was found serenely sitting under a small table intact.

Population of Ware County and Waycross, Georgia, so far as shown at each Federal census:

CENSUS WARE COUNTY, WAYCROSS

Year	Ware County	Waycross
1930	26,558	15,510
1920	28,361	18,068
1910	22,957	14,485
1900	13,761	5,919

1890	8,811	3,364
1880	4,159	*
1870	2,286	—
1860	2,200	—
1850	3,888	—
1840	2,323	—
1830	1,205	—

* Waycross was shown in a list of unincorporated places in Georgia in the 1880 census report on population, with a population of 628.

CHAPTER XI

UTILITIES IN WAYCROSS

GAS—Gas for the city of Waycross is furnished by the Consumers Gas and Coke Company, a subsidiary of the Central Public Service Corporation, Chicago, Ill.

The plant has a capacity of 225,000 cubic feet, while the present average daily send out is 100,000 cubic feet.

Bills are rendered at the gross rate. The discount is allowable if the bills are paid in full within ten days following the date of presentation.

WATER—The City of Waycross receives its domestic and industrial water supply from deep wells.

The pumping stations and distribution system are municipally-owned and operated.

The present average daily consumption is approximately 1,400,000 gallons, which is less than half of the estimated maximum flow of the existing wells. Two wells are held in reserve at all times.

This water supply is not affected by prolonged dry spells which sometimes effect other cities in various parts of the country, and regardless of consumption the static head remains practically the same.

At regular intervals samples of the city water are taken from the mains at three different points in the city and are tested by the State Department of Public Health. The water has always been reported as excellent for drinking purposes. It contains a little over 17 grains mineral matter and a little over 1 1-2 grains organic matter per gallon.

Ware's First Board of Health

In August, 1888, in view of yellow fever being prevalent in Florida, a Board of Health was organized in Waycross composed of the following named citizens: Mayor F. C. Folks, Dr. Alexander Carswell, Dr. J. L. Walker, Dr. J. H. Redding, A. M. Knight, H. P. Brewer, H. Murphy and William English. At the first meeting they declared a quarantine against Jacksonville and all other Florida towns.

Waycross Water Works

On September 19, 1889, Governor John B. Gordon signed the charter of the Waycross Water Works and Sanitary Commission. On December 28, 1889, the commissioner, W. M. Wilson, B. H. Williams, M. Albertson, W. A. Cason, H. W. Reed and H. Murphy, qualified before Judge Warren Lott, ordinary of Ware county. Work was immediately started and by April, 1893, the standpipe, two artesian wells, and a considerable part of the mains were completed.

A new air compresser with a capacity of 50,000 gallons per hour was added in 1895. The present capacity is over three million gallons every twenty-four hours.

The Waycross water works plant is located in the business center of Waycross, part of it on a triangular block on Plant Avenue near the railroad.

The second commission consisted of H. Murphy, W. M. Wilson, V. L. Stanton, E. H. Reed, W. A. Cason Lemuel Johnson, and R. P. Bird, clerk.

The water furnished Waycross is pure and wholesome. The first chemical analysis was made by State Chemist, Mr. White, in 1893, as follows:

Solids dissolved _____ Grains per U. S. Gallon
Carbonate of lime _____ 7,502
Carbonate of iron _____ 0,120
Sulphate of magnesia _____ 0,162
Sulphate of potash _____ 0,061
Sulphate of soda _____ 0,084
Sodium chloride (common salt) _____ 0,349
Silica _____ 0,582
Organic matter, combined water _____ 0,965
                                       _____
                                       10,356

Prof White said: "This water contains the dissolved solids usually found in the artesian waters of Southern Georgia. It contains them, however, in rather smaller quantities than usual, and it is one of the best of such waters that I have examined. It is pure and excellent water, suitable for domestic and manufacturing purposes."

Mr. H. Murphy, formerly a native of New Jersey, served in an efficient way as the first chairman of the commission. He was one of the early settlers of Waycross, and was ever considered one of the city's most progressive citizens and business men. He always took a leading part in any enterprise that helped in the building of the city. For a number of years he was the president of the First National Bank, retiring of his own volition.

Mr. R. P. Bird, clerk of the city council and of the water works commission, was a man well fitted for this place. Mr. Bird was ever faithful in the performance of every obligation placed upon him. He was born in Liberty county in 1842, was a gallant soldier under General Wheeler during the War Between the States and was a member of the South Georgia Camp of Confederate Veterans. He and his family came to Waycross in 1888, from Jefferson county. He died in Waycross.

The water works superintendent, D. B. Finn, came from Pennsylvania to Georgia in 1889. He completed the artesian wells in 1893, was employed as superintending engineer, and served for several years. He was an efficient mechanic, having a great understanding of machinery. He was long employed in the oil and gas regions of Pennsylvania, Ohio and West Virginia. In addition to being a thoroughly proficient worker, he was always popular with all classes of people.

The members of the commission were engaged in the following avocations: W. M. Wilson was for a number of years clerk of the Ware Superior Court, and was also a prominent Waycross merchant. V. L. Stanton was a leading insurance man; E. H. Reed had a prominent position with the Plant System R. R. (A. C. L.); W. A. Cason was a member of the firm of Cason & Griffin, and one of the county commissioners. Captain Lemuel Johnson was president of the Ware Lumber Company in this city.

Waycross Fair Association

The Waycross Fair Association was organized in 1897 under the most favorable circumstances. This movement caught the public favor at once, and from the start its success was assured. Immense crowds thronged the place every day, from nearly every section of the South. Everybody was pleased with everything connected with the exposition. The races were of the most exciting character, stock the finest, attractions the cleanest ever seen in South Georgia, and the people were surprised at the city's wonderful resources.

The second annual fair, notwithstanding the Spanish War excitement, was even better than the first. This is saying a great deal, but it is nevertheless true, and every indication is that each year will surpass all previous years.

Although thirty-four years have passed since the first fair was held, Ware county is still having annual fairs, which displays tempting arrays of fruits, vegetables, preserves, jellies, fancy patch work, and magnificent specimen of hogs, fine cattle and chickens of many different kinds.

WAYCROSS CONCERT BAND

In 1899 Professor C. L. Merriam organized the Waycross Concert Band. When the "big fair" was opened, this band furnished the music, from November 7th to 11th, inclusive, at which time the public was given an opportunity to judge for themselves of the rapid progress made by the first organized band of Ware county.

Following are names of members of this musical organization: C. L. Merriman, leader, saxaphone; A. P. Perham, Jr., solo B flat clarinet; G. P. Hamilton, 1st B flat clarinet; Elijah Cushing, 2nd B flat clarinet; B. M. York, solo B flat cornet; W. B. Folks, solo B flat cornet; G. W. Deen, 1st B flat cornet; F. W. Gerber, E flat cornet; G. R. Brinson, solo alto; C. R. Pitman, 1st alto; Ed Knox, 1st tenor; Dell Salisbury, 1st trombone; S. D. Pitman, 2nd trombone; A. F. Bergman, B flat baritone; H. A. Williams, E flat bass; Aug. Schomber, E flat bass; P. C. Archibald, bass drum; Tom Crawley, small drum.

THE WAYCROSS RIFLES

"Among the military organizations of Georgia none has made a grander showing than the Waycross Rifles. The boys have not tried by actual conflict with the enemy, but they have always responded when their state or country called. They have never been known to shirk a duty, and being composed of the best young men of the city, they are the pride of Waycross."

In July, 1889, in the office of the Southern Express Company, the idea of organizing a military company was conceived. Through the efforts of Mr. U. J. Williams, Dr. Carswell (then Mayor), and D. B. Sweat, editor of the Waycross Reporter, the organization was effected in August following under Captain J. S. Williams, First Lieutenant Benjamin Sirmans, Second Lieutenant Dr. J. E. W. Smith. Captain Williams resigned in January, 1890, and the company was reorganized under Captain J. McP. Farr.

This company passed one of the best inspections that was ever shown by a company in the state under Colonel Peter Riley in April, 1890, and was immediately admitted into the state service. In August, 1891, "The Rifles" became a part of the Fourth Regiment.

During the same year they were called upon by Governor Gordon to proceed to McDonald's Mill to quell one of the worst riots in the history of South Georgia. They arrived at that place at midnight, marched ten miles through a drenching rain, swam a swollen creek and reached Varn's Still, the scene of the trouble about 9 A. M. They dispersed the rioters and took charge of the dead bodies. In their armory hangs a framed letter from Governor Gordon, complimenting the Rifles for their good work, and expressing his appreciation for their prompt response. The Rifles have been called out four times on account of riot, serving fourteen days.

During the ten years of their existence the Rifles have passed four inspections and have stood first and second each time. No higher compliment was ever paid a military company than was paid the Rifles by Lieutenant-Colonel Setterlee Feb. 2, 1892. The Rifles have been called to arms eleven times, have attended every state and regimental encampment, and have attended more military gatherings than any similar organization in the state. Their last trip was on account of the big Dewey reception in New York. On this occasion they took forty-five men, and from reliable sources we learn that there was not a better drilled company in the parade. Our people have only to refer to the report of Col. Brooks to find out how the Rifles stood in New York, while recently there.

Following are the first and present rolls of the company. It will be seen that the best men of the city have been members of the Waycross Rifles, and that only two of the charter members are now with the company.

Roll August 26, 1889:

J. S. Williams, Benjamin Sirmans, Dr. J. E. W. Smith, C. E. Murphy, J. H. Gillon, A. W. Carswell, U. J. Williams, Warren Lott, C. A. Armstrong, C. I. Allen, Jeff Darling, John Hogan, B. H. Williams, B. H. Burnett, F. L. Hall, Charles Hohenstein R. C. King, J. L. Crawley, E. H. Crawley, D. J. Crawley, Robert Atkinson, C. E. Stead, W. H. Bullard, James Knox, W. B. Folks, W. L. Knox, C. A. Hilton, G. T. Nungazer, B. J. Smith, R. W. White, W. A. Burney, Mack Buchanan.

Roll Oct. 1, 1899:

Captain James McP. Farr, First Lieutenant John Hogan, Second Lieutenant J. C. Brewer, First Sergeant J. G. Bird, Second Sergeant J. P. Ulmer, Third Sergeant G. P. Hamilton, Fourth Sergeant W. A. Lowther, Corp. W. B. Fenton, Corp. G. A. Carney, Corp. J. W. Moor, Corp G. M. Kempton; Privates— C. D. Allen, H. Agathon, E. L. Babbitt, J. W. Baxley, W. M. Baxley, C. K. Brewer, M. E. Brinson, T. Broom, C. E. Cason, A. L. d'Avergne, P. L. Dickens, F. L. Evans, P. M. Teltham, J. F. Garrett, W. E. Haile, ―― Hayes, Hansell Hall, R. J. Hinson, C. D. Holmes, C. Hohenstein, M. Isaac, J. H. James, T. E. Kennedy, W. E. Knight, C. H. Lowther, W. M. Mash, W. H. Mercer, L. H. Mallon, E. A. Moore, F. C. McQuaig, H. P. McNeill, H. A. McDonald, M. J. Murray, A. P. Perham, Jr., C. W. Parker, B. E. Roberts, R. M. Gassett, A. J. Sweat, W. W. Sweat, J. L. Spence, R. A. Summerall, R. F. Smith, S. E. Shults, W. H. Ulmer, R. H. Walden, S. T. Walden, I. P. Woodward, J. V. Woodward, M. L. Whitehead, F. H. Williams, E. L. Young.

*Information from D. B. Sweat.

PLANT SYSTEM, LATER A. C. L. HOSPITAL

This hospital was built at a cost of $60,000 by the Plant System in 1896, and was opened for use in 1897.

It was presided over by Dr. Frank H. Carldwell, Dr. R. P. Izler, and Dr. Spratt.

The Plant System Hospital was taken over by the A. C. L. and Dr. G. G. Thomas, of Wilmington, N. C., was the first superintendent of the A. C. L. Relief department, which was organized in 1899.

The hospital, since being taken over by the A. C. L., was operated under the supervision of Dr. G. G. Thomas. He died while in office in Sept., 1920.

In Feb., 1821, he was succeeded by Dr. Robert Slocum, who is the present Superintendent and Medical Director with office in Wilmington, N. C. The hospital was renovated in 1923 under the supervision of Miss Ruth Kuhn (Mrs. C. M. Stephens). It was furnished throughout with the finest hospital equipment available. In Oct., 1924, it was placed on the list of a classified hospital by the American College of Surgeons. Dr. Kenneth McCullough was the surgeon in charge of this hospital at that time.

The Atlantic Coast Line Shops

The greatest of Waycross' industrial enterprises are the Atlantic Coast Line Shops, which are larger than any owned by the Coast Line south of Rocky Mount, N. C. They were in the course of construction from April 1, 1906, until the latter part of the year 1907. In normal times they give employment to hundreds of men.

A list of the principal buildings is as follows:

A brick round house where twenty locomotives can be stored under roof at one and the same time.

A coach shop, cabinet shop and a pipe and tin shop.

A dry lumber shed and a flooring shed.

A machine shop 200 x 312.

A blacksmith shop and a boiler shop 110 x 312.

A car repair shed having a capacity of 150 cars under roof at one and the same time.

A three-story paint shop, varnish room, stock room and upholstering room 160 x 312.

A planing mill 70 x 160 feet.

An engine and boiler room 50 x 117 feet, with electric dynamo room attached, equipped with modern electrical machinery capable of generating about 6,000 horsepower.

A store house for scrap iron, steel, etc.

A pattern shop 40 x 100.

A two-story house 35 x 220.

An oil house, 30 x 35, with office rooms attached.

A foundry 160 x 200.

An $85,000 sewerage and water works system through shop yards.

A large dry-kiln with cooling shed.

Two 50,000-gallon water tanks for supplying the numerous shop buildings.

Numerous small buildings.

The machinery and tracks for these shops cost about $750,000.

CHAPTER XII

FIRST MERCHANTS OF WAYCROSS *

COUNTY SEAT. A town of about 100 inhabitants, situated near the head of the Okefinokee Swamp and within two miles of Satilla river. It is at the junction of the S. F. & W. Ry. and B. & A. Ry., 97 miles from Savannah and 269 miles from Atlanta. The town is new, and is growing very rapidly. There are four churches—two Methodists, Presbyterian and Baptist—and good common schools. Telegraph, Western Union, Express, Southern. Miss M. E. Shine, P. M.

Anderson, Robert—saloon
Bennett, Daniel H.,—county tax receiver
Bennett, William T.—county surveyor
Branck & Smith—saloon and groceries.
Butler, Jesse E.—ordinary
Cason, W. A.—groceries
Cason & Knight—general store
Colcord, J. T.—saw mill
Cottingham, C. A., Mrs.—Grocer
Folks, William B.—physician
Folks, W. B. & Son (W. B. and G. P.) druggists
Geiger & Butler—general store
Green, W. H.—carpenter
Happee, O. T.—manufacturer naval stores
Hassett, Frank—Rev., Baptist
Highsmith, E., Mrs.—general store
Hill, Henry S.—publisher Waycross Reporter

*Copied from the Georgia State Gazeteer, Business and Planters Directory, For 1881-1882.

Hohenstein, R.—general store
Hollingshead, N. A.—dentist
Jenkins, M. E.—millinery and fancy goods
King, A. E.—proprietor Satilla House
Knox, James—general store
Kunitzki, Koppel—physician and druggist
Lang House—E. Lang, proprietor
Lang, Edward—proprietor Lang House
Leventhal, H.—general store
Lott, Daniel—wine manufacturer
Lott, Warren—clerk superior court
McDonald, John C.—lawyer
McQuaig, C., Mrs.—general store
Miller, Stephen F.—sheriff
Mock, J. B.—constable
Mock, J. B. & Bro.—Contractors
Morehouse, N. D.—Rev., Baptist
Morton, Thomas H.—county tax collector
Murphy, H.—contractor
Parker, O. D.—exp. agent
Paxton, D. B.—manufacturer naval stores
Quarterman, J. W.—Rev., Presbyterian
Roach & Blackburn (G. S. Roach and D. J. Blackburn)—grocers
Rowell, David—coroner
Shine, Mary E., Miss—P. M.
Smith, J. G.—blacksmith
Smith, W. I.—livery and sale stable
Stanton, Valentine L.—railroad agent and telegraph operator
Styles, Carey W.—associate editor Waycross Reporter
Sweat, Burrel—county school commissioner and ex-officio justice
Sweat, T. M.—general store.
Tillman, Joseph—editor Waycross Reporter
Todd, C. D.—confectioner

Waycross Reporter, J. Tillman, editor; Henry S. Hill, publisher
Williams, Henry C.—lawyer and general store
Wilson, Leon A.—lawyer
Wilson Bros. & Co.—saw mill
Wilson, D. G.—
Woodward, Wm. N.—Grocer

The Grace-Brantley Company

The Grace-Brantley Company was a corporation owned by C. C. Grace, J. T. Brantley, W. N. Beach, A. Sessoms, George W. Deen, C. W. Deen and S. D. Pitman. The immense business was under the joint care and supervision of Captain C. C. Grace, the president, who managed both the wholesale and retail grocery department, and Mr. John T. Brantley, vice-president, gave his time to the direction of the wholesale dry goods department. Mr. S. D. Pitman, the secretary of the company, was in charge of the office.

CHAPTER XIII

GLIMPSE INTO PAST ACTIVITIES

POLITICS

MANY YEARS ago a story was told of a well-known professional politician, who on his return from church one Sunday, was met by a newspaper reporter, who remarked to him in substance: "Mr. A., I do not understand how so regular an attendant at church as you are can be also so great an adept in stuffing ballot boxes, fixing juries, and witnesses, and plugging corporations." "Mr. B.", replied the statesman, "I never mix up politics and religion."

Since the women have been given the ballot they have been rapidly schooled by experience throughout the entire county, and are fast acquiring definite ideas of the right relationship of the political party to government, of the citizens and of the state. They rarely mix politics with their religion unless prohibition becomes an issue, for on that vital question some have been known to bolt the Democratic party, which party has always been the most forceful one in the South. It was organized mainly for the protection of the women and children during the Reconstruction Days.

In the early days of Ware, we find her representatives belonged to the Whig party, and when the legislature of Georgia met in Milledgeville in 1850, things were red hot and the secessionists were running things high. A pretty strong effort was put forth to get the legislature to declare Georgia free and independent of the United States. The Ware county delegates were in the thickest of the fight. A resolution favoring secession was referred to the State committee of the Republic, and the committee reported a substitute resolution directing the Governor to call a convention of the people to pass upon it. The legislature thus washed its hands of the matter and passed it on, which was probably a wise thing as events finally proved.

On Nov. 24, 1850, Ware county elected Union men to the convention which was to meet Dec. 10, 1850. Clinch also elected Union men, but Lowndes sent delegates in favor of secession. Ware's representatives to this convention was James Fulwood, who carried 199 votes for the Union.

The result of the election was a great majority for the Union advocates. They had turned—secession was defeated. The total votes cast were 71,115 and the Union men, mostly Whigs, had a majority in the State and controlled two-thirds of the convention.

Ware went Democratic in 1853 when Governor, Congressmen and county officers had to be elected. The Whigs, which had taken the name of the American or Union party, put forth Charles J. Jenkins for Governor; the Democrats put up Governor Cobb for re-election. Jenkins was defeated, but in 1866 was elected Governor of Georgia.

In 1882 the Whigs made a determined effort to retain control of the government through electing Daniel Webster for president. The Democrats put up Franklin Pierce. Ware went for Pierce, casting 273 votes for him; Webster received in this county 150 votes. Ware county officers, with one or two exceptions, were Democrats.

Ware, in the long ago, had some Populists or Third Party voters, and in sporadic places there now exists a few in Ware who vote the Republican ticket, but Ware is universally known to be a Democratic county.

Prohibition

In 1882 a prohibition contest began and a license of $20,000 was established by legislation and went into effect in 1883.

In 1890 the population had increased to 3,364 and the taxable value of the county five times as much. The license was increased in 1892 to $30,000 and Waycross at that time became an object lesson, showing that towns could progress and become permanent without the sale of intoxicants. The population has steadily increased since that date and in 1900 numbered 5,919. In the census of 1910 the population of Waycross had increased more than any other city in Georgia and gave the phenomenal figures of 15,485. In 1891 Mr. Leon Wilson was elected to represent Ware county in the General Assembly of the State upon the prohibition issue, the contest being a memorable one. Mr. Wilson won a great victory. It was through the untiring interest of a teetotaler, Mr. W. W. Sharpe, of Waycross, that the license was raised five thousand more, making a total of $35,000, which was prohibitive in the days of bar rooms in Georgia.

Loving Cup Given Mr. H. Murphy*

There was a very affective scene at the First Methodist church on Christmas night, at the prayer meeting service, when at the close of the prayer, a handsome loving cup was presented by the membership of the church to Mr. H. Murphy, the venerable chairman of the Board of Stewards. The idea of the presentation was very appropriate, coming at the Christmas time, to one who since his coming to Waycross in 1879 has been a most faithful and loyal member of the Methodist church and had done more perhaps than any one man toward the work of RIGHTEOUSNESS, wrought by this church, and who had administered in deeds of love to so many of the needy of Waycross for all the years of the past.

The cup was a most beautiful specimen of the silversmith's art, and was presented for the church by Mr. V. L. Stanton in the following words:

"In the year 1879 when Waycross was but a CROSSING of the railroads, a small hamlet, and when the pine

*Copied from the Waycross Journal-Herald, 1913.

trees were in all their primeval luxuriance and beauty, when the soft, sweet south wind sung its love songs through the umbrageous branches; when the deep stillness of the forests was only broken by the whistle of Bob White, of the low long blast of the once-a-day locomotive that brought the passenger train from Savannah, there came one day a man and his family FROM THE PLAINFIELDS of New Jersey and cast his lot with the South.

"From almost the very day of his arrival, he began to clear away the virgin pine from the spot of ground where now he lives, and to erect thereon his modest home; from the very first he identified himself by certificate with the Methodist church and declared himself enlisted on the side of righteousness and for the moral side of every question. No man who ever came from the north to make his home in the south, has ever been more loyal in his words or deeds to the south than has this man been, and I verily believe that God did not more truly thrust out into a land that he knew not of, Abraham, than did the Almighty hand send out from his home land and guide into a new land, this man whose life has meant so much to Waycross and South Georgia.

"In all matters that are fitting and take hold of the sentiment and heart of humanity, it is always our noble women who take the initiative, and so, it was Mrs. J. L. Walker who conceived the idea of expressing our love and appreciation for this noble man and his long and faithful service to the church. Surely this man has written his epitaph not on monuments of marble or brass but he has written upon the deathless tablets of human hearts, he has laid up his treasures where neither moth or rust can corrupt, nor where thieves break through and steal; and so we come tonight to present this loving cup inscribed 'To Herbert Murphy whose devoted life and service, has quickened our faith, inspired our love, from the members of First Methodist church, Waycross, Ga., 1913.'

"We take, therefore, great delight in presenting to you, our precious brother, this loving cup filled to the brim and running over with our unfeigned love and pray God that He may spare your consecrated life many more years to gladden our hearts and to bless the church and Waycross."

At the conclusion of Mr. Stanton's presentation speech, Mr. L. J. Cooper said: "I cannot add to what Mr. Stanton has said, as I have not known Mr. Murphy long, but I have known him long enough to learn his worth to this community and to esteem him highly for his work's sake, a man valuable in the moral and religious life as well as the business life of this community, a man whose presence in any community is worth more than a police department in its restraining influence and in its stimulus for righteous living. I think this is a scene long to be remembered, one whose fitness crown the Christmas day's close with a fervent benediction. I believe that we should plant the roses in the life while it is yet alive, rather than to cover the coffin lid with wreaths of extravagant and often unmeaning flowers."

Mrs. J. L. Walker said in a few words how much it gladdened her heart to be a participant in the event and how gladly those who aided her had responded with their contributions of love.

Indeed it was a most appropriate gift and worthily bestowed and will live long in the memory of those who were present.

CHAPTER XIV

NEWSPAPERS

Waycross Newspapers

WAYCROSS was four years old when the first newspaper published in the village made its appearance. The early settlers had passed through four years of hardships and changes had brought to them a broader vision of progressiveness and the little town throbbed more freely with life and thrift.

Dr. William B. Folks, with a spirit of enterprise, assisted by the strong hand of Dr. Daniel Lott began in 1876 the publication of the Waycross Headlight. Doubtless the name Headlight was suggested by the lights from the engines that often shone at night through the darkness of the primitive town.

This paper was published in one corner of the first railway station, which was later demolished by the Western fast mail, on the Plant System, which collided with a passenger train that crossed near the station. The Waycross Headlight was the only paper between Valdosta and Savannah, along the line of the Atlantic & Gulf Railroad and the only one between Pearsons and Brunswick & Albany railroad.

The next owners of the Headlight were Messrs. Ward and Darcey, with Mr. James Freeman as editor. In 1885 Thomas Lanier owned this paper with James Freeman as editor. In 1886 Mr. Lanier and Mr. George Youmans were proprietors and James Freeman editor. Mr. William Parker, moving in at that time from Coffee County, purchased the Headlight, and published it for several years. The associate editor in the office was Mr. James Freeman, who now lives in Douglas, Georgia. Ill health forced Mr. Parker to suspend his publication and the Headlight merged into The Waycross Reporter under the management of Judge Joseph Tillman from Quitman. With Cary Styles as associate editor. Later Mr. James Freeman assumed the entire editorship of the paper.

THE HEADLIGHT HAD A BEREAVEMENT*

BY JAMES FREEMAN

In the death of the late Dr. W. B. Folks the Headlight feels its bereavement, and desires in a last tribute to a noble man, one of the original founders of a former "Headlight" to drop a tear over the grave of our departed friend and brother. In years gone by Dr. Daniel Lott owned a printing office here and from it was sent forth the original Waycross Headlight, Dr. Folks filling the editorial chair. The little journal did well, was well received, because it handled no subject except with a spirit of fairness and honor.

Subsequently the paper was suspended, Dr. Lott having sold it and the Headlight's name went down. Two years ago the writer came to this place to publish a paper after obtaining permission from Dr. Folks to use the old name, the present Headlight sprang into existence as if by magic. One request that was made of us by Dr. Folks was, that we should use the name for throwing light on subjects which deserved the people's attention, and that we would, as he had, "Hew to the line", with justice and moderation". We have endeavored to keep the trust, we believe that the Headlight is undimmed, we hope we have been faithful to the promises made to the lamented deceased and as we turn from the face of our dead brother editor, with his farewell ringing in our ears, we grapple duty with a firmer hold declaring that the Headlight's banner shall never trail in the dust while our hand helps to guide it.

*This tribute appeared in the Headlight, 1886.

Waycross Reporter

Judge H. P. Brewer was for a short while editor of The Reporter; he resigned and this paper became the property of Mr. Daniel Sweat, who not only was the proprietor but also editor. It was he who laid the foundation for the future Journal-Herald, Mr. Sweat, desiring to publish a church paper, sold The Reporter to a stock company. New Equipment was purchased and upon the grave of The Reporter was born The Waycross Herald, with the Hon. Ben. E. Russell, of Bainbridge, as editor and business manager. This paper was published in one of Mrs. Fannie Sharp's stores on Plant Avenue. Captain Russell was an experienced newspaper man, having served as editor of the Bainbridge paper for a number of years, and was conceded to be among the five men known as the galaxy of Georgia Editors: namely, Charles Pendleton, Henry McIntosh, Judge A. P. Perham, Ben. E. Russell, and Captain John Triplett.

The next owner of the Herald was Judge A. P. Perham, who came to Waycross from Quitman, and made his home here in 1891. His son, A. Paris Perham, was associated with him in the printing office and was business manager of The Herald. Young Paris was accidentally killed by a live wire that had fallen in the street during a storm. This deplorable sorrow occurred in the early part of October, 1909, and the shock proved almost unsurmountable to Judge and Mrs. Perham.

Judge Perham was a strong, gifted writer and always advocated those things that tended to make the community more moral and prosperous. He did much for the upbuilding of Waycross and Ware County. He was a clear thinker and many sought his advice and counsel on weighty subjects.

Judge Perham published the first daily paper in this city, The Evening Herald, and Waycross was exceedingly appreciative of this progressive movement on the part of Judge Perham. In 1912 he relinquished the editorial chair, retiring from active newspaper work.

Mr. L. J. Cooper became owner of The Evening Herald and Mr. and Mrs. C. R. Hawks and Mr. Fort Andrews had charge of the paper for a year.

On October 17, 1895, the first issue of The Waycross Journal came from the press. This tiny weekly struck a popular chord at once. Its neat typographical appearance was a great improvement over many of the small town weeklies. It was filled with fresh, crisp news and each copy found many interested readers. The printing office was located in the old Parker building. Later it was moved into the old Masonic building. Mr. Dan B. Sweat was the efficient editor, whose life had been almost exclusively devoted to newspaper work. He was ever on the right side of every political question. His force consisted of ten men and some boys. Mr. A. G. Wesley was the foreman; Mr. John T. Blanchard, local reporter; John E. Wesley, a son of Mr. Wesley, was an assistant foreman and was said to be one of the swiftest compositors in Georgia, and was a superior job printer and pressman. R. G. Sweat served his apprenticeship on the Waycross Reporter, when the Journal editor published that paper. He occupied a place in the Journal composing rooms as long as that paper existed under that name. Charles Wesley was a printer. Blondel Brown was a printer and pressman. The Journal's force of carriers were Masters Willie Wesley, Eddie Peeples, Ernest Summerall and John Young.

In 1902 Mr. John Greer became assistant editor of The Waycross Journal and in the latter part of 1902 he became sole owner and publisher of the paper. Mr. Sweat retiring and entering other fields of activities.

In 1904 Mr. W. A. Price was made president and Mr. Volney Williams became one of the lessees and business managers, Mr. John Greer continuing as editor for The Journal. This paper was considered one of the best semiweekly papers of its class in the South. Neat, clean and newsy it truly pursued its course honorably throughout the nine years of its existence.

In 1911 The Journal became a daily morning paper, Mr. Volney Williams, manager, and Mr. John Greer, editor. This paper had a guaranteed circulation of two thousand five hundred subscribers which steadily increased during the years of its publication.

In 1914 The Waycross Evening Herald and The Waycross Daily Journal consolidated. Mr. C. Fort Andrews was made managing editor; Mr. Jack Williams, business manager; Robert F. McLendon, newspaper foreman, and Mrs. A. S. Anderson, office clerk. To perpetuate the names of the two papers, it was called The Journal-Herald.

In 1916 Mr. Jack Williams, who is now one of the outstanding newspaper editors in the state, and at this time president of the State Press Association, assumed the ownership of The Journal-Herald. This paper has gone steadily forward and the well-equipped, up-to-date office has no semblance to the office in which it had its beginning. The Journal-Herald is a valued visitor in nearly every home in Ware County, and is considered one of the best daily papers in the state.

The Headlight, the first newspaper of Ware County, is shining out today through the pages of The Journal-Herald in whose body it had its transmigration. Some of the editors are living in other towns and some have gone to their Eternal Home, but the present editor, Mr. Jack Williams, still abides with us.

The Millwood Advance

Mr. Lee Herrin, an enterprising young man of Millwood, established in 1903 the first newspaper in his home town. He named it The Millwood Advance. In his office equipment was a small, second-hand job press he had purchased from the Waycross Journal, owned at that time by Mr. John Greer. The old job press was cleaned up and moved to Millwood without any guarantee from the former owner to give much service, the buyer having no experience in the printing business secured the service of Mr. B. B. Allen, of Pearson, Georgia, to come down and rig up the press and put it in working order and teach Mr. Herrin how to become a practical printer. Mr. Allen arrived at the 10 x 12 room which was to be the home of the newspaper and job printing office. Mr. Allen was to receive five dollars per day for his services. He began to work but continued only a few hours when he quit the job, stating that the press was no good.

That day was the beginning of an unbounding spirit of self-confidence in the editor of The Millwood Advance. He made up his mind, right then and there, that he would learn the printing business. In a few months he had the printing and pewspaper plant on a small scale in operation, he acting as printer, devil, editor, solicitor, manager and sole proprietor.

In the latter part of 1907 Mr. Herrin bought out The Alapaha Ledger, at Alapaha, Georgia. This newspaper plant was run by him at Alapaha for only a few months and then moved to Millwood where the two papers were consolidated. This weekly paper grew rapidly, and Mr. Herrin decided it needed a new name, so it became The Ware County News. This Millwood paper is still being published under that name.

THE WAYCROSS GEORGIAN

The Georgian was established as a weekly newspaper and printing plant, the first number of the paper being issued on Thursday, May 29, 1924, with twenty pages. The Georgian was continued as a weekly for three years and then made a twice-a-week newspaper and published on Tuesdays and Fridays. Up to the present time (1931) The Waycross Georgian Publishing Company has enjoyed a very prosperous business for more than eight years under the management of the undaunted editor,

Mr. Herrin, who has demonstrated his ability to override many of life's difficulties, he is the son of Ware County pioneers, Mr. William Herrin and Mary (Hargraves) Herrin, who were born in Ware County, and have always been progressive people. Mrs. Herrin descending from one of the oldest and most historic families in this county, the Hargraves, who trace their lineage through an unbroken line of ancestry to John Hargreaves, of Hair's House, England.

CHAPTER XV

CO-OPERATIVE EXTENSION WORK

4-H Clubs of Ware County

N 1924 the Home Economic work became more than an active necessity for the Ellis Health Law had taken a firm hold on the people of Ware County and better health called for better food and better homes and this better home improvement necessitated trained workers.

During the first years of the home demonstration work in this county only 115 girls were enrolled for active improvement along the lines of canning, better gardens, home, health and sanitation, model kitchens, poultry raising, home furnishings, better bread-making and sewing. The demonstrations were sometimes given by the teacher of home economics in the rural schools and on other occasions the classes were held in the community house, where the 4-H Club Girls do the greater part of their canning.

During January, 1932, four hundred and fifty enrolled as members of the 4-H Club and are now doing outstanding work for the improvement of better homes.

Each year large classes graduate after having taken the full course under capable teachers who have received training at the Georgia State College of Agriculture.

The Ware County 4-H Club girls are truly trained in head, home, hands and health and are well equipped for the useful duties of a well-established home.

Pure Bred Pigs in Ware County*

The growing of pure bred pigs in Ware County has been progressing for the past ten years. It began mostly

---
*This information furnished by Dr. R. D. Heyde, Ware County farm demonstrator

with pig club boys in 4-H Club work, and at first progressed very slowly because most of the farmers had the idea that the pure bred pig had to be taken up, fed with a spoon and would cost more than he was worth. It was up to the county agent, at that time, to find the best pure bred pigs he could in the neighboring counties, go and pick them out and take them to his club boys' home, and see that they were properly fed.

In a year or so the pure bred boars were crossed on some of the common woods hogs, and the improvement shown in these pigs caused more talk among the farmers because the pigs were larger, more plump, and just as tough as the common woods hog. Neighbors began buying them from the club boys' fathers to grow a brood sow of their own, and more boys were enrolled in the 4-H Pig Club. The members began competing with each other in trying to have a larger and fatter pig than the others. Type, quality and conformation came on slowly until after our first pig club exhibit at the Georgia State Fair, held in Savannah about 1923. The boys were more interested in quantity at first, but after the fair they learned to realize what type and quality meant. From this fair, however, a roll of money and quite a number of ribbons were brought home.

This caused more interest and constructive breeding. Fathers and mothers became so interested that we ordered pigs from some of the best breeders, who showed in the open ring at the Georgia Fairs.

The next year we followed all of the largest fairs in Georgia, where pig club premiums were offered, and this stimulated interest in livestock judging. For the first two years our 4-H Club boys won the District Judging Contest, which contest has been held in Waycross for the past seven or eight years because of the livestock available in this county. Winning this contest meant a free trip to the Southeastern Fair in Atlanta, and each year we carried a carload of our oustanding club pigs for exhibit. One year we carried two carloads of club pigs, ton litters, and 4-H club barrows. Not only did these 4-H Club pigs bring money prizes, but after the exhibit the ton litters and barrows were sold at Chicago market prices, which were extremely high at that time. The other pigs were brought back, and the boys began with a greater interest to work toward more constructive breeding.

The advertising received from our Fair exhibits added to the sale of pigs in this county. Other counties and near-by States began ordering pigs from our pig club boys, the boys taking in more than a thousand dollars a year on their club pigs for several years. This profit caused the fathers of the club boys to become still more interested, and they increased the stock until small herds started in the county, and they began selling pigs throughout the counties far and wide. Then ton litter work became of interest when August Fechtel, a 4-H Club boy, grew a ton litter of ten pure bred Black Poland China pigs to 2,376 pounds in a hundred and eighty days. This was the first ton litter grown by a Club boy in Georgia. We put them on exhibit at the Southeastern Fair, where he made a wonderful showing, first prize litter, first and second pen of barrows and champion barrow. From that time we have grown from two to five-ton litters in the county each year.

The woods hog has become a scarce article, and we are still doing constructive breeding, and have a reputation for growing some of the most outstanding pure bred hogs in Georgia. We are now trying to grow our pigs under a more sanitary system as is being demonstrated by the U. S. Department of Agriculture at Moultrie. This will increase the size and quality of our swine industry as parasites have been a handicap to many of our farmers.

The First Canning Club of Ware County

The first canning club organized in Ware County came into active existence through the untiring efforts of Mrs. W. N. Jones and Mrs. J. L. Walker. These women were undaunted in their determination to have this project put over for the benefit of the young girls living in the rural sections of this county. In 1915 they set about in an efficient way to open the hearts and minds of all who had it in their power to help in this far reaching endeavor of securing funds to match the Federal appropriation set aside for that special work. These two women have had the joy of seeing the great projection that had its beginning seventeen years ago, merge into co-operative extension work in Agriculture and Home Economics.

MRS. ATWELL AND ONE OF HER CANNING CLUB GIRLS

Those interested in the canning clubs were most fortunate in securing the services of Mrs. Tallulah Brinson Atwell for the important office as County Demonstrator to carry on the work. After her appointment she carefully proceeded to organize the club in an able and logical way, and soon created a deep interest among the girls as well as the men and women of the county, who gave her their hearty co-operation.

Small plots of ground were measured off for the gardens that were to be planted and tended by the ninety-six girls who had enlisted for the canning club work.

They were enthusiastic in their desires to make a success of their gardens in which they only planted tomatoes for their first year's canning. There were forty-five clubs organized in the county and Mrs. Atwell became active in them all, by teaching in each, bread-making, preserving, canning, poultry-raising, sewing, etc. She visited in the homes, creating a neglected privilege of bringing about a better acquaintance between those living in town and those residing in the rural sections of the county. Mrs. Atwell was a welcome visitor in all sections of the county and organized four women's clubs that were a power in their respective communities. When the canning season began, God blessed the girls with sunshine and rain and a bountiful tomato crop was made.

The girls put up thousands of cans of tomatoes, supplying many homes for nominal prices with their products. The mothers became interested and attended the demonstrations given by Mrs. Atwell in the art of canning beans, corn, okra and other vegetables, also fruits and jelly-making. When Mrs. Atwell made her first visit to the Okefinokee Swamp in the interest of the canning club and garden planning, she was informed by the parents of the girls whom she had hoped to enroll as memmers of her club, that there was no use to try to raise tomatoes in the Okefinokee, for they would not grow in swamp soil. Before leaving Billy's Island, Mrs. Atwell organized a club and that club the following season was awarded the first and second-year prizes for tomatoes.

During the World War period the Governor requested that a great increase in planting be put forward. The canning club girls contributed much for public consumption. At the end of four years of useful work Mrs. Atwell retired, leaving an enrollment of over two hundred girls and several woman's clubs who have kept alive through the years her progressive undertaking in the interest of War.

Agricultural Products

The products of Ware County are corn, sea-island cotton, oats, hay, sugar cane, sweet and Irish potatoes, peanuts, rice, melons, figs, grapes, strawberries, snap-beans, lettuce, celery, velvet beans, cabbage, beets, turnips and various other vegetables. A truck growers and curb market association has been organized, fruits and vegetables are daily being hauled by trucks from this county to northern and eastern markets.

A Ware county agricultural federation has been doing constructive work along the lines of farming in Ware with the following active members:

Dr. R. J. Heyde	A. J. Moran
D. N. Stafford	C. E. Gibson
D. J. Wagner	W. D. O'Quinn
Dan Cowart	Jack Williams
B. G. Parks	G. R. Hatfield
Roy McDonald	J. M. Norman
O. E. Davis	T. L. Everett
R. C. Cavender	J. S. Elkins, Chairman

The Plant Memorial Park

No non-resident ever took a greater interest in any city than Henry B. Plant took in Waycross during his lifetime. He liked this little city in the wiregrass, and in it he had many friends. On every occasion Mr. Plant showed his appreciation in a most substantial way. That he was largely responsible for the rapid growth of this place is universally conceded. Few railroad magnates shared the confidence and esteem of the general public to the extent that did Mr. Plant, and few railroads have had less trouble from their employees than had the Plant System during its existence under that name.

A short time after Mr. Plant's death, a meeting was called in Waycross which was attended by nearly every prominent person in the city. At this meeting a movement was started for the erection of a lasting monument to his memory.

Committees were appointed and a fund started for that purpose. Many plans were made, but they were never carried out. Finally the extensive memorial fell through and only a fountain was placed in a park, that previously has been donated by Mr. Plant.

Other parks in the city are: Phoenix Park, World War Memorial Park, Winona, Trexler Park, Folks Park and a nameless park on Brunel Street.

CHAPTER XVI

SOCIAL AND CIVIC ORGANIZATIONS

WAYCROSS CLUBS

SOME OF the leading organizations in Waycross and Ware County are: The Chamber of Commerce, Kiwanis, Rotary, Lions, American Legion, Elks, Moose, Merchants' Association, Waycross Golf Club, Ware County Medical Society, two Masonic Lodges, Woman's Club, The Georgians, The Georgianas, two D. A. R. Chapters, American Legion Auxiliary, Woman's Auxiliary to the Ware County Medical Society, 4-H Clubs, Woodward Godwin Club, Emmerson Park Club, The Knights of Pythias, The Junior Order of United American Mechanics and Auxiliary, Pythian Sisters, Central Labor Union, Woodmen of the World, Y. M. C. A., Boy Scouts, United Daughters of the Confederacy, City Library, Welfare Board, Safety Commission, Atlantic Coast Line Better Business Club, Salvation Army, City and County Health Department.

HOSPITAL ASSOCIATION

The town of Waycross has merged into a city before the idea of a local hospital became prevalent. The ministers and doctors of the city held a meeting at the pastor's study of the First Methodist Church on July 21, 1902.

The committee appointed to draw up the constitution for a City Hospital made their report and it was adopted.

A provisional board of directors was then elected. They were as follows: Rev. W. H. Scruggs, Dr. R. P. Izlar and Dr. J. C. Rippard, Mrs. P. N. Harley, Mrs. E. H.

Reed, Hon. Warren Lott, A. M. Knight, Sr., C. E. Murphey and Oscar Lott.

On July 25, 1902, the board of directors of the Waycross Hospital Association held their first meeting. The attendance was good, only one member being absent. Rev. W. H. Scruggs was elected president, and C. E. Murphey, secretary and treasurer. A committee of ladies was appointed to solicit subscriptions in their respective wards, and to ask donations from City Council and the County Commissioners. The committee was: First Ward, Mrs. J. C. Rippard; Second Ward, Mrs. G. R. Youmans; Third Ward, Mrs. E. H. Reed; Fourth Ward, Mrs. J. G. McDonald; Fifth Ward, Miss Belle Blackshear; Sixth Ward, Miss Mattie Williams.

The hospital was not built until 1907, when the county donated $1,600 and the citizens of Waycross also donated a large sum for the establishing of this charitable institution. In the latter part of 1907 the Kings Daughters took over the work. This hospital was erected at a cost of about $30,000. It has a capacity of thirty-six beds and maintains charity wards. It is known as the King's Daughters Hospital.

THE KINGS DAUGHTERS AND SONS

An order founded by Mrs. Margaret Bottome for the purpose of stimulating Christian activity and usefulness, was organized in Waycross in February, 1888, by Mrs. J. H. Redding. There were two circles with a limited membership of ten each who worked together under one management. The work of this organization has never ceased. Every case of sickness or need that applied has been aided.

In April, 1905, a city union was formed consisting of three circles, Mrs. P. N. Harley was elected as president. Much good has been done by this little band of workers which has not only been a blessing to the sick and the poor but of personal good to the workers. Clothes, food, medicine and nursing, with many other little kindnesses, carry good cheer the year around, though at Christmas a special effort is made to give extra supplies with toys and fruit. In 1906 the state convention of the order met in Waycross with 70 delegates. We have now (1907) as a special work the building of a charity hospital. All arrangements are about perfected and we are anxiously anticipating the realization of our labor. (The Kings Daughters hospital has been built and has done a most humane work for Waycross and Ware county).

SUNSHINE CIRCLE NO. 1—Mrs. Lemuel Johnson, Leader; Mrs. J. E. Wadley, Mrs. J. M. Cox, Mrs. Robt. Odum, Mrs. Claude Ost, Mrs. J. C. McDonald, Mrs. P. N. Harley, Mrs. H. S. Redding, Mrs. E. A. Pound, Mrs. J. W. Bellinger, Mrs. Rad Hitch, Mrs. Chas. Shelton, Miss Georgia Wright, Miss Bessie Wright Miss Sara Cooper, Mrs. J. W. Seals, Mrs. J. C. Humphreys, Mrs. Lem Johnson, Mrs. A. L. Johnson, Mrs. C. H. Redding, Mrs. Willis Swain.

GOLDEN RULE CIRCLE NO. 2—Mrs. J. H. Redding, Leader; Mrs. E. H. Reed, Mrs. Herbert Murphy, Mrs. George Deen, Mrs. T. J. Darling, Mrs. Young, Mrs. Louis Campbell, Mrs. T. W. Morrison, Mrs. F. A. Bates, Mrs. J. R. May, Miss Suvilla Monroe, Miss Jessie May McCall.

WILLING WORKERS CIRCLE NO. 3—Mrs. W. W. Sharpe, Leader; Mrs. P. A. Hay, Mrs. A. M. Knight, Mrs. Henry Dubose, Mrs. R. D. Brown, Mrs. George Feltham, Mrs. W. W. Ansley, Mrs. W. A. Price, Mrs. J. P. Stewart, Mrs. Hatttie Gurr, Mrs. Agnes Findley.

FRANCIS S. BARTOW CHAPTER DAUGHTERS OF THE CONFEDERACY*

Francis S. Bartow Chapter No. 8, Daughters of the Confederacy, organized April, 1896—Charter received September, 1896.

Presidents from 1896 to 1907:

First President, Mrs. F. C. Owens, 1896-1898. Second President, Mrs. J. H. Redding, 1898-1900. Third Presi-

---
*Copied from the Industrial Edition of the Waycross Evening Herald of 1907.

dent, Henrietta Fitzsimmons, 1900-1903. Fourth President, Mrs. C. A. Sheldon, 1903-1907.

Charter Members:

Mrs. J. H. Redding, Mrs. Henry Covington, Mrs. E. C. Johnson, Mrs. Lemuel Johnson, Mrs. S. W. Hitch, Mrs. A. P. Perham, Mrs. J. E. Wadley, Mrs. E. A. Pounds, Mrs. A. Sessoms, Miss Blanche Sessoms, Mrs. Eugene McCall, and Mrs. F. C. Owens.

The first Memorial Day observed at Waycross, was in the Public School. Prof. E. A. Pound of the Public School arranged a programme among the children.

In 1896, 1897, 1898 and 1899, Prof. Pound assisted our Chapter materially in the celebration of Memorial Day. He also delivered the Memorial address in 1898 and 1899.

In February, 1900, Gen. John B. Gordon, visited the town and delivered his famous lecture, "The Last Days of the Confederacy". The Daughters extended an invitation to the veterans to attend his lecture. Forty accepted, a number of these gallant veterans having followed him to battle for a cause that can never be lost "while song and story record their deeds of valor."

In April, 1900, Mr. John T. Boifeuillet, of Macon, Ga., was the Memorial orator and made one of his characteristic eloquent addresses. Through the influence of the Daughters all the business houses were closed.

In 1901, Capt. S. T. Kingsberry, of Valdosta, Ga., was Memorial orator and the first "Crosses of Honor" were presented by the Daughters to the veterans of Waycross Camp.

In 1902 Hon. W. M. Toomer, of Waycross, delivered an address that was replete in historical facts and logical discussion of the causes which led to secession. In June of this year we were indebted to Prof. E. A. Pound for a lecture delivered for the benefit of the Winnie Davis Memorial fund on Robert E. Lee, which was an eloquent tribute and delivered in his usual graceful manner and thoroughly enjoyed by those who were fortunate enough to be present. The proceeds of the lecture amounted to $20, which were forwarded to Mrs. Ida Eve, Treasurer of the Winnie Davis Memorial fund.

In 1903 the Memorial address was by Rev. Harry Cassils, of Brunswick, Ga. It was one of the most eloquent and interesting addresses ever delivered here on Memorial Day.

In 1904 new life and growth in our Chapter was perceptible when they decided to furnish a room in the Winnie Davis Memorial Hall at Athens, Ga. After the amount of $60 was forwarded to the Treasurer for the furnishing of the room, our Chapter decided to add rocker and rugs. Miss Sallie Harley, of Thomasville, Ga., and Miss Cook, of Milledgeville, Ga., were the first occupants. In 1904 Memorial Day was fittingly observed on the 26th of April. Prof E. A. Pound, of Waycross, Ga., was orator of the occasion. A line of march was formed at the Public School building, including school children, veterans, Waycross Rifles and Daughters of the Confederacy. On October, 1904, the annual election took place resulting in the re-election of Mrs. C. A Sheldon, President; Mrs. E. A. Pound, 1st Vice-President; Mrs. J. E. Wadley, 2nd Vice-President; Miss Mattie Williams, Treasurer; Mrs. Lee Sheldon Moore, Corresponding Secretary; Miss Virginia Lyon, Recording Secretary and Miss Anne Willis Paine, Historian.

In 1905 Southern History was introduced as a study into the Chapter by the President, Mrs. C. A. Sheldon and has always proved a source of great interest and enthusiasm. In the March meeting of 1905 Mrs. E. A. Pound, President protem, agitated the question of placing marble markers at the graves of our Confederate Veterans in the city cemetery, which met with the hearty approbation of all present. She appointed the following committee to solicit: Misses Paine, Lyon, Beck and Harris. The public responded liberally and with a small assessment and annual dues we were enabled at a cost of $132.50 to have the marble head and foot stone markers placed at the graves of every Veteran buried in Lott cemetery by Memorial Day. Major R. P. Bird gave efficient help to us in the identification of graves. Memorial day, 1905, Major Bird accepted an invitation from the Daughters to deliver the Memorial address, thus honoring us in so doing. The Major is a gallant Confederate Veteran and always loyal to the "Lost Cause" and the Daughters of the Confederacy. On this occasion Capt. Thomas Spalding Paine was master of ceremonies, Capt. Charles A. Sheldon introducing his comrade, Major Bird, in a short appropriate speech. Little Miss Edna Lee Paine was color bearer for U. D. C's.

In 1906 Col. B. G. Park, a son of a gallant Confederate veteran, responded to an invitation from the Daughters to make the Memorial address. The exercises were conducted in the Public School auditorium. Capt. Chas. A. Sheldon introduced the speaker who delivered a fine oration, paying high tribute to the Confederate Army. soldiers and officers, also to the Southern women. Capt. T. S. Paine was master of ceremonies and little Miss Dorothy Sessoms was the color bearer of the Daughters. During the year 1906 the Daughters held Memorial service to Gen. Joseph Wheeler and Mrs. Jefferson Davis. They also contributed to President Jefferson Davis' monument fund, Major Henry Wirz's monument, Rabun Gap Dormitory and Gen. John B. Gordon's monument, to be erected at Atlanta. The Daughters always participate in the memorial exercises of Robert E. Lee on Jan. 19, held at the Court House under the auspices of the Veteran's Camp No. 819 U. C. V., Georgia Division. The exercises of 1907 were especially interesting, readings songs of the sixties by the Daughters and Children of the Confederacy, Prof. E. A. Pound's grand speech on Robert E. Lee and the Veterans' impromptu speeches were enjoyable. Little Claude Aldine Moore was color bearer for the Daughters.

We have awarded 57 Crosses of Honor to the following Veterans, Camp 819:

In 1900: Jackson Grimes, Co. G., 20th Regt., Inf., Ga. Vol., C. S. A.; R. P. Bird, Co. D., 5th Fegt., Ga. Vol., C. S. A.; J. B. K. Smith, Co. A., 4th Regt., Mississippi Vol., C. S. A.; W. M. Harbin, Co. H., 38th Regt., Ga. Vol., C. S. A.; Capt. C. A. Sheldon, Co. R., 8th Ala. Reg. Cav. Forest's Corps C. S. A.

In 1901: W. R. Harbin, Co. I., 8th Regt., Ga. Inf., Vol., C. S. A.; Charles West, Co. K., 63rd Regt., Ga. Inf., Vol., C. S. A.; James A. Waters, Co. A., 5th Regt., Ga. Vol., C. S. A.; J. B. Jones, Co. F., 4th Regt., Ga. Vol., C. S. A.; C. D. Todd, Co. B., 61st Regt., Ga. Vol., C. S. A.; Joseph McQuaig, Co. B., 26th Regt., Ga. Inf., Vol., C. S. A.; James Tomlinson, Co. H., 4th Regt., Ga. Cav. Vol., C. S. A.; William Wilson, Co. B., 4th Regt., Ga. Art. Vol., C. S. A.; W. R. Newsome, Co. B., 55th Regt., North Carolina Vol., C. S. A.; J. W. Strickland, Co. G., 4th Regt., Ga. Cav. Vol., C. S. A.; W. R. Youmans, Co. C., 4th Regt., Ga. Cav. Vol., C. S. A.; W. J. Carmon, Co. D., 6th Cavalry Regt., South Carolina Vol., C. S. A.; E. D. Hendry, Atlantic & Gulf Guards, 26th Regt., Ga. Vol., C. S. A.; J. L. Sweat, Co. G., 4th Reg. Cav., Ga. Vol., C. S. A.; C. T. Holmes, Co. H., 6th Fla. Reg., Vol., C. S. A.; A. J. Wainwright, Co. F., 4th Reg. Cav., Ga. Vol., C. S. A.; A. P. Perham, Sr., Co. F., 4th Regt., Ga. Inf., Vol. C. S. A.; J. J. Wilkinson, Co. K., 26th Reg. Ga. Inf., Vol., C. S. A.; E. Cottingham, Co. H., 1st Reg. South Carolina Vol., C. S. A.; Elliott C. Johnson, Co. Chatham Art., Savannah Vol., C. S. A.; J. W. Booth, Co. B., 1st Bat. Ga. Sharpshooters, Vol., C. S. A.; P. S. Barber, Co. C., 6th Reg. Ga. Inf., Vol., C. S. A.; Lemuel Johnson, Co. F., 26th Reg. Ga. Inf., Vol., C. S. A.; R. D. Harris, Co. H., Cobb's Legion, Reg. Ga. Vol., C. S. A.

In 1902: Wm. H. Sebring, Co. E., 2nd Reg. Tennessee Vol., C. S. A.; Holiday Sauls, Co. E., 25th Reg. Ga. Vol., C. S. A.

In 1903: John M. Lee, Co. I., 5th Reg. Ga. Vol., C. S. A.; W. H. Barbee, Co. E., 2nd Reg., North Carolina

Vol., C. S. A.; A. L. D'Augergne, Co. Lyon S., Reg. Ga. Reserves, C. S. A.; A. Sessoms Co. C., 36th Reg. North Carolina Vol., C. S. A.; J. R. Knight, 2nd Reg. Ga. Reserves, C. S. A.; G. T. Nungezer, Co. G., 26th Reg. Ga. Vol., C. S. A.; J. A. Cason, Co. C., 4th Cavalry Reg. Ga. Vol., C. S. A.; John R. Harris, Co. H., 26th Reg. Ga. Vol., C. S. A.; J. J. Henderson, Co. F., 26th Reg. Ga. Vol., C. S. A.; B. A. Johnson, Co. B., 48th Reg. Ga. Vol., C. S. A.

In 1904: J. C. Proctor, Co. K., 71st Cav. Reg. Ga. Vol., C. S. A.; J. S. Bailey, Co. I., 11th Reg. Ga. State Troops, Vol., C. S. A.; P. S. Barbee, Co. A., 61st Reg. Ga. Vol.; C. S. A.; W. P. Numez, Co. K., 26th Reg. Ga. Vol., C. S. A.; R. T. Cottingham, Co. C., 11 Reg. Florida Vol., C. S. A.; J. H. Clark, Co. A., 41st Cav. Reg. Ga. Vol., C. S. A.; J. J. Mershon, Co. B., 56th Reg. Ga. Vol., C. S. A.; J. W. Leigh, Co. D., 4th Cav. Reg. Ga. Vol., C. S. A.; H. J. Stone, Co. G., 7th Reg. Stuart's Cav., Vol., C. S. A.; M. J. Mock, Co. K., 25th Reg. Ga. Vol., C. S. A.; Elias Stanfield, Co. A., 4th Cav. Reg. Ga. Vol., C. S. A.; W. S. Carter, Co. A., 50th Ga. Reg., Vol., C. S. A.

In 1906: E. S. Aycock, Co. B., 30th Reg. North Carolina Vol. C. S. A.; A. Robbins, Cape Fear Light Art. Attachees, Co. C., 36th Reg., Vol., C. S. A.

Mrs. J. H. Redding, second President of the Chapter, has the honor of having named the Chapter Francis S. Bartow for our distinguished Georgia General, who was killed on the battlefield of Manassas in 1861.

Mrs. E. A. Pound was Historian from the organization of the Chapter until two years ago she was elected Vice President, and Miss Annie Willis Paine was elected her successor. We are indebted to Mrs. Pound for much of the Chapter history. She also presented three volumes, beautiful hand-painted covers, to the Chapter. First Volume, "Muster Roll"; second volume, "Reminiscences"; third, "Sketches of Women"; fourth, "Confederate Relics"; fifth, "Chapter History".

Many a faithful heart has grown cold since the above article was written, and the work in behalf of our Confederate dead is still being carried on by faithful members.

THE CHILDREN OF THE CONFEDERACY*

The 26th Georgia Regiment Chapter of the Children of the Confederacy, was organized in Waycross in the summer of 1903, under the direction of Mrs. James Stacy Bailey, with the following officers:

Miss Edith Lockhart, President.
William Morrison Toomer, Jr., First Vice-President.
Miss Magdalene Izlar, Second Vice-President.
Miss Ruby LeHardy Sessoms, Recording Secretary.
Ralph Bayard Sessoms, Treasurer.
Andromache Porter Taylor Bailey, Corresponding Secretary.
Walter H. Paine, Historian.

The 26th Georgia holds in its membership, residents of Georgia, Florida, Missouri and New Mexico, and is adding new recruits to its roll.

The chief work accomplished since its organization is the furnishing of a room in the Winnie Davis Memorial Hall, at Athens, it being one of the few Children's Chapters in the state to vie with the "Daughters" in this work, for which it received the special commendation of the state officers of the U. D. C.

JONATHAN BRYAN CHAPTER DAUGHTERS AMERICAN REVOLUTION*

In 1898 the National Board D. A. R. appointed Mrs. J. H. Redding to organize a chapter in Waycross. In February, 1900, 12 members secured the charter and elected Mrs. J. H. Redding regent; Mrs. P. N. Harley, treasurer; Mrs. J. M. Cox, secretary and Miss Bessie Wright, registrar.

The chapter was named for one of the fathers and

*Copied from the Industrial Edition of the Waycross Evening Herald of 1907.

founders of Georgia, and its social and literary life has been delightful.

Work on educational lines through prizes awarded the schools has aroused great interest among the children in the study of history.

The chapter in 1907 had 28 members:

Mrs. J. H. Redding, Mrs. C. H. Murphy, Mrs. P. N. Harley, Mrs. H. S. Redding, Mrs. J. M. Cox, Mrs. R. P. Izlar, Mrs. W. M. Toomer, Mrs. C. T. Holmes, Mrs. Eugene McCall, Mrs. J. E. Wadley, Mrs. R. O. Lee, Mrs. W. H. Payne, Mrs. J. S. Bailey, Mrs. S. S. Fitzsimmons, Mrs. A. C. Snowden, Mrs. Otto Bruch, Mrs. E. A. Pound, Mrs. B. F. Bullard, Miss Elizabeth Wright, Miss E. E. Blackshear, Miss A. G. Bass, Miss Sarah S. Letford, Miss Annie Willis Paine, Miss Virginia Lyon, Miss Grace Taylor, Mrs. Jelks, Mrs. Ham and Mrs. Walters.

LYMAN HALL CHAPTER—D. A. R.

This chapter, named in honor of Dr. Lyman Hall, a native of Wallingford, Conn., where he was born April 12, 1724. He represented Georgia at the Continental Congress, 1775-1777, and was one of the signers of the Declaration of Independence. Lyman Hall also served as Governor of Georgia in 1783.

The Chapter was organized June 5, 1907, by Mrs. Aldine Pound at her home on Williams Street. Those present at the meeting and who made up the list of charter members were: Mrs. Carrie Alston Andrews, Mrs. Arley Murphy Albertson, Miss Willie Rabun Beck, Mrs. Valeria North Burnet, Miss Caroline Mason, Mrs. Sarah Jackson Stewart, Mrs. Laura Singleton Walker, Mrs. Henrietta Lane Wadley, Mrs. Rena Mason Wright, Mrs. Genevive R. Young Phelan and Miss Mary Campbell Young.

LYMAN HALL CHAPTER MARKS THE SITE OF COLERAINE

On June 30, 1912 Lyman Hall Chapter of the Daughters of the American Revolution unveiled at Coleraine, in Charlton County, a large marble boulder to commemorate at this place the signing of the Treaty of Peace and Friendship between the President of the United States and the Indians. The site of the old trading post is forty-five miles above St. Mary's on the St. Mary's River. It witnessed in years past many bloody conflicts between the white settlers, Indians and Spaniards; but the dramatic episode which gives a sure place in American annals was the signing here in 1796 a treaty of peace and friendship between the President of the United States and the Creek Nation of Indians. History states that among those taking part in the momentous gathering were twenty-two Indian Kings, seventy-five principal Chiefs, and one hundred and fifty-two warriors besides officers of the garrison, commissioners of the government and representatives of the State. The pipe of peace belonging to the old Chief Tallassee was smoked by the various participants and was afterward presented to Governor Early.

The oaks under which the historic scene was enacted are standing yet, magnificent in their age and grandeur and here on the old site of the treaty of peace was erected the handsome boulder. The following inscription appears on the monument:

> "This boulder is to commemorate the signing of the Treaty of Peace and Friendship at Coleraine on the 29th of June, 1796 between the President of the United States and the Kings and Chiefs and Warriors of the Creek Nation of Indians. Ratified March 18, 1797. The Commossioners on the part of the United States were: Benjamin Hawkins, George Clymer and Andrew Pickens. Placed here in memoriam by the Lyman Hall Chapter Daughters of the American Revolution, Waycross, Georgia."

The boulder was unveiled by Walter Eustace Sirmans, Jr., a direct descendant of Gen. James Jackson, one of the Commissioners who signed the treaty 116 years ago. Nearly 2,000 people attended the ceremonies and gave an attentive audience to the following program:

> Invocation, Rev. Osgood Cook, Waycross; Address of Welcome from Charlton County, Joseph Mizell; Introductory Addresses, Judge John T. Myers and Judge T. A. Parker, Waycross; Address, Fred Saussy, Esq., Savannah; Presentation of Monument, Mrs. J. L. Walker, Waycross; Acceptance of the monument for Camden County, Judge David Atkinson; J. B. Sanders, of Waycross was marshal of the day and J. B. Lewis, Sr., host.

CHAPTER PRESIDENTS

Lucy Murphy Pound (Mrs. Aldine) 1907-1912
Laura Singleton Walker (Mrs. J. L.) 1912-1918
Edith Lott Dimmock (Mrs. Eugene D.) 1918-1920
Mary Carswell Redding (Mrs. Benj W.) 1920-1921
Henrietta Lane Wadley ,Mrs. John E.) 1921-1925.
Edith Lott Dimmock (Mrs. Eugene D.) 1925-1927
Marion Elizabeth Carswell (Mrs. Henry J.) 1927-1932.

Mrs. Lucy Murphy Pound served as Regent of the Chapter for five years but due to her change of residence from Waycross to Atlanta she resigned in 1912. Mrs. Pound not only organized the Lyman Hall Chapter but it was largely through her efforts that the Confederate Monument was erected in Phoenix Park. She also served most efficiently for several years as President of the Frances S. Bartow Chapter U. D. C. She cherished the ideals and deeds of her ancestry and was keenly interested in the records of the past but held the sentiment that the final test of merit after all was in individual achievement.

WAYCROSS WOMAN'S CLUB
ORGANIZED 1928

The publication of the History of Ware County was sponsored by the Waycross Woman's Club whose President is Mrs. Ellen Goodrich Townsend. The officers and board members are:

President _____ MRS. WILLIAM G. TOWNSEND
First Vice-President _____ MRS. J. R. WHITMAN
Second Vice-President _____ MRS. ARTHUR LOTT
Rec. Secretary _____ MRS. HARRY WILSON
Corres. Secretary _____ MRS. C. C. HAMILTON
Treasurer _____ MRS. JACK WILLIAMS
Parlimentarian _____ MRS. EDITH L. DIMMOCK
Advisory Board—MRS. EDITH DIMMOCK, MRS. J. A. ROLLISON, MRS. HERBERT BRADSHAW.
Special Committees—MRS. JACK WILLIAMS, MRS. J. R. WHITMAN, MRS. EDITH DIMMOCK, MRS. A. V. KENNEDY, MRS. C. M. PROPST, MRS. M. C. THOMAS, MRS. G. B. SCOTT, MRS. E. V. SPEER, MRS. C. C. HAMILTON, MRS. J. MAC JENNINGS, MRS. D. W. LANE, MRS. A. V. BALDESCHWEILER.

DEPARTMENTS OF WORK

Tallulah Falls Industrial School— CH., MRS. HERBERT BRADSHAW
Student Aid—CH., MRS. A. V. KENNEDY
Department Fine Arts—MRS. MACK BARNES
Music—MISS ISABELLA SMITH
Singing—MRS. CHARLES VAN WINKLE
Art—MRS. DOLLIE HIGHSMITH
Drama—MISS LUTIE NEESE
Literature —MRS. JOHN R. GLENN
Georgia Writers and Legislation—MRS. EDITH DIMMOCK
Department of Education—MRS. J. A. ROLLISON

OFFICERS AND BOARD MEMBERS
WAYCROSS WOMANS CLUB

Left, top to bottom, Mrs. J. R. Whitman, first vice-president; Mrs. Harry M. Wilson, recording secretary; Mrs. Charles C. Hamilton, corresponding secretary. Center Mrs. William G. Townsend, president. Right, top to bottom, Mrs. Arthur Lott, second vice-president; Mrs. Jack Williams, treasurer; Mrs. Edith Lott Dimmock, parliamentarian.

Adult Education—Miss Mamie Phillips
Pre School Education—Mrs. Glenn Harn
War Veteran—Miss Leila Summerall
Department Public Welfare—Ch., Mrs. J. L. Walker
Child Welfare—Mrs. J. Mac Jennings
Community Service—Mrs. J. M. Fesperman
Department of American Home—Ch., Mrs. D. S. McClellan
Home Demonstration—Mrs. C. L. Mattox
Ware County Products—Mrs. Russell King
Department of American Citizenship and Training—Ch., Mrs. M. C. Brinson
Department of International Relations—Ch., Mrs. E. V. Speer
Junior Club—Mrs. R. L. Scott
Co-operation—Mrs. J. Lee Parker
Custodian—Mrs. C. M. Propst
Scrap Book—Miss Mamie McKnight
Auditor—Mrs. Harry Wilson, Miss Winnie Quarterman
Publicity Chairman—Mrs. M. C. Thomas

Advisory Committee

Col. Leon Wilson
Judge Lee Crawley
Jerome Crawley
Jack J. Williams
Cecil V. Stanton
Mrs. F. B. Folsom

The County Commissioners

Joseph D. Mitchell
D. A. Woodard
John M. Cox

Commemorating Georgia Bicentennial Year 1933.

MRS. EDITH LOTT DIMMOCK
Organizer
President, 1928-1930

MRS. J. A. ROLLISON
President, 1930-1931

MRS. HERBERT M.
BRADSHAW
President, 1931-1932

MRS. WILLIAM G.
TOWNSEND
President, 1932-1934

CHAPTER XVII

MILITARY

REVOLUTIONARY SOLDIERS OF WARE

THE FOLLOWING Revolutionary Soldiers were living in Ware, when they drew their land lottery for service in the War. This information was obtained from pages of the book "Cherokee Land Lottery," which gives not only their place of residence (the soldiers) but their county precincts:

William Cason (Green) _____ Ware County
Willis Cason (Green) _____ Ware County
Willoughby Cason (Miller) ___ Ware County
Winiford Dyess (Miller) _____ Ware County
John McClain (Thomas) _____ Ware County
Specey Rusheon (Sweat) _____ Ware County
William Tompson (Thomas)___Ware County
Thomas Simmons (Williams) __ Ware County
William King (Sweats) _____ Ware County
Charles Griffis _____ Ware County
John Lee _____ Ware County
William Miller _____ Ware County
David Sutton (Motes) _____ Ware County
Joshua Sharpe _____ Ware County
Levi Lee _____ Ware County
Henry Stone (Sweats) _____ Ware County

WARE'S UNKNOWN SOLDIER

During the years of 1812 and throughout the intervening lapse of the time from 1838 to 1848 there was constant warfare between the white settlers of Ware and the Georgia and Florida Indians.

The Indians were a constant menace to the pioneers; they stole cattle, murdered families and burned homes, and Ware came in quite frequently for her share of enormities from the hands of the Seminole, Cowetas and Creek Indians.

An intersession for protection was made to the United States government, and troops were immediately sent to garrisons at various points to repel the approach of the invading enemies.

Captain David J. Miller's Company of Mounted Men were ordered into service by Colonel Thomas Hilliard, commanding officers of the militia of Ware.

These troops were stationed at Fort Mudge, and it was during one of their skirmishes with the Indians that one of the recruits who had joined the forces the day before was fatally wounded. The story of this Unknown Soldier of Ware was told by one of Captain Miller's soldiers to his daughter who is still living and retains a storehouse of interesting memories of the far-off times. I shall tell the story of The Unknown Soldier as she told it to me.

"Firing had been heard at intervals all during the day by the soldiers stationed in camp at Fort Mudge, and apprehensions were felt for the safety of those who lived in a small settlement near the southwestern side of the Okefinokee Swamp.

"Orders were given by the senior officers, not of the military sort, but still the best that could be given by untrained men in authority, and on this occasion they directed that each man go into the field and fight 'upon his own hook.' This order was carried into execution at once with surprising success. A close range of fire at random by the Indians, as if phased, but were still invincible in their approach. Each moment they saw their best men falling, and soon found themselves obliged to retreat, without obtaining revenge for which they were fighting. The appalling war songs filled the air and their watch fires were alternately blazing afar through the forests.

"Closely the soldiers followed the retreating Indians throughout that day, and felt triumphant, when looking over the field where their fallen enemy lay.

"My father said that although his powder had given out, he went across the field not far from the Fort; the first of the fallen that he saw was the young stranger who had the day before reached their camp and enlisted for service. He found that he had received a wound in his breast and was lying alone by the wayside. He observed a calm repose in the expression of the wounded soldier's features which he had often seen in those who were dying from gunshot wounds; his lips seemed like one neither dead nor sleeping, but profoundly wrapped in meditative thoughts on distant scenes and absent friends. He went to where the soldier lay, with a proud feeling that he had maintained throughout the battle, an assured victory, that they had won. However, when he saw the soldier lying there, in his youthful beauty he confessed that he had to sit down by the poor boy and wept like a child. He took the dying boy in his arms and carried him to the camp where he closed his eyes in sleep 'From which there was no awakening' and just a little off the road at Race Pond is the grave of the Unknown Soldier of Ware."

INDIAN WARS

The following information was contributed to the History of Ware County by the State Historian, Miss Ruth Blair, which consists of some old letters and Muster Roll of the 19th day of August, 1838:

Waresboro 1st March 1838

To His Excellency
    George R Gilmer
Dear Sir

I have seen you have Requested all persons haveing in thare poseshion public arms to in form you of the same the Quantity Quality &c—

I have in my poseshion 60 muskets and thare are 40 more at Centerville in Camden County all of which ware sent for the use of the citizens of this county the 40 at Centerville ware never brought from thare Two Boxes of cartrages Belts cartrage Boxes Bayonetts &c the sixty Guns in this county haveing been used some little and Boxed up again I have no doubt wants cleaning and if not done soon they will be more or less injured those yet remaining at Centerville have not been opened unless by some person without my consent should you think proper to have those in this county put in Good order inform me of the same and I will have them attended to I should like for them to remain here untill the Indians are removed &c

       Respectfully Yours &c
         Thomas Hilliard

     On Reverse

Letter

     Waresboro Ga
      3 March
       18¾

          His Excellency
Thos Hilliard Public Arms George R Gilmer
Public Arms   Milledgeville
            Georgia

Original letter on file in office of Georgia Department of Archives.

       Ware County

    Waresboro 4th June 1838

To His Excellency
George R Gilmer

  Sir

   I have Received information that a considirable Number of Indians have left Florida and are at this time in the limits of this county the Number I have not bin able to correctly assertain but suposed to be one hundred warors by those who have been enganed (*sic*) with them it appears that thare are different ages of thare sign and it is believed other companys have come before them and have taken up thare Residence in the Okafanoka Swamp two Battles have been fit (*sic*) by them and our citizens on the 27th and 28th May last the paticulars of which I have not bin able to assertain

Two of the whites ware wounded one suposed mortally no Indian kild or wounded as has been known the last battle ware in the limits of this county on the Sawanna River

The citizens are leaveing thare homes several familys have already left and many more will leave in a few days as they are hourly Exspecting the Indians to fall on them they have reached those deep and dense Swamps of the Okafanoka and from my knowledge of those Swamps it will be almost impossible for them to be removed

I hope thare fore your Excellency will Grant us the athaurity to raise one company of mounty (*sic*) men to continue in Service and to Guard our familys and property untill such times as our citizens can remain at thare Homes in peace and Safety.

with this company and the forces that will be raised in Lowndes I have no doubt we can protect our selves the citizens of this county are continually Exsposed to the mercy of those Savage in consequence of thare being no Guard to protect them from those marching from Florida and taking thare residence in those Swamps which makes it the more important that a guard should be kep on the line of Florida and Ware to keep them from reaching those Swamps

I have ordered a company to be organised amediately to keep them from commiting any depredations untill such times as we can drve (*sic*) them from our borders as our citizens are daily in danger while they remain amongst us

I think your Excellency will see the importance of amediate action in the case

> I am Sir verry
> Respectfully your obt.
> Servant
> Thomas Hilliard

To
His Excellency
George R Gilmer
Milledgeville
Georgia

On Reverse

Letter
Col Thos Hilliard
Invasion of Ware Co
by Seminole Indians

His Excellency
George R. Gilmer
Milledgeville
Georgia

per John S Henderson
Express bearer

Original letter on file in office of Georgia Department of Archives.

Waresboro July 3rd. 1838

His Excellency
George R. Gilmer

Sir :-

The Indians still remain in this county & part of the citizens are in distress Having to leave their Homes and property for the safety of their lives,—provisions cannot be had or obtained in this Section of the country to Support a sufficient force to drive them from the Swamp., I Have five companies in the field & Have been compeld. to purchase supplies on my own Responcibility for their support.

I do believe could I be furnished with supplies, with those already under my command & several other companies who have tendered their servises to me I could drive them from our borders.

I Hope therefore your Excellency will have supplies

sent to camp (*sic*) pinkney (*sic*) on the St Marys River or furnish me with the means to do so

the Indians have burnt already one House & farm in this county & killed considerable stock &c

I Have Established a line of posts sufficient to protect our frontiers, and have Employed waggons &c to furnish them with supplies.

I Have also purchased camp Equipages ammunition &c

I Hope your Excellency will Please write me Immediately on the reception of this

I Have the Honor to Remain

your Excellencys
obdt servt.
Thomas Hilliard coll.
commanding

Letter

Thomas Hilliard
3rd. July 1838.

On Reverse

His Excellency George R. Gilmer
Milledgeville
Georgia
Politeness of
Coln. G. J. Williams,
Col. Hillard (in pencil)

Original document on file in office of Georgia Department of Archives

Copy

Head Quarters—Army of the South
Suwannee river, near the
mouth of the Suwanonchee

Ware Co. Geo. July 13, '38

Sir—I have the honor to acknowledge the receipt of a copy of your letter of the 29. Ulto. from St. Mary's addressed to the Commanding Officer at Black Creek on the subject of the various reports which are in circulation relative to the number of Indians on the frontiers of Georgia, and which this moment reached me.

A short time since while at Black Creek, I was informed that a party of Indians had taken refuge in the Okefanoke Swamp within the limits of the State of Georgia; that they had passed up through the settlements from the regions around the Ocklawaha, but without committing depredations of any sort on the persons or property of the inhabitants. I immediately despatched an officer to the neighborhood of the Swamp, where it was reported the Indians had entered it; and at the same time took measures to have a quantity of supplies sent to that vicinity; I learned that the volunteers had pursued the hostiles (no doubt refugee Creeks), and supposed to be 40 or 50 men with their families, that they came up with them on two occasions, in each of which after a slight skirmish, two or three white men wounded, the volunteers retired to their homes—Two companies of Dragoons and two of Infantry were immediately ordered to the borders of the Swamp, of which, one company of Dragoons and one of Infantry occupy this Station—A company of Infantry occupies a Station intermediate between this and Trader's hill; and a company of Dragoons will be located near Waresborough; these four companies, in addition to one of militia just organised and mustered into the Service, along the dividing line between Georgia and Florida, to act as guides to the regular troops, I flatter myself will afford ample protection to the inhabitants around the Swamp; should this however not be the case, Major Dearbourn, who will locate the Post, is authorised to call into Service, such militia force as he may find requisite to effect that object. A Depot of Provisions etc. has been established at Trader's hill or Camp Pinckney, where Capt. Waite U. S. M. is ordered to ensure the regular supplies to the troops garrisoning the several posts around the Okefanoke, as well as to any others which may be called out.

I have just received from Lt. Col. Harney, a report of an expedition made by him up the St. Johns river to Fort Lane—(80 or 100 miles) He reports no signs of Indians—and believes there is not one in that Section of country.

I shall leave this in a few days for Tampa, when it will afford me much pleasure at all times to hear from you and of the well doing of yourself and family, to each of whom be so good as to present me most kindly.

    With respect and esteem
    Your friend and obedt. Servt.
    Z. Taylor, Bt. Br. Gen. U. S. Army

MS copy on file in office of Georgia Department of Archives.

    Ware County Ga
    Waresboro 25th July 1838

Sir

Last Sunday morning 22nd Inst between day break and sun rise the house of Maxey N Niles resident about seven miles from this place was attacked by a party of Indians supposed to be about fifty in number, and barbously murdered Niles, his wife, and six Children together with one of his neighbors Children who happened to be there at the time, four only out of thirteen made their escape to tell the sad news. they plundered and burnt the House to the ground (*sic*) Imediately on the alarm being given by Niles oldest son who is one of those escaped, Capt. Dade of the United States Dragoons who were stationed within three miles of the scene of depredation with about forty men went in pursuit of the indians and reached the place by one hour by sun the Indians were then gone but not more than half hour in advance but succeeded in reaching the swamp before the troops could overtake them. It was not considered advisable that so small a party of men would enter so dense a swamp where there were so much sign." (*sic*)

The situations of this county is truly distressing all the teretory south & south west of Blackshear's road is entirely abandoned which is the greatest part of the county, from every circumstance connected with Indians affairs in Ware it is evident that they are numerous, for there is no part of Ware bordering on the Okefanoke Swamp but there sign can be seen—There is at this place at this time upwards of thirty families who have fled their homes and the number increasing hourly. They of course left their all subject every moment to be destroyed.

It is highly necessary that some means should be adopted to secure the safty of the people We have men enough at our command to effect this if we had the necessary suplies such as provisions and amunitions—

I have appointed Elijah Mattox of this place Quarter Master for this Regiment and it is necessary that your Excellency would send him a commission, and means for enabling him to obtain the necessary supplies

Very Respectfully
your Obd Servt
Thos Hilliard
Coln Comandt

On Reverse

Letter from

Col Thomas Hilliard
Ware

July 25th. 1838.

Indian Hostilities

His Excellency
    Geo. R. Gilmer
        Milledgeville
pr Jas Fullwood Esq) Georgia

Original letter on file in office of Georgia Department of Archives.

Waresborro 14th, Aug. 1838

His Excellency

George R. Gilmer

Sir your orders of the 17th of Last month was received on the 6th. Inst requring me to discharge all the Troops under my command which orders has been promptly obayed—But the Citizens of the county having received no aid or protection from the United States Government, I Have again been cald on by the Inhabitants of the country to call the malitia into the field to render them protiction untill such a time as they receive it from the U. S. Government—

as regards the assistance rendered us by the u. s. troops is mere mockery for there is but one small company of Dragoons stationed about five miles below this place of about fourty men who cannot do much more than to Guard their own Quarters

I Have forwarded on Express to Maj. Derbourne some days since but the distance to his station, (or Quarters) is so far that I have not as yet been able to hear from that officer a large number of the citizens have already left the country and the balance of them is obliged to keep Embodied to gether for the safety of themselves and families—having finally to abandon their farms and property entirely exposed to the mercy of the savage

Should Maj. Dearbourn not render further assistance to this section we shall finally be obliged to abandon the country or continue our troops in the field

I Hope that your Excellency will advise with me on the subject as as Early a period as circumstances may per mit

I Have the Honor to be
your Excellency' most
obdt servt

Thomas Hilliard
Coln. Commanding

Letter

Col. Thos Hilliard
14th August 38

On Reverse

Waresboro Ga
14th Augt
18¾

His Excellency
George R. Gilmer
Milledgeville
Georgia

mail

Original letter on file in office of Georgia Department of Archives.

Ware County January the 19th, 1838
Waresboro

His Excellency
Geor R Gilmer

Dear Sir

the citizens of this country again feel Grate alarm in consequence of the Indians beeting back on our borders on the Fronteers of this county

thare being no post or station to keep them back from our swamps thare is no doubt of thare being some Indians at this time that had took shelter in the swamps of this county for the purpose of stealing from the citizens.

I have Received Information from the citizens that Indians have been seen lately thare sign have been seen also Guns have been heard at late hours of the night which confirm the belief that they have taken up to stay several of Our citizens have left thare Homes for fear of thare familys being murdered by the savage thare being no station to prevent them from marching from Florida and seeking thare vengance on the helpless woman (*sic*) a children an driveing of Our property at thare Own disposual

from my knowledge of this section of country I know they have every advantage over the citizens the sparce population of the country the deep and impenatrable (*sic*) swamps should they reach them it would almost be imposible to drive them away

I thare fore hope your Excellency will take the case into consideration and consider the importance of thare being a station of at least one company of mounted men keep on or near the line of Florida and Georgia to pataroll the country and protect the citizens from the savage murder

the company can be raised from the Battalion which I have the Honor to command shouould (*sic*) your Excellency think proper to authorise me to do so

any instruction your Excellency may think proper to give will be thankfully received and promptly attended to

I have the Honer to be Sir your most obedient servt.

        Thomas Hilliard

His Excellency
  George R Gilmer
    Milledgeville
      Georgia

      Letter

    Thomas Hilliare (*sic*)
      Hilliard
    Seminole Inds

     On Reverse

His Excellency   1834
  George R. Gilmer
    Milledgeville
Waresboro   Georgia
18th Jan.

Original letter on file in office of Georgia Department of Archives.

Waresboro' February 2nd 1839

His Excellency
   George R. Gilmer
      Sir,

         Having seen your Excellency's call for a regiment of volunteers to consist of Eight companies for the protection of the frontiers of this state against the attacks of the Creek and Seminole tribes of Indians, which measure I deem of paramount importance to this section, and as I reside on the border of the Okefenoke swamp, I tender to your Excellency the offer of my services to command said regiment which I can raise before the return of my Express as several companies have already made me a tender of ther services

                I have the honor
                 to be Sir, very respectfully
                  Your most obdt. servant
                    Thomas Hilliard
            Brigr. Gen: 2nd Brge. 6th Dvision
                      G. M.

Letter

1839
Gen Hilliard
                On Reverse

             On public service
Okefenokee   His Excellency
                       George R. Gilmer
                          Milledgeville

          Per Dr. R. M. McDonald
              Express Bearer

Original letter on file in office of Georgia Department of Archives.

Georgia   } Know all men by these presents that we
Ware County } Capt. David. J. Miller Jas. Lee, and R. McDonald are held and firmly bound unto his Excellency George R Gilmer Governor of said State, and his succes-

sors in office, in the just sums of Ten Thousand five hundred & five 14/100 Dollars, for the payment of which we bind ourselves, our heirs Executors and administrators, jointly and severally firmly by these presents.

Sealed with our seals and dated this 12th day of April 1839.

The condition of the above obligation is such, that whereas the above bound Capt. Davd J Miller has this day received of Yelverton P King commissioner for the State, the sum of Five Thousand two Hundred & five dollars & seven cents for the purpose of paying off the accounts of the persons composing his company, for the pay subsistence and allowances due them, while engaged against the Indians in the Okefenokee swamps: Now if the said David J Miller shall punctually and truly pay to each individual belonging to his command, the amount which has been allowed him by the commissioner, then the above obligation to be void otherwise to remain in full force and virtue

	David J. Miller	(L.S.)
Samuel G. Norman J. P.	James Lee	(L.S.)
	R. McDonald	(L.S.)

On Reverse
Bond
David J. Millers
Bond
Ware
County

Original document on file in office of Georgia Department of Archives

Georgia } Waresboro November 8th 1839
Ware County } To his Excellency
Charles J McDonald

Sir I have just returned from A Scout on the fronteer part of this county I found two Indian incampments in the Sewanuchee Swamp there was from the sign About forty or the Rise that Ocupied the camps the whole Nomber Of Indians In this County from Information from Good authority Is about sixty or seventy at least.

The exposed part of our county is about 70 miles and almoste A continual swamp And the Inhabitance nearest the Oakefankee swamp have left their places and property exposed to the Savage

I have Ordered out three Companys of mounted militia to protect the exposed part of this County the companys are under necessaty (sic) of furnashing (sic) their own supplies as I have no means of furnishing them, provisions is not in our county to be had, the companys are continually Scouting the fronteer part of this county, there is A number of Indian trails been discovered leading tward the Oakefanokee swamp the troops will Remain in service untill further Orders, &c,

  Richard Bourn   To his Excellency
   Major   Charles J. McDonald
Commanding 158. batt. G.M.   Governor of Georgia

Richard Bourn
 8th Nov. 1839

 per Wm. A. McDonald   His Excellency
   Express bearer   Charles J. McDonald
            Milledgeville, Georgia

Original letter on file in office of Georgia Department of Archives.

        Waresboro 24th Novr. 1839

Dear Sir

Your letter of the 13th Inst by William has been duly received.—Our head men in this little World of *Ware* and of Wonders are carrying on a large scale of *mighty* things, Maj. Bourne has appointed the Hon. James Fulwood Quarter Master Purchasing Commissary, of subsistance, contracts, and assistant Major and is going to request his Excellency to have him commissioned (so says my Informant) he has also ordered two companies in the field, Captains Sweat & Johnson, a Surgeon I suppose is to be Elected, I do not know who the lot will fall upon, I understand that 1000, bushels of corn has been purchased & one doz steel mills, for the use of the companies, Capt. Johnson has made accquisition for camp Equipage munitions of War &c &c

Corn sells at two Dollars per bushel freely, Pork 10 cts, Beef 6¼ and so goes the times.—

Please tender my Respects to Mr Mattox & say to him all is well—its now raining and I will quit Excuse Brevity

I remain yours Truely

to
Gen Thos. Hilliard } R. McDonald

On Reverse
Copy of a Letter from
R McDonald
to
Genl Hilliard

Original letter on file in office of Georgia Department of Archives.

Extract from a letter written by A. McRae of Waresboro to Genl Thomas Hilliard dated Waresboro Nov. 24th 1839.

"I have no Indian news of any importance to communicate to you Capt D Johnson was here yesterday he had returned a few days back from a scout: saw some little sign low down the Suwnnochee, (sic) could not say whether it was very new sign or not, his company is now out under command of his Liut—He came down to see the newly made Quarter Master, Contractor, Commissary &c &c (Fulwood) lately appointed by the Major for the furnishing his Johnson's Company with subsistence Camp Equipage and so on. We are doing big things down here to Ware I tell you—The Quarter Master is to leave to morrow morning with three carts to St. Marys for

Sugar Coffee &c This I have from Cobb who is now on his return from the Quarter Masters where he was seeking employment in the great train"

On Reverse
Extract of a Letter from
A. McRae to Genl Hilliard

Original document on file in office of Georgia Department of Archives

Georgia { Know all men by these presents, that
Ware County { we Jas. A Sweat, Thomas Hilliard & Jno. S Henderson are held and firmly bound unto his Excellency George R Gilmer Governor of said State and his successors in office, in the just sum of Nine Thousand & thirty dollars & sixty six cents for the payment of which we bind ourselves our heirs, executors and administrators, jointly and severally firmly by these presents.

Sealed with our seals and dated this eleventh day of April 1839.

The condition of the above obligation is such, that whereas the above bound Jas. A Sweat has this day recieved (*sic*) of Yelverton P King commissioner for the State, the sum of Four Thousand five Hundred & fifteen dollars & 66 cents for the purpose of paying off the accounts of the persons composing his company, for the pay, subsistence and allowances due them, while engaged against the Indians in the Okefenokee Swamp: Now if the said Jas A Sweat shall punctually and truly pay to each individual belonging to his command, the amount which has been allowed him by the commissioner then the above obligation to be void, otherwise to remain in full force and virtue.

Samuel G Norman, J.P.   Jas. A. Sweat   (Seal)
                         Thomas Hilliard   (Seal)
                         John S. Henderson   (Seal)

On Reverse
Capt Sweats Bond
Ware County.

Original bond on file in office of Georgia Department of Archives.

Georgia } Know all men by these presents that
Ware County } we Jas. Walker, Jas. Fulwood & Jas. Jones are held and firmly bound unto his Excellency George R Gilmer Governor of said State, and his successors in office in the just sum of six thousand & four 80/100 Dollars for the payment of which we bind ourselves our heirs executors and administrators, jountly (sic) and severally firmly by these presents sealed with our seals and dated this eleventh 11th day of April 1839.

The condition of the above obligation is such, that whereas the above bound Jas Walker has this day recieved (sic) of Yelverton P King commissioner for the state, the sum of Three thousand & two 40/100 dollars for the purpose of paying off the accounts of the persons composing his company, for the pay subsistence and allowances due them while engaged against the Indians in the Okefenokee Swamp. Now if the said Jas Walker shall punctually and truly pay to each individual belonging to his command, the amount which has been allowed him by the commissioner, then the above obligation to be void, otherwise to remain in full force and virtue

Samuel G Noman, (sic) J. P.   James Walker   (L.S.)
        James Fulwood   (L.S.)
        James Jones   (L.S.)

On Reverse

Jas Walkers
Bond
Ware county

Original bond on file in office of Georgia Department of Archives.

Georgia } Know all men by these presents, that
Ware County } we Nathaniel J Holton S. Hall, Benjh (sic) Smith are held and firmly bound unto his Excellency George R Gilmer Governor of said State and his successors in office, in the just sum of Ten Thousand seven Hundred & ninety nine 98/100 dollars for the payment of

which we bind ourselves our heirs Executors and administrators jointly and severally, firmly by these presents.

Sealed with our seals and dated this 10th day of April 1839

The condition of the above obligation is such, that whereas the above bound Nathaniel J Holton has this day recieved (*sic*) of Yelverton P King commissioner for the state, the sum of Five thousand three Hundred & ninety nine 99/100 dollars for the purpose of paying off the accounts of the persons composing his company for the pay subsistence and allowances due them while engaged against the Indians in the Okefenokee swamp: Now if the said Nathaniel J Holton shall punctually and truly pay to each individual belonging to his command, the amount which has been allowed him by the commissioner, then the above obligation to be void, otherwise to remain of full force and virtue

Test	N. J. Holton	(L.S.)
Wm Parker J (*sic*)	Seaborn Hall	(L.S.)
	Bnager (*sic*) Smith	(L.S.)

On Reverse
Nathaniel J Holtons
Bond
Ware county.

Original bond on file in office of Georgia Department of Archives.

Head Quarters Fort Floyd
Ware County 9th Decr 1839

Sir

in obedience to your order number *one* by Express McDonald, I have discharged one company & have retained two in the Service. My absence from the post in procuring Supplies &c for the two companies under my command is my apology for not writing at an Earlyer period and informing your Excellency of my procedings in due time —in consiquence of the Scarcity of Provisions & forage in this section of the country I have appointed James Fulwood Esq to act as quarter master for the present & untill such time as I Should hear from your Excellency on the subject.—

I Have also appointed Doctor R. McDonald Surgeon in charge of the Several post under my command, for the benefit of the sick &c the Doctor furnishes his own medicines camp equipage and all the necessary supplies within himself—

by next mail I shall forward on to your Excellency my monthly report when I shall be more able to write you more fully on the subject.

    I Have the Honor to be with much
     Respect your Excellencys very
      obedient servant.
       Richard Bourne, Major
        Commanding Vol Militia
         Ware County Georgia

To His Excellency
 Charles J. McDonald
  Milledgeville Georgia

      On Reverse

Major Bourn   Waresboro Ga
 Major Comding   Dec 9th   18 ¾
 Ware County His Excellency Charles J. McDonald
  1839   Milledgeville Georgia
      mail

Original letter on file in office of Georgia Department of Archives.

      Waresboro 28th. July 1836

His Excellency
 William Schley

Sir it becomes my duty to inform you from undoubted information that several strolling Partis of the Creek Tribes of Indians are now within the limits of this County and are Generally suposed to be making thare way to the okefenoke (*sic*) swamp

Under these Circumstances Grat alarm prevails amongst the Inhabitants of this County being daily under the apprehension of an attack from the savage foe

I have thare fore to request of your Excellency to order the Redgement Consisting of Appling & Ware to hold themselves in redaness to act as the Exigencies of the Case may require as I do not believe a sufficient force Can be raised to repell them in any other way

I think some imediate Exetive (sic) action necessary for the safety and to relieve the fears of the People

Should any Murders be Committed I will inform you immediately

                Verry Respectfully
                   I have the Honor to be your
obt servent   Thomas Hilliard

                Letter
           Col. Thomas Hilliard
             28 July 1836
             Creek War

              On Reverse

Col. Thos Hilliard   Waresboro Ga
Answered   28th July   18¾
16th August 1836   His
                   Excellency
                      William Schley
                       Milledgeville
                         Georgia

Original letter on file in office of Georgia Department of Archives.

                Waresboro
             26th August 1836

To His Excellency
    William Schley

Dear Sir

I wrote to you by mail on the 28th of July last concerning our Indian affairs in this county and from some unknown cause to me I have not received your answer thare ware some partys of Indians at that time in the limits of this county and from every circumstance yet remain here and still continue to come

On the 23rd. Instant a small party cosisting of nine said to be in Nomber ware discovered making thare way down the St. Tilla River they ware persude by a small company of whites they came on them on the Bank of the River they charged on them put them to flight kild three dead on the Ground fired on the ballance as they crosed the River and suposed they kild three more of the whites one ware wounded but suposed not mortally another party was discovered the next day the 24th Instant suposed mostly woman and children of about fifteen in Nomber and a company are in pursuit of them at this time but I have not herd the result other partys have bin seen pasing through the county on the direction for the Okafanoka Swamp they Go consealed as much as posible and are commiting depredations continually by robing our corn fields and kiling our stock thare sign have also bin seen in different parts of the county making thare course for the Swamp it also has bin discovered on the borders of the swamp and as thare course is in that direction and not in the direction for Florida it is believed they intend taking up thare residence here

The nature of the country is such around the swamp that should they stop thare it will be troublesome to remove them should they be let gather thare.

The citizens have taken alarm and are leaving the country and if means are not taken to remove them the country will be left the citizens are daily petitioning to me to take measures to have such an armd. force out as will secure protection to thare lives and property but I have bin waiting to receive your Excellencys answer before I proceeded to act as I am doubtfull of my being authorised as commanding officer of the Battalion of this county to order out a suficent Guard and compell them to act without a sufficient athaurity from you, but I have bin compeld for the safety of our property to call out a suficent force and shall commense operations on the 29th. Instant and shall purchas such provisions amunitions &c as we are compeld to have untill I be otherwise directed by your Excellency I have sent this by Exspress Mr. Fulwood the bearer of this is a man of high responceability and can give you better information than I have in this

Could I be authurised to call out a sufficent force of mounted men with athaurity to furnish nessary suplies thare is no doubt they can be removed in short time

Your Excellency will tharefore act as to you the nature of the case may seem best any orders or instructions that you may see proper to give will be thankfully received and promptly attended to

Very respectfully
I Remain Your umble
Serv.
Thomas Hilliard

On Reverse

Letter
  Col. Thos. Hilliard, 26 August 1836. Creek War—
  Col. Hilliard Ware County orders issued 30th Aug. 1836
  To His Excellency William Schley Milledgeville Ga.
    Care of Mr. Fulwood

Original letter on file in office of Georgia Department of Archives.

Waresboro Oct. 5th 1836

Sir,

In pursuance of your order by my Express (Mr. Fulwood) I proceeded to raise and organize a company of mounted men (volunteers) Exclusive of officers which duty I completed on the 10th Sept. when the company was organized by the Election of the following officers Viz. Simon Howard Captain David J. Miller 1st Lt. James A. Sweat 2nd do & George B. Williamson Ensign—

Having been satisfactorially informed that a murder had been commited on the body of one Thomas Fulwood of this county on the Suwannee river near the mouth of the Sawanonchie Creek distant about sixty miles from this place, by a party of Indians (tribe unknown) and having also learnt that the Indians we Embodied to a considerable number I deemed it my duty, but the authority confided to me in Your Excellency's order, to call upon the commanding officers of the counties of Appling and Wayne for their respective quotas of men. *After* giving this order, I received information from an undoubted source, that the Indians were not so numerous as at first represented and thinking it improper to run the State to any unnecessary Expense, I judged it Expedient to countermand my former order and proceed with the troops already organized in this county to the scene of Expected hostilities, which I did in person: I am sorry to say that the troops from Wayne arrived at this place before receiving the countermanding orders on the Friday Evening after we had left on Tuesday—The men from Appling did not start

The following statement will embrace the movements of the Ware troops.

On the 13 Sep. we left Waresboro, our place of rendezvous, for the Suwannee, and after some promiscuous scouting, we arrived on the 18th at the place where the murder had been committed, and although we found considerable Indian sign; we could find no traces of the way they had gone. While in camp this night I received intelligence that Captain William B. in command of a company of Ware County and Florida Militia, had had two several Engagements a few days previous with parties of the Creek tribe of Indians, in which fights the Indians were supposed to have had between fifteen and twenty killed and a number wounded—From this information I directed a letter to Capt. North desiring his opinion relative to the movements of those Indians, in reply he informed me that after these engagements he had trailed them, up the south side of the Suwannee, to the Edge of the Okefenoke, where finding the trail very large, (supposed to be large

Enough for 100) he thought it imprudent to pursue farther, his force consisting at that time of only sixteen men, and that he believed that the Indians had gone into some of the islands and encamped.

In consequence of this information I directed my course for the residence of Capt. North it being a convenient place for crossing the Suwannee and obtaining supplies— The morning after my arrival (the 20th) I was joined by Capt. North and a small portion of his company, and proceeded up the Suwannee to the place where Capt. N. had left the trail: it being impossible to pursue farther on horseback, I directed Capt Howard to dismount his men & detail a sufficient guard for the protection of the horses—

With the remainder we pursued the trail, through the dismal and almost impassable bays of the Okefenoke for about four miles, when we came upon a very large Encampment situated in a large island, which had been abandoned only a few days (not more than four or five) and had all the appearance of having been occupied for some length of time—. From this camp we could not distinguish the way the Indians, had gone, from the heavy rains which had fallen after the camp had been Evacuated—in this island the grass was very short and the woods very bad to trail on at *any time*. in trailing through the bay the case was different, the broken bushes &c giving sure indications—After sometime spent in fruitless attempts to trail them, we returned to our horses, and made our way for the settlements, being very short of provisions.

I have given Capt. Howard instructions to use the utmost diligence and vigilance in patroling the county as it is strongly believed that a considerable number of Indians remain concealed in the swamps and bays with which this county abounds—

In consequence of my absence from this place I did not receive your Excellencies order of 3d Sep. until the 25th Ult.—On the 10th inst. the company will rendezvous for the purpose of mustering into the service of the United States

I believe that one company will be sufficient to protect this county at present—should more be required your Excellency will be immediately informed of it.

His Excellency   I have the honor
  William Schley   To very respectfy &c
    Milledgeville   Thos. Hilliard
      Georgia   Major

           On Reverse
       Col Thomas Hilliard
Waresboro Ga Oct. 6th.   18¾
  His Excellency William Schley
    Milledgeville Georgia
Letter
  Col. Thos Hillard
    5th Octr 1836. Creek War

Original document on file in office of Georgia Department of Archives

            Waresboro October 18th 1836

His Excellency
  Governor Schley
    Dear Sir

Since my letter to you of the 6th Instant I have received your orders to furnish Majr Dearborn with any amount of men he may see proper to call for the call has not yet bin made should it be it will be attended to with prompness

  the company raised under your orders of the 30th August. after one months service has bin discharged believing as I do that Indians are done pasing through and the most of them Gone to Florida I thought it best to discharge them Your orders of the 3rd of Sept. to raise a full company of mounted volunteers and muster them in to the United States service was not received on the account of my absence with the company as stated in my last till the 25th Sept.—and in consequence of that nothing had bin done before I received your orders of the 24. and as I am doubtful a full company of mounted volunteers cannot be raised in this county that will Muster in I have thought best to await Mjr Dearborns orders before the attempt is made which will be done when ever cald on or such amount of men as he may call for

I neglected to state to you in my last that had bin four Indian prisianers brought to Waresboro which still remains thare two of which ware badly wounded they ware taken on the east side of the Sttilla some time sinse in this county they ware discovered at camp at knight a small company of men about ten in No went on them next morning before they left camp and captured them all being ten in No six of which ware kild the prisuaners consists of two male one quite small and two female as thare ware no Jail near and they not able to travel in consequence of thare wounds they ware left at waresboro whare they have bin attended to and are well of thare wounds or nearly so I don't know what better to do with them than to send them to Telfair Jail to await your Excellencys orders The arms, ammunitions, &c. have been received that were sent to this county.

I shall be at Milledgeville shortly whare I can communicate to you more fully on the Indian subject.

    Respectfuly your most obed. servt.
          Thos. Hilliard

     Letter
    Col. Thos. Hilliard
    October 18, 1836.
      Creek War
      On Reverse

Col. Thos. Hilliard

  Waresboro
  20th Oct.
         18¾
   His
    Excellency
     William Schley
      Milledgeville
       Georgia

Original letter on file in office of Georgia Department of Archives.

Georgia   } At an (*sic*) held at Waresboro in and
Ware County } for the 451st dist Company G.M on Saturday the 3rd day of November 1849 for a First &

second Lieutenant for said Company the following persons appeared and voted Viz

1 Duncan Bohannon
2 Elijah Thompson
3 Reuben Wilds
4 W. G. Reggins
5 Thos. Fulwood
6 Wm. B Boothe
7 R G. Dickerson
8 J T. Clough
9 Geo B Williamson
10 Wm Taylor
11 Edmund Corbet
12 David Geiger
13 John W Boothe
14 Franklin Young
15 Thos. Hutchison
16 D B Smith
17 William H. King
18 Richd. Pellam
19 Wm. H. Miller
20 James G Sweat
21 Martin E. L. Blackburn
22 James E. Boothe
23 Wm. W. Smith
24 Allison Cason
25 James Wilds

Candidates Names
    For 1st Lieut

        Donald J McDonald 25

For 2nd.

        Cuyler W. Hilliard 25

Georgia   ⎫ We the undersigned superintendents do
Ware County   ⎬ certify that the foregoing Election was
opened held and closed in due form of law and that the foregoing is a true Exhibit of the Polls

Given under our hands and seals this 3rd November 1849—

            John T. Clough J P   (LS)
            R G Dickerson F H   (LS)
            Geo B Williamson F H.   (L.)

Georgia   ⎫ We Robert G. Dickerson and Geo B
Ware County   ⎬ Williamson freeholders do solemnly
swear that we will faithfully superintend this days Elec-

tion and make a true return thereof according to law, and the best of our skill and understanding so help us God
Sworn to and subscribed } R G Dickerson   F. H
before me 3rd. November 1849 } Geo B Williamson F. H
John T. Clough J. P.

                On Reverse
                451st Ware
                   CMS
              24th Nov 1849
Waresboro 5 Nov   5
       His Excellency
            George W. Towns
                  Milledgeville Ga

Original document on file in office of Georgia Department of Archives

MUSTER ROLL.

Of Captain James A. Sweats (mounted) Company, from the ninth day of June 1838 to the nineteenth day of August 1838 ordered into service by Thomas Hilliard commanding officer of the Militia of Ware County, to repel the invasions of the Indians into that County in the year 1838, by the authority of his Excellency Governor Gilmer.

No.	NAMES Present and absent—(Privates in alphabetical order.)	Rank	Date of arrival at general rendezvous, when service commences.	When mustered into service	By whom mustered into service	Period	TRAVELLING		SUBSISTENCE AND FORAGE FURNISHED BY THEMSELVES	
							To place of rendezvous, No. of miles	From place of rendezvous, No. of miles	Sub. No. of days	For. No. of days
	James A. Sweat	Capt.	9th June	9th June	Thomas Hilliard	71 days	20	20	71	71
	Servant	Servant	"	"	"	"	"	"	71	71
	Thomas Crafford	1st. Lieut.	"	"	"	"	"	"	71	71
	Servant	Servant	"	"	"	"	"	"	71	
	Berrian Henderson	2nd. Lieut.	"	"	"	"	"	"	71	
	Servant	Servant	"	"	"	"	"	"	71	
1	Richard Bourn	1st. Serj.	"	"	"	"	"	"		
2	William Sweat	2nd. Serj.	"	"	"	"	"	"		
3	John Minchew	3rd. Serj.	"	"	"	"	"	"		
4	William Crafford	4th. Serj.	"	"	"	"	"	"		
1	Arnold B. Fussell	1st. Corpl.	"	"	"	"	"	"		
2	George W. S. Waldron	2nd. Corpl.	"	"	"	"	"	"		
3	Calaway King	3rd. Corpl.	"	"	"	"	"	"		
4	Gideon Crafford	4th. Corpl.	"	"	"	"	"	"		
1	Altman, Richard	Private	"	"	"	"	"	"		
2	Beasley, William	"	"	"	"	"	"	"		
3	Bennett, John	"	"	"	"	"	"	"		
4	Beasley, Nathan	"	"	"	"	"	"	"		
5	Coursen, Joshua	"	"	"	"	"	"	"		

MUSTER ROLL—(Continued)

No.	NAMES Present and absent (Privates in alphabetical order.)	Rank	Date of arrival at general rendezvous, when service commences.	When mustered into service	By whom mustered into service	Period	TRAVELLING To place of rendezvous, No. of miles	TRAVELLING From place of rendezvous, No. of miles	SUBSISTENCE AND FORAGE FURNISHED BY THEMSELVES Sub. No. of days	SUBSISTENCE AND FORAGE FURNISHED BY THEMSELVES For. No. of days
6	Davis W. George	Private	9th June	9th June	Thomas Hilliard	71 days	20	20		
7	Davis, Randal	"	"	"	"	"	"	"		
8	Gainey, Isaac	"	"	"	"	"	"	"		
9	Guy, William	"	"	"	"	"	"	"		
10	Hilliard, Silas	"	"	"	"	"	"	"		
11	Hires, Joseph	"	"	"	"	"	"	"		
12	Hilliard, Benjamin	"	"	"	"	"	"	"		
13	Jourden, John	"	"	"	"	"	"	"		
14	Jenkins, George	"	"	"	"	"	"	"		
15	Johnson, William	"	"	"	"	"	"	"		
16	King, William	"	"	"	"	"	"	"		
17	Lightsey, Jacob	"	"	"	"	"	"	"		
18	Lee, Jacob	"	"	"	"	"	"	"		
19	Milton, Benjamin	"	"	"	"	"	"	"		
20	Minchew, Isaac	"	"	"	"	"	"	"		
21	Minchew, Jacob	"	"	"	"	"	"	"		
22	Mercer, William	"	"	"	"	"	"	"		
23	Music, William	"	"	"	"	"	"	"		
24	Nettles, Martin	"	"	"	"	"	"	"		
25	Nettles, Glenn	"	"	"	"	"	"	"		
26	Newborn Thomas	"	"	"	"	"	"	"		
27	Newborn, John	"	"	"	"	"	"	"		
28	Prescoatt, John W.	"	"	"	"	"	"	"		
29	Prescott, Isham	"	"	"	"	"	"	"		

MUSTER ROLL—(Continued)

No.	NAMES Present and absent (Privates in alphabetical order.)	Rank	Date of arrival at general rendezvous, when service commences.	When mustered into service	By whom mustered into service	Period	TRAVELLING To place of rendezvous, No. of miles	TRAVELLING From place of rendezvous, No. of miles	SUBSISTENCE AND FORAGE FURNISHED BY THEMSELVES Sub. No. of days	SUBSISTENCE AND FORAGE FURNISHED BY THEMSELVES For. No. of days
30	Rodenbury, Henry	Private	9th June	9th June	Thomas Hilliard	71 days	20	20		
31	Reevis, John	"	"	"	"	"	"	"		
32	Strickland, Abraham	"	"	"	"	"	"	"		
33	Strickland, Mathew	"	"	"	"	"	"	"		
34	Strickland, Levi	"	"	"	"	"	"	"		
35	Sweat, Samuel	"	"	"	"	"	"	"		
36	Sweat, Nathan	"	"	"	"	"	"	"		
37	Spradley, William	"	"	"	"	"	"	"		
38	Stone, Allen	"	"	"	"	"	"	"		
39	Sulivant, Bud	"	"	"	"	"	"	"		
40	Sweat, Burrell	"	"	"	"	"	"	"		
41	Smith, Charles	"	"	"	"	"	"	"		
42	Stone, Daniel	"	"	"	"	"	"	"		
43	Stone, Henry	"	"	"	"	"	"	"		
44	Sweat, James	"	"	"	"	"	"	"		
45	Sulivant, Jackson	"	"	"	"	"	"	"		
46	Smith, John W.	"	"	"	"	"	"	"		
47	Sweat, Mathew	"	"	"	"	"	"	"		
48	Stanley, Shadrick	"	"	"	"	"	"	"		
49	Stanley, Wiley	"	"	"	"	"	"	"		
50	Thomas, Edward	"	"	"	"	"	"	"		
51	Thorington, Ezekiel	"	"	"	"	"	"	"		
52	Thomas, James R.	"	"	"	"	"	"	"		
53	Thomas, Lewis	"	"	"	"	"	"	"		

MUSTER ROLL—(Continued)

No.	NAMES Present and absent (Privates in alphabetical order.)	Rank	Date of arrival at general rendezvous, when service commences.	When mustered into service	By whom mustered into service	Period	TRAVELLING To place of rendezvous, No. of miles	TRAVELLING From place of rendezvous, No. of miles	SUBSISTENCE AND FORAGE FURNISHED BY THEMSELVES Sub. No. of days	SUBSISTENCE AND FORAGE FURNISHED BY THEMSELVES For. No. of days
54	Thorington, Samuel	Private	9th June	9th June	Thomas Hilliard	71 days	20	20		
55	Underhill, Joseph	"	"	"	"	"	"	"		
56	Walker, Andrew	"	"	"	"	"	"	"		
57	Waldron, Asbury	"	"	"	"	"	"	"		
58	Waldron, Elias D.	"	"	"	"	"	"	"		
59	Wilkinson John	"	"	"	"	"	"	"		
60	Wynn, Joseph	"	"	"	"	"	"	"		
61	Wilkinson, William R.	"	"	"	"	"	"	"		
62	Walker, Littleberry	"	"	"	"	"	"	"		
63	Highsmith, Isaac	"	"	"	"	"	"	"		

REMARKS

The pay for the risk of horse is included in the aggregate amount opposite each officer & privates name on the Pay Roll.

I certify, on honor, that this Muster Roll exhibits the true state of Captain James A. Sweats mounted company, of the county of Ware for the period herein mentioned; that the remarks set opposite the names of each officer and soldier are accurate and just, and that the recapitulation exhibits in every particular the true state of the company.

JAS. A. SWEAT, *Commanding the Company.*

11th April 1839.

Original muster roll on file in office of Georgia Department of Archives. That underscored part is printed on the original. The part that is not underscored is written on the original.

MUSTER ROLL

Of Captain James Walker (Mounted Company, from the 9th day of June 1838 to the 19th day of August 1838 ordered into service by Col. Thomas Hilliard commanding officer of the Militia of Ware County, to repel the invasions of the Indians into that County in the year 1838, by the authority of his Excellency Governor Gilmer.

No.	NAMES Present and absent— (Privates in alphabetical order.)	Rank	Date of arrival at general rendezvous, when service commences.	When mustered into service	By whom mustered into service	Period	TRAVELLING To place of rendezvous, No. of miles	From place of rendezvous, No. of miles
	James Walker	Capt.	9th June 1838	9th June 1838	Col. Thomas Hilliard	71 days	20	20
	Servt.	Servant	"	"	"	"	20	20
	Joseph Lowther	1st Liut.	"	"	"	"	20	20
	Servant	Servant	"	"	"	"	20	20
	Burrell Stokes	2nd Liut.	"	"	"	"	20	20
	Servant	Servant	"	"	"	"	20	20
	Elias Stewart	1st Serj.	"	"	"	"	20	20
	James Griffin	2nd Serj.	"	"	"	"	20	20
	Arthur Allbritton	3rd Serj.	"	"	"	"	20	20
	Henry Allbritton	4th Serj.	"	"	"	"	20	20
	William Griffin	1st Corpl.	"	"	"	"	20	20
	James Highsmith	2nd Corpl.	"	"	"	"	20	20
	James Allbritton	3rd Corpl.	"	"	"	"	20	20
	Westberry Rolison	4th Corpl.	"	"	"	"	20	20
1	Allbritton, Thomas sen.	Private	"	"	"	"	20	20
2	Allbritton, Noah	"	"	"	"	"	20	20
3	Allbritton, Thomas Jun	"	"	"	"	"	20	20
4	Altman, Jesse	"	"	"	"	"	20	20
5	Cason, David	"	"	"	"	"	20	20
6	Cassey, Abslom E.	"	"	"	"	"	20	20

MUSTER ROLL—(Continued)

No.	NAMES Present and absent— (Privates in alphabetical order.)	Rank	Date of arrival at general rendezvous, when service commences.	When mustered into service	By whom mustered into service	Period	TRAVELLING To place of rendezvous, No. of miles	TRAVELLING From place of rendezvous, No. of miles
7	Cooper, Willoby	Private	9th June 1838	9th June 1838	Col. Thomas Hilliard	71 days	20	20
8	Cooper, John	"	"	"	"	"	20	20
9	Crews, Alexandr	"	"	"	"	"	20	20
10	Dowling, Dooling	"	"	"	"	"	20	20
11	Dowling, James	"	"	"	"	"	20	20
12	Dowling, David	"	"	"	"	"	20	20
13	Griffin Dempsey	"	"	"	"	"	20	20
14	Horris, Jimpsey	"	"	"	"	"	20	20
15	Highsmith, William	"	"	"	"	"	20	20
16	Highsmith, John	"	"	"	"	"	20	20
17	Highsmith, Allen	"	"	"	"	"	20	20
18	Jones, Horley	"	"	"	"	"	20	20
19	Jones, James	"	"	"	"	"	20	20
20	Jones, Robert	"	"	"	"	"	20	20
21	Knox, John	"	"	"	"	"	20	20
22	Knox Reddeck	"	"	"	"	"	20	20
23	Lowther, Isham	"	"	"	"	"	20	20
24	Petty, Edward	"	"	"	"	"	20	20
25	Robson, Wiley	"	"	"	"	"	20	20
26	Rolison, Josiah	"	"	"	"	"	20	20
27	Stokes, Elbert	"	"	"	"	"	20	20
28	Stokes, Richard	"	"	"	"	"	20	20
29	Stephens Isham	"	"	"	"	"	20	20
30	Stephens, Samuel	"	"	"	"	"	20	20

MUSTER ROLL—(Continued)

No.	NAMES Present and absent— (Privates in alphabetical order.)	Rank	Date of arrival at General rendezvous, when service commences.	When mustered into service	By whom mustered into service	Period	TRAVELLING	
							To place of rendezvous, No. of miles	From place of rendezvous, No. of miles
31	Trescoat, William	Private	9th June 1838	9th June 1838	Col. Thomas Hilliard	71 days	20	20
32	Wayneright, Joseph	"	"	"	"	"	20	20
33	Cason, Purnel	"	"	"	"	"	20	20
34	Kella, George	"	"	"	"	"	20	20

REMARKS

The pay for the risk of horse is included in the aggregate amt opposite each officer & privates name.

JAMES WALKER, Capt.

I certify, on honor, that this Muster Roll exhibits the true state of Captain James Walker mounted company, of the county of Ware for the period herein mentioned; that the remarks set opposite the names of each officer and soldier are accurate and just, and that the recapitulation exhibits in every particular the true state of the company.

11th April 1839— .

JAMES WALKER, Commanding the Company.

Original muster roll on file in office of Georgia Department of Archives. The underscored part is printed on the original. The part that is not underscored is written on the original.

Captain North's Militia Company

The following is a muster roll of Capt. John J. North's company which served around Blount's Ferry in the Indian War, from April, 5, 1842, to April 30, 1842, a period of twenty-five days. These men were all mounted and the company was under Brigadier-General Thos. Hilliard.

Captain, John J. North; First Lieut., W. Whidden: Second Lieut., Wm. B. Crews; First Sergeant, Robt. T. Seynes; Second Sgt., David Hunter; Third Sgt., W. W. Tumblin; Fourth Sgt., John G. Slade; First Corporal, Rigdon Brown; Second Corporal, John Forbus; Third Corporal, Noah Whidden; Fourth Corporal, John Cook.

Privates: Sampson Altman, Thos. Altman, Wm. Bryant, John Bennett, Grandison Barber, Stephen Crews, Wm Crews, Joseph Crews, Sr., Joseph Crews, Jr., Joseph Crews, 3rd., Alex Crews, Jr., Lemuel Crews, Ed. Crews, Jr., D. D. Crews, Isham Crews, David Cannon, Wm. Cannon, Aaron Douglas, Chas. Fletcher, Geo. Fletcher, Daniel Green, Jas. C. Green, Henry Herrington, Josie Hicks, Josie Hunter, Jas. Hunter, Hunton Hunter, Malachi Harper, Josiah Johnson, Patrick Jordan, Wiley Keen, Wm. Levins, Elijah Lochalin, David Morgan, Jas. North, Jas. Olesby, Sr., Jas Olesby, Jr., Jas. Parish, John Padgett, Jesse Pennington, Franklin Raulerson, David Raulerson, Stephen Slade, Robt. Sanderlin, Jesse Sanderlin, Samuel Scott, Chas. Scott, David Summerall, Thoa. W. Smith, Stephen Tucker, Isiah Thomas, Aaron Vickers, Isaiah Williams, Maxfield Whiddon, Wm. Whiddon, Jas. Wright and Thomas Wright.

In order to facilitate the pay of his soldiers it seems that Captain North often drew the total pay from the government to his company and paid it to them individually or accepted orders from them to their friends or creditors as attested by the following:

Capt. J. J. North:

Be so good as to pay Matthew A. Stewart what money

Third Sergeant, Wm. Van Zant
Fourth Sergeant, Isham Peacock
First Corporal, Allen Dixon
Second Corporal, Benajah B. Morris
Third Corporal, William Lee
Fourth Corporal, Daniel Byrd

Privates

1 Addison, Mark L.
2 Anthony, Lawrence
3 Bennett, Richard
4 Brooker, Wm. P.
5 Bohannon, Duncan
6 Byrd, Isaiah
7 Brown, Thomas
8 Corbett, Daniel
9 Carver, John B.
10 Cason, McGinty
11 Cransby, Silas
12 Cason, Willoughby
13 Cason, A.
14 Carter, William, Jr.
15 Carter, William, Sr.
16 Capps, Hezekiah
17 Cobb, John
18 Corbitt, William
19 Crawford, Archibald
20 Dunaway, James
21 Dryden, Benj.
22 Fulwood, John
23 Guest, Miles J.
24 Griffis, Samuel
25 Guest, Wm. P.
26 Guest, Benj. W.
27 Gill, Dennis
28 Gainey, Henry
29 Gibson, James
30 Henderson, John S.
31 Hopps, Daniel
32 Hall, Hardie
33 Inman, James
34 Inman, John
35 James, Benj.
36 Joyce, Cornelius
37 Jeffords, H. V.
38 James, Wm. T.
39 Kite, Hiram
40 Knowles, Washington
41 Lee, Richard
42 Lee, Lewis
43 Lee, George
44 Lee, Isham W.
45 Lane, Bryant
46 Lane, Edward
47 McQuaig, James
48 McCandle, Able
49 McKey, Francis R.
50 Miller, Ezekiel S.
51 Norman, R. G.
52 O'Steen, John
53 Padgett, Elijah
54 Pittman, Lorenzy
55 Peacock, Henry
56 Peacock, John
57 Pierce, George
58 Padgett, William

59 Rowell, James
60 Smith, Lawrence
61 Smith, James C.
62 Smith, John
63 Smith, Peter
64 Smith, William
65 Stone, George W. R.
66 Sasser, Josiah
67 Stafford, Nathaniel B.
68 Thomas, Banner, Jr.
69 Thomas, James, Jr.
70 Thomas, Thomas
71 Thomas, Benj.
72 Taylor, Lewis

73 Taylor, William
74 Tatum, Henry
75 Thomas, James R.
76 Thorrington, Elbert
77 Williams, Stephen
78 Wilkerson, John, Jr.
79 Wilkerson, Daniel
80 Wilkerson, Willis
81 Wilds, Maxey M.[1]
82 Ward, Jackson
83 Williamham, Wm. A.
84 Wilson, Hezekiah
85 Wilson, George

WARE HEROES OF 1838

Ware County had six companies during the Indian invasions in 1834. The Roster includes:

Officers: Captain, James A. Sweat; First Lieutenant, Thomas Crawford; Second Lieutenant, Berrien Henderson; First Sergeant, Richard Bourn; Second Sergeant, William Sweat; Third Sergeant, John Minchew; Fourth Sergeant, William Crawford; First Corporal, Arnold B. Fussell; Second Corporal, George W. Waldron; Third Corporal, Carraway King; Fourth Corporal, Gideon Crawford.

Privates: Richard Altman, William Beasley, John Bennett, Nathan Beasley, Joshua Courson, George W. Davis, Randol Davis, Isaac Gainey, Wm. Guy, Silas Hilliard, Joseph Hughes, Benjamin Hilliard, John Jordan, George Jenkins, Wm. Johnson, Wm. King, Jacob Lightsey, Jacob Lee, Benjamin Milton, Isaac Minchew, Jacob Minchew, Wm. Musick, Martin Nettles, Glynn Nettles, Thos. Newbern, John Newbern, John W. Prescott, Isham Prescott, Henry Roddenberry, John Reaves, Abraham Strickland, Nathan Strickland, Levi Strickland, Samuel Sweat,

---

[1] Maxey M. Wilds killed by Indians July 25th, 1832. Total pay of Company $5252.07. Paid at Waresboro on July 25th, 1838.

Nathan Sweat, Wm. Spradley, Allen Stone, Byrd Sulevant, Burrell Sweat, Chas. Smith, Daniel Stone, Henry Stone, James Sullivan, John W. Smith, Matthew Sweat, Shadrack Stanley, Wiley Stanley, Ed. Thomas, Ezekiel Thorington, Samuel Thorington, Jas. R. Thomas, Lewis Thomas, Joseph Underhill, Andrew Walker, Asbury Waldron, John Wilkinson, Joseph Wynn, Wm. R. Wilkerson, Littleberry Walker, and Isaac Highsmith.

COMPANY "K" 26TH GEORGIA INFANTRY

This company was organized of men from Clinch and Ware Counties, in 1861, and saw service in Virginia. The first Captain was William A. McDonald, while Cuyler W. Hilliard was later elected. Both were residents of Ware County, while Thomas J. Ivey, the last captain, was at this time a resident of Clinch. Captain Ivey is buried in Lott Cemetery at Waycross.

Captains: William A. McDonald, Cuyler W. Hilliard, Thomas J. Ivey.

First Lieutenants: Cuyler W. Hilliard, Thomas J. Ivey, John L. Morgan, Jr., John T. Harris, B. L. McLendon.*

Second Lieutenants: William Miller; Vinson A. Hodges.

Privates: Alcox, Jesse*, Alcox, Henry*, Agee, William, Agee, John, Box, Allen, Box, Richard A., Agee, Andrew, Box, Josep, Bailey, Aaron, Bailey, Tharp, Bailey, Joseph, Boatright, C. J. D., Booth, James, Booth, William*, Booth, Jessee, Bennett, Tom, Bennett, D. H., Bennett, Randall, Bennett, John, Bennett, Martin, Carmichael, John, Carmichael, D. C., Courson, Pliney W., Courson, John T., Cason, B., Chauncey, John M., Chauncy, Samuel, Chauncey, Mark*, Griffis, Joel, Goette, Allen, Goette, Jeff, Hodges, Vinson A.*, Hodges, Francis M.*, Henderson, Andrew J., Henderson, J. T., Holt, Greenberry, Harris, Joseph, Hall, Bill, Hall, Hiram, Howell, Joe*, Inman, James M., Johnson, Benj., Jones, John*, Joyce, William, Jefferds, J. M., Kight, John, Kight,

James M., Miller, James*, Moore, Elias L., Morgan, Martin Z., Morgan, Thomas F., Morgan, Hampton, Morgan, Lemuel*, McLendon, Ephriam, Miller, Tom, Miller, James M., Miller, John H., Murray, S. C., Nettles, James, Nettles, Thomas, Nunez, Nunez, W. P., Cole, Riberon, David M., Roberts, Gray*, Rowland, Bill, Strickland, W. J., Smith, William, Smith, Harrison*, Smith, Lawrence, Smith Moses, Smith, Manning, Smith, Lewis, Smith, Benjamin, Smith, James M., Smith, Daniel, Smith, Wade, Smith, Allen, Smith, Charles, Smith Alfred, Stephens, James, Sears, Hiram, Jr., Sweat, Farley, Sweat, John F., Sweat, Roland, Sauls, Holliday, Sauls, O. J., Summerlin, Payton, Summerlin, Julius, Summerlin, John, Sweat, John, Jr., Tooten, Alex, Williams, H. P., Williams, Bill,* Wilkerson, Jack, White, Tom.*

War Between the States

Ware County although sparsely settled took an important place in the ranks of the Southern Army. The endless controversy over the slavery question had wearied the brave men and all who could possibly leave home enlisted, some were boys who joined the army and were not only willing to fight to the bitter end, but desired that their last dollar be contributed to continue the great struggle.

Captain William McDonald was largely responsible for the organization of a company of soldiers from Ware and Clinch during the early part of 1861. This company was known throughout the War as Co. "K", 26th Georgia Infantry.

Records of the War Between the States*

Waresboro, Ga., Dec. 31, 1860.

To His Excellency
  Joseph E. Brown,
    Governor.
Dear Sir:

The Wiregrass Minute Men are very anxious for

NOTE:—Those which are marked with an * were killed or lost in the war. Information obtained from History of Clinch County, Georgia, by Folks Huxford.

guns. Permit me to ask when we can be supplied and with what character of arms.

We are getting our uniforms as fast as possible.

We are all for Secession. I am much indebted to you for your views expressed in your letter. I published your letter in an Extra and scattered it broadcast. It has done the cause much service in the Wiregrass region.

Our Union Candidates, on Saturday last, abandoned their cause and withdrew from the contest.

I have caused the Fourth to be sent to the Executive Department. I trust in God men are on the right line, and that all may be well; but if we are to have trouble, please remember that *I* desire to have a "place in the picture."

Give us arms.

With high consideration,

Your Obedient Servant,
C. N. Styles.

Georgia } At an Election held this day at the
Ware County. } Parade Grounds of the "Forest Rangers' of said County for a Captain, one first Lieutenant and two second Lieutenants to command said company, the Following named duly enrolled members of said corps appeared and voted, viz.,

1 Wm. L. Evans
2 M. Bedell
3 Daniel Lott
4 James Bennett
5 W. T. Bennett
6 Wm. S. Bailey
7 Wm. B. Folks
8 R. McDonald
9 Joseph McQuaig
10 James C. L. Bennett
11 James Linn
12 Thos. Sweat
13 George Goethe
14 James Corbitt
15 John B. Cason
16 E. S. Miller
17 E. M. Rigdon
18 Wm. A. McDonald
19 Joseph Davis
20 A. Davis
21 Richard Bennett
22 Thomas Lott
23 James J. Sweat
24 Wm. Herrin
25 Robert Holton
26 Jesse Deen

27 Thomas H. Morton
28 J. N. Tuten
29 A. Tuten
30 David A. Butler
31 Thomas Hilliard
32 T. Dayley
33 C. W. Hilliard
34 B. Wilds

35 H. R. Roberts
36 D. Smith
37 D. E. Knoles
38 D. Davidson
39 I. B. Bedford
40 L. W. H. Pittman
41 Wm. Millison
42 James B. Smith

Candidates Named

For Captain

WM. A. MCDONALD _____41

For First Lieutenant

WM. B. FOLKS _____41

For First 2nd Lieutenant

CUYLER W. HILLIARD _____41

For Second 2nd Lieutenant

DAVID E. KNOLES _____23
THOMAS SWEAT _____17

Georgia
Ware County

We the undersigned superintendent of the foregoing election do hereby certify that the foregoing election was opened, held and closed in due form of Law, and that the foregoing is a true statement of the Poles.

Given under our hands and seal this 1st day of June, 1881.

        C. L. Walker, J. P. (Ls)
        Geo. B. Williamson, F. H. (Ls)
        James J. Sweat, (Ls)

---

*Copied from the Archives of History, Atlanta, Georgia.

HISTORY OF WARE COUNTY, GEORGIA 243

CONFEDERATE GRAVES IN WARE ARE MARKED

Marble Memorials Placed Under Auspices of Francis S. Bartow Chapter.

The Francis S. Bartow Chapter, United Daughters of the Confederacy in Waycross has placed handsome marble markers at the graves of the following Confederate veterans:

Dr. Daniel Lott, 4th Ga. Cavalry.
Dr. W. B. Folks, Surgeon, 26th Ga. Inf. Reg.
W. S. Bailey, 26th Ga. Regiment.
James Knox, Capt. Co. D. 26th Ga. Reg. Inf.
W. L. Evans, Co. 2, 26th Ga. Reg.
E. H. Crawley, Capt. Co. K., 26th Ga. Reg. Inf.
J. S. Lyon, Adj. 26th Ga. Reg.
A. P. Perham, 1st Lieut. Co. F., 29th Ga. Reg. Capt. of Staff.
W. F. Parker, Co. C., 10th Ga. Battalion.
H. P. Brown, Co. 1, 5th Reg. Ga. Cavalry, Effingham Hussars.
Lemuel Johnson, Co. F., 26th Ga. Reg.
Mitchell M. Sweat, 26th Ga. Reg.
T. J. Ivey, Co. K, 26th Ga. Reg.
J. R. Knight, Ga. Militia.
T. L. Brown, 20th Ga. Reg. Gen. Toomb's Brigade.
D. B. Smith, John B. Gordon's Brigade, 26th Ga. Reg.
R. D. Brown, Cobb's Legion.
R. T. Cottingham, Co. C, 11th Florida Volunteers.
J. H. Faust, Co. E, 5th Ga. Cavalry.
J. J. Wideman, Co. I, U. C. V.
Dr. B. F. Williams, McIntyre Regiment.
J. W. Highsmith, Co. A, 4th Ga. Cavalry.
T. H. Morton, Co. K, 25th Ga. Reg.
J. W. Quarterman, Co. B, 20th Ga. Cavalry.
Jeff Davis, Legion, Com. Ga.
W. R. Newsome, 55th N. C. Cavalry

Charles E. Walden, Co. H, 26th Ga. Reg.
W. J. Strickland, Co. A, 4th Ga. Cavalry.
T. M. Sweat, Co. H, 26th Ga. Reg.
J. L. Morgan, Co. G, 4th Ga. Cavalry.
N. M. Parker, 5th Florida Volunteers.
Judge J. L. Sweat, Co. G, 4th Ga. Cavalry, Brigadier General Commanding South Georgia Brigade, Confederate Veterans.
A. J. Sweat, Co. A, 26th Ga. Reg.
J. M. Lee, Co. E, 7th Ga. Cavalry.
J. D. Smith, Georgia Militia.
William A. McDonald, Co. H, 26th Ga. Reg. Inf.
Joseph Knight, Jr., 7th Ga. Cavalry.
John M. Purse, Joe Brown's Pets.
Rev. B. A. Johnson, 48th Reg. Co. B, Wright's Brigade.
W. H. Bradley, Co. D, 5th Ga. Cavalry.
R. P. Bird, Co. D, 5th Ga. Cavalry.
C. C. Buchanan, Co. G, 4th Ga. Cavalry.
C. M. Eunice, Co. C, 26th Ga. Reg.
A. M. Britt, 2nd Ga. Militia.
E. S. Aycock.
A. Robbins.
J. G. Clough, 4th Ga. Cavalry.
Capt. C. W. Hilliard, 26th Ga. Reg.
B. G. Waldron, 4th Ga. Cavalry.
Robert Charles West, Co. K, 63rd Ga. Inf.

Reminiscences of War Life
(J. W. Quarterman)

I was a student at Oglethorpe College in Georgia, my native state, when the first gun of the War Between the States was fired in 1861. I left the halls of college to take up arms in defense of our dear Southland. As soon as necessary arrangements could be made I joined a company in cavalry service and my first experience in war life was doing picket duty along the coast of dear old Georgia. But it was not long before the company of which I was a member was detached from the command and was stationed on James Island, near Charleston, S. C., and a heavy picket from our company was placed at a point on Stone River, about two miles from Secessionville.

Capture of a Federal Gunboat

The enemy gunboat took pleasure in making weekly visits to our picket post and their shot and shell forced us away to take refuge in a neighboring wood. This continued for some time, much to our inconvenience. But our authorities decided on an effort to put a stop to that business. A gun was placed a short distance from the river, just at our picket post and was masked. Everything in readiness we impatiently waited for her next visit. We did not have long to wait, in a few days she was seen coming up the river and anchored in easy reach of our gun. Only two shots from our gun were needed to bring her to terms of surrender, and the white flag went hurriedly up her mast. This was an occasion of great rejoicing to us, and we were not molested any more in that way.

After twelve months' stay on James' Island our company returned to the command and for seven months did picket duty along the coast of Georgia.

My Marriage

Well, young people seem to have a strange propensity to fall in love and think about getting married. I had previously met a fair damsel whose charms won my heart. I ventured to propose to her and she gave her consent; the hardships of war-days, the shadow of the war-cloud, and the dangers of the battlefield, did not serve as an obstacle to prevent our union, and on February 21, 1864, the words were spoken that linked our destiny. But our honeymoon was of a very short duration; on the third day after our marriage I was again in camp; and only a few days later our command was ordered to report to Gen. R. E. Lee for duty in Virginia.

A Long March

Our command was not long in getting ready to move to the front. We were required to march all the way from Savannah to Richmond and our commanding officer reported to General Lee the latter part of May, 1864. This was quite a long ride for us Georgia boys, but we were soldiers now, and our cause was very dear to us, and no hardship too great to be endured in the hope that a brighter day would soon come to us.

A Brave Officer

Our first engagement in Virginia was on May 28, 1864, in what is known as the Hawes-Shop Battle. Dismounted and used as infantry we were taken into a wood and found the enemy in very strong force. In the hottest of the fight, the members of our company falling on the right and on the left, our Major Wm. Thompson, a gallant officer of splendid physique and in beautiful uniform stood only a few steps from me. He turned to me and pointing to a certain tree, said: "John, a Yankee is hid behind that tree and is shooting our boys down; he will shoot again directly, and as he puts his head in sight be ready and take him down." I did my best at him, and—well, he did not shoot from that tree any more. Only a few minutes later this noble officer received a wound from which he never recovered.

My Dear Brother Killed

I had seen comrades, friends and kinfolks fall in battle, but it was a dark day in my war-life when my own dear brother fell dead, shot from the enemy's line in one of the engagements around Pittsburgh. We wrapped him in his blankets and with bleeding hearts laid him in a soldier's grave quietly to rest till the glorious resurrection morn.

In January, 1865, our command was transferred to the army of Gen. Jos. E. Johnson, then in South Carolina. I had varied experiences about Columbia, Chiraw, and other places till we crossed the state line into North Carolina. At one time during the three days' hard fighting at Bentonville, I was separated from my command amid the rattle of small arms and the rain of shot and shell, and I thought I was a "Gone Reb," but they did not get me, and I succeeded in getting back into our line.

Something I Greatly Regretted

Early in the morning of an eventful day after two scouts had taken in the enemy's pickets without firing a gun, Gen. Wade Hampton surprised Gen. Kilpatrick's camp and it was the most complete surprise I ever witnessed. In the hottest of the fight I put my pistol in the face of a stout Yank and told him to surrender; he threw up his hands and plead for his life, for Yanks seemed impressed that to fall into the hands of the Rebs was certain death. I took him to the rear and turned him over to the guard. But in the midst of his most earnest pleadings for life, he persistently offered to give me anything and everything he had about his person. I swapped hats with him then put him in the hands of the guard. In the afternoon I was put on the detail to take the prisoners to Fayettsville. Of course our detail was mounted and sitting in our saddles in line ready to move off with the prisoners, a member of our company, a Mr. Keener, was lazily smoking his pipe, but he had his eyes wide enough open to notice a little protrusion in the waistband of the pants of my big prisoner who was directly in my front line. Keener speedily had him to bring to light, and it proved to be

$40 in silver. Well if I had known that fellow had that money on his person when he offered me everything he had about him, you may just know this, that Keener would never have been keen enough to get that money.

Coming Home

The war ended in the early part of 1865 and, with the army of Gen. Jas. E. Johnson, I laid down my war weapons and surrendered to Gen. Sherman. I took a bee-line for Georgia and found myself wife-hunting again for I did not know what may have become of my fair damsel, all communication having been cut by Gen. Sherman's army, and not a line having passed between the good lady and myself for about three months; I did not even know where she was, if indeed, she had survived the horrors of the war. But I found her after a while, and our honeymoon was resumed and has continued even until now.

Reminiscences By J. L. Sweat and How He Became a Confederate Soldier

At eleven years of age I was attached to politics by the election of my eldest brother, Dr. James Sweat, the Democratic candidate as the first representative from Pierce County in 1858.

During the memorable presidential campaign of 1860, when only thirteen I was an ardent advocate of Breechenridge and Hamlin, attending political rallies addressed by Henry R. Jackson, Julian Hartridge and John C. Nicholls, the latter two then being brilliant young lawyers, and subsequent to the war succeeding each other in Congress from the old Fourth District. In 1861 I was attending a school taught out on Kettle Creek by Miss Mary Lane, when on Sunday while we were all at the old Kettle Creek church, the news came that Fort Sumter had been fired on, and Miss Lane immediately left for her home in Boston.

Returning to the old plantation just north of Blackshear, where I was reared I continued to live there with my Grandmother Strickland, my parents being dead, attended school at Blackshear Academy, then taught by Miss Mary Campbell, now the widow of the late Robert B. Rippard.

Early in 1862 a military company composed of the boys of Blackshear between the ages of 12 and 15 was organized and I was elected captain and my schoolmate, Bob Hendry, the son of Capt. E. D. Hendry, First Lieutenant. We tendered our services to President Davis assuring him, that although young, we were fully capable of whipping the Yankees if he could only let us come to Virginia, but while assuring us that our valor was not doubted, yet on account of our youth we could not be received in the army. Meanwhile a cavalry company had been organized and my uncle, Allen Strickland, elected captain. Fearing the war would soon be over and that I would miss the glory of helping whip the Yankees, I applied to Captain Strickland for membership in his company, who told me I was too young and must remain with my grandmother and at school.

Still determined I went to Alex McMillan, clerk in the store of D. B. Brantley, father of Congressman W. G. Brantley, who had been chosen First Lieutenant of the Cavalry Company, and was told by him that as several who had joined would fail to appear, if I would get a horse and be at Tebeauville, now "Old Nine" in Waycross, on the day an officer of the Confederate Army was to muster the company into service, keep in the rear out of sight of Capt. Strickland until the company was ordered to form in line and then ride into the ranks, I would be mustered in before he knew it.

I acted on his suggestion, sold a lot I owned in Blackshear, bought a pony, saddle and bridle and thus at the age of fourteen and a half years became a Confederate soldier.

Col. Ed. Atkinson

Atlanta, Ga., May 20, 1908.

Miss Mamie Atkinson,
  Brunswick, Ga.

Dear Miss Atkinson:

Your relative, Spencer R. Atkinson tells me you desire to know something about the military career of your father. It was my good fortune to know him intimately during the war, although we were in different commands. He was, when I knew him Colonel of the 26th Georgia Regiment. I was a captain in the 31st Georgia in the same Brigade, commanded first by Gen. Alex R. Lawton, then by Gen. John B. Gordon and last by Gen. Clement A. Evans. The Brigade consisted of six regiments as follows: the 13th Ga., 26th Ga., 38th Ga., 60th Ga., and 61st Ga. regiments. In 1864 the 12th Ga. Battalion of infantry was added to this brigade and served with it until the surrender at Appomattox, Va., April 9, 1865.

Col. Ed. Atkinson served some few months as Adjutant of his Regiment under Col. Carey W. Styles. When the regiment re-entered the war, and new officers were chosen, Adjutant Atkinson was elected Colonel and served with distinction throughout the war. As an officer he was, perhaps, the most popular one in the brigade. The men of his own regiment all loved and honored him. Those of the other regiments applauded him and joined in according to him the highest praise as a brave, daring leader in battle; and a considerate, thoughtful commander, who mingled with his men on most friendly terms, yet without lessening his authority, or weakening his discipline. He was full of sympathy for his men, protected them, saw to it that their wants were supplied as far as could be, and oftentimes he would dismount from his horse and allow some sore-footed or faltering soldier to ride, while he walked along with the boys who bore the muskets.

Whenever Gen. Gordon or Evans desired a regiment to do some particular work, or they needed a capable brave commander to lead them, Col. Atkinson and his gallant 26th regiment were generally selected and the task was always well done.

Returning from Gettysburg, Pa., in July, 1863, Gordon's brigade for a part of the time "brought up the rear", and it became necessary at times to turn upon the Federals who were following our column. Col. Atkinson, with his fighting regiment of Wiregrass boys, was sent back to face the somewhat exultant Yankees who were annoying us with their artillery from nearly every hilltop behind us, and with strong lines skirmishing in advance. We had just entered a typical body of timber, rectangular in shape, covering possibly 50 acres of land. Through this large grove of heavy trees the road over which our men were traveling ran. Col. Atkinson deployed his regiment across the road just before passing the body of woodland. The rest of our corps went on and left the 26th and its Colonel to do the proper thing— to check the enemy until our trains might gain time and get beyond the reach of the annoying Yankee shells. Col. Atkinson waited quietly in these woods until the advanced line of Federals came close up to where he had his men lying down waiting for them. With a yell (at his command) the regiment arose and charged the enemy (numbering more than twice his own command) and drove them pell-mell back through the woods across the open space beyond. He halted his men at the edge of the grove and continued firing as long as there was a Yankee to be seen. Then, quickly facing one-half of his men to the left—the other to the right, they opened a gap in the center and turning back he filed both wings of his command to the rear, and quickly vacated the woods, and re-entering the road soon overtook the brigade. The Yankees, supposing from the noise the 26th made, and the execution they did, that this big body of woods "was just swarmed with rebels", hurried up to the support of their retreating line several pieces of artillery and a body of infantry. The guns were run into battery and for half an hour they vigorously shelled the woods, while the Confederates were leisurely retreating over the hills three or four miles from the scene. We never heard or saw the Yankee column after that well-planned and brilliantly-executed moment.

I distinctly remember with what genuine glee and delight Col. Ed. Atkinson talked about the affair as he rode along that evening after he rejoined us on the road. We could hear the angry cannon as they belched forth their singing shells, and could see the smoke curling above the woodland long after we were rejoined by the 26th regiment, and were well out of their reach. The only damage done by this furious bombardment was to the beautiful trees in this park-like body of woods, which doubtless had been tenderly preserved for years by the thrifty Pennsylvania landowners in the neighborhood.

Another incident is recalled by me in which Col. Atkinson led a charge and restored our line at Spottsylvania court house on May 10, 1864. The Yankees massed ten picketed regiments against a part of our little line of entrenchments late on the afternoon of that day, and broke over a part of Dole's brigade. Gordon's brigade was hurried up to restore the line. We drove the Federals back but part of them held a section of our works, fighting behind our own entrenchments, facing to our rear. It was necessary to dislodge these. Col. Atkinson was ordered to take his regiment to a part of our line, which had not been broken, and to spring over the works and charge down upon the Yankees, who were occupying the captured line. His Men moved quietly until they reached the place where they had been ordered. They formed in column—four men abreast—and moved, as we called it, "by the flank." As a signal for their trusted leader this little command charged and routed the Yankees from their position, and almost in a moment's time restored our line. Col. Atkinson, in a jolly way was to the writer, "Captain Tip that was the first time I ever charged with my regiment endways." He led (with sword waving above his head) and joined in the yelling as this movement was made.

No Yankee ever stood his ground long when he heard the Rebel Yell on his flank. They moved and moved promptly.

I love to think of this gallant officer—one of the best in Gordon's brigade. A man who was as brave as Marshal Ney, and as kind and tender as Robert E. Lee. There are few officers more honored and beloved by their men. There are none who record for gallant service surpassed that of Edmond N. Atkinson.

His daughter and his other relatives can point with pride to his career as a soldier.

Long live the memory of this noble gentleman, this heroic officer who illustrated Georgia on so many battlefields. Long live the memory of the gallant men who eagerly followed where he led and shared with him the glory of the South.

Respectfully,

W. H. HARRISON.

An Old War Relic

In 1894 Dr. T. S. Paine received from Capt. W. S. Rockwell, of Savannah, the old flag of the Ochlochnee Light Infantry from Thomas county used during the war.

The flag was recently found in Cincinnati, Ohio, in a box of old papers by Col. R. T. Coverdale.

It was supposed to belong to the Oglethorpe Light Infantry, of Savannah, and was sent to that company by Col. Coverdale.

Dr. Paine wrote to Capt. Rockwell stating that he thought that the flag belonged to the Ochlochnee Light Infantry. Capt. Rockwell, after seeing the flag, soon found that it did belong to the Oglethorpe Light

Infantry and he sent it to Dr. Paine. This flag was stored with Messrs. Johnson and Duncan when the Ochlochnee Light Infantry joined the regiment at Savannah and was captured during Sherman's raid.

The flag is made of blue silk and was given to Ochlochnee Light Infantry just before the war commenced by the ladies of Thomasville and was presented by Miss Lena M. Seixas, now Mrs. T. S. Paine of this city.

One side of the flag is painted the coat of arms of Georgia, surrounded by eleven stars on the other "O. L. I.", Sept. 28, 1860. Painted on the bottom are the words "Captured at Savannah, Ga., by the 2nd Division, 20th Army Corps, December 21st, 1865."

Dr. Paine was First Lieutenant in the Ochlochnee Light Infantry and there are only four of the original members of the company living. The flag was given to him by the members and he now has it in his possession and it is in a good state of preservation.

Below is the presentation speech made by Miss Lena Seixas, now Mrs. T. S. Paine, at Thomasville, June, 1861.

Soldiers of O. L. I.:

In behalf of your lady friends I am here to entrust this flag to your charge. They present it to you as a token of their confidence in your valor and honor and as a testimonial of their high appreciation of your patriotism. We need not ask you to guard it well. We know the hands in which we trust it and we know that with you it can suffer no dishonor; that no stain can ever rest upon its folds and if it ever sinks upon the battlefield, it will only be when deeply dyed in the life's blood of its brave defenders. It bears upon it the broad shield of our noble state. She has won a high position among her southern sisters and the daughters of Georgia proudly entrust the honor of her great name in your keeping. You go forth in a holy cause.

"To fight in a just cause for our country's glory
Is the best office of the best men."

We can not join you in the battlefield, but we can always appreciate true patriotism, for we know that he who does not love his country is unworthy of woman's love.

Should you be called to the field, our thoughts will follow you full of interest and expectation and our hearts will go up in earnest prayer to Him who rules the destinies of men for your safety and success.

Then take the flag, and while you guard it, as we know you will, may Heaven guard and protect our gallant young Ochlochnee's."

A Confederate Hero

I remember in my early childhood of having my lamented father tell of a heroic incident in the life of one of my uncles, Jacob Sikes, during the Civil War. In April one of his old comrades, realizing that he had done his duty in putting on historic record this brave act of one who wore the gray, wrote the following article to the Jesup Sentinel:

"For a long while I have felt that I have failed to discharge a duty that I owe to one of my old comrades from '61 to '65, but before giving an account of this case will say that in the company of which I was a member, there were four men from Wayne County— Robert Sloan, killed at Spottsylvania; John Strickland, one of the five members of the company that surrendered at Appomattox; and John and Jacob Sikes, brothers. It is the latter of these, Jacob Sykes, who, in my estimation, deserves a monument and to be enrolled with such men as Sam Davis in the honor rolls of history.

Jacob Sykes was charged with threatening the life of a superior officer, was tried, condemned and ordered to be shot at noon of a certain day. An appeal was made to the President for pardon, which was refused. Some three hours before the hour of his execution, we got into an engagement with the enemy. Soon after he made his escape from the guard, joined the company, got a dead man's gun and accutrements, and went through the fight with us. As soon as the fight was over we advised him, as he was now free, to give himself up to the Yankees and stay North until the war ended. His reply was, "No, I am not guilty of the crime for which I was convicted. They can shoot me tomorrow, but I am not going to run," and with thus stating the circumstances, he walked off and hunted up the guard from whom he had escaped and said, "Boys, here I am, aren't you glad to see me back?" "I was lucky enough to get one more whack at the Yankees before you got a chance to put me under the ground."

He had to be re-sentenced and another hour set for his execution. This gave us a chance to start another appeal for pardon as above stated, which was granted, and Jake was ever at his post seeming to have a charmed personage until after the evacuation of Petersburg. In one of the engagements the day before the surrender at Appomattox, he received the fatal bullet and was left lying where he fell.

For a verification of above facts I would most respectfully refer you to Captain N. Dixon, who was captain of the company, address, Tampa, Fla.; James M. Flinn, Pensacola, Fla.; Horace Dart and James G. W. Harris, of Brunswick, Ga.

Yours truly,
D. D. Spear,
Waycross.

History South Georgia Camp, U. C. V.
(By Maj. R. P. Bird)

The first meeting of this camp of which there is an authentic record was held Jan. 19, 1898. The book containing minutes, etc., of the camp prior to that date was misplaced or lost, yet we believe that the camp was organized for many years before this date. Before this time we recall there was a great review of the veterans in Waycross in which there were 300 Confederate soldiers and 8 Federals. The parade formed at the court house, where they listened to an address by Col. Benn Russell. Much enthusiasm was aroused. A great dinner was served by the ladies to the Veterans in the old Crawley store and the boys feasted like princes.

At the first meeting, Jan. 19, 1908, Judge J. L. Sweat was Commander; H. H. Sasnet, Adjutant; C. C. Grace, First Lieutenant, A. P. Perham, Sr.; Second Lieutenant, W. H. Sebring; Third Lieutenant, J. Johnson, Fourth Lieutenant; H. P. Bird, Officer of the Day.

Another meeting was held July 4, 1898, and the roll perfected. At this meeting Miss Annie Paine was unanimously elected the first Camp Sponsor and presented with a badge.

The next meeting was held Jan. 19, 1899, at the court house. Judge Sweat was re-elected Commander for the next year and the other officers were also elected. At this meeting announcement was made of the death of one of the "Daughters of the Confederacy," and suitable resolutions were passed by the Camp. A communication was received from the Waycross Rifles tendering the use of their armory, which was gratefully received, and that the members of the South Georgia Camp has been elected honorary members of the Waycross Rifles.

Meetings were held in April, 1899, and January, 1900, and officers were elected as follows: C. T. Holmes, Capt. Commanding; R. P. Bird, Adjutant; T. S. Paine, 1st Lieut.; A. P. Perham, Sr., 2nd Lieut.; W. M. Harbin, 3rd Lieut.; H. D. Harris, 4th Lieut.

On Feb. 4, 1900, Gen. John B. Gordon addressed a large and enthusiastic concourse of Veterans and citizens at the opera house. This address was much enjoyed and was frequently interspersed by applause. The subject was "The Last Days of the Confederacy". Resolutions were passed by the Camp expressing the appreciation of the Veterans.

On Jan. 19, 1901, met at the court house and elected

the following officers: T. S. Paine, Capt., Commanding; R. P. Bird, Adjutant; A. P. Perham, Sr., 1st Lieut.; W. M. Harbin, 2nd Lieut.; R. D. Harris, 3rd Lieut.; W. P. Humphreys, Officer of the Day. The following delegates were elected to the reunion at Memphis, Tenn.: T. S. Paine, J. L. Sweat and T. L. Brown.

Another meeting was held April 20. Committees were appointed to arrange a reunion of the South Georgia Brigade to be held at Waycross July 4. The general committee consisted of C. T. Holmes, W. M. Harbin, T. S. Paine, T. L. Brown and H. P. Bird. The ladies appointed to secure funds to defray the expenses were Misses Maggie Crawley, Hattie Grace, Lizzie Bird, Kate Johnson, Virginia Lyon, Genevieve Young, Daisy Perham, Beulah Knight and Susie Sasnett. Miss Susie Sasnett was elected sponsor of the Camp for a year. A committee was appointed to arrange for a basket dinner on July 4, which all the Veterans were invited. Gen. P. McGlashan, of Savannah, was Brigade Commander and presided over the ceremonies. It was at this reunion that Comrade J. B. K. Smith made his famous oration, which was pronounced very eloquent. The expenses of this dinner amounted to $332, which was promptly paid.

Several meetings at the Camp were held this year and the interest kept up. Saturday, January 18th, the Camp met, Capt. T. S. Paine presiding; R. P. Bird, Secretary. Ninety-six members were reported as in good standing. Officers for 1902 were elected as follows:

Chas. A. Sheldon, Captain Commanding; R. P. Bird, Adjutant; T. L. Brown, 1st Lieut.; H. D. Harris, 2nd Lieut.; R. T. Cottingham, 3rd Lieut.; W. M. Russell, 4th Lieut. The following delegates were elected to the reunion at Dallas, Texas: J. L. Sweat, W. M. Harbin, T. S. Paine, R. D. Harris and T. L. Brown. Alternates: C. A. Sheldon, S. P. Bird, W. R. Harbin, W. M. Russell and W. H. Miller.

On April 11 a meeting was held and arrangements made for the observance of Memorial Day. On this occasion Hon. W. M. Toomer was orator of the day, being introduced by Capt. L. Johnson. His address was one of the best expositions from a constitutional standpoint that we ever heard.

Memorial services in honor of Gen. Lee were held Jan. 19, 1903. All officers were re-elected for the ensuing year. At this meeting resolutions were passed in memory of Adjt.-General Moorman, U. C. V.

Rev. Harry Cassils, of Brunswick, delivered the address on this ocassion and was highly complimented by the press and people. Memorial day fell on Sunday in 1903. The procession was one of the largest that ever marched to the cemetery. Maj. R. P. Bird was Marshal of the Day with E. J. Berry, John T. Myers and B. H. Thomas as his aids. Miss Grace Taylor was appointed sponsor for this year, with Miss Lillian Nicholls and Miss Lula Sweat as her maids of honor.

On Jan. 14, 1904, memorial exercises in honor of Gen. John B. Gordon were held at the First Methodist Church and appropriate resolutions passed commemorative of his life and service. On Feb. 6, 1904, the following officers were elected: R. P. Bird, Capt. Commanding; T. S. Paine, Adjutant; D. C. Carmichael, 1st Lieut.; R. D. Harris, 2nd Lieut.; R. T. Cottingham, 3rd Lieut.; J. J. Wilkinson, 4th Lieut.; Comrade J. L. Sweat was elected Commander of the South Georgia Brigade and C. A. Sheldon, Adjutant-General, of the brigade.

Memorial services were held this year at the cemetery. Prof. Pound delivered the oration and made a masterful address. Miss Lillias Nicholls was elected sponsor for the Camp, with Misses Acosta and Lyon, Maids of honor for 1904.

The officers, sponsors and maids of honor were re-elected for the year 1905 and the necessary meeting held for the year.

Memorial exercises were held at the Central School in 1905. Maj R. P. Bird being the orator of the day.

For 1906 the same officers, etc., were re-elected. Memorial exercises were again held at Central School. Hon. B. G. Parks being the orator of the day. His address was a splendid effort. Maj R. P. Bird was Grand Marshal.

In 1907 Memorial exercises were again held at Central School. Hon. W. W. Lambdin was the speaker of the day and made a masterly address on the constitutional rights of the South in the great conflict.

Officers elected for 1907 were: R. P. Bird, Capt. Commanding; T. S. Paine, Adjutant; T. L. Brown, 1st Lieut.; R. D. Harris, 2nd Lieut.; D. C. Carmichael, 3rd Lieut.; C. M. Eunice, 4th Lieut. Sponsor Miss Lillian Nicholls, Maids of Honor, Misses Acosta and Lyon.

This brief sketch closes the history of the South Georgia Camp No. 819, U. C. V.

> "They fought fair Liberty for thee,
> They fell, to die was to be free."

List of Veterans of South Georgia Camp 819, Oct. 20, 1908:

J. L. Sweat, A. P. Perham, Sr., L. Johnson, W. P. Humphrey, W. M. Harbin, Jackson Grimes, R. D. Brown, T. S. Paine, B. A. Johnson, R. P. Bird, J. J. Wilkinson, E. Cottingham, E. D. Hendry, T. L. Brown, J. W. Strickland, M. Tomlinson, W. R. Youman, Blackshear, C. M. Eunice, William Wilson, Geary Lang, T. H. Morton, R. T. Cottingham, R. D. Harris, A. J. Wainwright, J. D. McKinney, A. L. D'Auvergne, C. D. Todd, A. J. Sweat, D. H. Bennett, L. Dowling (Folkston), L. R. Thompson, W. S. Carter, J. W. Roddenberry (Folkston), J. W. Booth, W. R. Newsome, J. W. Wade (Blackshear, B. H. Spivey, Daniel Taylor (Blackshear), J. S. Bailey, W. H. Bradley, W. P. Brewer, J. S. White, N. B. Ham (Blackshear), N. W. Martin, H. Sauls (Blackshear), J. J. Davis, Chas. J. West, Handall C. Crews, Newton Sweat, W. B. Keel, J. B. Jones, L. Florid (Fla.), John E. Cleland, D. C. Carmichael (Manor), Peter Griffin, John Aldrich (Blackshear), D. N. Campbell, J. J. Henderson (Blackshear), W. P. Eunice (Blackshear), J. H. Strickland, (Blackshear), E. L. Aycock, C. J. Thomas, J. M. Alexander, W. J. Strickland, A. I. Hendry, M. D. (Hinesville, Liberty Co.), G. N. Hendry (Blackshear), H. W. Stone, W. H. Reville, E. V. Haygood, C. A. Sheldon, W. H. Hilliard.

> *"He folded the drapery of his couch about him,*
> *And lay down to pleasant dreams."*
> *"The Confederate Soldier."*

RECOLLECTIONS OF THE CONFEDERACY
MRS. BENJAMIN F. WILLIAMS

My recollections of the Confederacy are mostly of the cares and responsibilities which crowded upon us at that time.

My husband was one of the two physicians retained for home service, so my burdens were made lighter than those of many others. And yet, my duties seemed very hard at times. Clothing was to be provided, not only for our family but for servants, a large number of whom worked in turpentine. The cloth had to be spun and woven. I had to learn to weave. After one or two failures, which caused bitter weeping, I succeeded and wove most of the cloth on the place.

We had to substitute dried sweet potatoes browned for coffee. We gathered Pinckneya Puben from branches, put the twigs in barrels and shipped them to hospitals to be used as quinine. (Pinckneya Puben, better known as "fever tree")

When the last call of "On to Richmond" was made, my husband was compelled to go, leaving me sick in bed. His was the bravest company I heard of, for there was but one gun in the company. It was carried by Mr. Alexander Cooper—their wives refusing to let their husbands take the guns away. They went as far as Savannah, led by Col. McIntyre. There they camped for about a month, and then heard of Lee's surrender and returned home.

When returning from the battle of Olustee, Gen. Colquitt's brigade camped on the site of our present home and adjoining land. (Located in the central part of the present city of Waycross, in the section where Lee Avenue and Williams Street intersect). While here they received their last call, "On to Richmond".

First Canteen Service in Ware County

One day we had word that a company of soldiers was to pass through on the train, so the ladies prepared baskets, and when the train stopped at Tebeauville, went on board and served them and a northern prisoner they had with them. Just before being sent north, the Andersonville prisoners were camped at Blackshear for a short time.

Cannon in Phoenix Park

The cannon in Phoenix Park was moved from Doctortown to Waycross in 1887. Its valuation is estimated through the part it played in the War Between the States. During the War it had been placed on the Altamaha river banks to protect the draw bridge which lay along Sherman's line of march to the sea. Cannon were placed on different points along the river but only this one was left after the Yankees paid their respects to the dangerous firearms of our Confederate soldiers. The Yankees "spiked" the cannon and left it, and for many years everyone who passed that way was afraid to move it. Finally Mr. W. W. Sharpe, road master of the Savannah district, had it loaded on a wreck train and brought it to Waycross. The railroad company placed it in a park where the express company now is located. For a long time, above the cannon was a signboard, telling the history of its feudal days. This relic of the War was later moved to Phoenix Park, just in Front of the Confederate Monument.

Hon. Jefferson Davis Once a Visitor in Waycross

The train bearing this distinguished American passed through Waycross on May 8, 1886. The notice of his intended arrival was not sufficiently confirmed in time to allow any preparation for his reception, which was deeply deplored. The brass band and all of our citizens who had heard of his contemplated passage through Waycross were at the station when he came, and with speeches, flowers and a lusty yell greeted the beloved representative of the "Lost Cause". Mr. Davis responded in a few words at the close of which cheers again rent the air. He then seated himself on the rear platform of the car and shook hands with quite a number of Waycross citizens, principally ladies. When the time for departure came the band played "Nearer My God, to Thee". It was during the rendition of this beautiful hymn that the train with its precious passenger moved away with its beautiful decorations of flags and flowers on the engines and coaches. Winnie Davis, the real Daughter of the Confederacy, was with her father on this occasion and extended her deepest gratitude for the heartfelt tributes extended her father by the patriotic men and women of Waycross.

That day was one that is still revered by many Waycross citizens, and they carry in their memory the Ex-President of the Confederacy, the tall proud form that had suffered so much in prison walls, whose limbs were bound with iron, and manacled for the loyalty to the people of the Sunny Land that he loved so well.

"GOING AWAY"

By Frank L. Stanton

(Lines on a Departure from Fort McPherson)

Going away, boys, going away,
But not as you went in that other day,

When we glimpsed, in the homeland, the battle-skies,
And the beautiful Mothers, with rainy eyes,
Giving all in life—or the life to be
To the ships that sailed to sea.

Going away, boys, going away,
But you made Life's winter Love's dream of May,
And we never kept one heartache bright
But you made its light!—you made its light!
It came from the far skies whose stars you made free—
From the ships that sailed the sea.

Going away, boys, going away,
But your Country's great arms are around you today,
And when the last Night comes, with bells that ring
"Rest",
You will sleep on her breast, boys—her own—on her breast!
She will dream—as you dream, in the long years to be,
Of the Ships that sailed the sea.

World War Veterans—Ware County

Adams, Albert	Waycross
Adams, Guy A., 116 Plant Ave.	Waycross
Adams, Joe (c), 177 Thomas St.	Waycross
Albert, Prince (c), 68 Berwick St.	Waycross
Alexander, Joe (c), 82 Pendergrass St.	Waycross
Allbritton, Andrew (Jackson), RR 5	Waycross
Allen, John S.	Waycross
Allen, Joseph B.	Waycross
Allen, Love (c), 2 Camilla St.	Waycross
Allen, Wm. G., RR 1	Waycross
Ammons, Walter A.,	Glenmore
Anderson, Robert (c), 161 Maron St.	Waycross
Andrews, Charlie (c)	Fairfax
Arthur, James K.	Waycross
Arthur, David F.	Waycross

HISTORY OF WARE COUNTY, GEORGIA

Arnett, Wm. J. _____ Waresboro
Arnold, Barney _____ Millwood
Ashley, William (c), 22 East St. _____ Waycross
Atkinson, Robert W. _____ Waycross
Aycock, George W. RR 2 _____ Waycross
Baisdon, Cleophus (c), 60 Berwick St. _____ Waycross
Baisden, Rufus (c), 7 Pitman St. _____ Waycross
Bagley, Dan, RR 2 _____ Nichols
Bagley, Leo V., _____ Waresboro
Bagley, Daniel R. _____ Waycross
Bagley, Horace, _____ Fairfax
Bagley, Daniel H. _____ Fairfax
Baldwin, Barney O., 77 Brewer St. _____ Waycross
Baldwin, Samuel (c), Box 89, RR 1 _____ Fairfax
Barber, Everett O. _____ Manor
Barker, Clarence W., _____ Hebardsville
Barker, William E. _____ Hebardsville
Barnard, John I., 31 Morton Ave. _____ Waycross
Barnard, Bailey J., RR 2 _____ Waycross
Barnes, Erliss (c), 63 Wadley St. _____ Waycross
Barnes, Will (c) _____ Waycross
Baum, Joe I., 21 Pendleton St. _____ Waycross
Beall, Charles M., _____ Waycross
Beaton, Everette M., 94 Gilmore St. _____ Waycross
Beaton, Wilbur E., _____ Waycross
Beck, Alfred F., _____ Hebardsville
Bell, Leon, RR 2 _____ Waycross
Bennett, Eulica, _____ Millwood
Bennett, Joseph R., _____ Millwood
Bennett, Willie, _____ Millwood
Bennett, William T. _____ Millwood
Best, Arthur (c), 17 Camelia St., _____ Waycross
Biggs, Edward E., 10 Fad St., _____ Waycross
Bingham, James H., 3 Alpha St., _____ Waycross
Bird, Robert P., _____ Waycross
Blackburn, Robert W., RR 3, _____ Waycross
Blalock, Lonie (c), 10 Everett Lane _____ Waycross
Boatright, Walter L., RR 2, _____ Waycross

Bohler, Benjamin F., 89 Elizabeth St., _____ Waycross
Bolton, Neal R., 15 Reynolds St. _____ Waycross
Bowen, William H., _____ Waycross
Boyd, Isaac, RR 1, _____ Manor
Boyd, Richard, _____ Manor
Bradham, Bowens (c), 70 Pittman St. _____ Waycross
Bradley, Henry (c) _____ Waycross
Brady, Stacy H., 10 Eads St. _____ Waycross
Brannen, William C., 187 Albany Ave., _____ Waycross
Branch, Robert (c), 21 Wadley St., _____ Waycross
Branch, John, _____ Millwood
Brantley, John D., _____ Waycross
Braswell, Cornelius (c), 41 Bailey St., _____ Millwood
Brewer, Geo. N., _____ Hebardsville
Bridges, Cliff (c), 35 East St., _____ Waycross
Brinson, Dixie T., 62 Pendleton St., _____ Waycross
Broach, Norman H., _____ Waycross
Brock, David (c), 95 Butler St., _____ Waycross
Brown, Geo. D., _____ Waycross
Brown, Grover (c), 5 Effie St., _____ Waycross
Brown, John M. (c), _____ Beach
Brown, Oliver _____ Waycross
Brown, Robert, 225 Albany Ave, _____ Waycross
Bryant, James (c), 25 Pitman St., _____ Waycross
Bryan, Reginal, _____ Waycross
Buckins, John O., _____ Waycross
Buchanan, John L., 18 Jane St., _____ Waycross
Burch, John (c), 35 Sycamore St., _____ Waycross
Burley, Henry H., 420 Jones Ave. _____ Waresboro
Burney, Augustus L., 98 Plant Ave., _____ Waresboro
Burns, Charlie (c), 86 Butler St., _____ Waresboro
Butler, Ben (c), _____ Darien
Butler, Johnnie Willie (c), 125 Reynolds St.,__ Waycross
Byck, Sylvan _____ Waycross
Byrd, Dewey G., _____ Millwood
Byrd, Walter (c), 45 1st St., _____ Waycross
Cadle, Edgar F., _____ Hebardsville
Calhoun, John H., _____ Beach

Campbell, Mitchell H. (c), Box 22 _____Beach
Campbell, Roy Alexander (c), RR 1, _____ Waycross
Cannon, William J., _____ Waresboro
Carter, Alfred E. _____ Haygood
Carter, Charlie, 60 Alpha St., _____ Waycross
Carter, Geo. D., Box 34, RR 3, _____ Olive
Carter, Luther, Box 85, _____ Manor
Carter, Otis, _____ Waycross
Carter, Robert Lee (c), 37 Eade St., _____Waycross
Carter, Robert W., _____ Olive
Carter, Willie Lee (c), 8 Pittman St., _____ Waycross
Carver, William J., Albany Ave., _____Waycross
Cason, Alvie Berry, Box 85, RR 1, _____ Waycross
Cason, Edward M., Jr., 47 Brewster St., ____ Waycross
Cason, George, _____ Waycross
Cason, Henry G., 48 Elizabeth St., _____ Waycross
Cason, Roy P., _____ Waycross
Cavender, Ledford W., _____ Millwood
Chancey, William S., _____ Waycross
Christian, John, (c), 42 First St., _____ Waycross
Clark, Dwellie (c), 139 Reynolds St., _____ Waycross
Clark, James C. (c), 8 Jones St., _____ Waycross
Clark, Joe S., _____ Waycross
Condurelis, Steve G., 28 Satilla Lane, _____ Waycross
Cone, George H., _____ Waycross
Cobb, Arthur (c), 87 Thomas St., _____ Waycross
Cobb, George Eugene, 53 Byrd St., _____ Waycross
Cobb, Harry _____ Hebardsville
Cobb, Willie (c) _____ Folkston
Cooper, Willis (c), 9 J. Street, _____ Waycross
Corbett, Charlie C., _____ Manor
Corbitt, Walter S., RR 1, _____ Manor
Courson, Allen W., RR 4, _____ Waycross
Cowart, James H., _____ Waycross
Cox, Isham, _____ Waycross
Cox, John M., 69 Gilmore St., _____ Waycross
Cox, Simon (c), _____ Waycross
Craven, Charles W., _____ Waycross

Craven, Thomas J., _____ Hebardsville
Craven, William T., RR 5, _____ Waycross
Crawley, Jerome, 71 Albany Ave., _____ Waycross
Crawford, Oliver M., _____ Waycross
Creel, Earl R., _____ Waycross
Crews, Lester A., _____ Waycross
Cribb, Daly N., _____ Waresboro
Cribb, George H., _____ Manor
Cribb, John C., RR 1, _____ Manor
Cribb, Mack L., RR 1, _____ Manor
Cribb, William P., 45 Brunswick Ave., _____ Waycross
Crosby, George E., 189 Albany Ave., _____ Waycross
Currie, Robert L., _____ Waycross
Currie, Sam M., _____ Waycross
Curtain, Frank, Box 242, _____ Waycross
Damren, Joseph O., _____ Waycross
Daniel, Frank A., _____ Waycross
Daniels, John A., _____ Manor
Darling, Charles LeCount, _____ Waycross
Davis, Alfred B., _____ Millwood
Davis, Edwin (c), 28 J. St., _____ Waycross
Davis, Joe (c), 2 Everett St., _____ Waycross
Davis, John (c), 92 Brownell St., _____ Waycross
Davis, Jorden S., _____ Millwood
Davis, Leon P., _____ Beach
Davis, Robert (c), 24 "I" St., _____ Waycross
Dawson, Edgar A., _____ Waycross
Deen, George, 74 Pendleton St., _____ Waycross
Deen, Jessie, RR 1, _____ Fairfax
Dell, Allen, _____ Waycross
DeMaurice, Renee W., _____ Waycross
Dickinson, William S., Box 242, _____ Waycross
Dolley, Sam (c), _____ Waycross
Dorsey, DeWitt T., _____ Fairfax
Dotson, Sam (c), _____ Waycross
Douberley, Archie Locky, _____ Waycross
Dowling, Perry L., RR 5, _____ Waycross
Dreggors, Norman P., _____ Waycross

Dugger, Everett (c), 27 Wilkinson St., _____ Waycross
Ellis, George (c), 20 Highsmith St., _____ Waycross
Ellis, John I., _____ Waycross
Ellis, Rozier (c), _____ Waycross
English, Clifton C., _____ Waycross
English, Connie C., 12 Washington Ave., ____ Waycross
Ernstine, Charles (c), 62 Jones St., _____ Waycross
Erwin, Jerry, 15 Jones St., _____ Waycross
Estes, Brantley L., 30 Dewey St., _____ Waycross
Eunice, Joseph G., _____ Waycross
Evans, Richmond (c), 106 Reynolds St., _____ Waycross
Finn, Charles H., 57 Albany Ave., _____ Waycross
Finley, Remer G., _____ Millwood
Fishburn, Thomas (c), _____ Waycross
Fitzgerald, Robert L., _____ Waycross
Flanders, Raleigh (c), 12 Glenmore St., ____ Waycross
Flowers, Robert H., _____ Waycross
Fobbs, Charlie (c), Box 89, RR 4, _____ Waycross
Folks, Fleming C., 87 Mary St., _____ Waycross
Folks, Robert L., 87 Mary St., _____ Waycross
Frasier, Cleveland (c), _____ Manor
Fraser, Marvin D., _____ Waycross
Fraser, Sidney C., _____ Waycross
Freeman, James (c), 161 Marion St., _____ Waycross
Friar, Clarence (c), _____ Waycross
Fullwood, Ernest (c), 20 Brown Alley, _____ Waycross
Fullwood, James A., _____ Waresboro
Garrett, Henry (c), _____ Waycross
Gaster, Harvey C., _____ Waycross
Gaskin, Clyde (c), 36 Glenmore St., _____ Waycross
Gaskin, Elijah (c), Everidge Lane, D. St., __Waycross
Gassett, Eilbur F., 250 B. St., _____ Waycross
Gill, Oliver, _____ Fairfax
Gillis, Nathaniel, RR 1, _____ Fairfax
Glander, Willis (c), 93 Brewil St., _____ Waycross
Godwin, Joseph (c), _____ Beach
Godwin, Will, RR 1, _____ Waycross
Goodson, Allen D., _____ Waycross

Goodson, Russell B., _____ Waycross
Gordon, James (c), D., 27th St., _____ Waycross
Graham, Lucius A. (c), 105 Glenmore Ave., Waycross
Graham, Walter, _____ Waycross
Green, Lacey O., _____ Waycross
Green, Leon (c), 260 Thomas St., _____ Waycross
Green, Tracy E., _____ Waycross
Green, Jesse (c), 72 Parallel St., _____ Waycross
Griffn, Avery C., RR 4, _____ Waycross
Griffin, George (c), 115 Walter St., _____ Waycross
Griffin, Ornie L., 43 Pendleton St., _____ Waycross
Griffin, Wesley Gaines (c), 70 Satilla St., ___ Waycross
Griffiin, Willie, _____ Waycross
Griffis, Claude H., _____ Millwood
Griffis, Thomas Eustace, _____ Millwood
Grovenstein, Sidney L., _____ Waycross
Guy, Jesse, _____ Waycross
Hack, Arthur G., _____ Waycross
Hall, Clarence (c), 2 Camilla St., _____ Waycross
Hall, Charlie Other, Albany Ave., _____ Waycross
Hall, George (c), RR 2, _____ Waycross
Hall, Sawyer (c), 21 Wadley St., _____ Waycross
Hall, Willie (c), _____ Millwood
Hancock, William H., _____ Beach
Handley, Barney J., 49 Brunswick Ave., _____ Waycross
Hannah, Albert (c), 31 Camilla St., _____ Waycross
Harbin, Roy C., _____ Waycross
Hardin, Dines H., _____ Fairfax
Hardy, James C., 24 Lot St., _____ Waycross
Hargraves, Leon D., _____ Waresboro
Harper, Deleware (c), _____ Manor
Harper, Willie (c), _____ Waycross
Harrington, James A., _____ Beach
Harris, Isaiah (c), _____ Glenmore
Harris, James H., 138 Plant Ave., _____ Waycross
Harris, Will (c), _____ Fairfax
Harrison, James T., Box 68, _____ Hebardsville
Hart, Roy, _____ Hebardsville

Hatcher, Will (c), 19 Wadley St., _____ Waycross
Haygood, John (c), _____ Manor
Heidt, Redding E., 36 Tebeau St., _____ Waycross
Hemingway, Albert J. (c), _____ Waresboro
Hengeveld, Fred William, _____ Waycross
Henderson, Eddie B., _____ Waycross
Henderson, Julius C. (c), 51 Nichols St., ___ Waycross
Hendley, Holt D., 55 Gilmore St., _____ Waycross
Hendrix, Otto, _____ Manor
Henry, Ben (c), _____ Waycross
Heerndon, Carrie H., _____ Waycross
Herren, Arney L., _____ Millwood
Herrick, Hubert C., 45 Lee Ave., _____ Waycross
Herring, Barney M., _____ Millwood
Herrin, James D., Jr., _____ Millwood
Herrin, William L., _____ Glenmore
Herrington, Charles J., _____ Waycross
Heyward, Crist (c), 59 Brunell St., _____ Waycross
Hickox, James, RR 5, _____ Waycross
Hickox, Matthew F., _____ Hebardsville
Hickox, Nathan J., _____ Waycross
Higginbotham, Jesse, Hopkins, _____
Hightower, Ashley (c), RR 1, _____ Ollington
Hill, Gus, 13 Alford St., _____ Waycross
Hill, William H., _____ Waycross
Hilton, Frances E., _____ Waycross
Holt, Martin B., RR 1, _____ Waycross
Hopkins, William Hart, 10 Thomas St., _____ Waycross
Horner, Archie F., 65 Plant Ave., _____ Waycross
Huggins, Lawrence Y., _____ Waycross
Hughes, Carl W., _____ Waycross
Hurst, John H., _____ Waycross
Hurst, Seaborn D., 61 Brunel St., _____ Waycross
Hurst, Charles W., _____ Waycross
Humphries, Amos E., _____ Waycross
Ingram, Francis (c), 105 Daniel St., _____ Waycross
Iven, George Walter (c), 66 Railroad St., ___ Waycross
Jackson, John (c), 121 Wadley St., _____ Waycross

Jackson, Sam R., ---------------------- Waycross
Jacobs, Jesse (c), Box 48, RR 1, ----------- Fairfax
James, Carlie D., RR 1, ------------------ Manor
James, Ossie C., 105 Carswell Ave., ------- Waycross
Jeffers, Charles, ------------------------ Waycross
Jeffords, Herbert L., 47 Folks St., --------- Waycross
Jeffords, Jeremiah S., 27 Alice St., -------- Waycross
Jeffords, John O., ---------------------- Waresboro
Jenkins, Hugh M., --------------------- Waycross
Johns, Jacob M., ----------------------- Millwood
Johnson, Arthur, RR 4, ------------------ Waycross
Johnson, Carl E., ---------------------- Waycross
Johnson, George W., -------------------- Millwood
Johnson, Isham (c), RR 2, --------------- Waycross
Johnson, Robert (c), 26 Alice St., --------- Waycross
Johnson, Thomas M., ------------------- Waycross
Johnston, Carrie M., 53 Elizabeth St., ----- Waycross
Joiner, Cecil P. ------------------------ Waycross
Jones, Doc (c), ------------------------ Manor
Jones, Ernest R., 3 Alpha St., ------------ Waycross
Jones, Ernest, RR 3, -------------------- Waycross
Jones, Fred T. (c), 130 Reynolds St., ------ Waycross
Jones, Frank (c), 18 Pennigraph St., ------- Waycross
Jones, Isiah (c), 114 Brewer St., ---------- Waycross
Jones, John B., Jr., RR 3, ---------------- Waycross
Jones, Jesse (c), 71 Walters St., ---------- Waycross
Jones, Jake (c), 15 Robert St., ----------- Waycross
Jones, Luther (col), 93 Brewer St., -------- Waycross
Jones, Nicholls C., 60 Miller St., ---------- Waycross
Jones, Silas (c), ----------------------- Hebardsville
Jones, Sin (c), 20 Browns Alley, ---------- Waycross
Jones, William (c), 26 Ete St., ------------ Waycross
Jordan, Mack W., RR 5, ----------------- Waycross
Jowers, Charlie DT, -------------------- Waycross
Kammerer, Albert G., 84 Albany St., ------- Waycross
Kammerer, Ralph W., 84 Albany St., ------- Waycross
Keel, Joseph H., ----------------------- Waycross
Kellam, James A., 60 Reed St., ----------- Waycross

Kelsie, Ira C. (c), RR 1, _____ Beach
Kennedy, Henry, _____ Waycross
Kennedy, John L., _____ Waycross
Killens, Pomby (c), 27 Clough St., _____ Waycross
Kimbrell, Silas L., _____ Waycross
Kinnon, Benjamin F., _____ Millwood
King, Daniel R., _____ Waycross
King, Dewey H., _____ Fairfax
King, James Harvey, _____ Manor
Kite, Dave (c), 45 K St., _____ Waycross
Knight, Aldine W., 39 Tebeau St., _____ Waycross
Knight, Gerald B., _____ Waycross
Knight, Given (c), 89 King St., _____ Waycross
Knight, Will (c), 31 1-2 H St., _____ Waycross
Korb, Leon A., 2 Carswell Ave., _____ Waycross
Lanier, Gus H., _____ Waycross
Lanier, John C., _____ Waycross
Laroche, Frank I., 41 Tebeau St., _____ Waycross
Layton, Frank E., _____ Waycross
Layton, Fred H., _____ Waycross
Leapheart, Solon (c), 119 Butler St., _____ Waycross
Leapheart, William M. (c), 119 Butler St., __ Waycross
Leeks, Loomis (c), 10 Glenmore Ave., _____ Waycross
Lee, Andrew Z. (c), Box 29, RR 1, _____ Beach
Lee, Andrew J., _____ Beach
Lee, Andrew J., _____ Beach
Lee, Banner, Box 35, _____ Beach
Lee, Hamilton B., Jr., _____ Waycross
Lee, Henry Newton, RR 1, _____ Beach
Lee, John S., _____ Beach
Lee, James, _____ Manor
Lee, Lonnie J., _____ Beach
Lee, Thomas S., _____ Waycross
Lee, Walter E., 36 Mary St., _____ Waycross
Lee, Wyley M., RR 1, _____ Beach
Leggett, Horace G., _____ Millwood
Lesesne, Joseph B. (c), 244 A. B. & A. Ave., Waycross
Lesesve, Solomon (c), 244 Brewer St., _____ Waycross

Lester, Anderson (c), 12 G St., _____ Waycross
Lester, Christopher C. (c), 77 Parallel St., __ Waycross
Lovett, Simon (c), RR 5, _____ Waycross
Lewis, George (c), _____ Bolen
Lewis, Herbert L., _____ Waycross
Lide, James R., _____ Waycross
Lide, Robert M., _____ Waycross
Liles, James L., _____ Waycross
Locklier, John (c), _____ Millwood
Lott, Daniel J., 72 Church St., _____ Waycross
Lott, John H., 158 Plant Ave., _____ Waycross
Lott, Roy (c), _____ Fairfax
Love, Tommie (c), RR 2, _____ Haywood
Lowther, Alexander C., _____ Waycross
Luster, Charles (c), 34 Glenmore Ave., _____ Waycross
Luther, Sidney H., _____ Waycross
Lynn, Grady, _____ Millwood
Lynn, William _____ Millwood
Lyons, George (c), 228 Thomas St., _____ Waycross
McClellan, Everett J., RR 5, _____ Waycross
McConner, Peter (c), 30 Effie St. Lane ___ Waycross
McCoy, Granville (c), _____ Fairfax
McCoy, Nathan (c), 41 Eads St., _____ Waycross
McCray, Cornelius, 17 Ivey Lane, _____ Waycross
McDew, Ellis (c), 100 Parallel St., _____ Waycross
McDaniel, Edmond L., _____ Waycross
McGlone, Daniel P., Gen. Delivery, _____ Waycross
McIntyre, Will (c), 79 D St., _____ Waycross
McIver, Charles H. (c), Box 5, RR 1, _____ Beach
McIver, Will (c), 115 Blackwell St., _____ Waycross
McMullen, Joseph C., 9 McDonald St., _____ Waycross
McMillan, Willie (c), 61 Thomas St., _____ Waycross
McNeil, Ben, _____ Fairfax
McPhaul, Andrew (c), 164 Reynolds St., __ Waycross
McQuaig, Baxley, _____ Waycross
Malone, Grant (c), _____ Glenmore
Manor, Rich (c), 29 Mosley St., _____ Waycross
Marable, Doctor (c), 123 Thomas St., _____ Waycross

Marr, Joseph P., _____ Waycross
Marr, William M., 36 Sweat St., _____ Waycross
Marshall, James B., 38 Glenmore Ave., _____ Waycross
Marshall, James Joe (c), 113 Brewer St., _____ Waycross
Marvin, Willie (c), RR 3, _____ Waycross
Martin, Green (c), 105 Parallel St., _____ Waycross
Martin, Ira A., _____ Waycross
Martin, Marvin M., _____ Waycross
Martin, Robert B., _____ Waycross
Matchette, Herbert L., _____ Hebardsville
Mathes, Richard (c), 75 Lee St., _____ Waycross
Maxwell, Harry (c), _____ Waycross
Melton, Aaron M., Box 82C, RR 4, _____ Waycross
Mercer, Joe A., RR 1, _____ Manor
Merritt, Leon (c), 60 Railroad St., _____ Waycross
Midgett, Joe (c), 8 Jones St., _____ Waycross
Milligan, Ed., _____ Waycross
Miller, Andrew H., 29 Butler St., _____ Waycross
Miller, Bailey (c), 7 Parallel St., _____ Waycross
Miller, John (c), 112 Thomas St., _____ Waycross
Miller, John F., _____ Waycross
Miller, William D., 28 Izlar St., _____ Waycross
Mills, Charlie (c), 112 Brewer St., _____ Waycross
Mitchell, John (c), _____ Waycross
Mixon, Perry A., _____ Manor
Mixon, Scott I., _____ Manor
Mixon, Exley, _____ Waycross
Mixson, Jesse E., RR 4, _____ Waycross
Montgomery, Scriven (c), Box 106, RR, _____ Waycross
Moore, Charlie (c), 278 Butler St., _____ Waycross
Moore, Ivy (c), 62 Jones St., _____ Waycross
Moore, Lonnie S., _____ Fairfax
Moore, Nathan (c), RR 3, _____ Waycross
Morgan, Baxton (c), 25 Mays St., _____ Waycross
Morgan, William (c), 25 Mays St., _____ Waycross
Morris, Benjamin I., 64 Gilmore St., _____ Waycross
Morris, Alfred, _____ Waycross
Morris, Harry W., _____ Waycross

Morris, Robert C., 199 Elizabeth St., _____ Waycross
Morriston, Jesse L., 11 William St., _____ Waycross
Mosely, Kiler, _____ Waycross
Mullis, Charles H., _____ Waresboro
Murry, Lorraine J., _____ Waresboro
Murphy, Edwin LeCount, _____ Waycross
Music, Lewis, _____ Waresboro
Music, Thomas, RR 1, _____ Fairfax
Nesby, Robert (c), 176 Congress St., _____ Waycross
Nettles, Robert L, 15 Alice St., _____ Waycross
Nelson, Lee (c), 11 10th St., _____ Waycross
Nixon, Charlie (c), RR 1, _____ Waycross
Norman, Jim (c), _____ Waycross
Norton, Herschel V., 40 Moorehouse St., ___ Waycross
Norwood, Andrew S., _____ Waycross
Nunn, Julius (c), 31 Highsmith St., _____ Waycross
Odol, William (c), 51 Jones St., _____ Waycross
Orovitz, Sam, 62 Howe St., _____ Waycross
Orrell, Eugene D., _____ Waycross
Osburn, Cecil J., _____ Waycross
Overstreet, John E., _____ Beach
Pasco, Rosevelt (c), 16 Camellie St., ____ Waycross
Parker, Cortez Eason, _____ Waycross
Parker, Sellers _____ Waycross
Parker, William Cling, _____ Waycross
Parsons, James (c), _____ Waycross
Patterson, Alfred H., 351 Mary St., _____ Waycross
Patterson, Harry (c), _____ Waycross
Patterson, Isham L., Florence Hotel, _____ Waycross
Payne, Will (c), 118 Railroad St., _____ Waycross
Peckham, William A., _____ Waycross
Peacock, Isham G., RR 2, _____ Waycross
Perham, Alexander P., _____ Waycross
Perry, Isaiah (c), _____ Manor
Persons, Carl P., 24 Jane St., _____ Manor
Petty, Sam, _____ Manor
Phelps, Harry Truman, RR 4, _____ Manor
Plummer, Emanuel (c), 96 Wadley St., _____ Manor

Ponder, George (c), 23 Putnam St., _____ Manor
Poppell, Donnie Mc D., _____ Manor
Porter, Karl R., 47 Nichols St., _____ Manor
Pridgeon, Eldon W., _____ Manor
Proudfoot, Charles C., _____ Hebardsville
Price, Carey E., _____ Waycross
Price, Ralph L., 37 Mary St., _____ Waycross
Pridgon, Jesse C., 45 Hicks St., _____ Waycross
Pryde, Herbert (c), 111 Butler St., _____ Waycross
Quail, Blain (c), 94 Ead St., _____ Waycross
Rahn, John L., 37 Thomas St., _____ Waycross
Raybon, William A., 206 Nichols St., _____ Waycross
Reddick, Dewey (c), 17 F St., _____ Waycross
Reese, Dock (c), 22 Archie St., _____ Waycross
Reeves, James J., _____ Waycross
Register, Isaac M., _____ Waycross
Register, John C., 44 Carswell St., _____ Waycross
Reid, Cliff, 16 1-2 Johnson St., _____ Waycross
Rieger, William E., _____ Kineva
Rittenhouse, William Henry, _____ Waresboro
Rosier, James, _____ Manor
Roberson, Jesse D. J., _____ Ruskin
Roberts, Floyd (c), Box 37, RR 3, _____ Waycross
Robison, Charles (c), 50 J St., _____ Waycross
Rogers, Edwin H., 78 Albany Ave., _____ Waycross
Rogers, Lee (c), 10 Gilmore St., _____ Waycross
Rogers, William M., _____ Waycross
Roper, James (c), 62 Reynolds St., _____ Waycross
Rouse, Holton A., _____ Waresboro
Rowland, Manning, _____ Waycross
Rowland, Travis G., 34 Jane St., _____ Waycross
Royal, James H., _____ Waycross
Ryan, John P., _____ Millwood
Sanders, Willie C., _____ Waycross
Saxon, Henry T., _____ Ruskin
Scarlett, Theodore (c), 108 Reynolds St., ___ Waycross
Scher, Harry W., 58 Plant Ave., _____ Waycross
Scott, Preston (c), _____ Manor

Sessoms, Lewis C., 60 Tebeau St., _____ Waycross
Session, Thelma W. (c), 22 East St., _____ Waycross
Shannon, James C., 37 Miller St., _____ Waycross
Sharp, Lott W., 176 Plant Ave., _____ Waycross
Shaw, Eliga, _____ Waycross
Sikes, Bernard N., 220 Albany Ave., _____ Waycross
Simmons, Fred, Phoenix Hotel, _____ Waycross
Sims, Johnnie (c), 122 Walton St., _____ Waycross
Sims, Wiley (c), _____ Millwood
Smith, Arthur J., _____ Waycross
Smith, Ben (c), Box 13, RR 1, _____ Beach
Smith, Cyrus G., 44 Carswell Ave., _____ Waycross
Smith, Earnie, RR 1, _____ Fairfax
Smith, Hoke V., _____ Waycross
Smith, James (c), _____ Millwood
Smith, James L., _____ Beach
Smith, King (c), _____ Waycross
Smith, Robert O., 118 Albany Ave., _____ Waycross
Smith, Sampson (c), 93 Sampson St., _____ Waycross
Smith, Rufus (c), _____ Hebardsville
Smith, Tom (c), 127 Daniel St., _____ Waycross
Smith, Tom (c), 45 D St., _____ Waycross
Smith, William W., _____ Waycross
Spaulding Wilford W., _____ Waycross
Spaulding, Charlie C., _____ Hebardsville
Sprouse, William Lee, _____ Waycross
Spell, Julius R., 12 Washington Ave., _____ Waycross
Spivey, Needham N., _____ Waycross
Stafford, Daniel (c), _____ Beach
Stafford, William Thomas (c), _____ Beach
Stallings, Harry B., _____ Waycross
Steedley, John F., _____ Manor
Steedly, William H., Box 615, _____ Waycross
Stephens, Cyrus M., _____ Waycross
Stewart, Charlie L. (c), _____ Waycross
Stewart, Dave (c), 57 F St., _____ Waycross
Stokes, Ellis (c), _____ Waycross
Story, Isaac, _____ Manor

Strawter, Charlie (c), _____ Fairfax
Streeter, Johnie (c), _____ Waycross
Strickland, Allen H., _____ Waycross
Strickland, Charlie _____ Waycross
Strickland, Dock, Box 68, RR 5, _____ Waycross
Strickland, George B., _____ Waycross
Strickland, Gus P., _____ Waycross
Strickland, Harley, RR 5, _____ Waycross
Strickland, Harvey, _____ Manor
Strickland, Henry A., _____ Waycross
Strickland, Henry W., _____ Waycross
Strickland, Oliver, _____ Waycross
Strickland, William A., Box 68, RR 5, _____ Waycross
Strong, George W. (c), _____ Waycross
Sturdivant, Moses (c), RR 1, _____ Fairfax
Summerall, Charles H., _____ Waycross
Summer, Troy A. (c), Box 7, RR 1, _____ Beach
Sutton, Carlton S., _____ Waycross
Sutton, Isaac (c), _____ Fairfax
Sweat, Gus L., _____ Beach
Sweat, Henry, RR 1, _____ Beach
Sweat, Leroy, _____ Beach
Sweat, Robert L., _____ Waycross
Simpson, James (c), 15 Cornelius St., _____ Waycross
Simpson, Randolph (c), 44 Jones St., _____ Waycross
Sirmans, William (c), 97 Reynolds St., ____ Waycross
Taylor, Arthur (c), 15 Robinson St., _____ Waycross
Taylor, Alexander, _____ Beach
Taylor, Clifton L., _____ Waycross
Taylor, Jesse, 112 Albany Ave., _____ Waycross
Taylor, Joseph, _____ Beach
Taylor, Joseph E., _____ Fairfax
Taylor, Wilbur, RR 4, _____ Waycross
Teaser, Willie (c), _____ Waycross
Templeton, Shelby, _____ Waycross
Temple, Clarence W., _____ Waycross
Thigpen, Ira L., RR 1, _____ Beach
Thigpen, Ward S., _____ Waycross

Thomas, Anderson (c), Box 30, RR 1, _____ Beach
Thomas, Ephriam F., _____ Hebardsville
Thomas, George Preston, _____ Waycross
Thomas, Gordon, _____ Manor
Thomas, Henry (c), 45 12th St., _____ Manor
Thomas, Lester Lonnie _____ Manor
Thomas, Oscar (c), 65 D St., _____ Manor
Thompson, Henry C., _____ Manor
Thompson, Horace G., _____ Manor
Thompson, William R. (c), _____ Fairfax
Thrasher, John T., _____ Hebardsville
Thrift, Gordon, _____ Manor
Thrift, Louie, _____ Hebardsville
Thrift, Nathan _____ Hebardsville
Thrift, Russell, _____ Hebardsville
Thrift, William H., _____ Hebardsville
Tootle, Grant (c), 78 Grover St., _____ Hebardsville
Tootle, Dave (c), 18 Grover St., _____ Hebardsville
Troup, William D. (c), 10 Bowen St., ___ Hebardsville
Tutum, Isaiah J., RR 3, _____ Waycross
Tucker, Elisha (c), _____ Manor
Tullis, James T., _____ Manor
Tullis, Johnie H.. _____ Manor
Tuten, Harman, _____ Hebardsville
Tuten, Joseph H., RR 2, _____ Waycross
Ulmer, Charles E., _____ Waycross
Verdery, Charles E., _____ Waycross
Vickers, Newsome E., _____ Manor
Waddell, John E. (c), _____ Fairfax
Waldron, Bryn J., RR 3, _____ Waycross
Waldren, David H., RR 3, _____ Waycross
Waldren, Percival P., _____ Waycross
Waldren, Thomas H., _____ Waycross
Walker, Arthur W., 99 Reynolds St., _____ Waycross
Walker, Cleve (c), Box 1, RR 3, _____ Beach
Walker, Robert C. 38 Gilmore St._____ Waycross
Walker, Samuel E., 38 Gilmore St., _____ Waycross
Walker, Sidney P., 38 Reed St., _____ Waycross

Warren, George H., RR 1, _____ Waycross
Warren, James (c), 111 Parallel St., _____ Waycross
Washington, Drew (c), _____ Waycross
Washington, Julius (c), _____ Waycross
Washington, Theodore (c), _____ Waycross
Watson, Joe (c), Box 39, RR 5, _____ Waycross
Wells, LeRoy, _____ Waycross
Wells, Moses T., 34 Stevenson St., _____ Waycross
Wells, Will (c), 107 Parallel St., _____ Waycross
Westberry, Herbert H., _____ Waycross
Westberry, James R., _____ Waycross
Westberry, Willis R., _____ Waycross
White, Cary, _____ Manor
White, Lonnie W., _____ Manor
White, Mack, _____ Fairfax
White, Simon (c), _____ Glenmore
Whitfield, Arthur (c), 55 F St., _____ Waycross
Wiggins, Marvin, _____ Hebardsville
Wildes, James E., _____ Waycross
Williams, Benjamin F., 9 Ave St., _____ Waycross
Williams, Charles M., 73 Gilmore St., _____ Waycross
Williams, Derby L., _____ Beach
Williams, Frank Allonia (c), 15 G St., _____ Waycross
Williams, George C., 62 Albany Ave., _____ Waycross
Williams, Jimmie, _____ Waycross
Williams, Jimmie, _____ Waycross
Williams, Ralph (c), 43 Jones St., _____ Waycross
Williams, Richard (c), 60 Mosely St., _____ Waycross
Williams, Sandy (c), 10 St., ?? Lane, _____ Waycross
Williams Ely M. (c), 125 Reynolds St., ____ Waycross
Williams, Walter M., _____ Waycross
Wilson, George A., _____ Waycross
Wilson, Ishmael (c), 15 Robert St., _____ Waycross
Wilson, John E., 205 Gilmore St., _____ Waycross
Wilson, Thomas H., _____ Fairfax
Wilson, Will (c), 95 D St., _____ Waycross
Woodard, Ira C., _____ Waycross
Wright, John H. (c), 42 Johnson St., _____ Waycross

Wright, Sharpe R., _____ Waycross
Wright, Warren (c), 36 Nunn St., _____ Waycross
Wynne, Osgood C., _____ Waycross
Yarbrough, Reppard W., _____ Waycross
York, Dekle B., _____ Waycross
Youmans, Fred L., 28 Parallel St., _____ Waycross
Youmans, Judge, _____ Waycross
Young, Elgan W., _____ Manor
Young, Joseph (c), _____ Beach
Young, James Russille (c), 42 Eye St., _____ Waycross

Officers

Allen, Henry T., Jr., _____ Waycross
Beall, Charles M., _____ Waycross
Bennett, Ernest K., 22 Williams St., _____ Waycross
Bradley, Daniel M., 229 Nichols St., _____ Waycross
Brown, Blanton Johnson, _____ Waycross
Carroll, Edward Joseph, 1620 Plant Ave., ___ Waycross
Carswell, Henry J., 71 Brewer St., _____ Waycross
Chandler, Cyril Clifton, 60 Hicks St., _____ Waycross
Crawley, Edward H., 144 Plant Ave., _____ Waycross
Dorsey, Charles Raymond, _____ Waycross
Ellington, Thomas H., _____ Glenmore
Estes, Brantley Lawton, 30 Dewey St., _____ Waycross
Folks, William M., 87 Mary St., _____ Waycross
Gray, Walter O., 88 Gilmore St., _____ Waycross
Green, Millard Meyer, 25 Georgia St., _____ Waycross
Griffin, James R., _____ Waycross
Groover, Charles Elliott, _____ Waycross
Harper, William Harold, 132 Plant Ave., ___ Waycross
Jeffords, James Ernest, 35 Reed St., _____ Waycross
Johnson, Raymond Lovejoy, 72 Gilmore St., Waycross
Knox, George Edward, 35 Reed St., _____ Waycross
Lane, Paul Peyton, _____ Waycross
Lewis, David Justin, _____ Waycross
Lott, Warren, 158 Plant Ave. _____ Waycross
Lucas, Maitland Baynon, 33 Stephenson St., __Waycross

MacCallum, Robert Nelson, _____ Waycross
Marshburn, Herbert Edgar, _____ Waycross
McClure, James Henry, Box 558, _____ Waycross
Minchew, Benjamin Harvey, _____ Waycross
Morrison, Frank Gilmore, _____ Waycross
Oliver, James Alpheus, Box 683, _____ Waycross
Parker, William Cling, _____ Waycross
Pedrick, Larry Esteen, _____ Waycross
Carl, Burgwin, 62 Elizabeth St., _____ Waycross
Purse, Benjamin Snider, 201 Screven Ave., __ Waycross
Redding, Chs. Leonidas, Isabella & Ware Sts., Waycross
Scully, John Reginald, _____ Waycross
Sessoms, Robert Lee, _____ Waycross
Smith, James Matthew, _____ Waycross
Stokes, Edgar Eugene, 35 Gilmore St., _____ Waycross
Thomas, William Rastus, 36 Church St., ___Waycross
Todd, William, _____ Waycross
Walker, Robert Carroll, 38 Gilmore St,, _____ Waycross
Wilson, William Bernard, 136 Plant Ave., __ Waycross
Witmer, Chester Anderson, Box 193, _____ Waycross

Navy

Baker, Dan, _____ Waycross
Booth, Herschel Alex, _____ Waycross
Braxton, Edwin Irvin, Box 304, _____ Waycross
Byrd, William Haywood, 16 Hicks St., _____ Waycross
Campbell, Alfred Rollins, Jr., 23 Brunel St., Waycross
Cannon, Richard Farris, _____ Waycross
Cavender, Ralph Clifton, _____ Millwood
Churchill, Albert, 91 Washington St., _____ Millwood
Collins, Alvin Frederick, _____ Waresboro
Combs, Robert Leon, _____ Manor
Crib, Jennings, _____ Manor
Dowling, Tollie Edgar, _____ Waycross
Dun, David Owen Slane, 77 Gilmore St., ____ Waycross
Estes, Andrew Broaddus, Jr., _____ Waycross
Farris Taylor Henry, 48 Tebeau St., _____ Waycross

Fendt, Louis M., 39 Brunel St., _____ Waycross
Frier, William Ashley, _____ Fairfax
Goodwin, Martin Luther, 72 Church St., ____ Waycross
Gramling, George Francis, 20 Brunell St., ___ Waycross
Hart, Noah, _____ Waycross
Henry, Robert Lee, 7 Hicks St., _____ Waycross
Herrin, Thomas Lester, _____ Millwood
Hill, Thomas Jefferson, 37 James St., _____ Waycross
Hood, Anderson St. Elmo., 110 Screven Ave., Waycross
James, Clifford Randolph, _____ Waycross
Jenkins, Orville Parker, 1 Brunel St., _____ Waycross
Joiner, Cecil Perry, 67 Folk St., _____ Waycross
Langford, Joseph Dale, 13 Knox St., _____ Waycross
Layton, William Roger, Box 573, _____ Waycross
Lewis, Frank Hammond, Box 21, RR 1, _____ Waycross
Lide, Rufus Lee, _____ Waycross
Lott, Walter Matthews 52 Church St., _____ Waycross
McCullough, Robert Allen, _____ Waycross
Mercer, Monroe Hudson, 15 Hicks St., _____ Waycross
Mixon, John Abram, _____ Manor
Mitchell, William Leon c-o Col. L. A. Wilson, Waycross
Norton, Earl Vandorn, _____ Waycross
Norton, Joe Hubert, 40 Morehouse St., ____ Waycross
Owen, John James, 130 Screven Ave., _____ Waycross
Parker, Charles Orville, 46 Mary St., _____ Waycross
Pelham, Jay Betts, 47 Howe St., _____ Waycross
Pitman, Nathan Alford, Box 666, _____ Waycross
Plant, Walter Lee, 68 Wadley St., _____ Waycross
Polkinghorne, James Rickard, 9 Hicks St., __ Waycross
Priddy, Oscar Truitt, 8 Lincoln St., _____ Waycross
Raybon, Clarence Madison, Jr., 206 Nichols St., Waycross
Ridgley, Willie, Ridgley Place, Rt. 1, _____ Gough
Robbins, John Horace, 14 Lincoln St., _____ Waycross
Rowling, Henry Herschel, Jr., _____ Waycross
Smith, Alfred Wilkens, _____ Waycross
Smith, Frank McGill, _____ Waycross
Smith, Warren Lott, RR 2, _____ Waycross
Stanton, Walter Hicks, 26 Gilmore St., _____ Waycross

Stewart, Cecil Crawford, _____ Waresboro
Summerall, William James, 63 Gilmore St., __ Waycross
Sweat, Herley, _____ Beach
Tatum, William Robinson, RR 4, _____ Waycross
Washington, Colbert, _____ Waycross
Woodruff, Bruce Franklin, 210 Virginia St., Hopkins
Wynne, William Allen, 56 Carswell Ave., ___ Waycross

America Answers

No modern war poem has elicited more interest from the public and the press than "In Flander's Field", written by Lieutenant Colonel McRae of the Canadian forces and printed some time ago in the Constitution. Below is the American soldier's answer to the mission left him by the dead that lay in the fields of France, written by a member of the forces at Camp Gordon.

IN FLANDERS FIELDS

By Lieut. Col. John D. McRae

(Written during the second battle of Ypres, April, 1915. The author, Dr. John D. McRae, of Montreal, Canada, was killed on duty in Flanders January 28, 1918.)

In Flanders fields the poppies blow
Between the crosses, row on row,
That mark our place; and in the sky
The larks, still bravely singing fly,
Scarce heard amidst the guns below.
We are the dead. Short days ago
We lived, felt dawn, saw sunset glow
Loved and were loved and now we lie
In Flanders Fields.

Take up our quarrel with the foe!
To you from falling hands we throw
The torch. Be yours to hold it high
If ye break faith with us who die
We shall not sleep, though poppies grow
In Flanders Fields.

AMERICA'S ANSWER

(Written after the death of Lieut. Col. McRae, author of "In Flanders Fields", and printed in The New York Evening Post.)

Rest ye in peace, ye Flanders dead,
The fight that ye so bravely led
We've taken up. And we will keep
True faith with you who lie asleep
With each a cross to mark his bed,
And poppies blowing overhead,
Where once his own life blood ran red.
So let your rest be sweet and deep
In Flanders Fields.

Fear not that ye have died for naught
The torch ye threw to us we caught,
Ten million hands will hold it high
And Freedom's light shall never die!
We've learned the lesson that ye taught
In Flanders Fields.

WAYCROSS CANTEEN

No more efficient service was rendered during the World War by any organization than was given by the Waycross Canteen Service. The real patriotism and hospitality of the city was extended through this organization to the soldiers passing this way. The expressions of appreciation which the soldiers manifested on being given refreshments and courttesies were forcible and sincere and the work and service was truly patriotic as well as direct. This service was organized under military requirements in companies, each of which had a captain, two lieutenants and sergeants. Each member was regularly enrolled and when on duty wore a standard uniform and distinctive badge. Members only of the Red Cross were eligible to enrollment.

Mr. O. T. Waring was director of the canteen service of the Waycross Division during the World War, and was one of the most capable officers that served in the local war activities. It was through his efficiency that the canteen service was carried on in a real military way, everything being done according to rules of order. The roster enlisted and duly qualified as the regulations demanded were:

Mrs. J. L. Walker	Commandant
Mrs. W. W. Sharpe	Vice-Commandant
Mrs. J. M. Cox	Secretary
Mrs. Mary E. Peabody	Treasurer
Mrs. J. McP. Farr	Capt. Co. No. 1
Mrs. W. T. Seaman	1st Lieut. Co. No. 1
Mrs. Joel Lott	2nd Lieut. Co. No. 1
Mrs. W. D. O'Quin	Supply Clerk Co. No. 1
Miss Carrie Perham	Mail Agent Co. No. 1

The following is a list of members constituting Company No. 1:

Mrs. T. Atwell	Miss Maud Jenkins
Mrs. A. L. Bowden	Miss Susie Sharp
Mrs. H. C. Bunn	Miss Leila Summerall
Mrs. J. F. Everett	Mrs. H. D. Herefored
Mrs. W. H. Fendt	Mrs. W. R. Hunt
Mrs. A. Fleming	Mrs. A. M. Litch
Mrs. P. A. Hay	Mrs. Warren Lott
Mrs. J. J. Moore	Mrs. Arthur Lott
Mrs. P. N. Harley	Mrs. C. W. Leary
Mrs. W. F. Reavis	Mrs. J. Ludlam

Mrs. C. C. Nettles
Mrs. W. D. O'Quin
Mrs. J. C. Rippard
Miss Mary Letford
Miss Nan Smith
Miss Annie Laurie Walker
Mrs. W. P. Sims
Mrs. F. B. Sims
Mrs. James Sinclair
Mrs. Robt. Singleton
Mrs. H. J. Sweat
Mrs. J. E. Vann
Mrs. S. W. Walker
Mrs. Chas. N. Wilson
Miss Bernice Gettis
Miss Clara Harris
Miss Carrie Perham
Miss Cleo Strickland

CANTEEN SERVICE—COMPANY NO. 2

Mrs. Delevan Salisbury _____ Captain
Mrs. L. G. Jinkins _____ 1st Lieut.
Mrs. Albert Mason _____ "2nd Q"
Mrs. J. M. Hopkins _____ Supply Agt.
Mrs. Albert Mason _____ Chairman Drinks
Mrs. Harry Wilson _____ Chairman Box Lunches
Mrs. J. A. Wall _____ Chairman Sandwiches
Mrs. O. T. Waring _____ Chairman Magazines
Mrs. W. E. Sirmans _____ Chairman Flowers
Mrs. Basil Cole _____ Chairman Cigarettes
Miss J. W. Andrews _____
Miss Carrie Perham _____ Mail Agt.

Mrs. John W. Bennett
Mrs. J. L. Crawley
Mrs. Jerome Crawley
Mrs. Raymond L. Johnson
Mrs. Oscar Lott
Mrs. Charles Ost
Mrs. C. A. Pedrick
Mrs. Henry Redding
Mrs. J. L. Waldrup
Mrs. A. H. Reddick
Mrs. H. P. Myers
Mrs. Amie Rolofson
Miss Annie Laurie Walker
Miss Susie Sharp
Miss Etta Lula Walton
Miss Elizabeth Wilson
Miss Magdalina Islar
Miss Juanita Bennett
Miss Stella Williams
Miss Ruth Kuhn
Mrs. Walter Ealen
Mrs. Arthur Hack
Miss Eula Long
Mrs. Clarence Hill

This Canteen Unit No. 2 served the last car load of soldiers that passed through Waycross on Thanksgiving day, 1918:

MEMORIAL BRIDGE

"An old man going a lone highway
  Came at the evening cold and gray,
To a chasm vast and deep and wide.
  The old man crossed in the twilight dim,
The sullen stream had no fear for him;
  But he turned when safe on the other side
And built a bridge to span the tide.
"Old Man", said a fellow pilgrim near
"You are wasting your strength with building here:
  You never again will pass this way
You've crossed the chasm deep and wide,
  Why build you this bridge at evening-tide?"
The builder lifted his old gray head.
  "Good friend, in the path I've come," he said,
"There followeth after me today
  A youth whose feet must pass this way.
This chasm has been as naught to me,
  To that fair-haired youth may a pitfall be,
He, too, must cross in the twilight dim,
  Good friend, I am building this bridge for him."

How forcibly the beautiful poem, "A Builder", brings to mind one of the outstanding citizens of Waycross, who first suggested the building of the Waycross-Blackshear bridge as a memorial to the boys of Ware and Pierce Counties who made the supreme sacrifice in the World War.

Dr. Carswell whose inspiration made possible the bridge to "span the tide" is a prominent professional man, full of enthusiasm, ever in the procession, pulling for the betterment and the beautification of his home town.

He worked out a plan for the memorial and presented it to the Ware County Post Number 10 of the American Legion for consideration. The post adopted the plan presented and voted to make it a big thing for the Legion to put over during the year 1923-24.

Dr. Henry J. Carswell, Dr. Paul K. McGee, Q. L. Garrett and William C. Parker were appointed a committee to lay this matter before the Ware County Bond Commission and request their co-operation in doing this work. The Bond Commission favored the idea and called a joint meeting of the Ware and Pierce County Bond commissioners where the proposition was discussed. At this meeting the plan was unanimously adopted and the Memorial Bridge was made possible.

The bridge is built in two sections. The main bridge over the stream is made of reinforced concrete and is 750 feet long. It spans the historic Satilla River at the point where it divides Ware County from Pierce County. The wonderful bridge has twelve lights and on a section of the bridge are two large posts of special design built to hold the bronze memorial tablets. These tablets were donated by the Ware County Post Number 10 of the American Legion and cost $330. The bridge over the river slough is 550 feet long, built of the same material as the main bridge and has ten white way lighted posts. The memorial bridge as a whole is one-fourth of a mile long and has twenty-two lights which are lighted by Ware and Pierce Counties as a tribute to their World War Dead.

Inscribed on the bronze tablets are the following names:

WARE COUNTY MEN

J. C. Barber	Nicholas Eugene Campbell
James Jules Beaton	Claude Dewitt Chambless
Alvin Claude Bozeman	Norman Earnest Daniels
James A. Brown	Early Davis
Atkinson Fred Capps	Dellie Gilliard

Lewis Gillis
Franklin L. Henderson
Lewis H. Hopkins
Aaron Holt
Lonnie James
Archie B. Liles
L. D. Moody
Clyde Mott
James A. Pierce
Milton Worth Porter
Leon Ray
William Rogers

Wadley Everingham Sharp
Ralph Smith
John Spaulding
Jefferson D. Strom
Frank Tuten
Andrew Thrift
Peter Archie Thrift
Peter Archie Thrift
Alfred Wiley Turner
Dewey D. White
Charles S. Walden
Gerald Yarbrough

COLORED

Calvin Baldwin
Norman Joseph Thomas
Fell Hall
Daniel Monroe
Sam Miller

Buster Sutton
Isaac Preston Starling
Thomas Herman Larkins
Arthur Caraway

PIERCE COUNTY MEN—WHITE

Ivey Lee Gunter
Alva Crawford
Jessie L. Dixon
John K. Dykes
Harvey Dubose

Charlie Martin
William J. Kelley
Edward J. Chauncey
David M. Manning
Onas K. Delk

THE AMERICAN LEGION AUXILIARY, WARE COUNTY UNIT NO. 10

The American Legion Auxiliary Ware County Unit No. 10, was organized Thursday, April 28, 1921. The meeting was held in the parlors of the Phoenix Hotel. The following officers were elected:

Mrs. L. G. Jenkins _____ President
Mrs. John W. Bennett _____ Vice-President
Mrs. Walter Lee _____ Secretary

Mrs. C. L. Redding _____ Treasurer
Mrs. E. D. Dimmock _____ Historian

Mrs. J. H. Redding, Mrs. H. B. Lee, Mrs. S. B. Parker, Executive Committee.

From the best records we have the following chapter members:

Atkinson, Mrs. R. W.
Bennett, Mrs. John W.
Bennett, Mrs. Juanita
Biggs, Mrs. John
Biggs, Mrs. Earl
Booth, Mrs. W. S.
Bowden, Mrs. A. L.
Cason, Mrs. Glenn
Christian, Mrs. C. H.
Dimmock, Mrs. E. D.
Garrett, Mrs. Q. L.
Hardy, Mrs. J. C.
Harris, Miss Clara
Harris, Mrs. H. A.
Harris, Miss Jessie
Jenkins, Mrs. L. G.
Jenkins, Miss Maude
Lee, Mrs. H. B.
Lee, Mrs. Thad
Lee, Mrs. Walter E.
Lewis, Mrs. J. B.
Lott, Mrs. Hattie J.
Lott, Mrs. Warren
Morrison, Mrs. A. R.
McGee, Mrs. Paul
Nettles, Mrs. C. C.
Nettles, Mrs. Gertrude
Owens, Mrs. E. P.
Pedrick, Mrs. C. A.
Pedrick, Mrs. L. E.
Parker, Mrs. S. B.
Parker, Mrs. Will C.
Polkinghorne, Miss Sarah
Polkinghorne, Mrs. James
Redding, Mrs. Charles L.
Redding, Mrs. J. H.
Salisbury, Mrs. D.
Scully, Mrs. J. B.
Sharpe, Mrs. Fannie L.
Sharpe, Miss Susie
Sims, Mrs. W. P.
Sykes, Mrs. B. N.
Sykes, Mrs. J. M.
Summerall, Mrs. J. I.
Summerall, Miss Leila
Trexler, Mrs. R. E.
Witmer, Mrs. C. A.
Wright, Mrs. Julius
Walker, Miss Annie Laurie
Walker, Mrs. J. L.
York, Mrs. B. M.
York, Mrs. Dekle

The Second Annual Convention of the American Legion Auxiliary, Department of Georgia, was held in Waycross, Georgia, July 17, 18 and 19, 1922.

The War Record Blanks, compiled by Mrs. E. D. Dimmock were adopted by the National Convention.

At the State Convention held in Savannah, June, 1924 Ware County Unit No. 10 presented a Historical Cup in honor of the State Historian, Mrs. E. D. Dimmock who was a member of Ware County Unit. This cup is a rotating one and each year is presented to the Unit which has done the best historical work.

Ware County Unit No. 10 won the membership cup, which was presented at the State Convention in Brunswick, June, 1929.

In 1930 Mrs. J. L. Walker, a member of the Ware County Unit, was appointed by the County to write the history of Ware County.

Members of Ware County Unit No. 10 who have helt state offices and have been members of the State Committees are:

Mrs. E. D. Dimmock, Historian, ____ 1922-1923- 1924. 1925.

Mrs. Clem Hardy
Mrs. Walter Lee } ___ Emblem Chairmen, 1927-28

Mrs. J. A. Rollinson, Member Nominating Committe, 1928-1929.

Mrs. Paschal Philips, F. I. D. A. C., _____ 1929-1930.

Miss Leila Summerall, District Committee Woman, 1928-1929; First Vice-President, 1929-1930; Second Vice-President, 1930-1931; First Vice-President, 1931-1932, 1933 President.

Mrs. Thad Lee, District Committe Woman, 1929-1930.

In September, 1924, Miss Gertrude Nettles was a State Page to the National American Legion Auxiliary Convention held in St. Paul, Minn. Miss Leila Summerall was a State Page to the following National Conventions:

    Louisville, Ky. _____ October, 1929
    Boston, Mass. _____ October, 1930
    Detroit, Mich _____ September, 1931

During the National Convention in Louisville, Ky., Miss Leila Summerall represented the State on the National Defense Committee. At the Convention in Boston, Mass., Miss Summerall was appointed to serve on the Membership Committee.

THE AMERICAN LEGION WARE COUNTY POST NO. 10

The Waycross Journal-Herald, dated July 3, 1919, gives the information that the local lodge of the B. P. O. Elks made the arrangements for the organization of the veterans of the World War. Rev. R. N. MacCallum, B. H. Minchew and W. E. Lee were elected by the Elks on an organization committee.

The organization meeting was held in the Elks Home Friday, July 4, 1919, at 4:30 o'clock P. M. The following officers were elected:

Warren Lott _____ Chairman
C. L. Redding _____ Vice-Chairman
W. L. Sprouse _____ Corresponding Secretary
W. E. Lee _____ Recording Secretary

The following names are on the charter of the American Legion Ware County Post No. 10:

Beaton, Wilbur E.
Booth, Hershel A.
Campbell, A. R.
DeMaurice, Rene W.
Henry, R. C.
Jenkins, Orville P.
Joyner, Cecil K.
Knight, Aldine W.
Lee, H. B., Jr.
Lee, Thad
Lee, Walter
Lott, John Henry

Lott, Warren
MacCallum, Robert N.
Minchew, B. H.
Parker, Charles O.
Pittman, N. A.
Polkinghorne, James B.
Porter, Karl R.
Redding, Charles L.
Scully, John R.
Sutton, Carlton S.
Witmer, C. A.

The fourth annual convention of the American Legion, Department of Georgia, was held in Waycross, Georgia, July 17, 18 and 19, 1922.

In 1925 Dr. H. J. Carswell suggested the project of a Wilson Memorial Highway from Washington, D. C., to Florida, from there to Los Angeles California. The Ware County Post entered into the project. It was also endorsed by the State Department of the American Legion. Dr. Carswell was elected President of the Wilson Highway Association.

The Highway has already been marked from Washington to Pensacola, Fla., with Legion markers. A worthy project in honor of a great American, Woodrow Wilson.

The following have served as members of the State Executive Committee:

Dr. Paul McGee, Vice-Commander _____ 1922-1923
    Americanization Officer, 11th District 1928-1929
Mr. John Henry Lott, 11th Dist. Com'man 1922-1923
Dr. H. J. Carswell, Member Exec. Com. __ 1926-1927
    Member Legislative Committee _____ 1928-1929
    Appointed to represent Georgia in F. I.
        D. A. C. Congress in Europe _____ 1928-1929
Mr. J. A. Rollinson, Commander 11th Dist. 1929-1930
    State Vice-Commander _____ 1930-1931
    Member of Rehabilitation Committee __ 1931-1932
    Member of Membership Committee __ 1931-1932

The Past Commanders of Ware County Post No. 10 are:

Warren Lott _____ 1919-1920
Larry E. Pedrick _____ 1920-1921
John Henry Lott _____ 1921
Dr. Paul K. McGee _____ 1922
Q. L. Garrett _____ 1923
Dr. B. H. Minchew _____ 1924
Dr. H. J. Carswell _____ 1925
J. Clem Hardy _____ 1926
Dr. L. E. Atwood _____ 1927
J. A. Rollinson _____ 1928
Walter E. Lee _____ 1928-1929
Thad Lee _____ 1929-1930
E. J. Wylie _____ 1930-1931

HISTORY OF WARE COUNTY, GEORGIA

Branch Lee _____ 1931-1932
   The past-Presidents of the Unit are:
Mrs. L. G. Jenkins _____ 1921
Mrs. Walter Lee _____ 1922-1923
Miss Leila Summerall _____ 1924
Mrs. Paul McGee _____ 1925-1926
Mrs. B. N. Sykes   ⎫
Mrs. Clem Hardy   ⎬ _____ 1927-1928
Miss Montine Rowling ⎭
Mrs. Thad Lee _____ 1928-1929
Mrs. J. A. Rollinson _____ 1929-1930
Mrs. E. E. Brannen   ⎫
                              ⎬ _____ 1930-1931
Mrs. C. C. Nettles   ⎭
Miss Leila Summerall _____ 1931-1932

"For God and country we associate ourselves together for the following purposes:

"To uphold and defend the Constitution of the United States of America; to maintain law and order; to foster and perpetuate a one hundred per cent Americanism; to preserve the memories and incidents of our association during the Great War; to inculcate a sense of individual obligation to the community, state and nation; to combat the autocracy of both the classes and the masses; to make right the master of might; to promote peace and good will on earth; to safeguard and transmit to posterity the principles of justice, freedom and democracy; to participate in and to contribute to the accomplishment of the aims and purposes of The American Legion; to consecrate and sanctify our association by our devotion to mutual helpfulness.

The American Legion Ware County Post No. 10 serves the veterans of the World War and serves the families of these veterans. The Post takes an active part in community welfare work and teaches Americanism to the boys and girls who are the men and women of the future. The aim of the Post is to have the stars and stripes floating above every schoolhouse in this section.

Information furnished by Miss Leila Summerall.

CHAPTER XVIII

WARE COUNTY OFFICERS

THE election for Justice of the Inferior court was had in February, 1825, and resulted in the election of the following citizens of the county: William Smith, Solomon Hall, John L. Stewart, Jr., Philemon Bryan and Absalom Thomas, all of whom were commissioned March 2, 1825. The Inferior Court in those days exercised the powers of the present Board of County Commissioners, Court of Ordinary, Board of Education and the old County Court. From the nature of its duties and the broad scope of its jurisdiction over county affairs, this court was the most important office or tribunal in the county, and as a rule the most intelligent and upright men were elected. The above-named justices served until 1829, when the following citizens were elected and commissioned April 20, 1829: Mark Addison, John J. H. Davis, John O'Steen, William G. Henderson and Thomas I. Henderson. The latter resigned April 28, 1830 and was succeeded by Thomas Newborn.

At the same time that the justices of the Inferior Court were elected in 1825 Philemon Bryan was elected state senator from Ware county and John L. Stewart, Sr., as representative. The next year Mr. Bryan was succeeded by Joseph Dyall, and two years later Mr. Stewart was succeeded by John J. H. Davis.

The election for other county officers held in January, 1826, resulted in the election of the following: William G. Henderson, sheriff; Joseph Bryan, clerk of the Superior Court; Zachariah Davis, surveyor, and Joshua Sharpe, coroner. They were commissioned Feb. 11, 1826, and served two years, when (in 1828) William B. Hooker was elected sheriff; Thomas Hilliard, clerk of the

(297)

Superior Court; Thomas Newborn, surveyor; and Elisha Green, coroner.

The first tax collector and tax receiver of Ware county, according to the records, were appointed in 1828. There must have been appointments made for the years 1826 and 1827, but there is no record. In those days these officers were appointed by the Inferior Court, and a certificate of their appointment or a commission issued by the Governor. Thus, Daniel J. Blackburn qualified as tax receiver March 17, 1828 and Edwin Henderson as tax collector the same date.

Edwin Henderson served as tax collector until 1832. He served in the Indian War under Captain Levi J. Knight and was mortally wounded in a skirmish near Brushy Creek in Lowndes county in 1836, and died on the battlefield. Daniel J. Blackburn emigrated from Bulloch county, where he served as a justice of the peace in the 44th or Jones district, being commissioned as such justice Feb. 21, 1818, and serving until May 21, 1822, when he resigned. Mr. Blackburn served continuously as tax receiver until 1840. This old citizen held many other offices of trust in Ware county, the last one being the clerk of the Superior Court, to which he was elected in 1873.

The first bond given by Tax Collector Henderson in 1828 was signed by William Smith and Thomas Hilliard as securities in the amount of $4,000. The State bond (for collection of state tax) dated July 4, 1828, was signed by Duncan Henderson and Thomas Hilliard in the amount of $2,000. The bond of Tax Receiver Blackburn given in 1828 was signed by Thomas Newborn and B. Milton. The state bond for same year was signed by Lewis Greer. Both were for $2,000 each. Mr. Fulwood was long a political figure of Ware county, and was often honored by his fellow citizens with positions of trust and honor. Perhaps no better attestation of the confidence and esteem in which a man is held, can be found than one's election to a position of honor and trust. Mr. Fulwood bought a good deal of Appling county land (now in various counties carved from Appling and Ware) at the state land lotteries in Milledgeville. He was born in 1787 in North Carolina. His wife's name was Mary, and they had no children, most of his property going to his nephews, William, John and Randall Henderson, children of Mr. Fulwood's sister, Pollie Henderson, and John S. Henderson. Mr. Henderson is buried at Homerville where he died in 1879. Mr. Fulwood, besides serving as justice of the peace, served continuously from 1827 to 1843 as representative from Ware county, and continuously from 1833 to 1857 as a justice of the Inferior Court. He died about 1874 and is buried in Ware county.

Ordinaries of Ware County

NOTE:—Previous to 1852, the Inferior Court discharged the duties of the Court of Ordinary.

George B. Williamson	Jan. 17, 1852-1856
Daniel Lott	Jan. 11, 1856-1858
Daniel Knowles	Jan. 13, 1858-1862
Nathan Brewton	Jan. 24, 1862-1864
L. R. Thompson	Feb. 16, 1864-1866
Jesse E. Butler	Mar. 27, 1866-1868
Daniel Lott	Sept. 19, 1868-1871
Isidore Wilson	Feb. 19, 1871-1874
James Smith, (resigned)	Mar. 11. 1874-1875
C. E. Walden	Aug. 27, 1875-1877
J. J. Wilkinson	Jan 26, 1877-1881
Jesse E. Butler	Jan. 13, 1881-1885
Elias D. Walden	Jan. 15, 1885-(died)
Warren Lott	Jan. 15, 1885-1908
Warren Lott, Jr.,	Jan. 16, 1908-1909
B. H. Thomas	Nov. 10, 1909-1921
C. L. Mattox, (died in service)	Jan. 1, 1921-

Sheriffs of Ware County

William G. Henderson	Feb. 11, 1826-1828
William B. Hooker	Feb. 11, 1828-1830
Allen O'Steen	Apr. 5, 1830-1832

John Newbern _____ Jan. 23, 1832-1834
Thomas J. Henderson _____ Mar. 1, 1834-1836
Miles J. Guest _____ Jan. 28, 1836-1838
Richard Bowen _____ Jan. 26, 1838-1840
David J. Miller _____ Jan. 28, 1840-1842
Richard Bowen _____ Jan. 20, 1842-1844
Miles J. Guest _____ Jan. 16, 1844-1846
William Tomlinson, (resigned) ____ Jan. 26, 1846-1847
Daniel Lott _____ Feb. 8, 1847-1848
Burrell Sweat _____ Jan. 22, 1848-1850
Miles J. Guest _____ Jan. 15, 1850-1852
William Johnson _____ Jan. 17, 1852-1854
George Delk _____ Jan. 11, 1854-1856
Henry Jordan _____ Jan. 11, 1856-1858
Richard Bowen, (resigned) _____ Jan. 13, 1858-1858
Suffee B. Lamb _____ Nov. 6, 1858-1861
Joel Walker _____ Jan. 11, 1861-1862
William D. Murray _____ Jan. 24, 1862-1864
T. H. Morton _____ Feb. 16, 1864-1866
Randall M. Bennett _____ Jan. 22, 1866-1868
Edward M. Cribb _____ Sept 14, 1868-1871
I. Foreman _____ Jan. __, 1871-1875
Michael J. Mock _____ Jan. 18, 1875-1881
S. F. Miller _____ Jan. 13, 1881-1887
Thomas B. Henderson _____ Jan. 10, 1887-1891
S. F. Miller _____ Jan. 9, 1891-1897
Thomas J. McClelland _____ Oct. 14, 1896-1903
S. F. Miller _____ Jan. __, 1903-1907
D. A. Woodward _____ 1907-1911
Dave Pittman _____ 1911-1915
H. J. Sweat _____ 1915-1924
L. C. Warren, (still in office) ____ 1924-____

Treasurers of Ware County

Randall McDonald _____ Jan. 11, 1861-1862
William Brantley _____ Jan. 24, 1862-1868
Joseph McQuaig _____ Feb. 8, 1871-1873

HISTORY OF WARE COUNTY, GEORGIA 301

Edward H. Crawley _____ Jan. 18, 1873-1879
W. S. Bailey _____ Jan. 16, 1879-1891
E. H. Crawley, (died) _____ Jan. 9, 1891-1893
E. H. Crawley, Jr., _____ Oct. 7, 1893-1895
J. A. Jones _____ Jan. 9, 1895-1905
D. A. Williams _____ Oct. 17, 1905-1911
J. F. Harbin _____ Nov. 5, 1911-1915
W. E. Steedley _____ Nov. 30, 1915-1921
W. K. Booth _____ 1921-1928

JUSTICES OF THE INFERIOR COURT WARE COUNTY
Created by Acts of Dec. 15, 1824, Dec. 20, 1824

William Smith _____ Mch. 2, 1825-Apr. 20, 1829
Solomon Hall _____ Mch. 2, 1825-1827
Philemon Bryan _____ Mch. 2, 1825-1827
John L. Stewart, Jr. _____ Mch. 2, 1825-1827
Absalom E. Thomas _____ Mch. 2, 1825
Mark Addison _____ Feb. 20, 1827
Samuel Scott _____ Feb. 20, 1827
John Jones, Sr. _____ Feb. 20, 1827
William G. Henderson __ Feb. 11, 1828-Apr. 20, 1829
William Murray _____ Feb. 11, 1828-Apr. 20, 1829
James A. Sweat _____ Feb. 11, 1828-Apr. 20, 1829
Mark Addison _____ Apr. 20, 1829-Feb. 11, 1833
John Osteen, Jr. _____ Apr. 20, 1829-Feb. 11, 1833
William G. Henderson ___ Apr. 20, 1829-Feb. 11, 1833
William G. Henderson ___ Apr. 20, 1829-Feb. 11, 1833
John J. H. Davis _____ Apr. 20, 1829-Feb. 11, 1833
Thomas J. Henderson _____ Apr. 20, 1829-1830
Thomas Newbern _____ Apr. 28, 1830-Feb. 11, 1833
James Fullwood (Ful-
  wood) _____Feb. 11, 1833-Jan. 17, 1837
Thomas Hilliard _____Feb. 11, 1833-Jan. 17, 1837
William G. Henderson _____ Feb. 11, 1833-1835
Randal McDonald _____Feb. 11, 1833-Jan. 17, 1837
Benjamin James _____Feb. 11, 1833-Jan. 17, 1837
John S. Henderson _____Mch. 10, 1835-Jan. 17, 1837

James Fullwood (Ful-
　wood) _____Jan. 17, 1837-Jan. 14, 1841
Thomas Hilliard _____Jan. 17, 1837-Jan. 14, 1841
Randal McDonald _____Jan. 17, 1837-Jan. 14, 1841
Benjamin James _____Jan. 17, 1837-Jan. 14, 1841
Oliver Walden _____Jan. 17, 1837-1837
Banner Thomas (Jr.) ____Oct. 14, 1837—an. 14, 1841
Thomas Crawford _____Jan 14, 1841-
Harman V. Jeffords _____Jan 14, 1841-
Banner Thomas (Jr.) _____Jan 14, 1841-
Benjamin James _____Jan. 14, 1841-Mch. 19,1845
James Fullwood (Ful-
　wood) _____Jan. 14, 1841-Mch. 19,1845
Richard Brown _____Jan. 23, 1844-Mch. 19, 1845
John P. Wells _____Jan. 23, 1844-Mch. 19, 1845
Thomas Crawford
　(resigned) _____Mch. 19, 1845-1847
Jehu Murray _____Mch. 19, 1845-Jan. 15, 1849
Banner Thomas, Jr.
　(resigned) _____Mch. 19, 1845-1847
Manning Smith _____Mch. 19, 1845-1864
George B. Williamson _____Mch. 19, 1845-1864
John T. Clough _____Oct. 29, 1846-Jan. 15, 1849
James Inman _____Oct. 29, 1846-Jan. 15, 1849
Austin Smith _____July 5, 1847-Jan.15, 1849
John F. Sweat _____July 5, 1847-Jan.15, 1849
James Fullwood (Ful-
　wood) _____Jan. 15, 1849-Mch. 22, 1853
William A. McDonald ___Jan. 15, 1849-Mch. 22, 1853
John F. Sweat _____Jan. 15, 1849-Mch. 22, 1853
Tyre (Tyry) Mathis
　(removed to Clinch
　County _____Jan. 15, 1849-1850
Jehu Murray _____Jan. 15, 1849-1850
William T. James _____Jan. 18, 1850-Mch. 22, 1853
James Jones _____Apr. 30, 1850-Mch. 22, 1853
James Fullwood (Ful-
　wood) _____Mch. 22, 1853-Feb. 12, 1857

HISTORY OF WARE COUNTY, GEORGIA 303

Early Davis _____ Mc. 22, 1853-1856
Cuyler W. Hilliard _____ Mch. 22, 1853-Feb. 12, 1857
Daniel Lott _____ Mch. 22, 1853-1856
William W. Smith _____ May 12, 1853-1856
Randal McDonald _____ Feb. 25, 1856-Feb. 12, 1857
Burrell Sweat _____ Feb. 25, 1856-Feb. 12, 1857
Gordon S. Taylor _____ Feb. 25, 1856-Feb. 12, 1857
Randal McDonald _____ Feb. 12, 1857-Jan. 10, 1861
Gordon S. Taylor _____ Feb. 12, 1857-1858
Charles S. Youmans _____ Feb. 12, 1857-1859
James E. Booth _____ Feb. 12, 1857-Jan. 10, 1861
Daniel E. Knowles _____ Feb. 12, 1857-1858
William Brantley _____ May. 5, 1858-Jan. 10, 1861
William Bardin Folks ___ May. 5, 1858-Jan. 10, 1861
John B. Cason _____ June 25, 1859-Jan. 10, 1861
John L. Courson _____ Jan. 10, 1861-Jan. 23, 1865
Jesse Deen _____ Jan. 10, 1861-Jan. 23, 1865
John A. Thompson _____ Jan. 10, 1861-Jan. 23, 1865
John W. Booth _____ Jan. 10, 1861-Jan. 23, 1865
John B. Cason _____ Jan. 10, 1861-1863
L. W. H. Pittman _____ Feb. 7, 1863-Jan. 23, 1865
Daniel Lott _____ Jan. 23, 1865-
L. W. H. Pittman _____ Jan. 23, 1865-
John A. Thompson _____ Jan. 23, 1865-
D. J. McDonald _____ Jan. 23, 1865-
J. N. McQuague (Mc-
  Quaig) _____ Jan. 23, 1865-
Harman V. Jeffords _____ Sept. 2, 1867-1868
Austin Smith _____ Sept. 2, 1867-1868
John Fitzgerald _____ Dec. 21, 1867-1868

CLERKS OF INFERIOR COURT, $3,000 EACH

Isham Walker, clerk, June 14, 1827; Sureties, James
  Fulwood, William P. Dennison.
Thomas Hilliard, clerk, Mar. 17, 1828. Sureties, James
  Roberson and Benj. Milton.

CLERKS SUPERIOR COURT:

Thomas Hilliard, clerk, March 17, 1828. Sureties: James Robertson and Benj. Milton. Amount $3,000.
Thomas Hilliard, clerk, June 7, 1830. Sureties: James Fulwood, Mark Addison. Amount, $3,000.
Elijah Mattox, clerk, Mar. 24, 1834. Sureties: Mark Addison, James A. Sweat. Amount, $3,000.
David J. Miller, clerk, March 5, 1838. Sureties: John S. Henderson, Mark Addison, Miles J. Guest. Amount $3,000.
George B. Williamson, clerk, Feb. 15, 1840; sureties: Elijah Mattox, Richard Bourn. Amount $3,000.
Thomas Hilliard, clerk, May 5, 1842; Sureties: R. McDonald, James Inman, Richard Bourn. Amount $3,000.
Thomas Hilliard, clerk, Mar. 4, 1844. Sureties: John T. Clough, M. J. Guest, Elijah Guest. Amount $3,000.
William A. McDonald, clerk, Apr. 27, 1846. Sureties: Thomas Hilliard, John T. Clough. Amount $5,000.
Geo. B. Williamson, clerk, March 1, 1847. Sureties: Thomas Hilliard and Austin Smith. Principal $2,000.
Geo. B. Williamson, clerk, March 6, 1848. Sureties: Thomas Hilliard and R. McDonald. Amount $2,000.

CORONERS:

Thomas Newbern, coroner, dated March 17, 1828. Surety: D. J. Blackburn. $500.
Wilkins Fullwood, coroner. (no date). Surety: John Williams. Amount $500.
John Jordan, coroner, June 11, 1844. Sureties: Jacob Minshew, Andrew Walker. Amount $4,000.

SURVEYORS:

John O'Steen, surveyor, date June 7, 1830. Sureties: D. J. Blackburn and T. Hilliard. Amount $10,000.
Elijah Mattox, surveyor, date March 4, 1844. Sureties

Thos. Hilliard and M. J. Guest. Amount $10,000.

Nathan Brewton, surveyor, date March 2, 1846. Surety: James Fullwood. Amount $3,000.

Elijah Mattox, surveyor, date June 5, 1848. Sureties: James A. Sweat and R. McDonald. Amount $2,000.

WARE COUNTY OFFICER'S BONDS
(From Executive Dept. Records, Atlanta)

TAX COLLECTORS:

Edwin Henderson, Tax Collector; March 12, 1828; amount $4,000. Sureties: William Smith, Thomas Hilliard.

Edwin Henderson, Tax Collector; July 4, 1828; amount $2,000. Sureties: Duncan Henderson, Thomas Hilliard.

James A. Sweat, Tax Collector; June 22, 1832; amount $4,000. Sureties: Joseph Winn, Thomas Hilliard.

James A. Sweat, Tax Collector; June 22, 1833; amount $4,000. Sureties: Joseph Winn, Thomas Hilliard.

James A. Sweat, Tax Collector; June 22, 1834; amount $4,000. Sureties: Joseps Winn, Thomas Hilliard.

Joseph J. Winn, Tax Collector; June 22, 1835; amount $4,000. Sureties: James A. Sweat, Thomas Hilliard.

Onslow G. Keith, Tax Collector; June 22, 1840; amount (blank). Sureties: Wm. A. McDonald, Randall McDonald, Richard Bourn.

Randall McDonald, Tax Collector; Mar. 6, 1843. Amount $2,000. Sureties: James Inman, William Yarboro, John B. Cason.

Randall McDonald, Tax Collector; June 11, 1844. Amount $2,000. Sureties: Wm. A. McDonald, James Inman, Willie Sweat.

David J. Sirmans, Tax Collector; May 5, 1845; amount $2,000. Sureties: David Johnson, William Lastinger.

Randall McDonald, Tax Collector, May 2, 1846; amount $1,500. Sureties: James Fullwood, Nathan Brewton.

Randall McDonald, Tax Collector, April 3, 1847;

amount $1,500. Sureties: James Fullwood, Nathan Brewton.

Randall McDonald, Tax Collector, April 3, 1847; amount $1,500. Sureties: James Fullwood, Nathan Brewton. Joel Lott.

Daniel E. Knowles, Tax Collector; date March 6, 1848; amount $1,500. Sureties: Randall McDonald, William A. McDonald.

Benjamin Cornelius, Tax Collector; date March 5, 1849. Amount $1,600. Sureties: O. A. Walden, J. Dowling, Geo. W. Newbern, Nathan Brewton, Thomas Crawford and Benj. James.

TAX RECEIVERS' BONDS:

Daniel J. Blackburn, principal, dated March 17, 1828. Amount $2,000. Sureties: Thomas Newbern, Benj. Milton.

Daniel J. Blackburn, principal, dated July 4, 1828. Amount $2,000. Surety: Lewis Greer.

Daniel J. Blackburn, principal, dated June 7, 1830. Amount $2,000. Surety: John O'Steen.

Daniel J. Blackburn, principal, dated Apr. 26, 1834. Amount $2,000. Surety: R. McDonald, Thomas J. Henderson.

O. G. Keith, principal, dated June 22, 1840. Amount $2,000. Sureties: R. McDonald, Richard Bourn, A. McDonald.

Randall McDonald, principal, dated March 6, 1843. Amount $1,000. Sureties: James Inman, Juniper Griffis, William Yarboro.

David J. Sirmans, principal, dated May 5, 1845. Amount $2,000. Sureties: David Johnson, William Lastinger,

(Remainder, same as tax collectors' list above)

CLERKS, COURT OF ORDINARY: $2,000 each

Elijah Mattox, clerk, April 26, 1834. Sureties: Thomas Hilliard and Randall McDonald.

George B. Williamson, clerk, June 22, 1840. Sureties: Randall McDonald, Richard Bourn.

Thomas Hilliard, clerk; May 2, 1842. Sureties: R. McDonald, Richard Bourn, James Inman.

Thomas Hilliard, clerk; July 7, 1845. Sureties: James Fullwood, George B. Williamson, dated March 1, 1849; sureties: Thomas Hilliard and Austin Smith.

George B. Williamson, dated Mar. 5, 1849; sureties: Thomas Hilliard, John T. Clough.

REPRESENTATIVES OF WARE COUNTY

John L. Stewart	1825-1826
John H. Davis	1827-1829
Thomas Hilliard	1830-1839
Josiah Stewart	1840
Thomas Hilliard	1841
William A. McDonald	1842
John S. Henderson	1843
Thomas Hilliard	1844-1846
Wm. A. McDonald	1847-1850
Daniel Lott	1851-1852
Matthew Sweat	1853-1854
C. W. Hilliard	1855-1856
Wm. Guy (resigned)	1857-1858
Wm. Brantley (2nd session)	1858
John R. Cason	1859-1860
L. W. H. Pittman	1861-1865
D. T. Sumner	1865-1867
Joseph D. Smith	1868-1870
D. Morrison	1871-1872
J. B. Cason	1873-1874
W. H. Miller	1875-1876
W. A. McDonald	1877
T. J. Ivey	1878-1879
Wm. M. Denton	1880-1881
Warren Lott	1882-1883
W. H. Miller	1884-1885
L. C. Wilcox	1886-1887
Wm. A. McDonald	1888-1889

J. A. Cason _____ 1890-1891
Leon A. Wilson _____ 1892-1893
Wm. A. McDonald _____ 1894-1895
C. C. Thomas _____ 1896-1897
Jesse R. McDonald _____ 1898-1899
W. M. Toomer _____ 1900-1901
J. M. Spence, Jr. _____ 1902-1905
W. H. Buchanan _____ 1906
N. A. Frier _____ 1907-1909
S. F. Miller _____ 1909-1911
L. P. Taylor _____ 1911-1913
L. J. Cooper _____ 1913-1915
J. L. Crawley _____ 1913-1915
C. W. Parker (resigned) _____ 1915-1918
Volney Williams _____ 1915-1917
David M. Parker _____ 1917-1919
W. A. Seaman _____ 1919-1921
J. L. Sweat _____ 1919-1921
J. E. T. Bowden _____ 1921-1923
J. D. Blalock _____ 1921-1923
Calvin W. Parker _____ 1923-1924
W. W. Griffis _____ 1923-1924
John H. Quarterman _____ 1924-1927
Robert L. Folks _____ 1924-1925
Scott T. Beaton _____ 1926-1927

DISTRICT AND COUNTY SENATORS

Philemon Bryan _____ 1825-1826
Joseph Dyall _____ 1826-1827
James Fulwood _____ 1827-1834
Randall McDonald _____ 1835-1836
James Fulwood _____ 1836-1839
Elijah Mattox _____ 1839-1840
James Strickland _____ 1840-1841
James Fulwood _____ 1841-1843
Jacob Lightsey _____ 1843-1845
Daniel Lott _____ 1853-1854

William A. McDonald _____ 1855-1858
Burrell Sweat _____ 1859-1860
Thomas Hilliard (Ware) _____ 1861-1862
Peter B. Bedford (Ware) _____ 1865-1866
Newsom Corbitt (Clinch) _____ 1868-1869
T. A. Corbitt (Coffee) _____ 1869-1870
M. Kirkland (Clinch) _____ 1871-1874
George W. Newbern (Clinch) _____ 1875-1877
William B. Folks (Ware) _____ 1878-1879
C. A. Smith (Clinch) _____ 1880-1881
William McDonald (Ware) _____ 1882-1883
J. M. Wilcox (Coffee) _____ 1884-1885
F. B. Sirmans (Clinch) _____ 1886-1887
F. C. Folks (Ware) _____ 1888-1889
J. W. Boyd (Coffee) _____ 1890-1891
F. B. Sirmans (Clinch) _____ 1892-1893
Leon A. Wilson (Ware) _____ 1894-1895
Jefferson Wilcox (Coffee) _____ 1896-1897
R. G. Dickerson (Clinch) _____ 1898-1899
Lemuel Johnson (Ware) _____ 1900-1901
Frank L. Sweat (Coffee) _____ 1902-1904
F. B. Sirmans (Clinch) _____ 1905-1906
George W. Deen (Ware) _____ 1907-1908
Calvin A. Ward (Coffee) _____ 1909-1910
M. T. Dickerson (Clinch) _____ 1911-1912
J. L. Sweat (Ware) _____ 1913-1914
Calvin A. Ward (Coffee) _____ 1915-1916
R. G. Dickerson (Clinch) _____ 1917-1918
J. E. T. Bowen (Ware) _____ 1919-1920
Dan Wall (Coffee) _____ 1921-1922
Henry C. Morgan _____ 1923-1924

CIVIL COURTS AND THEIR OFFICERS

Brunswick Circuit

Many men of ability have filled the position of Judge of the Brunswick Circuit since 1858, at which time A. E. Cochran, father of the late A. E. Cochran, of Waycross, sat on the bench. He was succeeded by Judge Wm. M. Sessions, who served during the war up to 1871. John L. Harris, M. L. Mershon and Courtland Symmes presided in succession up to 1886. Judge Spencer R. Atkinson served from 1886 to 1892, when he was succeeded by Judge Sweat, who served with distinction until Jan., 1899, when he in turn was succeeded by Joseph W. Bennett. Judge Bennett later resigned and was succeeded by F. W. Dart. Then followed Thomas A. Parker, who served from 1902 to 1908; C. B. Conyers from 1908 to 1913; and J. P. Highsmith from 1914 to 1925.

CONGRESSIONAL

Solicitor Generals

Little is known of the men filling the positions in the early days of the circuits. The first man whose record as Solicitor found is J. S. Wiggins. He was followed by Isaac W. Christian and Peter B. Bedford, who in time was succeeded by Col. S. W. Hitch of this city. He served for twelve years and being a man of broad views and high legal attainments, filled the office with entire satisfaction. G. B. Mabey and J. J. Carter served, each one term. Their terms extended from 1880 to 1884, for the former, the latter until 1888, when Hon. W. G. Brantley was elected. Mr. Brantley's abilities and services are well known to everybody in the circuit. He was re-elected in 1892, and served with success for eight years, being considered one of the ablest of the state's officials. In 1896 he resigned to make the race for Congress, to which position he was elected by an overwhelming majority. Col. W. M. Toomer was appointed to fill Mr. Brantley's unexpired term. This position was filled by Mr. William Toomer in a highly satisfactory manner. He was succeeded by Hon. John W. Bennett, who was elected to the office in 1896.

Editor Lawton Walker was elected in 1908 to suc-

HISTORY OF WARE COUNTY, GEORGIA 311

ceed Col. John W. Bennett but died before assuming his office. Mr. M. D. Dickinson went into office after Mr. Bennett and was a very popular official, serving from 1909 to 1918. Hon. Allen B. Spence began in 1918 and is still the present Solicitor-General.

CONGRESSIONAL DISTRICTS

WARE COUNTY

7th—December 22, 1825-December 18, 1826
1st—December 23, 1843-September 26, 1891
11th September 26, 1891-August 25, 1931
8th—August 25, 1931-date.
(Dawson, pp. 161, 168; Acts 1843, pp. 54; Acts 1890-91, I, pp. 193; Acts 1931, pp. 46)

GEORGIA CONGRESSIONAL DISTRICTS

There was no 8th congressional district until 1843. Prior to that year the largest number of districts in the state had been 7. But on December 23, 1843 the 8th congressional district was created, and consisted of Wilkes, Lincoln, Columbia, Richmond, Burke, Screven, Jefferson, Warren, Hancock and Washington counties. This arrangement continued with minor changes, which included the removal of Washington and Hancock into the 7th district on February 22, 1850, and the addition of Elbert on February 22, 1850, of Oglethorpe and Taliaferro on January 22, 1852, and of Glascock on December 19, 1857 to the 8th district. At the time of secession in 1861, the number of districts was increased to 10 for Confederate representation, not one of the old counties remaining in the 8th district according to the new apportionment made on March 23. By this new arrangement the 8th district consisted of Campbell, Carroll, Cobb, Coweta, DeKalb, Fulton, Haralson, Heard, Paulding and Polk counties. On October 26, 1865 the number of districts was reduced to 7. From October 26, 1865 until July 30, 1872, there was no 8th congressional district. However, on July 30, 1872, 9 congressional districts were established and the 8th district consisted of Columbia, Elbert, Glascock, Greene, Hancock, Hart, Jefferson, Johnson, Lincoln, McDuffie, Oglethorpe, Richmond, Taliaferro, Warren, Washington and Wilkes counties. On Aug. 28, 1883 the number of congressional districts was increased to 10 and the 8th district then included Clarke, Franklin, Elbert, Greene, Hancock, Hart, Madison, Morgan, Oconee, Oglethorpe, Putnam and Wilkes. When the number of districts was raised to 11 on Sept. 26, 1891, the 8th district lost one county, Hancock, and gained one in its place, Jasper, making the number of counties in the district the same as before. Congress provided that the state should have twelve congressmen in 1911 and on Aug. 19, 1911, the congressional districts were again reapportioned. By this arrangement the counties in the 8th district were Greene, Franklin, Hart, Elbert, Wilkes, Oglethorpe, Madison, Clarke, Oconee, Morgan, Newton and Walton. Putnam was added to the 8th district on July 19, 1912. These counties remained in the 8th district until 1931 when the number of districts was reduced to 10 on Aug. 25, and the new 8th district was given the following counties: Atkinson, Appling, Bacon, Berrien, Brantley, Camden, Charlton, Clinch, Coffee, Cook, Echols, Glynn, Irwin, Jeff Davis, Lanier, Lowndes, Pierce, Telfair, Ware and Wayne. There have of course been no changes since.

Eighth Congressional District

(The Eighth Congressional District of Georgia was first provided for by an act assented to Dec. 23, 1843. Prior to that time 7 districts had been the largest number into which the state had been divided.)

1843-1861

"An act to lay off and divide the state into 8 congressional districts. ... . That the counties of Wilkes, Lincoln, Columbia, Richmond, Burke, Screven, Jefferson, Warren,

Hancock and Washington shall compose the 8th district. ... Dec. 23, 1843." (Acts 1843, p. 54). On Feb. 22, 1850 Hancock and Washington counties were placed in the 7th district and Elbert county was placed in the 8th (Acts 1849-50, p. 115). Oglethorpe and Taliaferro, were added to the 8th district on Jan. 22, 1852 (Acts 51-52, p. 88), and Glascock was added to the 8th on December 19, 1857 (Acts 1857, p. 35).

1861-1865

"An ordinance to organize the congressional districts of the state. ... That the congressional districts of this state shall be arranged by counties, as follows: ... The eighth district shall be composed of the counties of Campbell, Carroll, Coweta, Cobb, DeKalb, Fulton, Haralson, Heard, Paulding and Polk ... Mch. 23, 1861" (Confederate Records I, p. 732; Code 1860).

From the passage of an ordinance on October 26, 1865 there were only 7 districts until the passage of an act on July 30, 1872, when 9 congressional districts were established. (Confederate Records IV, p. 146).

1872-1883

"An act to lay out and establish congressional districts in this state, in conformity with the last apportionment of representation in the Congress of the United States.... That from and after the passage of this act, there shall be in this state nine congressional districts, which shall be as follows, to-wit: ... 8. The eighth district shall include the counties of Columbia, Elbert, Glascock, Greene, Hancock, Hart, Jefferson, Johnson, Lincoln, McDuffie, Oglethorpe, Richmond, Taliaferro, Warren, Washington and Wilkes.... July 30, 1872." (Acts 1872, p. 12).

1883-1891

"An act to apportion and divide the state of Georgia into ten congressional districts.... 8. The eighth congressional district shall be composed of the following counties: Clarke, Franklin, Elbert, Greene, Hancock, Hart,

Madison, Morgan, Oconee, Oglethorpe, Putnam and Wilkes. . . . Aug. 28, 1883." (Acts 1882-83, p. 121).

1891-1911

"An act to divide the state of Georgia into eleven congressional districts, in conformity to an act of the congress of the United States, approved February 7, 1891. . . . That the districts shall be composed of the following counties respectively: . . . Eighth District—Jasper, Putnam, Morgan, Greene, Oconee, Clarke, Oglethorpe, Madison, Elbert, Hart, Franklin, Wilkes . . . Sept. 26, 1891." (Acts 1890-91, I, p. 193).

1911-1931

"An act to reapportion the several congressional districts of this state, in accordance with the act of congress, increasing the number of the congressmen from Georgia to twelve. . . . The districts shall be composed of the following counties, respectively: . . . Eighth District: Greene, Franklin, Hart, Elbert, Wilkes, Oglethorpe, Madison, Clarke, Oconee, Morgan, Newton and Walton. . . . Aug. 19, 1911." (Acts 1911, p. 146). Putnam was added to the 8th district on July 19, 1912. (Acts 1912, p. 108).

1931-date

"An act to reapportion the several congressional districts of this state, by abolishing the twelve (12) districts created by the reapportionment Act of 1911, and creating in lieu thereof ten (10) congressional districts in this state, in accordance with the act of congress decreasing the number of congressmen from Georgia to ten (10); . . . The districts shall be composed of the following counties, respectively: . . . Eighth District: Atkinson, Appling, Bacon, Berrien, Brantley, Camden, Charlton, Clinch, Coffee, Cook, Echols, Glynn, Irwin, Jeff Davis, Lanier, Lowndes, Pierce, Telfair, Ware and Wayne. . . . Aug. 25, 1931." (Acts 1931, p. 46).

HISTORY OF WARE COUNTY, GEORGIA 315

SENATORIAL DISTRICTS
Ware County

5th—December 23, 1843-January 19, 1852
5th—July 2, 1861-date.
(Acts 1843, pp. 15, 17; Acts 1851-52, pp. 48; Constitution 1861, art. 11, sec. 2 and Confederate Records, 1 pp 490.)

SUPERIOR COURT TRANSFERS
Ware County
(Dec. 15, 1824)

Southern Circuit, December 15, 1824-Feb. 8, 1856
Brunswick Circuit, Feb. 8, 1850-Oct. 17, 1870
Alapaha Circuit, Oct. 17, 1870-Dec. 4, 1871
Brunswick Circuit, Dec. 4 1871-Jan. 1, 1910
Waycross Circuit, Jan. 1, 1910-date.
(Dawson, pp 127; Acts 1855-56, pp 215; Acts 1870 Ex., 37; Acts 1871-72, pp. 31; Acts 1909, pp. 94)

CHAPTER XIX

STORY OF A TRAGIC DEATH

(Although Addie Smith lived in the adjoining county of Pierce, there are many of the older residents of Ware county who will be interested in this story.)

BACK in the late seventies there lived in Blackshear Miss Addie E. Smith, daughter of Mr. and Mrs. H. J. Smith, and a sister of Mrs. W. W. Lambdin, of Waycross. The little girl was bright and fond of books and writing. Young as she was her work showed signs of promise and attracted the attention of Joel Chandler Harris, himself a young writer whose work was just beginning to win for him fame, and in the course of time, a correspondence sprung up between them. In June, 1876, a party went to the Satilla river to fish, little Addie Smith being one of the party. She was accidentally drowned, her death being a great shock to her family and friends. Joel Chandler Harris, (Uncle Remus) hearing of it, wrote a poem in her memory, which was published in The Savannah Morning News of June 24, 1876, and which was reproduced in an edition of that paper in 1907. The poem, which follows, is one of the few which Mr. Harris penned, for his work, though showing the true poetic spirit, was almost entirely confined to prose:

IN MEMORIAM

Dear child; a stranger mourning,
　Slips from the worldly throng,
To weave and place beside thee
　This poor frayed wreath of song.

O'er him the seasons falter,
   The long days come and go,
And Fate's swift-moving fingers
   Fly restless to and fro.

O'er thee, the west wind sighing,
   Slow sways the slumb'rous pine.
And through the shifting shadows
   The bright tears gently shine.

When Springtime's murmurous gladness
   Filled all the listening air,
And old Earth's rarest favors
   Bloomed fresh, and sweet, and fair;

When waves of perfumed sunshine
   Rolled o'er the ripening wheat
May laid her crown of blossoms
   At Summer's waiting feet.

And Nature's pulses bounded
   As though infused with wine;
Life! was the season's token—
   Life! was the season's sign.

And yet—ah, me! the mystery
   Of this unbroken rest!—
June sheds her thousand roses
   Above the pulseless breast.

Bright hopes, nor fond endeavor,
   Love's passion, nor Life's pain,
Shall stir thy dreamless slumber,
   Or waken thee again.

The fragrance of the primrose
   That opens fresh and fair
In the deep dusk of evening,
   Still haunts the morning air.

The song of the wild bird warbles
   With nature's art and grace,
Are wafted on forever
   Through the vast realms of space.

Dear child; thy pure life cadence—
   A sad, yet sweet, refrain—
Shall wake the hearts now broken
   To life and hope again.

And fall a benediction,
   When, at the day's decline,
Pale Sorrow, lowly bending,
   Weeps at Affections' shrine.

            —JOEL CHANDLER HARRIS.

AN OLD SOUTHERN MAMMY, THE LAST OF HER RACE

"The love we feel for the negro race, you can neither measure nor comprehend. As I attest it here, the spirit of my old black Mammy from her home up there looks down to bless me and through the tumult of this night steals the sweet music of her croonings, as thirty years ago she held me in her black arms and led me smiling into sleep."—*Henry Grady.*

CHAPTER XX

THE NEGROES OF WARE

THIS history would not be complete without devoting a few pages to the lives of some of Ware's early settlers of the negro race.

Ware county has no problems connected with the negro citizens, for they have always worked harmoniously whenever called upon to join in the industrial development of their surroundings. They are grateful for favors shown them and are often willing to reciprocate. They are musical and are generous with their singing of the negro spirituals, a talent handed down to them from generation to generation. Rhythm and melody with them is truly a natural gift.

The story of five of the negroes who are still living and were reared in Ware county before Waycross came into existence follows:

EVELINA HILLIARD

My pen fails me when I attempt to write about this wonderful woman, who served in the family of Dr. J. L. Walker for twenty years. She is original and has a way exclusively her own. She was always honest, upright, truthful and loyal, putting forth the best that is in her in whatsoever she undertook to do. Her chief pride has always been in her full assurance of knowing her capabilities, never failing to try her hand in doing intricate things; and always intrepid when a question of right or wrong was at stake. I once asked her if she did not think Mrs. A— was a good woman. Her answer was: "God knows, darling, I ain't never lived with her."

No guest ever came to the house, for any length of time, without forming the acquaintance of Evelina, and through her excellent cooking and her cheerful manner, she never failed to receive unstinted praise from them. Few dignitaries ever phased her. A certain Governor of Georgia was dining in the home, and she, not having faith in the ability of the girl who ordinarily served the meals, imperiously ordered her to retire to the kitchen, putting on a well-starched apron and served herself. The Governor, who had on a previous visit, made the acquaintance of Evelina remarked, "What fine biscuits you make, Evelina, I shall be pleased to have another." Her reply was, Governor, honey, I can make better biscuits than these when the milk is not too sour."

JOE AND EVELINA HILLIARD

Evelina was married to Joe Hilliard when quite a young girl. The marriage took place in Waresboro during the dark days of the Reconstruction and times proved hard for them. However, they were undaunted in their efforts to supply their home in moderate comforts. This couple lived to celebrate the fiftieth anniversary of their marriage. They truly represent a type of servant of the ante-bellum days who are now passing away. Joe drew a pension for many years before he died as a soldier of the War Between the States. He went to the War with Captain Hilliard, to whom he belonged before the War. Evelina is pensioned as his widow. She was born at Waresboro in 1857; her mother was also born there. Evelina owns her own home, pays her taxes and insurance when they fall due, and through self-abnegation and strict economy paid cash, $400, for the paving on McDonald Street that passes along her property.

KING SCARLETT

King Scarlett came to this county in the spring of 1869 from Glenn county, and made his home for a while at Old Nine. King has always had the respect of the Waycross people and by his industry and frugal habits he has accumulated valuable property. He owns his home and is in the grocery business on Reynolds Street.

He is a valued member of Antioch Baptist Church and is the only one of the charter members living. This church was the first building erected on what is known as Hazzard Hill. The founder of this house of worship was the Rev. Frank Hazzard, for whom Hazzard Hill was named.

King has only changed his place of residence twice since becoming a citizen of this county sixty-two years ago. He has been living at his present home on Reynolds Street thirty years. Dr. H. C. Scarlett, a successful physician of Waycross, is the son of King Scarlett.

STYLES SCARLETT

Styles Scarlett was living here before Tebeauville or Waycross was created. He came here in March, 1869, accompanied by his mother and other members of his family, and settled at Old Nine. He tells the following history of his old home.

"There were three stores, two of which were grocery and merchandise combined, and the other a barroom. There was one tavern for the accommodation of the railroad employees and travelers. The stage coach from Milledgeville to Traders Hill and St. Marys passed that way, and people then as now, were coming and going. There were a few tenement houses at Old Nine, mostly for negroes. There were very few people living there at that time and they were: the Grovenstines, Tebeaus, Reppards, Remsharts, Parkers and Sweats."

Styles has always been a leader among his people, ever ready to do his part toward the upbuilding of Waycross. He has many friends among both white and colored citizens. He and Amanda, his wife, have the respect of all who know them, and have filled their place in their home town in a highly creditable way.

FLOYD SNELSON

Floyd Snelson came to Waycross in the latter part of 1886, from Liberty County. He was a man of marked ability, and diligent in the pursuit of his professional duties. It was through his untiring efforts that the first Negro High School was built in Waycross. He was the first principal of the Reedsville School, situated on Snelson Street. Floyd Snelson was truly a good citizen, always ready to lend a helping hand in constructive work for the upbuilding of the town; he was justly regarded as among the leading men of his race. His passing from earth truly carried sorrow into not only the homes of his negro friends but those of many of the white citizens of Waycross.

ADELLA DAWSON

Were washer-women pensioned for long years of service, Adella Dawson would certainly be retired. As it is, she is working into her thirtieth year for two Waycross families, that of Mrs. Robert L. Singleton and of Miss Willie Beck. Either will tell you that she never counts her clothes because there is no use; "Della" is not careless. Out of these earnings "Della" has paid for and furnished a nice little home, and taxes and insurance are paid up to date.

"Della's" good, faithful, and worthy character, together with her long residence in Ware county entitles her to a place in its history. A short life history of her as she told it to me, follows:

She was born "four years after Freedom" in Dougherty county of former slaves brought from the West Indies. They were owned before Freedom by the Outler family of that county. "Della" came to Waycross when she was eleven years old with an aunt. Grown to womanhood she married George Welch, who was killed several years later in a railroad accident. Later she married Robert Dawson. "Della" had one child who died in infancy.

(Contributed by Sara Singleton King)

CHAPTER XXI

HUNDREDTH ANNIVERSARY OF WARE COUNTY

VARIOUS epochs in the one hundred years of Ware county's history were strikingly and impressively portrayed on Dec. 15, 1924, in a beautiful and highly dramatic pageant staged at the baseball park and participated in by more than eight hundred boys and girls and men and women of Waycross and Ware County.

The vari-colored costumes and period effects intrigued the eyes of the spectators. From the beruffled tissue paper frocks of the score or more little sprites who put the butterfly dance on up to the mantillas and scarfs of the Spanish grande dames the costumes were correctly in detail, according to the periods or incidents which were being portrayed.

One hundred years ago, on the very spot where the pageant was given, the Indians and early settlers were in controversy as to which would hold possession of the wilderness that gave way to farming settlements, one of which has grown into the important beautiful city of Waycross.

There were seven episodes to the pageant, which was preceded by a long and interesting parade that wound its way from the Waycross High School, in the center of the city, to the baseball park. At the park a large force of workmen, under the direction of a group of women who arranged the pageant, had transformed the smooth barren grounds into a forest scene, designed to represent a section of the great Okefinokee Swamp, which is but twelve miles distant.

Living water oaks, palmettos, pines and other trees and shrubbery had been transplanted, and hanging from the boughs of the trees were great quantities of Spanish moss. The grounds in this forest bower were carpeted with pine straw.

Both parade and pageant were conceived and executed by the Waycross Drama League, which is composed of many of the most cultured and talented citizens of this city, and the celebration was known as the Ware County Centennial.

The historic facts were compiled by Mrs. J. L. Walker and Mrs. E. D. Dimmock. The story was woven by Mrs. Oscar Lott and was dramatized by Mrs. J. A. Rollison and Mrs. Stafford Moody, who gave general direction to the presentation. Carlton Merck was director of music, and Mrs. Dimmock was also chairman of the program committee.

Episode One dealt with the Indian period and showed the Indians in amazement over a group of beautiful Spanish women who had come here from Florida. The Indian men were impressed with their white skins and the Indian women were exceedingly jealous.

White explorers appeared, followed soon after by state troops, sent to quell the Indians, who had just massacred a number of whites. The Indians were driven into the great swamp, and the episode concludes with the "Spirit of the Swamp" dance by a number of pretty girls.

Episode Two delineated the settlers' period, from 1824 to 1861. It showed the arrival of a number of families in wagons, oxcarts and on horseback. Immediately after the arrival of the settlers the first churches were built and religious services were held. Several noted men of that period were impersonated, some of them by their lineal descendents who live in Waycross and Ware county.

Episode Three reviewed the period of the Confederacy. It showed a group of girls in hoopskirts, a number of fine youths, dressed in Confederate gray, being sent to the front by their patriotic mothers, who wiped away their tears while they smiled a farewell, and after their boys were gone prayed for their safe return and the success of the Confederate cause.

This touching scene was followed by the arrival of refugees from an adjoining county who bring the news that the Confederates are being pushed back and that Sherman and his troops are driving them toward the sea. Then followed the visit of Robert E. Lee and Jefferson Davis to Ware county, after the war. They were preceded by singing children, who scattered flowers in their path.

Episode Four, covering the period from 1872 to 1882, introduced the founders of Waycross, who were preceded by the Queen of Waycross and her attendants. The founders were in almost every instance impersonated by their descendants. These founders are all men and women whose names are revered by the present generation, and therefore, episode four was one of the most interesting to the spectators.

Episode Five dealt with the period of development, and visualized in a most inspiring manner the spiritual, educational and material progress of the people of Ware county and the city of Waycross. Groups of people appropriately costumed represented the churches, schools, railroad shops, Women's Christian Temperance Union, King's Daughters, the Georgians, and the highway department.

Episode Six depicted the Spanish-American war period. Several groups of young people in scenes common to that period were shown.

Episode Seven covered the world war period and the present. This episode concluded with a review of noted visitors to Waycross. These were groups representing the Red Cross, Canteen, Girl Scouts, Boy Scouts, and the National Guards.

Several thousand people crowded the ball park to witness the pageant and many of the spectators came from miles around. For two hours it held close interest of all this large crowd and when it was over everyone who saw it had a better and clearer knowledge of the history of Ware county during the one hundred years since it was created by legislative action on December 15, 1824. In addition to the clearer knowledge all of the spectators were impressed with the heroism of the pioneers who settled this section and of the patriotism and noble achievements of their descendants.

It was a wonderfully comprehensive pageant and in itself marks a milestone in the culture of this most delightful city and prosperous and progressive county.

BIOGRAPHIES
1824 TO 1890

"The slight esteem in which genealogical investigations are sometimes held, can legitimately attach only to such as are pursued from unseemly motives of display. For, indeed, to the earnest man, the study of his ancestry must be regarded as the study of himself. Christian insight, no less than heathen wisdom, has sanctioned the ancient admonition, 'Know thyself', and if it be true that in order to know one's self one must know one's ancestors, then the practice of genealogical research must be regarded as a duty, and with peculiar fitness the Family Tree is inscribed in the Family Bible."

"As we build monuments and erect statues to preserve national memories, so family records deserve and should have a place in the domestic sanction."

CHARLES HAYNES ANDREWS

Mr. Andrews was a son of Charles and Florence (Harris) Andrews and a grand and great-grandson of some of the early settlers of Milledgeville, Georgia. Iverson Lewis and Mary Euphema (Davies) Harris were his grand parents. Judge Iverson L. Harris was considered one among the greatest jurists that Georgia ever had. He was born at Watkinsville, Georgia, in 1805 and his parents, Augustine and Anne (Byne) Harris removed early afterwards to Milledgeville, later making their home at their plantation "Pomona" four miles from the town. Anne Byne Harris (Mr. Andrew's great grandmother) was a sort of Major General in petticoats, if tradition can be relied on. This story is told of her by one of her great-granddaughters, Mrs. Mary Hunter Hall:

"She is described as being nearly six feet in height, straight as an arrow, hair the color of a raven's wing, eyes so black and piercing they seemed to be searching out the darkest secrets of one's soul, and to read at a glance the character of each one she met. Her children and servants naturally stood in awe of her, and many stories are told illustrating her devotion to duty, as well as her courage. One of these has to do with the War of 1812. When the British were approaching Milledgeville, then the state capitol, she was urged to come to the town, from her country home, for protection. Loading a four-horse wagon with things she valued most, including her children, she mounted to the seat with her negro foreman Peter, as driver. On reaching Fishing Creek, she found the bridge guarded by a squad of enemy soldiers, who gave the order to "halt", when Peter obediently pulled his team to a standstill. Without appearing to see the soldiers, his mistress calmly commanded "Drive on, Peter", and when he obeyed, the British with muskets aimed straight at his head, repeated the order to halt; again the team was stopped. The second time the voice, serene and untroubled, admonished, "Drive on, Peter", "La, ole miss, dem mens will kill us", remonstrated Peter. To relieve his fears she grasped the lines, rising to her full height, she plied the whip with such vigor, that the mules broke into a mad gallop, charging the enemy with such effect, that their precipitate flight opened the way, and "ole miss", with her treasures, drove triumphantly on her way."

Mr. Andrews had many family connections in Georgia through his descent of William Davies, of Savannah, and his wife, Mary Ann Baille, the daughter of Robert and Anne (Nancy) McIntosh Baille. Few families in Georgia have a prouder ancestrial line than the Andrews, Harris's, Halls, Kennons and Whites, of Milledgeville. All of whose names appear on the family tree of this Waycross family.

Charles Haynes Andrews was born Aug. 3, 1867 at Milledgeville, and was married to Carrie Alston Hall, of Milledgeville, April 24, 1888, and immediately after the wedding they came to Waycross to live. Mr. Andrews was a loyal citizen of Waycross and few men who have ever lived here had more devoted friends. He lived the life of a good and just man, and the records show him to have been always true to every trust. His talents were as a business man which made him a conspicuous figure in the commercial world of his adopted city. He died at his home in Waycross in 1921.

Mr. and Mrs. Andrews' children are:

Fort C., Louis, Florence (Mrs. Benjamin Wilson) Sadie, Carrie, (Mrs. Raybon) Charlie and Harris.

One of the Bible Records of Charles Andrews' Family

Thomas Haynes Junior was married to Martha Jones on Wednesday 2nd, of February 1708.

Andrew Haynes was married to Anne Eaton Thursday, the 11th, of July 1745.

John Pughe was married to Anne Haynes (widow of Andrew Haynes) on the 11th of January 1766.

Thomas Haynes was married to Frances Stith May 2, 1782.

Charles Eaton Haynes was married to Martha Hicks Harrison 1st of July, 1810.

Edwin Ruffin Andrews was married to Mary Ann McKinley Haynes 21st of June 1831.

Rev. John M. Bonnell was married to Cornelia F. Haynes in church at Sparta 18th December 1845.

FAMILY OF THOMAS AND MARTHA HAYNES

My son Herbert Haynes was born the 11th, Dec. 1709.
My son Anthony Haynes was born the 18th, Febr. 1711.
My son Thomas Haynes was born the 18th, July 1714.
My son Richard Haynes was born the 17th, July 1716.
My son Andrew Haynes was born the 16th, November 1718.
My daughter Elizabeth Haynes, was born the 28th, March 1721.
My daughter Martha Haynes was born the 17th, Jan. 1723.
My daughter Mary Haynes was born the 5th, March 1725.
My son Draughton Haynes was born the 23rd, May 1728.
My son William Haynes was born the 9th, of December 1730.

FAMILY OF ANDREW AND ANNE HAYNES

My son Anthony Haynes was born the 18th, of Jan. 1747.
My son Thomas Haynes was born the 19th, March 1748.
My daughter Mary Haynes was born the 11th, December 1751.

Family of John Pugh and Anne Haynes, Widow of Andrew Haynes

Eaton Pughe was born the 25th, June 1768.

Family of Thomas and Frances S. Haynes

Anne born Feb. 28, 1783
Charles Eaton, Apr. 15, 1784
Thomas, Dec. 3, 1785
Catherine, June 9, 1787
Frances, Apr. 27, 1789
Mary, July 28, 1790
John Wesley, Jan. 6, 1793
Elizabeth, June 17, 1794
Susan W., March 27, 1796
William P., Dec. 19, 1797
Martha M., July 25, 1799

Family of C. C. and M. Haynes

Mary, Nov. 20, 1812
John G., 1814
Cornelia, June 3, 1819
Charles E., Dec. 31, 1820

Deaths

Herbert Haynes died in London 22, Jan. Was interred in the middle aisle of Stepney church, 1736
Draughton Haynes died Aug. 30, 1742
Thomas Haynes died Sept. 14, 1742
Martha Haynes died March 3, 1744
Thomas Haynes died April 30, 1749
Anthony Haynes died July 9, 1759
Andrew Haynes died Oct. 9, 1753
Richard Haynes died Nov., 1754
Anthony (son of Andrew) died Nov., 1768
Anne Pughe died Nov. 10, 1772
Thomas Haynes died at his residence in Columbia County, Ga., 182_
Charles Eaton Haynes died in Milledgeville Aug. 29, 1841

Martha Hicks (his wife) Sparta, Ga., Jan. 11, 1821
Cornelia F. Bonnell died at Athens May 7, 1846
Edwin B. Andrews in Alabama, Dec., 1836
John Randolph Andrews March 4, 1834

The late Mr. Charles Haynes Andrews, Sr., of Milledgeville, Ga., son-in-law of Judge Iveson L. Harris, who was the son of Agustin and grandson of Walton Harris, before his death completed a genealogy of the family from the progenitor to present date, all from records left by Judge Iveson L. Harris, who had collected more data than any of his family previous to his death.

WILLIAM WESLEY ANSLEY

Mr. Ansley traced his ancestry back through his English line to that of Samuel and Susannah Wesley. Mr. Ansley was a very devout church member, he doubtless inherited some of his strong Christian tendencies from his forebears. He was never known to neglect the church, or remain from the "House of God" unless providentially hindered. He fully believed the teaching of Wesley as he himself defined it, Christian Perfection is in "the loving God with all our heart, mind, soul and strength."

When the First Methodist Church built an annex to the building Mr. Ansley put his strongest efforts in looking after the work, seeing that every detail was carried out according to specifications. He was born April 15, 1850. He married Anne Olevia Clark October 17, 1872. Mrs. Ansley was a direct descendent of General Elijah Clark. Mr. and Mrs. Ansley came to Waycross from Alabama October 15, 1896. The following are the names of their children:

Willie Olevia Ansley was born Sept. 23, 1876; William Thomas Seaman was born May 23, 1876; Willie Olevia Ansley and William Thomas Seaman were married Dec. 6, 1899. Their children's names are: Margaret, (Mrs. Hardy Jacobs) and Dr. Ansley Seaman. Mary Lois Ansley was born Mar. 8, 1878. James Weldon Seals was born Nov. 5, 1871. Mary Lois Ansley and James Weldon Seals were married Dec. 17, 1896.

Mr. and Mrs. Seals came to Waycross Jan. 1898. Their wedding was the second one in the First Methodist Church. All the children, three girls, have been christened at its altar, and one daughter, Annie Lois Seals was married there twenty-eight years later, on their anniversary.

JAMES T. AND FLORENCE BEATON

Mr. James Beaton came to Waycross in 1870, where for thirty-seven years he engaged in the mercantile business. He was a successful business man and believed in the future prosperity and advancement of Waycross, by investing his accumulated savings here. He was a deacon of the Baptist Tabernacle and his wife a member of the Methodist Episcopal Church.

Mrs. Florence Beaton, the wife of Mr. James Beaton, was born at St. Marys, Georgia, January 28, 1857, a daughter of John L. K. and Julia (Scott) Holtzendorff. Her father was born near St. Marys, Georgia; was a farmer and merchant, and died when between sixty-five and sixty-six years of age. During the War Between the States he served four years as a Confederate sharpshooter, and though once shot through the lung, he recovered. His father, Alexander Holtzendorff, a former native of Germany, married Sarah Spalding, of McIntosh County. Mr. Holtzendorff, after settling in Camden, joined forces in all of the Indian Wars, he being a trained soldier in the army of his native land. He proved an important leader among the white settlers in the sparcely-settled country in all of the Indian invasions.

Julia Scott, mother of Mrs. Florence Beaton, was also born near St. Marys, Georgia, and spent most of her life there, dying at the age of fifty-three. Her parents,

Alexander C., and Eliza (Brown) Scott, were natives of Scotland, where they were married, and as young people came to the United States, Alexander Scott becoming an extensive planter in Camden County, Georgia.

Of the five children born to James and Florence Beaton, two died in infancy; Clifford, formerly a successful Waycross merchant, died in El Paso, Texas, age twenty-eight years; Dr. James Julian (deceased) was a graduate of the Atlanta College of Surgeons, and was one of the leading specialists of Waycross.

Mr. Scott Beaton is the only one of the sons of Mr. and Mrs. Beaton now living. Scott Beaton has been a successful business man in Waycross and has held public office in different departments of city and county affairs. Mr. Beaton's first experience as a public official was in the office of alderman of the Fourth Ward, in which he served two years. Here he displayed untiring energy in his great desire to forward the interests of his constituents; this won him instant favor and placed him in the light of acceptable mayorality timber. In December, 1913, he was elected to the chief executive's office, and December 2, 1915, received re-election without opposition, which had only occurred once before in the history of the city. He has served as State Senator, and was a leader in promoting movements for the advancement of educational standards, and has served efficiently as a member of the school board of the city schools of Waycross.

DR. JAMES BAGLEY

Dr. Bagley is truly a native Georgian, having been born January 16, 1866 in Ware county, which was also the birthplace of his father and mother.

His paternal grandfather, Ransom Bagley, was born in Virginia, and while quite a young man, with two of his brothers removed to North Carolina, later one brother settled in Raleigh of that State, while the other settled in

Alabama. Ransom Bagley came to Ware County, Georgia, having purchased lands here; he carried on general farming, with the help of slaves, for a number of years, but later removed to Florida, where he spent the remainder of his life.

Born in what is now Ware County in 1815, Berrien Bagley was reared to agricultural pursuits, and when ready to begin life for himself bought land lying within three miles of the parental estate, and continued life as a farmer. There were no railroads in the state when he was young, and he was forced to haul the surplus production of his farm with teams to Centerville, Traders Hill, and Savannah, but before he died there was a railroad within six miles of his home. Honest, industrious, and a good manager, he was very successful in his calling, acquiring a competency. On the farm, in which he took great interest in improving, he spent his last days, passing away in January, 1908, at the venerable age of eighty-three years. Berrien Bagley married in early life Eliza Thompson, a daughter of Rev. Henry Thompson, for many years a Methodist preacher in Ware County. She passed to a higher life, aged eighty years. Of the twelve children born into that home, ten grew to years of maturity. Their names were: Mary J., Rachel, Julia, John W., Amanda, James B., Roan H., Thomas Berrien, Francis and Ella.

James Bagley, the subject of this sketch, attended school as opportunity offered, in the meantime becoming intimately acquainted with farm work of all kinds. When he was eighteen years old his father gave him one hundred acres of land, and he began his career as an independent farmer. Having been trained to habits of industry and thrift, and well drilled in the art and science of agriculture, he succeeded from the start, and continued a tiller of the soil until 1892. Desirous then of gratifying a long-cherished ambition, Mr. Bagley began the study of medicine, in the Atlanta Medical College of Physicians and Surgeons, from which he graduated with the class of 1894. Immediately beginning the practice of his profession at Millwood, Ware County, Dr. Bagley continued there fifteen years, meeting with unquestionable success. Locating at Waycross in 1909, he here built a large and remunerative patronage, the people of his native county having great confidence in his skill and ability.

Dr. Bagley married, when a youth of eighteen summers, Miss Lucinda Meeks, whose birthplace was in the northern part of Clinch County, Georgia, eight miles from Pearson, a daughter of Mr. and Mrs. William Meeks. Four children came to bless the home of Dr. and Mrs. Bagley, whose names are: Dr. William Francis (deceased) James Wesley, Daniel English and Loney.

Dr. Bagley and Mrs. Bagley are consistent members of the Primitive Baptist Church and their two older sons are affiliated by membership with the Methodist Episcopal Church.

JAMES STACY BAILEY

James Stacy Bailey's home was in Ware County; he owned and lived at a sawmill six miles from Waycross, located at a little settlement known as Duke, later Ruskin. He was born in Montgomery County, Georgia, October 9, 1848. His father, William Stacy Bailey, was born in Woolwich, Maine, March 5, 1818. His parents were Abner and Mahala Bailey Abner, descended from an Englishman, who accompanied a certain Duke on his mission to this country to lay out a grant of land he had acquired. Mr. Bailey's son met the daughter of the Duke, and this meeting proved a case of "love at first sight," and they ran away and were married. The lady was disinherited, but in the course of time, all other lineage having become extinct, the Government sought to find her, the only living heir of an estate amounting to over three million dollars. Her descendants were found, but during the Revolutionary War all records of the marriage had been destroyed. Unable to prove his marriage, nearly a century was spent in a vain attempt to prove their title to the estate, which eventually reverted to the treasury of the English government. Mr. Bailey's grandfather was a soldier in the War of 1812, and his great-grandfather was a soldier in the War of the Revolution.

William Stacy Bailey, Sr., after many vicissitudes settled in Montgomery County, Georgia, in 1846, where he married Miss Mary Elizabeth Pittman July 20, 1847, who died in 1886, after which he married Mrs. Nancy Clemens, widow of Senator Clayton Clements. In 1855 he brought his family to Ware county, and he is named as one of the founders of Waycross. He settled on some of the lands near the present site of Waycross, and bought 500 acres.

During the War Between the States Mr. Bailey served first as a private and later became a Captain, having charge of the Rifles in Atlanta. He was a successful sawmill man and owned several sawmills in Georgia. He served as treasurer of Ware for twelve consecutive years. He was a devout Methodist, also a member of the Masonic fraternity. His son, James Stacy Bailey, was but a child when the family moved to Ware County, where he received training from private tutors and in the common schools. He early developed remarkable business talent, especially along saw-mill lines, in which he became interested when but eighteen years of age. With his father and brother, John, he engaged in extensive lumber business on the Satilla river. Two years later he formed a partnership with his father and Captain Cuyler Hilliard, and three years later Mr. R. B. Reppard, of Savannah, purchased the entire business. Mr. Bailey then formed a new partnership with Captain Hilliard for the operation of a sawmill in Nassau County, Florida, in connection with a mercantile business, which was carried on for fourteen years. For two years of this time Mr. Bailey, with his brother, John, had an established business on the St. Marys River, known as

J. S. Bailey & Company. In 1890 he closed out both partnerships and bought an interest in the firm of W. T. Scott & Company, and about the same time he entered the Satilla Manufacturing Company, of which he served as president.

He was a member of the Methodist Church and a Master Mason, always taking great interest in both the Church and Masonic Lodge. On January 30, 1877, Mr. Bailey was married to Miss Margaret Hilliard, daughter of Captain Cuyler Hilliard, of Hilliard, Florida. After her death he married Miss Mattie May Taylor, daughter of Rev. John R. Taylor of the Florida Conference. Mr. Bailey died at Dublin during a visit there, and is buried in Lott Cemetery, Waycross, Ga.

JOHN W. BENNETT

Among the successful lawyers of Waycross is Honorable John W. Bennett, a member of the firm of Wilson, Bennett & Pedrick. He occupies a prominent place in the front ranks of his profession and is considered one of the leading attorneys of the State.

HON. JOHN W. BENNETT

Reared on a farm, he had time for the reading of books which infused into him a persistent ambition for some of the higher things of life, and through his untiring efforts he accumulated sufficient funds to pay almost for his entire college course.

Since 1889 he has been actively engaged in the practice of his profession in Southern Georgia and many times he has been a co-worker when neither fame nor emolument were considered features, nevertheless his part of every contract has always been fulfilled to the letter. This part of his nature may explain his great personal popularity. He has never been defeated for any office that he desired, within the gift of the people.

Judge Bennett has concentrated his activities on the practice of law, but has found time to serve his community and state, though largely in the line of his profession and in offices where the opportunities for work are greater than the remuneration. In August, 1889, he was appointed by the Governor, Solicitor of the County

Court of Wayne County and filled that post until 1892. He was elected for two terms to the legislature from Wayne County. He filled the office of Solicitor General of the Brunswick Circuit for four years, being elected in October, 1896; was re-elected in 1900 and again in 1904 and altogether gave twelve years to that important position. In 1904 he was appointed a member of the board of trustees of the University of Georgia and for over twelve years has served as a member of the City Board of Education and one term as President of the Board.

During the administration of President Woodrow Wilson Mr. Bennett was appointed District Attorney for the Southern District of Georgia. He now represents Ware County in the State Senate of the General Assembly. In Liberty County, on Dec. 31, 1889, Judge Bennett was married to Miss Gertrude Price. To this marriage have been born three children: Junita (Mrs. B. H. Minchew) E. Kontz (married Katie Dale Mitchell) and John W., Jr., (married Allie Madge Sanders). Mrs. Bennett died May 14, 1929.

MR. AND MRS. GEORGE W. BARNES

When Mr. and Mrs. Barnes moved from their home in Charlotte, North Carolina, to Waycross during March, 1888, they found this little town in southern Georgia just beginning to outgrow its primitive existence. A new brick court house had just been erected to replace the wooden structure that had proved itself inadequate to hold the people during "big court." There was talk of a Baptist Church being erected along with the court house, and the building of a Presbyterian Church in the early future.

A great part of New Waycross was swamp lands overgrown with pine trees and the only street lights were of kerosene which were stationed near the railroad crossing and along the corners of the streets in "Old Waycross".

Mr. and Mrs. Barnes soon identified themselves with the town. They always contributed gladly of their time and resources toward any movement for the moral or material welfare of the community and have ever been recognized as foremost citizens of Waycross.

Mr. Barnes is of a modest and retiring disposition, often setting in motion plans for achievements but carefully keeping himself in the background, preferring that others should receive credit. Easy of approach, once his word is given, it is to be depended upon.

Mr. Barnes has been an elder in the Presbyterian Church for many years, and is a faithful official and a loyal churchman.

He was born in Fremont, North Carolina, July 4, 1853 and was married to Miss Julia E. Moore at Titusville North Carolina, October 4, 1874.

Mrs. Barnes was born at Burgar, North Carolina November 9, 1856.

Mr. and Mrs. Barnes had two children: Mack, who married Miss Elsie Love, of Waycross; and Annie, who married Mr. Jesse M. Fesperman, of Thomasville.

Mr. and Mrs Barnes' only son, Mack Barnes, died in Waycross January 5, 1918, leaving one son, Mack Barnes, who is a prominent lawyer of Waycross.

Their daughter, Mrs. Fesperman has two children: Kate (Mrs. Arthur Lott), and George Fesperman, who married Miss Marion Cooper.

Mrs. Barnes entered her home eternal February 16, 1931.

Mr. Barnes has retired from active business and spends a great part of his time at St. Simons where he maintains a summer home.

OBEDIAH BARBER

When Governor George Gilmer appointed Mr. Crawford and J. Hamilton Couper as a committee to ascertain the true boundary line between the State of Georgia and the territory of Florida during the year of 1831, they met on this occasion near the Okefinokee Swamp Mr. Israel Barber, who said he was the first white settler living on the northern border of the Swamp and had been living in that vicinity for twenty-six years. Israel and Young Obediah Barber proved of great assistance to the state surveyors, due to their extensive acquaintance with that section of the country.

The Barbers originally came to Ware about one hundred years ago from Bryan County. Few individuals had more varied acquaintances among men than Mr. Obediah Barber. Authors of books and newspaper writers have written interesting nature stories revealing him to be an outstanding character in their narratives. It was through these writers that the sobriquet "The King of the Okefinokee" was acquired by him.

He was a nature lover and was a natural zoologist. It has been said of Mr. Barber that he was so familiar with animals that he was considered a sage among the young students of biologists seeking information on plant and animal life in the Okefinokee. He often told of having clubbed a bear to death, and catching a large yellow tiger in his back yard. The bear that he killed with a stick of wood, instigated a surprise attack upon him when he was unarmed, and he had to fight for his life. After a deathlike struggle Mr. Barber won the fight over the immense black bear by killing him.

Mr. Barber's snake stories would have been incredible had they been related by others, but snakes of immense size and length were killed by him in the heart of the Okefinokee.

He was married three times. His first wife was Nancy Stephens and he was the parent of 18 children, all of whom lived to reach maturity, except one, who was accidentally shot in early childhood.

Mr. Barber saw active service in the War Between the States, and was honored as a Confederate Veteran. He died at the age of 92 years in his old home situated several miles from the Okefinokee Swamp out on the Old Train Road.

THE BLACKSHEAR FAMILY

The Blackshears, of Waycross, are of distinguished ancestry which dates back through many centuries of English, Scotch, and German history. They have a complete family record that was compiled by their grandmother, Mrs. Mary H. Hamilton.

Their great-great- grandfather, Charles Floyd, was the son of Samuel Floyd and Susan Dixon, who were born in the state of Virginia. The date of Charles Floyd's birth was March 4, 1747, and in 1768 he married Mary Fendin, on Green Island, South Carolina, where she was born April 15, 1747. Mrs. Mary Floyd died at their home at Bellevue, Camden County, Georgia, of erysipelas, Sept. 18, 1804. Col. Charles Floyd died there Sept. 9, 1820.

While Savannah was in the possession of the British General Charles Floyd enrolled in a volunteer company known as the "Liberty Boys" and was captured and carried on board an English vessel. The commander of the ship thought from the prisoner's appearance that he was a fellow countryman and asked him:

"Mr. Floyd, are you not an Englishman?"

"No, sir, I am an American by birth, a native of the state of Virginia, and an enemy of King George."

The commander said, "I see that you are a good seaman; renounce your country, receive your bounty money that I offer you and you shall be put in immediate command of a sixteen-gun ship-of-war."

Mr. Floyd replied fearlessly, "Sir, were I in command of this vessel I would instantly pull down the colors now flying at her mast, nail those of the United States flag in their place, and turn her guns against you."

The only child of Charles and Mary Floyd was John

Floyd, grandfather of Mrs. Blackshear, who was born on the island of Hilton Head South Carolina, October 3, 1767. John Floyd was married on December 12, 1793, to Isabella Maria Hazzard. General John Floyd was a brave soldier of the War of 1812 and throughout that period of Indian Warfare was in active service until the Peace Treaty was signed at Ghent.

General David Blackshear was the grandfather of Misses Zoe, Isabella and Mr. Duke Blackshear. He at an early age took an active part against the Tories. He moved to Georgia from Jones County, North Carolina, in 1790 and settled in Laurens County, Georgia. He fought in the War of 1812 and in various ways General Blackshear served the state of Georgia, taking an active part in unearthing the Yazoo Fraud.

Mrs. Mary Hamilton Blackshear and her family came to Waycross in 1888. A book could be filled with interesting history of herself and children. Mrs. Blackshear was a well educated woman, being a member of the first graduating class of Wesleyan College. Her beautiful character shone at its best in her home, where, as a gracious and charming hostess, a devoted mother and a loyal friend, she manifested those qualities which have always marked the gentlewoman of the South. Her sons opened the first exclusive hardware store in Waycross. It was located on Albany Avenue. One by one this large representative family passed on to their home eternal, leaving here only three of the family, Misses Zoe, Isabella and Mr. Duke Blackshear. Mr. Blackshear died July 8, 1910. He loved his friends in adversity as well as prosperity and never neglected them and was a joy to his neighbors and family. He was a life-long member of the Methodist Episcopal Church, and was loyal to its faith and traditions.

Miss Zoe and Miss "Belle", with an unfailing courage and faith in the greatness of God's mercies, never gave up, although death's angel had almost demolished their beloved home. They have displayed in their natures the intrepid determination of their brave forefathers and are truly strong in their mental conception of weighty subjects. In their manner, they are individual and not of today but unmistakably women of the Old South.

Miss Belle's wonderful spirit has passed into the Great Beyond and the much-loved Miss Zoe is still bravely carrying on, living in the home once so replete with life and happiness.

Mrs. Blackshear's five sons and one daughter sleep in Lott Cemetery, and her grandfather, General John Floyd, is buried at Fairfield, in Camden County. This place has a historic past that dates back into the Colonial period. The "Mansion", the residence of General Floyd, was a typical southern home whose latchstring hung outside and around whose festive 'bode often gathered the Greens, Shaws, Butlers, Postells, Pages, McIntoshes, and many other people of note. The stately live-oaks that were planted by the Floyds are still standing with a distinction of age, but the "Mansion", like many southern homes, was burned in the early part of the nineteenth century. A singular coincidence is connected with Fairfield. It was not only General Floyd's abiding place in life, but his remains were interred on the site where his old home stood—a privilege that is not often accorded one.

Miss Zoe died July 8, 1933. She was the last of the Blackshears who came here from Laurens County, Ga., to Waycross in 1890.

DANIEL I. BLACKBURN

Daniel I. Blackburn was born in 1784 in South Carolina—exact date and place unknown. By occupation he was a school teacher and was one of the earliest teachers in Ware and Clinch counties. He is remembered by only the oldest of the people of these counties. It seems he lived in Bullock County for some years before migrating to Ware County about 1825. He was among the first settlers to move to Ware County after it was created. His first wife was Mary Ann (Polly) Miller, born 1790 in South Carolina. She was a daughter of William Miller, Revolutionary soldier of Ware County. She died about 1852, and his second wife was Sarah, widow of Henry Joyce, Sr., of Clinch County, but no children were born to them. Second wife was born in 1798 and was first married in 1818 in Tatnall county to Henry Joyce; She was Sarah (or Sallie) Triplett before marriage.

THE BLACKBURN FAMILY

One of the early settlers of Ware County was Daniel I. Blackburn, who came to this county from Bullock. He married Mary Ann Miller, who was the daughter of William Miller, the Revolutionary soldier who is buried at Kettle Creek Churchyard. Mr. Blackburn was a very progressive citizen of Ware, was ever ready to lend all help that would keep things on the move in the county. When the Kettle Creek School was opened in 1924 the patrons of the school could not secure a teacher and Mr. Blackburn (although actively engaged in the surveying of the lands in Ware, Coffee and Clinch, volunteered to teach reading, writing and spelling in the school until the place could be filled. He frequently served on Tax Receiver's Boards. On March 17, 1826, he furnished a bond of $2,000. Entaties: Thomas Newbern, Benjamin Milton, again Daniel I. Blackburn, principal dated, July 4, 1828, amount $2,000, Surety, Lenis Greer. Daniel I. Blackburn, dated June 7, 1830, amount $2,000, Surety John O'Steen. Daniel Blackburn, principal, dated April 26, 1834, amount $2,000. Surety Randal McDonald, Thomas Henderson.

Mr. Blackburn served as Justice of Peace of Ware County Feb. 12, 1833 to 1837. He served as a Ware County commissioner April 16, 1827-28. He served in the Ware County District, that later was a part of Clinch, 1845-1846-49 and 50.

Daniel Blackburn's son, Martin Ebenezer L. Blackburn, born 1824 in Ware County, Georgia, died while a prisoner of War at Elmira, New York. He was a private, Company "G", 7th Georgia Cavalry—died on Nov. 3, 1864. His grave is 841 Woodlawn National Cemetery, Elmira, N. Y.

The children of Daniel I. Blackburn and his wife, Mary Ann Miller Blackburn, who lived to maturity were:

Cynthia Blackburn, Julia, married John Inman, Ellie, married Jim Bullard, Lavinia, married Wm. Vansant, Mary, married James Sweat, Martin E. L. Blackburn, married Mary Cason.

The children born to Martin E. L. Blackburn and Mary Cason Blackburn were as follows: Elizabeth Blackburn (deceased), Daniel J. Blackburn (deceased) married Lizzie Barber, Mary Ann, married Jas. I. Barber, Margaret (deceased married Henry Waldron, Mattie, married T. T. Thigpen, Fred (deceased) married Florence Smith. These sons and daughters were residents of Ware county practically all their lives and the two still living are still residents of Ware. The four who have died are buried in Kettle Creek Cemetery.

Daniel I. Blackburn held many offices of trust in Ware County. The last services he rendered his county were that of clerk of the Superior Court, to which he was elected in 1873 for a term of two years.

DAVID HOPPS BENNETT

David Bennett was born in the southwestern portion of Ware County February 24, 1813. He was the son of Richard and Mary (McDonald) Bennett. Mrs. Mary M. Bennett was the daughter of Dr. McDonald and Catherine (Miller) McDonald.

Mr. Bennett served through the entire four years of the War Between the States. He was a member of Company E of the 26th Georgia Regiment, which formed a part of General Gordon's Brigade. He was a county commissioner for several consecutive years or terms and was a valued member of that commission due to his ability and his high-tone sense of truth and honor. He belonged to the old Democratic party as well as the new one and he was the recognized exponent of the principles of each. He married Miss Emma Smith, daughter of Austin and Mary Smith, and both were constant members of the Methodist church at Waresboro. Both of these pioneers sleep in the city of the dead at Waresboro, Georgia.

JUDGE H. P. BREWER

Judge Brewer was one of the greatest enthusiasts on the subject of schools and education that ever passed this way. He was made President of the first board of education that was established in Waycross under the local school system. He never lost his zeal in putting forward his best efforts for the educational work in Ware County and as long as he lived was connected in one way or another with the board of education.

He was born in Effingham County March 26, 1838, and remained in his native town until 1882 when he came to Waycross. He built his home on a street that was later named for him and where he and his family lived until his children were grown. It was there that Mrs. Brewer, (Mrs. Addie Kelley) died and where she lived since coming to Waycross with her interesting family from her old home in Effingham County.

In 1886 Judge Brewer was serving along with his other duties as senior editor of The Waycross Reporter. He remained with the paper three years and served six years as Judge of the City Court, he being a lawyer by profession. For a number of years he was an efficient employee of the Plant System, serving in the position of Claim Agent.

Judge Brewer enlisted in the Confederate Army on

Sept. 7, 1861, in the Effingham Hussars, which was made Company "I" of the 5th Regiment Georgia Cavalry, under Captain Edward Bird. He later served under Capt H. J. Strobar and remained in the service until he was taken very ill and went home on leave by authority of Dr. Martin, the Regimental Surgeon. The Army surrendered before he was able to return to service. He left just four days before the fight at Bentonville, N. C., and his Company of Troops was discharged from service at Appomattox court house.

Mrs. Addie Brewer, the wife of Judge Brewer, died in 1892 at the age of sixty years. She was survived by eight children, Joseph, Turner, Charles, Fred, Hallie, Eva (Mrs. D. P. Williams) Lollie (Mrs. J. R. Elerbee) and Effie (Mrs. C. H. Lowther).

Judge Brewer was later married to Miss Bell Williams, a woman of marked ability. Time passed happily with them, death intervening only a few years, Judge Brewer passing first, Mrs. Brewer dying suddenly in 1931.

PROFESSOR BRIDGES

Prof. R. M. Bridges, who was elected Superintendent of the Waycross schools in 1890, was a Virginian by birth and educated at Princeton. Immediately upon finishing his education he decided on teaching as his life's work and not as a stepping-stone to something else. He had taught in five states before coming to Georgia. During his stay in Waycross a city paper, The Herald, had this to say of him: "Prof. Bridges, the present head of the schools of Waycross, is a gentleman of high attainments, decided discipline, splendid equipment and thorough experience. His success in the past in other states is emphatic witness to his work as a teacher. The excellent system of public schools now being supported by the city, presided over as they are by one so competent, shows up to satisfying prominence the intellectual advancement of a people heartily in sympathy with higher education." Prof. Bridges' stay in Waycross was cut short by failing health, which he sought to benefit by a change to Florida and later to the west. After an absence of nine years, having remembered so kindly Waycross and her people, he returned and organized a private school, believing that the work would be less laborious than the conduct of a public school. He was only permitted to continue this work one year, when he was stricken with a fatal illness. A short time previous to his passing he wrote to a loved son as follows: "I do not think many of us believe that the providences of this life are making for our eternal good. There are many things of the past and present as well, that with our short vision we would have otherwise, but I have tried to see His ruling hand in each event of life and in my deepest sorrows I have been prone to believe that:

"*Somewhere the sun is shining,*
Somewhere the songbirds dwell."

Continuing, he quoted the following from Shakespeare: "Out, out, brief candle, life's but a walking shadow, a poor player that struts and frets his hour upon the stage and then is heard no more. It is a tale told by an idiot, full of sound and fury, signifying nothing." Then he added, "But how different this from the glorious hope that

"*Our God will take the clay His mercy warms,*
And mould it into heavenly forms."

How beautiful the thought that our failures and our hardships; our disappointments and our sorrows; our humiliations and our triumphs are rounding out the matchless symmetries of our eternal life."

MR. AND MRS. BUCHANAN

Waycross was once noted for being the most religious town in Georgia and Mr. and Mrs Buchanan were untiring in their efforts to help their home town to sustain that reputation.

Trinity Church was blessed in their membership. They loved the church; they loved the members who assembled there to worship and every Sunday found them in the same pew, ever in harmony with the minister, who happened to be stationed here to serve in this House of God.

C. C. Buchanan entered the service of the Confederate Army when he was twenty-one years of age in Savannah Volunteer Guards for six months in Company "B", commanded by Lieutenant George W. Stiles, under Captain John Screven, Battalion Commander, was mustered out of that branch and later enlisted in the Cavalry and served under Captain A. C. Strickland in Troop "G" of the 4th Georgia Cavalry, commanded by Colonel D. L. Clinch, and served in that branch until the close of the War. He enlisted as a private, later made an Orderly Sergeant, and at the close of the war was Regimental Adjutant. C. C. Buchanan served under Gen. John T. Morgan part of the time and under Gen. Joe Wheeler in the battle of Shiloh, and at Chickamauga. He was in the siege around Atlanta under Gen. Hardee June 22, 1864. His War record was remarkable in that he answered all roll calls throughout the four years of war, with the exception of three days while in the hospital suffering from sunstroke. He was never absent without leave, never under arrest, was never on extra duty and was in every fight in which his regiment engaged without receiving a wound. He was Capt.-Commander of the South Georgia Camp No. 819 United Confederate Veterans for eight or nine years.

Mr. Buchanan was an active business man for many years, but his latter days were devoted to the Ministry. Consecration, sympathy, intellectual grasp and soundness of judgment characterized his life work.

He was born December 4, 1840, in Montgomery County, Georgia. He married Mary Ann Harper January 29, 1865, at Blackshear, Georgia, and died in Waycross November 2, 1929.

The honesty, simplicity and frankness that characterized Mrs. Buchanan through her entire life was strikingly prominent. She resolutely refused to compromise any matter of principle and would often endure with unflinching steadfastness popular disfavor, if need be, to maintain the right. Her spirit was illumined like that of the Maid of Orleans in the prophetic vision of what she might do for her Divine Lord. Nothing to her looked impossible and she lived in an atmosphere too high for duplicity or selfish interest of any sort; and one of the most beautiful characteristics of her nature was cheerfulness. She had an abiding faith that everything happened for the best.

Mrs. Buchanan was born December 27, 1844, in Blackshear, Georgia, and died in Waycross, Georgia, November 29, 1916.

Mr. and Mrs. Buchanan were blessed with the following children: Margaret L. (Mrs. Henry Williams), born November 5, 1865; Minnie Lee (Mrs. Daniel Sweat), born May 17, 1867; Clinton C., born March 24, 1874, died January 20, 1926; and William H., born January 1, 1876, died January 9, 1924.

Mr. Christopher Buchanan's father was Duncan Buchanan and he married Jincy Gay and lived in Montgomery County, but later moved to Blackshear, Georgia. Duncan Buchanan's father was William Buchanan, who was born in Scotland in 1746, and died in 1849. He came from Pennsylvania to Raleigh, North Carolina, later settling in Georgia. He fought in the Revolutionary and the French and Indian Wars.

BUNN FAMILY

The name of Bunn appears in England long before surnames existed there, except among land owners. The name, as imported from Germany, was probably in the form of von Bonn (from Bonn), which was quickly rendered Bunne by the English, just as Bohn became Bunn elsewhere. It is found chiefly in the southeastern counties of England—Norfolk, Suffolk, Middlesex, Essex and Kent. Many names in common use in America today have undergone modifications and variations in comparatively recent years in England and America. The origin of those of the remote past is largely a matter of speculation. Apparently, the name Bunn came into use as a surname in Germany, whence it drifted down the Rhine into Holland and across the North Sea to England.

Of this we are quite certain, those bearing the name of Bunn have been good citizens, industriously plying their various vocations and attending strictly to their own affairs. J. R., Taylor and J. W. Bunn were the first of that name found in the annals of Ware County and the men of that name have taken their place among the most reliable and honorable citizens of this county. Mr. Taylor Bunn's parents were Applewhite and Mary (Pierce) Bunn. Mr. Bunn was born Sept. 25, 1855, at Earpsboro, Jones County, North Carolina, near Zebulon. He was educated in the public schools of his home town. At the age of twenty-one he went to Camden, South Carolina, where, in 1877 to 1884, he dealt in the turpentine business, and in the latter year moved to Leesburg, Florida, and continued in the same business two years. Since 1886 he has operated a saw mill, dealt in turpentine and engaged in farming and merchandising in Ware County. His home is in Fairfax, eight miles from Waycross, where he owns 11,000 acres of land, four hundred of this is under cultivation, devoted chiefly to corn and tobacco.

Mr. and Mrs. Bunn are constant members of the church. Mr. Bunn is a Mason and in politics, a democrat. He was married to Miss Elizabeth Whitley, February 27, 1881, in Johnson County, North Carolina, a daughter of Monroe and Martha Whitley. Their children are: Marvin (deceased), James Dudley (deceased), Estell (Mrs. Ben S. Gibson), Harvey C. and Lila (Mrs. R. B. Zachery).

JOHN BURNETT

Among the early settlers of Clinch county was John Burnett, a native of South Carolina, born in 1792. He came to this county while it was Ware county, about 1842, and lived in the 719th district of Ware county. This district is now in Echols county but in those days it embraced the present 1219th or Fargo district in Clinch.

This old settler was a son of John Burnett, Sr., and his wife was Sophia Harvey whose parents lived on Saltketcher Creek near Walterboro, S. C. She was born in 1806. To them were born seven children as follows:

1. Elizabeth, born 1838, in S. C., married Noah Langdale of Echols.
2. Richard, born 1839 in S. C., married Elizabeth, daughter of David Register of Clinch county.
3. Nancy, born 1841 in S. C., married Samuel Register, a son of John Register.
4. Mary, born 1843, in this county; married Giles Dryden: they moved to Florida.
5. John, born 1840 in this county, married Dunaway; lives at Sanderson, Fla.
6. Lucy, born 1847 in this county, married James Crews; they moved to New Smyrna, Fla.
7. James, born 1849 in this county, married Martha Daugharty, a sister of the late Francis Daugharty, and after her death he married Emily Zeigler of Echols county. He lives at Howell, Ga.

Mr. Burnett fought in the War of 1812 but what company and regiment we have not learned. After coming to this section, he served as a Justice of Peace of the 719th district from 1843 to 1846 and again from 1850 to 1852. He died in 1867 at the age of 75, and is buried at Bethel church in the eastern part of Echols county. His wife died in 1871.

About the same time he came to Georgia, he had three brothers to come to this state—Bryant, Benjamin and Richard Burnett. However we do not know where they settled, except Ben, who located in Bulloch county where some of his descendents live today.

WILLIAM J. CARSWELL

William J. Carswell was the third son of Matthew and Harriet Eliza (Kilpatrick) Carswell, and descended from Scotch and Irish ancestors who several generations ago settled in St. George's parish. His grandfather was a captain in the Revolutionary army, and the land on which he lived is still in the possession of the family. Matthew J. was a farmer, highly honored and a public-spirited man and was for a number of years a member of the board of education. He served in the Confederate army during the last year of the war. His eldest son was also a soldier and surrendered with Johnston's army.

William Carswell was born in Whitfield County August 19, 1854, was educated in the common schools of Hephzibah. He was a deacon in the Baptist church after coming to Waycross and served six years on the Board of Education. April 20, 1877, Mr. Carswell married Miss Mary Lyon, who died four years later leaving a daughter, Marion (Mrs. H. J. Carswell). On April 13, 1882 he married Miss Lilla T. Jones, and by this union had another daughter, Jessie (Mrs. Will C. Parker). Mrs. Carswell survives Mr. Carswell and is an honored and beloved citizen of Waycross.

DR. ALEXANDER CARSWELL

Dr. Carswell was born in Burke County, Georgia, March 9, 1852, and was a son of Matthew and Eliza (Kirkpatrick) Carswell. Matthew J. Carswell was born in the same county Jan., 1822, later moved to Richmond county where he died in 1887. His wife, Eliza Kirkpatrick, was also born in Burke County in 1825.

Dr. Alexander Carswell was reared in Whitfield and Richmond counties, and was a graduate of both Mercer University and the State University.

In 1874 he read medicine with Dr. J. William Jones of Dooley County, and graduated from the medical department of the University of Georgia in 1879. He located in Burke county, and in 1884 he removed to Waycross, where he soon built up a large practice, and he occupied an honored place in his chosen profession.

On February 16, 1882, Dr. Carswell was married to Miss Fannie Carswell, daughter of Matthew J. and Ellen (DuPree) Carswell, and their home was blessed by three charming daughters, Della D. (Mrs. Paine), Mamie (Mrs. Benjamin Redding), Alexander, Mrs. Isaac Suggs.

Mrs. Carswell, after the death of Dr. Carswell, was happily married to Mr. George Youmans of this city, whose devotion to her three daughters has been as great as if they were his own. Mrs. Youmans died from an attack of pneumonia in 1928. Mr. Youmans and daughters survive her.

DR. THOMAS JANES CARSWELL

On the 6th day of April, 1877, Thomas Janes Carswell was born at the Old Alexander home place in Burke county, Georgia, about twelve miles northwest of Waynesboro, and eight miles from the town of Hephzibah.

His father was Rev. John Hamilton Carswell, Baptist minister, educator and farmer, who in his later years made his home at Hephzibah, Ga.

His mother was, before her marriage, Mary Fannie Janes, daughter of Dr. Thomas P. Janes, physician and planter of Green county, Georgia. Dr. Janes was Georgia's first Commissioner of Agriculture.

A son of a Baptist minister and the third oldest of

eleven children, Dr. Carswell, as a boy, had to perform many and varied tasks about the home and on the farm.

After attending the common schools of Jefferson and Richmond counties, in order to further his education, Mr. Carswell found it to his advantage to teach awhile and go to school awhile. He, therefore, entered the State Normal School at Athens, where he was graduated in 1900 with L. I. degree. He then taught at Adrian, Ga., and later returned to Hephzibah High School for a year's study and received his diploma from that institution. He again taught at Adrian, Ga., and later entered Peabody College for Teachers at Nashville, Tenn., where he received the L. I. and B. Ped. degrees. Mr. Carswell then became superintendent of schools at Nicholls, Ga., continuing here several years and spending part of each year studying in the Medical Department of The University of the South, where he graduated in medicine and surgery, receiving the M. D. degree Oct. 1, 1908.

Dr. Carswell completed another year's teaching at Nicholls, Ga., and in the summer of 1909 he went to New York for post-graduate study. While here he stood a competitive examination and made the highest grade over 30 or more physicians and was appointed Head of the House Staff of Physicians of the New York Maternity Hospital. He held this position for two years, during which time he completed several courses of post-graduate study in Medicine and Surgery.

In the fall of 1910 Dr. Carswell came to Waycross in Ware county, Ga., and located to practice his chosen profession. He opened offices to himself and soon had the attention of the leaders in his profession in this city. Dr. J. L. Walker had a large practice, but on account of his age he decided that he needed a younger physician to associate with him in his practice, and accordingly invited Dr. Carswell to share his offices with him.

In this connection Dr. Carswell continued his practice in Waycross and Ware county until he lost his life as the result of an automobile accident Feb. 10, 1913. There were no eyewitnesses to the accident. He was discovered in the early morning hours in flames near his automobile which was burning. His clothing seemed to have become saturated with gasoline and doubtless caught fire from the acetylene lights with which his car was equipped. He was so badly burned that he died some ten hours later at the Kings Daughters Hospital in Waycross. His remains were carried to the home at Hephzibah and interred in the Hephzibah cemetery.

Dr. Carswell was never married. He was a member of the Baptist church and belonged to the order of Modern Woodmen of America. He was a good citizen, a lover of humanity, and sought to relieve suffering as far as lay in his power. The accident which caused his death came near the end of a night which he had spent in attendance upon two patients whose lives he was trying to save.

WILLIAM CASON

William Angus Cason was born in Ware County at what is now Waltertown, on the Satilla River, December 13, 1849. He was the son of J. B. and Amy Cason, the daughter of Dr. Randall McDonald.

Mr. Cason attended the public schools of the county and was a man of fine intellectual ability and began his life as a farmer in his home county. He was a merchant for a while and was later appointed Superintendent of public roads of the county and served as a county commissioner for nearly twenty years.

Mr. Cason married Miss Janie Williamson, daughter of Col. George B. Williamson, and the child of that union was Charles E. who was serving as deputy clerk of the court when he died, and whose mother preceded him to the grave.

Miss Gertrude duBignon, of Brunswick, Georgia, became the second wife of Mr. Cason and their children are: Misses Jewel and Virdie.

With his business interests so varied Mr. Cason naturally took a large part in civic works, giving generously of his time and experience to their success and attracting to him a large circle of friends throughout his life. His wife and two daughters survive him.

JONATHAN GILMAN CLOUGH

Jonathan Clough was born December 8, 1845, in Ware county, near Waycross. He married Isabella Hilliard, who was born July 23, 1849 in Ware county near Waycross. Jonathan Clough's father's name was John True Clough, who was born Feb. 5, 1814 at Bay Hill near Rochester, N. H., at the old Clough homestead. He married Serenia Catherine Miller, who was born May 2, 1828, in Bullock County, Georgia, and died October 3, 1883. Serenia Catherine was married twice. Her last husband was Captain James Sweat. Her father's name was Martin T. Miller, who was born June 22, 1797 in Tatnall County, Georgia. He married Nancy Brewton Miller. He died May 2, 1883. His wife, Nancy Brewton Miller, was born July 7, 1805, in Bullock County, Georgia, and died Dec. 7, 1890.

Jonathan Gilman Clough during the War Between the States joined Company K., Fourth Georgia Regiment. His company was under the command, at first, of Col. William A. McDonald and was attached to the 26th Georgia Regiment, known as Company K.

Jonathan Gilman Clough was a direct descendant of Captain Jeremiah Clough, Sr., the Indian fighter who was a pioneer settler of Canterbury, New Hampshire. Captain Jeremiah Clough's land deeds show him to have been a resident of the town before 1738, although tradition concedes him to have been the first settler. He was chosen a selectman by the proprietors in 1738, and, as he was the first inhabitant to be elected to office, he was probably the pioneer of the settlement. His first purchases included home lots 68 and 69 near the fort.

His son, Jeremiah Clough, Jr., whose birth was in 1736, is said to have been the first white male child born in Canterbury. Captain Clough served in the Continental army. He was appointed chairman of a committee "to inspect the inhabitants of the town of Canterbury and see that they observe and keep the resolution of our Grand Congress when sitting in Philadelphia last fall." This was Canterbury Committee of Safety. He was re-elected on this committee for the following year. He fought in the battles at Lexington and Bunker Hill. He was a member of the Provincial Congress of New Hampshire. Captain Jeremiah Clough was appointed as one of the "twenty able-bodied effective men to serve as soldiers in the Continental army during our contest with Great Britain or for three years, as they choose, unless regularly discharged".

The Clough family were truly Colonial people of affairs. They were founders of churches, towns and schools, and the men were prominent in the Colonial and Revolutionary War.

Mr. Jonathan Gilman Clough was an honored and highly esteemed citizen of Ware county. Mr. and Mrs. Clough's children are: Eva Lee, Forest True, Emily Margaret, Elizabeth Belle, John Gilman, Walter Hilliard, Annie Laurie, Loyd Brewton and Ira Dwight. Mr. Clough died Nov. 4, 1907.

MR. ROBERT Y. COTTINGHAM

Mr. Robert Cottingham's native home was Spartanburg, South Carolina, where he was born January 5, 1845. When only eight years old his parents moved to Madison, Florida, where he grew to young manhood, and Sept. 27, 1866, he was married to Miss Angilina L. Davis and in 1872 they removed to Waycross. There were only a few families living here at that time and Mr. Cottingham, being among the first settlers, became identified with the town in its infancy.

In those days the land was young and undeveloped, roads were bad, markets there were none, and it was a two days' journey to Traders Hill, the nearest approach to a trading place. Yet in this secluded locality, remote from marts and markets, Robert Cottingham worked and took fine care of his wife and family of young children. In this day of organized labor it is difficult to appreciate the kind and variety of talent then required in the development of a new subdivision of the state.

He entered into the industrial and commercial affairs of the thriving little village and was recognized as a progressive and a reliable business man and a public-spirited citizen. Mr. Cottingham most strenuously held to the principles advocated by the Democratic party and was always on the right side of political activities in his state. He was at one time a member of the city council. He cared little for public office, but was ever ready to help others into official service. He was a valued employee of the Plant System (later A. C. L.) and held an important place with the railroad as long as he lived.

Mrs. Cottingham was a woman of fine personality and took a deep interest in all religious affairs. She and Mr. Cottingham were consistant members of the Methodist Episcopal church and were strong in their Christian faith. They had six children: Francis (Mrs. J. W. S. Hardy), Susan, William, Charles, Robert and George. William, Charles and Susan sleep beside their parents in Lott's cemetery. Robert lives in Williamsburg, Va. George and Mrs. J. W. S. Hardy are valued citizens of Waycross.

JOHN MADISON COX

John Madison Cox was the son of James Madison Cox and was born February 27, 1868, in Woodsville, Green County, Georgia. His great-grandfather, Captain

Stemridge Cox, was a Virginian, born of Scotch-Irish ancestors, served as an officer in the Revolutionary War, having command of a company. The grandfather of Mr. Cox, who was J. S. Cox, was a life-long resident of Virginia. He was not old enough to bear arms during the Revolution, but he entered the employ of the government, being engaged in the manufacture of guns in a government factory.

James Madison Cox, Sr., was born and brought up in Mecklenburg County, Virginia. As a young man, seized by the wanderlust, he migrated to Georgia, locating in Green county where he engaged in farming and also in mercantile pursuits, opening a store at Woodville. Although past military age at the beginning of the War Between the States, he enlisted. During the second year of the struggle he went with his command to Virginia where he took part in several battles of note. Mr. Cox, Sr., married Miss Sarah Ann Newson, who was born on a farm at Union Point, Green County, Georgia, where her parents spent their last years. Four sons and three daughters were born of their marriage.

Mr. John M. Cox came to Waycross in 1896 and engaged in the brokerage business as a wholesale grocer. He recently was elected Ordinary of Ware county.

As a man and a citizen Mr. Cox is held in high esteem by all who know him. He is an active worker in the Democratic ranks and has always been regarded as a man whose integrity was of the highest order. He served two years as mayor of Waycross, and for two years was president of the Waycross Board of Trade. Fraternally, he is a member of the Waycross Lodge No. 369, Protective Order of Elks and of the Knights of Pythias.

Mr. Cox married December 29, 1897, Miss Willella Lockhart, who was born in Opelika, Alabama. Her paternal grandfather, Richard Puryear Lockhart, was born in Virginia of Colonial and Revolutionary stock. Migrating to Alabama while a young man, he settled in Chambers county, becoming owner of a large plantation which he managed successfully until his death. He married Sarah Hamilton Harris, a daughter of Judge Edmund Harris, a prominent lawyer of LaGrange, Georgia, and a granddaughter of Absolem Harris, whose father, Lieut. Benjamin Harris was an officer in the Revolutionary War. The Harris family came from Greensville County, Virginia, to Georgia, settling in Hancock county seven miles from Sparta. Judge Harris married Mary Rollings, who was a graduate of a Baptist College in LaGrange, and a woman of a high order of intellect, culture and refinement.

Mr. Jesse H. Lockhart, the father of Mrs. Cox, was educated in LaGrange, and during his active career was identified with the railway service of the state for a number of years, serving as Superintendent of the Louisville & Nashville Railroad. He married Ella Hurt, who was born in Hurtsboro, Alabama, and was educated in Georgia, having been graduated from Wesleyan University at Macon. She died at the early age of thirty-two years, her death occurring in Birmingham, Alabama, and her body was laid to rest in the cemetery at Auburn, Alabama. Her father, William Chappel Hurt, married Miss Jane McTyeire, a sister of Holland Nimmons McTyeire, who for many years was the senior bishop of the Methodist Church, South, and from the time of the establishment of Vanderbilt University at Nashville, Tenn., was one of its board of trustees.

Three children were born of the union of Jesse Hamilton and Ella (Hurt) Lockhart, namely: Willella, now Mrs. Cox, Jessie, the wife of G. W. Smith, of Brewton, Ala.; Edith, the wife of Cecil Valentine Stanton, of Waycross.

Mr. and Mrs. Cox are the parents of five children as follows: John M., Jr.; Virginia Hurt, who died at the age of two years; Sarah McTyeirre; William, and Elizabeth.

Mrs. Cox received her education in the schools of Birmingham and finished at Dr. Price's Female College at

Nashville, Tennessee. Mrs. Cox is a brilliant, cultured and accomplished woman. She is a member of the Methodist Church, Daughters of the American Revolution and the Colonial Dames.

CAPTAIN EDWARD CRAWLEY

Edward H. Crawley was born at Lexington, Kentucky, in 1839, and as a young man came to Ware County, taking up his residence in the vicinity of Waycross. When war was declared between the States, he enlisted as a private in a Georgia infantry regiment in the Confederate Army, and for gallant service won promotion, holding the rank of Captain when the war ended.

Captain Crawley commanded a company in the 26th Georgia regiment, which formed a part of General Gordon's brigade, and he served under him in Northern Virginia, and all through other hard fought campaigns during the war. He was with John B. Gordon, when he was made a Major General, and at the battle of Gettysburg, in which Gordon's Division took a prominent part, Captain Crawley, with his brave little company, shared the hardships with his gallant chief, who never forgot his able service.

When General Gordon was governor of Georgia he appointed Captain Crawley on his staff, aid-de-camp to the Governor with rank of lieutenant colonel of cavalry, an honor justly bestowed upon this loyal soldier of the South.

In 1886 Captain Crawley was a member of a committee of citizens who met at the court house to take in consideration the procuring of a site and erecting thereon a suitable building for school purposes. He at that time was county chairman of the County Board of Education. He was strongly instrumental in the drilling of the first Artesian Well in Waycross for public use. He headed the subscription with the sum of $232.50 and through his friends, Mr. and Mrs. Leopold Weise, he was given by them one hundred and fifty dollars. Captain Crawley, impatient when some of the citizens displayed a lack of enthusiasm in the drilling of the well, in a Waycross Headlight, dated September 8, 1886, had this to say:

"It will take but little more money to finish the well, with what we have, and if there was more work and less inquiry as to what has become of the sum already subscribed, we would have a well, but as matters now stand, I see but little chance to have one, and in order to keep from using the money, if nothing is done to complete the well soon, I shall divert my subscription to the first schoolhouse under construction in Waycross."

For many years Captain Crawley was a prominent and influential figure in democratic politics, and served as clerk of the Superior Courts and as county treasurer of Ware County for a long period. He was actively engaged in merchandising in Waycross at the time of his death, which occurred in 1893 when he was fifty-four years of age. Captain Crawley was a Mason of prominence and well known in that order in this part of the state.

He married Miss Martha McDonald, who was born in Ware, daughter of Col. William Angus McDonald, a distinguished citizen of Ware County. Mrs. Crawley was a woman of strong mentality and a wonderful personality. She was reared in the faith of the Methodist church. Of the twelve children of Captain and Mrs. Crawley four are living, Judge J. Lee; Jerome, Thomas B., and Mrs. Margaret Davis of Hurtsboro, Alabama.

BRYAN CREWS

Mr. Crews was born in 1844 near High Bluff Church, situated on Big Creek in the Northeastern part of Ware County. His father was Macajah and his mother Eminiza Crews.

When the call to the colors came Bryan Crews was one of the first to enlist and served in the Southern army until the end of the war when the entire army was mustered out of service.

Mr. and Mrs. Crews have twelve children, one hundred and six grand children and seventy-five great grand children. Although Mr. Crews is rounding out his 88th year of activities he still hunts and is considered a good fisherman, always generous with his bait.

Joseph Crews was a soldier in the Indian Wars of 1837-38, he was the great grandfather of Bryan Crews. Macajah Crews, his father, drew land in Camden County through the Cherokee Land Lottery which was granted previous to the first day of January, 1838.

FRANCIS ASHER BATES AND MAUD MUNROE BATES

On the roll of the progressive business men of Waycross, no name stands out more prominently than that of Francis A. Bates. During the years of his activities he filled many places of usefulness. He was earnestly interested in the well-being of mankind, and was always willing to lend financial and liberal aid and encouragement to those less fortunate than he. His life was characterized by a spirit of simplicity and truth, and he never deviated from the highest ideal of progress and human betterment. He was a member of the Board of Directors of the R. R. Y. M. C. A., an active member of the First Methodist Church, Past Eminent Commander of Damascus Commandery No. 18; Past High Priest of the Royal Arch Masons, Waycross Chapter No. 19; 32nd. Degree Scottish Rite Mason, and a member of the Alee Temple of the Shrine in Savannah.

Mr. Bates was born in Newbern, Alabama, Dec. 13, 1867. His mother was Johanna Ridgeway Bates, whose native home was Meringo County, Ala. The childhood home of his father, William Independence Bates, was Union, S. C. Francis Bates and Maud Munroe were married in Tuscaloosa, Ala., coming to Waycross when quite young, they contributed materially toward the activities and the building of the home of their adoption.

Mrs. Bates was the daughter of Andrew Munroe and Mary Ann Finley. She was of Scotch descent on both sides of the family. Her father was born in Dundae, Scotland, on April 8, 1835, and came to America when only nine years old. He followed the mercantile business the greater part of his life. He was the son of Major Donald Munroe of Glasgow, the grandson of Col. Andrew Munroe, and great-grandson of Sir Robert Munroe of "Foulis Castle," Rosshire.

Major Donald Munroe served while young in Ireland under Gen. Sir John Moore in the Reay Fencibles. On the disbandonment of the Reay Fencibles he was transferred to the 78th Rosshire Highlanders. "The Queens' own body-guard." He served in India and in France. A tablet commemorating the bravery of his regiment under fire is erected in St. Gile's Cathedral, Edinburg.

Col. Andrew Munroe served with Field Marshal James Keith in Russia and Prussia under the great Frederick and was wounded at Hachkirchen when Field-Marshal Keith was killed. Sir Hector Munroe is the present incumbent of the baronetcy.

On her mother's side, Mrs. Bates is the granddaughter of Jane Shropshire of Jasper County, Ga., and Mortimer Finley of Pickens County, Ga., members of old Virginia and South Carolina families, who migrated to Georgia and are still prominent in the affairs of their adopted state. Jane Shropshire was the daughter of James Shropshire and Elizabeth Cunningham, of Virginia. Three brothers, Col. James Cunningham of the "Flying Camp," Pennsylvania '76, Captain Charles Cunningham, and Chaplain Cunningham were among the Revolutionary soldiers. The Cunninghams owned vessels and sent out privateers, one was "The Surprise." The first American flag seen in the British Channel was that raised by Capt. Cunningham on The Surprise. The Barrons, Twoddles, Price McCleskys, Estwoods, Mights and others are related and intermarried.

Mrs. Bates entered actively into the work of the church

and the various civic and patriotic organizations of the city. She was never too busy to respond when called upon to write a paper or to aid in some civic enterprise. She served as Secretary of the State branch of the King's Daughters and was a member of the Executive Committee for many years. She was an active member of the Board of the King's Daughters Hospital at Waycross from its inception until it was closed in 1932.

William Braxton Bates, Mary Lucille Bates and Nell Glen Bates (Mrs. J. E. Penland) are the names of the three children of Mr. and Mrs. Bates. Lucille's successful and beautiful life ended November 17, 1920 and her last resting place is in Lott Cemetery, close beside that of her father who preceded her to the great life Eternal, March 27, 1920.

GEORGE W. CROOM

Captain Croom came to Waycross in 1881 and found only about four hundred people living here.

He built his home in a pine grove, and lived there during his entire citizenship in Waycross. The street on which he lived became known as Brunel Street.

Captain Croom was born in Watha, North Carolina, and was the son of Lott and Martha Frances (Onell) Croom. He married August 19, 1874 Sarah Carlton Puryear, daughter of Dr. W. C. Puryear, who was born in Columbus, Georgia, in 1818.

Captain Croom entered the service of the Atlantic Coast Line Feb. 17, 1881, and was in continuous service until July 1, 1925, when he retired on pension. There were only two entries on his page of the service record, viz., date of employment and date of retirement, no other mark ever appearing thereon, he closed his life with a clean record with his company and with his fellowmen. The following tribute was paid him by the Waycross Journal-Herald.

"Captain Croom was one of the most widely known conductors on the Atlantic Coast Line System, he was in active service of the road for forty-four years.

"When he reached Waycross June 30, 1925, at the termination of his last run from Thomasville, he was greeted at the Union Station here by a large delegation of railway officials and representative citizens who paid tribute to his remarkable career of service and faithful adherence to duty. There was a brass band at the station and the reception given Mr. Croom was a cordial and enthusiastic one."

In connection with Mr. Croom's last run the Press of Valdosta made the following comment:

"There are many people here who will be interested to know that on June 30, Captain George A. Croom, Sr., will make his last trip as a conductor on the Atlantic Coast Line. On that road trip Captain Croom will round out a long and honorable career with that road and its predecessors, forty-four years and four months, during which time he has always maintained the esteem and respect of higher officials and of the people from whom he has collected tickets during that time. He will be greatly missed by the many people along the road who have known him since their childhood days."

As President of the Y. M. C. A. Mr. Croom was a valuable leader and an efficient worker. He was associated with various branches of the Association work and was particularly interested in those activities that tend toward the moral and physical uplift of the young men of this section. Captain and Mrs. Croom's children's names are: Carlton E., Wm. P., George A., and Martha Frances (Mrs. A. R. Pittman). Captain Croom died August 14, 1925.

THOMAS JEFFERSON DARLING

Mr. Darling was born June 25, 1868, in Blackshear, Pierce County, Georgia. His father was Dr. Thomas Jackson Darling, who was born in Richmond County, Georgia, in 1828. He married Miss Bashabee Elizabeth Godbee, who was born in Alabama July 29, 1829; she was a daughter of Samuel Isaac Ivey Godbee, and granddaughter of Samuel Godbee, who married Elizabeth Moore, a daughter of Abner Moore. Samuel Isaac Ivey Godbee moved from Alabama to Georgia in 1830, and spent the remainder of his years in Richmond county, married Miss Elizabeth Mobley, a daughter of James Alexander and Sarah (Wimberly) Mobley. The Wimberlys, the Mobleys, and the Moores were among the prominent early settlers of Richmond county.

Mr. Darling's father, Dr. Darling, graduated from the Augusta Medical College, with the degree of M.D. Beginning the practice of medicine in Blackshear, Dr. Darling continued there until the beginning of the War Between the States, when he offered his services to the Confederacy, and as a surgeon in the army continued in active service until the close of the conflict. Resuming his medical practice in Blackshear he was recognized as one of the most prominent physicians and surgeons of that part of the country. Dr. Darling died June 14, 1873. His wife passed away October 9, 1903, leaving eight children, Rena, Mina, Dora, Will, Emma, Count, Thomas Jefferson, and Edward Lee.

Mr. Darling's grandfather was Joseph Darling who was born in 1784, his predecessors after coming to America, settled in Rhode Island. Mr. Joseph Darling was one of the early settlers of Richmond county, Georgia, owning a large plantation on the Washington road, eight miles from Augusta, where both he and his wife spent their last years, at the close of his life being buried side by side in the family churchyard, near their old home. His death occurred October 4, 1844. His wife's name was Mary Manning Dunevan, who was born March 5, 1783, and died April 14, 1847.

Mr. Thomas Jefferson Darling was married to Miss Laura Le Count, a woman of outstanding intellect, and one who in all of her undertakings has brought to bear rare judgment, discriminating tact, and generous enthusiasm. On both sides of her ancestral line, Mrs. Darling is descended from the earliest settlers of America, the best strain of both Puritan and Cavalier being blended in her lineage. Her grandfather, John Hendrix Le Count, a native of New Rochelle, N. Y., served in the war of 1812, and Mrs. Darling has in her possession his papers, giving him an honorable discharge from the service. Her great-grandfather, John LeCount, was of Huguenot ancestry, and was born at New Rochelle, New York.

Mr. and Mrs. Darling are blessed with four children whose names are: Thomas Jackson, Charles Le Count, Dorothea, and Sunshine Darling.

Politically Mr. Darling is a Democrat; religiously, Mr. and Mrs. Darling are members of the Methodist Episcopal Church.

W. M. (BILL) DENTON

Mr. W. M. (Bill) Denton was born in Bickley, Ware County, Georgia, June, 1842. He lived all his life at the place where he was born, and died there November 17th, 1928. Mr. Denton's mother was a Ward, a descendant of Mother Jones and her Ward boys. There were five of the Denton children, four sons and one daughter. The sons were: Tom, John, Bill and Jim Denton. Mary, the daughter, married Benjamin Minchew. The father and mother of the Denton children died while they were young, and they were reared by Mr. Jack Hargraves, their mother's uncle. Mr. Hargraves was a bachelor, but maintained a good home which was presided over by a negro slave known as "Lottie." The children called her "Black Mammy."

Mr. Denton served in the Confederate Army, and had an honorable record as a Confederate soldier. Early in life he married Miss Mary Hargraves, a daughter of Mr. Abe Hargraves, an English descendant, whose name was made famous in south Georgia by having received seventy thousand dollars in gold from England about 1865. There were no children born of this union.

Mary Hargraves Denton died about 1896. Mr. Denton later married Miss Olive Smith, daughter of Mr. Dan Smith, a pioneer citizen of Ware County. Two sons were born of this union: William Denton, Jr., and Max Denton.

Mr. Denton was regarded as one of the foremost citizens of Ware County. He owned extensive farming properties and pasture lands which was well stocked with cattle, sheep, hogs, etc. He operated a saw mill, cotton gin and a village store. His was the only grist mill operated by water power for a large area. The old mill dam at Bickley, Mr. Denton's home, which controlled the water, was built by Mr. Jack Hargraves more than a hundred years ago. Mr. Denton was very active in educational matters, and was a leading member of the Methodist Church in Ware County for many years. He often boasted that he was a Methodist and a Democrat. Mr. Denton went to the Georgia Legislature from Ware County about 1880, and was a valuable member of that body. Mr. Denton was at his best in his home. He loved to have his friends visit him, and kept an open house to all travelers. He was always glad to be of service to those in need. As a merchant he was worth a great deal to the people of his community. He had an ideal country home and his family life was truly ideal.

Like Zacheus in Bible times, he was a man of small stature, but he had a strong, healthy body and a clear, logical mind. He lived to be eighty-six years of age, and was blind two or three years before his death, but in his blindness, he was cheerful.

Mr. Denton lived a long and useful life. He "fought a good fight and kept the faith." Those who knew him will never forget him—his warm heart, smiling face and happy disposition will linger with many as long as they live.

CHARLES EDWARD DUNN

Charles Dunn, contractor and builder, was born at Columbia, Alabama, on the Chattahoochee River, December 30, 1867. His parents were George W. Dunn, and Elizabeth (Albritton) Dunn. Charles Dunn attended the public schools at Columbia where he obtained a good education and has acquired, since leaving school, a broad knowledge of the current literature of the times. He has a keen conception of the political issues on local, state, and national questions and has often turned the tide of votes in behalf of a friend who was seeking office. He is a Mason, Odd Fellow, and has served as Past Chancellor Commander of the local order of Knights of Pythias, and is also an Elk. He was married to Miss Amy Thomas, Sept. 24, 1899 and the following are the names of their children: Helen, Hilda, Tessie Lee, and Charles E., Jr.

GEORGE MILES ELLISTON

Mr. Elliston was a prominent and successful contractor of Waycross and a capable and intelligent business man. He was closely allied with the public interest of his community, and was ever active in doing his part in putting forward all progressive movements.

He was strong in loyalty to his friends. He never, without a cause, allowed that bond to be dissolved, being true to his friends, he proved himself worthy of many. He married Miss Nancy James, and both have entered into the life eternal. Their children are honorable citizens of Waycross and their names are Adrian, Otto, Walker, Stewart, Lenonora, Hazel, and Nina.

Mr. Elliston was born Jan. 9, 1860 and died April 20, 1905. His wife, Nancy (James) Elliston was born March 16, 1860 and died Feb. 4, 1931.

DR. WILLIAM BARDEN FOLKS

Dr. Folks was born in Jefferson County, Georgia, Nov. 6, 1830. He died in Ware County, in April, 1886. Dr. Folks received a good education in the common schools of his native county, and then devoted himself to the study of medicine, and in 1855 graduated from Oglethorpe Medical College, located in Savannah. After a year's practice in his old home, Dr. Folks established himself in Ware County, his home being located in Waresboro, at that time the county seat of Ware. He later became a citizen of Waycross, where he was not only prominent and popular as a physician, but as a citizen, honored and beloved. For a number of years he was mayor of Waycross, and for a term was senator from, at that time, the Fifth District in the general assembly. During the War he was a surgeon in the Confederate Army, in which service he contracted the disease that ultimately terminated his life. He was the second physician to locate in Ware County. He was also the first editor of Ware. He edited the Waycross Headlight for two years, which was devoted mainly to the upbuilding of the town and county.

Dr. Folks was married to Miss Mary Jefferson Miller, and to them were born four sons, Dr. Frank C., Chauncey M., William B., and Dr. Gustavus P. Folks.

HON. FRANK CLINGMAN FOLKS, M. D.

Hon. Frank Clingman Folks, a prominent and successful physician of Waycross, Georgia, not only gained marked prestige in his profession, but was known as a progressive and public-spirited citizen throughout his long and useful life. He was a man of the highest principles of honor. A native of Jefferson County, Georgia, he was born on a farm that is now included within the corporate limits of the city of Wadley. His father, Hon. William Brandon Folks, M.D., was born in 1830 at the same place while his grandfather, Amos Folks, was a native of North Carolina. His paternal great-grandparents were of English birth, or of English ancestry. After living for many years in North Carolina they migrated to Georgia, making the removal with private conveyances bringing with them their household goods, stock and slaves. Buying land in Jefferson County he improved a homestead and there both he and his faithful helpmeet spent their remaining days.

A young boy when his parents moved to Georgia, Amos Folks assisted his father to some extent in the pioneer labor of improving the farm, and during his active career was a successful planter. He died while yet in manhood's prime, in Jefferson County. His wife, whose maiden name was Celia Lofly, was a life-long resident of that county. Three sons and one daughter were born of their marriage, as follows: Green, the oldest son, enlisted during the Civil War in the Confederate Army, and died while in service, in Virginia; Solomon died in early manhood; William Brandon, father of Frank C. Folks, M.D., and Catherine, who married Dr. Seaborn Bell, of Emanuel County.

Acquiring his literary education in the schools of his native County, Dr. William Brandon Folks began the study of medicine under Dr. William Hauser, of Jefferson County, and was graduated from the Savannah Medical College with the class of 1855. Practicing but a short time in Jefferson and Washington Counties, he located, in 1856, in Waresboro, then the County seat of Ware County. At that early date neither railroad, telephone or telegraph lines spanned the country. Ware County, and all of the nearby counties, being then in their pristine wilderness. As the population grew his practice increased. His visits, which extended many miles in either direction, were made on horseback, oftentimes the trails which he followed having been those made by the Indians. At the outbreak of the Civil War he offered his services to the Confederacy, and was made Surgeon of the Twenty-sixth Georgia Volunteer Infantry. He went with his regiment to Virginia, joining the Army of the Potomac. He continued with his regiment until the close of the conflict, when he resumed his practice in Waresboro. He subsequently settled in Yankee Town, afterward in Tebeauville, where, in addition to his practice he engaged in mercantile business. Removing from there to Whigham, Decatur County, he was station agent on the Atlantic and Gulf Railroad for two years, and during the next two years practiced medicine at Valdosta, Georgia, after which he lived for a while in Savannah.

When Waycross was first started, Dr. W. B. Folks was the first physician to locate in the new town, and built the fourth house erected within its limits. Here he was actively and prosperously engaged in the practice of his profession until about two years prior to his death, which occurred in 1886. Energetic and public-spirited, he became exceedingly influential in public affairs, and served two terms as Mayor of the city, and represented the Fifth District, which included Ware, Clinch and Coffee Counties, in the State Senate, to which he was elected in 1878.

Dr. William B. Folks married Miss Mary Jefferson Miller, who was born in 1830, in Jefferson County Georgia. Her parents were life-long residents of Jefferson County. Her grandfather, Thomas McWatty, immigrated from Scotland to America, settling in Jefferson County, Georgia, in pioneer days. She survived her husband many years, passing away in 1906. Five children blessed their union as follows: Rosa, who died at the age of eighteen years; Frank Clingman, the special subject of this brief sketch; Chauncey M.; Augustus P.; and William B., Jr. The father was a staunch Democrat in politics and both he and his wife were members of the Methodist Episcopal Church.

After completing the course of study in the public schools of Ware County, Frank Clingman Folks read medicine with his father, and later with Dr. William Duncan, of Savannah. Matriculating at the Savannah College he was graduated there with the class of 1876, receiving the degree of M.D. Immediately entering upon private practice of his profession, Dr. Folks was for four years located at Homerville, Clinch County, where he made rapid progress along the pathway of success. In 1880 he returned to Waycross, where he continued in his field of labor until his death, having won a noteworthy position in the front rank of the medical fraternity of Ware County.

Dr. Folks took quite an active part in public affairs at all times. In addition to serving two terms as Mayor of Waycross, he represented the Fifth District in the State Senate, to which he was elected in the fall of 1888, just ten years after the election of his father to the same position from the same district.

It was while he was a member of the Georgia Senate that Dr. Folks introduced and secured passage of a bill to sell the State-owned and unsurveyed Okefinokee Swamp. This historical swamp, up to that time, was in its primeval state. No civilized person had crossed it or penetrated far into its depths. This was supposed to be the largest, densest and most difficult swamp in America and surveyors had abandoned attempt to survey it. Dr. Folks' foreseeing more, eventuated in the thriving and successful Hebardville development near Waycross, where the pine and cypress timber was converted into lumber and distributed over the whole civilized world. The constructive and foreseeing acumen in economic and development ideas was not the greatest of his service to his fellowmen. In the chosen field of medicine and surgery his talents were manifest, so much so that in his advanced treatment of typhoid, pneumonia, malarial and other fevers he was called upon and used not only by the local and surrounding counties, but the Health and State authorities of adjoining States sought his council in handling difficult situations and in formulating treatments for newly appearing diseases. This was notably true in the case of LaGrippe.

He was local surgeon and physician in charge of the handling of that most disastrous railroad wreck known as "Hurricane Creek" wreck in which twenty-two were killed and nearly one hundred injured. He was local surgeon for the A. B. & C. Railroad and from his residence in Waycross to the time of his death was connected with the medical department of the Atlantic Coast Line

Railroad Company and its predecessor, being called by this railroad to other points for expert consultation.

Fraternally, Dr. Folks was a member of the Ancient Free and Accepted Order of Masons and The Independent Order of Odd Fellows. Since his death The Frank C. Folks Lodge No. 192 F. & A. M. has been organized as a memorial to this loyal and beloved member of the Masonic Order. Religiously both the Doctor and his wife were valued members of the Methodist Episcopal Church, South.

In honor of Dr. Folks the Tree and Park Commission of Waycross some time before his death changed the name of one of its parks to "Folks Park" and ordered its beautification.

In 1877 Dr. Folks was united in marriage with Emma A. Morgan, who was born in Clinch County, Georgia, a daughter of Jonathan L. and Susan (Hargraves) Morgan, who were born in Georgia. Mr. Morgan having been of Welsh lineage and Mrs. Morgan of English ancestry. Eight children were born to Dr. and Mrs. Folks, namely, Ada, who died in infancy, Rosa, Mabel, Frankie, William Morgan, Fleming, Robert and Louise. Rosa married first George Bell, who died in early life leaving one child, Sarah Bell. She married her second husband, Peter K. Groff, of Akron, Ohio, and they have two children, Phillip Folks Groff and Rose Groff. Mabel, who married Charles E. Newton, had two children, Frances and Charles. She has since died. Frankie, who married Walter Rivers, died March 1st, 1912. William Morgan Folks, the doctor's oldest son, is a graduate of the Atlanta College of Physicians and Surgeons, and is engaged in the practice of his profession in Waycross. He is an outstanding member of his profession throughout the State, is a member of the American College of Surgeons, the Southern Medical Association, the American Medical Association, and various organizations throughout the South. He was selected by President Coolidge for appointment as a member of the Society formed for perpetuation of the memory of the celebrated Dr. Gorgas. His son's success in his chosen profession was a source of great joy to Dr. Folks during the last years of his life. Dr. William Morgan Folks was married December 6th, 1926, to Miss Antoinette Morris, of Uvalda, Ga. Fleming was graduated from the Atlanta School of Pharmacy. Robert, who was married on November 20th, 1926, to Miss Lucia Belle Sheppard of Waycross, resides in Waycross, as does Louise, the youngest daughter.

Dr. Folks' health was bad for a number of years prior to his death, which occurred on August 5th, 1926. His beloved wife preceded him just a few weeks, having died on June 5th, 1926.

WILKINS FULWOOD

Mr. Fulwood was the grandfather of Mr. Jack J. Murray of Waycross. He came from North Carolina to Appling County in 1840. He was an Englishman and was born in 1773. Mr. Fulwood remained only a few months in Appling, moving to Ware to be near his brother, James Fulwood, who held many political offices of trust in this county. He settled here the first year (1824) that the county was organized.

Mr. Wilkins Fulwood settled about eight miles above Waresboro between the lands where Fairfax and Millwood are now located. In those primitive days, household commodities were bought exclusively from trading posts, sometimes these trading places were fifty or sixty miles away from a settlement, and the journey was very much dreaded by the men for fear of an encounter with the predatory bands of Seminole Indians who often were roving through the forests of this section.

Mr. Fulwood and Mr. Abe Smith (his neighbor) being in need of supplies undertook the trip to Suwanee Shoulds where the nearest trading post was located and their only resource for transportation depended on both men riding one horse. Mr. Fulwood had on a previous visit to the trading post, bought a bolt of cloth and had it on his shoulder taking it to the place where his horse was tied, and on reaching there, was hailed by an Indian who shot at him, and instead of the shot reaching him it passed through the bolt of cloth. Mr. Fulwood laid down his bundle and chased the would-be murderer and stabbed him through the heart. The story of Indian animosity is always the same and the band of Indians, brooded in secret over the death of one of their tribe and nourished the deadly revenge that they contemplated against Wilkins Fulwood. When Mr. Fulwood and Abe Smith were on their journey homeward from the trading post, they had gone only a few miles when an Indian rose from an undergrowth by the side of the path and shot Mr. Fulwood through a vital part of his body. The murderous foe fled and Mr. Smith was left in the wilderness alone with his dying friend. It was already late in the day. The sun had sunk down and twilight was gradually closing in when Mr. Smith put Mr. Fulwood on the horse and carried him to a secluded place close by the road. Here he used his shot bag for a pillow for Mr. Fulwood and made him as comfortable as lay in his power.

Mr. Fulwood cried out for water, "Drink, give me drink." He burned with a mad thirst of fever, mere physical thirst expelled all horrors of his condition, and water was the sole object of his thoughts. Mr. Smith took from the foot of the dying man his shoe and retraced his journey to a creek, where he filled the shoe with water, but when he reached Mr. Fulwood he was no longer restless, but lay quiet and seemed out of pain. Mr. Smith left him to seek help from a squad of soldiers stationed at Stampede in Ware County. It took him thirty hours to make the trip to the camp, When Captain George Newburn and his soldiers who occupied the camp at Stampede reached the place where Mr. Fulwood lay, they found his faithful dog sitting by the dead body of his master, and he would allow no one to go near him, but finally Mr. Hunter (a friend of Mr. Fulwood's) came near and called the dog and he ceased his vicious barking at the soldiers, recognizing Mr. Hunter as one of the friends of his master. This murdered pioneer is buried at Fulwood Cemetery near Friendship Church.

"Passing away," is the destiny of the redmen, their council fires have long since gone out, they vanished before the march of the white settlers, a few, if any, now live on Georgia soil.

THOMAS FULWOOD, SR.

Thomas Fulwood, Sr., died in Wayne County in 1824, at a very old age, and was very probably a soldier of the Revolution. We do not know anything about his antecedents, and the Fulwoods are not so numerous in this section today so that data has been hard to obtain.

His will was dated Nov. 7, 1822, and was probated in Wayne County, July 5, 1824. In it, he left his personal property to his wife name Laana Fulwood and his daughter, Anna. A certain negro slave was to be leased out at five dollars and the proceeds divided equally between his children; and he directed that the lot of land he lived on, lot 250, was to be sold at public outcry. His wife, Jesse Moody and Samuel Knight were named as executors of the will.

The children were as follows:

1. Wilkins, born 1773. He was for many years coroner of Ware County and was living in 1850 with George Hunter in Clinch County. We presume Hunter married his daughter.

2. Andrew Fulwood. Though Andrew is mentioned in the will dated Nov. 1822, we find in Irwin County where Mary Fullwood was appointed administratrix of Andrew's estate on Sept. 18, 1822 and that the value of the estate was $3,000. We further find where on Jan. 6, 1823, Abel Chester qualified in Irwin County as guardian for David and Rachie Fulwood, orphans of Andrew, deceased. Whether this is the same Andrew mentioned in the will, we do not know but believe it is.

3. James, born 1787, the third son was a prominent old citizen of Ware County for fifty years, and died about 1875. He and his wife Mary, had no children. James Fulwood's first office was that of justice of peace of the 54th district in Montgomery county in 1812. He migrated to the new County of Ware and was justice of peace in the 451 district (now the Waresboro district) in 1825-26. After that he held various offices of clerk, senator, representative, Justice of Inferior Court and other offices. He granted a great many lots of land in the 6th, 7th, 8th, and 9th districts of Ware County. These districts are now in various counties in this section, Bacon, Coffee, Atkinson, Ware, Clinch, Pierce and probably other counties, so that his name is familiar to people who have occasion to read the records.

4. Thomas Fulwood, Jr., the fourth son, was married in Wayne County, to Mary Harrigan, Sept. 4, 1825. He and his wife removed to Ware County and he lost his life in the warfare against the Indians in 1837. Reference to his death can be found on page 13 of the "History of Clinch County."

5. Anna was apparently the youngest daughter, and was married to Wm. P. Dennison in Wayne County, Aug. 12, 1824. They moved to Ware County also where he became a captain of the militia in the 586th district in 1827 to 1830, and in the 719th district from 1830 to 1835. He was Justice of Peace of the 586th district in 1826. The 586th district was cut off into Clinch in 1850, and in 1920 into Lanier County, while as above stated the 719th district after being cut off into Clinch became a part of Echols County when it was created.

6. There were three other daughters but we can only refer to them by their married names as we do not know anything further about them: They were Mrs. Beady Henson, Mrs. Ester Fittes and Mrs. Catherine Hargraves. They were mentioned in the will as daughters.

JOHN W. GREER

There are few better known men in Georgia than John W. Greer. His wonderful ability as an organizer, and his special ability as an executive officer have put him forward in many leading roles of public work.

He was born in Dawson, Terrell County, Georgia, June 15, 1868, and attended the public schools for a while. Later he worked for his father until he was 21, and then went to Emory College at Oxford. After the first year he paid his own way, teaching school each summer until he graduated at the age of 26 years.

He taught school in Bibb County one year after graduation, edited Douglas Breeze one year, traveled for Macon Telegraph one year, read proof and was reporter on same one year, came to Waycross and with Mr. Dan Sweat organized the Waycross Journal. After two years he bought Mr. Sweat's interests; later sold an interest to Mr. L. V. Williams. After four years he sold to Mr. Williams and went with Mr. George W. Deen in real estate.

In 1908 Mr. Greer married Miss Edna Roberts of Hawkinsville, went to Fitzgerald as Secretary Chamber of Commerce, but soon organized and began publication of Fitzgerald News. Later organized and began publication of Wiregrass Magazine. He moved same to Tifton and along with this publication, handled Capt. H. H. Tift's large land interests.

After two years Mr. Greer went to Moultrie as Secretary of Chamber of Commerce. During two years in that work he promoted and built the Moultrie Packing Plant —first packing plant in Southeast.

With Mr. C. L. Brooks he organized Brooks Engineering Co. and built seventeen other meat packing plants in the Southeast, one in New York State, one in Virginia and one in Cuba. These plants gave the South its first market for live stock, which, in turn, created markets for other food crops in the South, which was the first break and relief from cotton planting of the Southern farmer since the War Between The States. The merchants and bankers talked "diversification" to the farmers for thirty years, but these packing plants unchained the Southern farmer from the all-cotton system overnight.

The World War came on and Mr. Greer was chosen to lead the war work in his county, which he did, raising all the funds required of Colquitt County; offered to go over seas and was selected to do Y. M. C. A. work, being over age for regular duty. Armistice came just before he started over seas.

After the war, before leaving Moultrie, Mr. Greer wrote "Looking Ahead, A Business Romance with a County Plan", a little book that has circulated over the South extensively and was the first and original of all the Five Year Plans in America, and, beyond a doubt, the origin of Russia's Five Year Plan.

For two years after the war he was Executive Secretary of the Municipal League of Georgia, making a fight for the development of the water power of Georgia.

For the next two years Mr. Greer was Secretary of Chamber of Commerce of Cordele, where he promoted and started the engineering on Crisp County's great hydroelectric plant.

While in Waycross he assisted in the promotion of the Car Factory, which made a profit equal to its capital stock the first ten months, bought old Georgia Car Factory of Savannah, was soon afterward burned. While Editor of the Waycross Journal he assisted in settling the big strike on the A. B. & A. Railroad. Also made a hard fight against peonage, and gave definite assistance to Judge Speer in putting an end to that kind of slavery in Georgia.

Mr. Greer is no doubt the most highly educated citizen in Lakeland and Lanier County, and well does he fill the bill of "a gentleman and scholar" and is so recognized by the people of his native state.

THE GOODRICH FAMILY

Eben B. Goodrich was born in Boston, Mass., and was reared and educated there. He was married in early life to the intelligent and accomplished home keeper, Elizabeth Burnett whose birth took place in Liverpool, England in 1828.

She came with her parents to Boston when a girl of sixteen, there she met Eben Goodrich and was

MR. WALTER GOODRICH

married to him when quite young.

During the War Between the States, they moved to Augusta, Georgia and made their home. During the reconstruction days, they removed to Savannah. Their family consisted of Mr. and Mrs. Goodrich and two children who were Hariett and Walter Goodrich.

MRS. WALTER GOODRICH

Among the family connection was Samuel G. Goodrich, American author who wrote under the name of Peter Parley.

Other relatives of this family were Daniel Goodrich (Mass.) Captain of Cady's Battalion, who served in the Revolutionary War and William Goodrich (Mass.) Captain in the Lexington Alarm, 1775.

The Goodrich Family tree shows that this family came to America from England in the sixteenth century and their coat of arms reveal that they belong to the nobility.

Walter Goodrich, when quite a young man, entered the Atlantic and Gulf Railroad service and was employed as a locomotive engineer at the time that he was transferred to Waycross. He worked for the railroad through the entire changes that took place during intervening years, from the Atlantic and Gulf to the Plant System and later the Atlantic Coast Line.

In 1898 Walter Goodrich and Miss Florence E. Archer of Oliver, Georgia, were married. Florence E. Archer was the daughter of David Isaiah and Sarah Elizabeth Archer. David Archer was a gallant soldier in the War Between the States and the Revolutionary records show that Mrs. Archer's (his wife) great grandfather fought in the Army.

Mr. and Mrs. Goodrich were blessed with three children: Irene Florence (married Charles Ralph Wolf), Walter B. (died in childhood), and Ellen Elizabeth (married William G. Townsend.)

Mr. and Mrs. Goodrich's grandchildren are Mary Wolf and Ralph Wolf.

Mr. and Mrs. Goodrich are members of the Baptist Church and as long as Mr. Goodrich lived he served as a deacon of the First Baptist Church and was a loyal Mason.

Walter Goodrich died August 2, 1924, and his body rests in Oakland Cemetery.

Mr. and Mrs. Eben Goodrich, along with other early citizens of Waycross, are interred in Lotts Cemetery.

THE HARGREAVES FAMILY OF WARE AND COFFEE COUNTIES

Through all of the vicissitudes of time and changes for more than a thousand years ago the Hargreaves of Colne in the County of Lancaster were recognized among the most prominent and distinguished families of the British Isles. At the time of the conquest of William 1st, Duke of Normandy in the year of 1052, the Hargreaves of England were prominent in the affairs of that period and their name is still to be found in the landed property of Normandy.

The Hargreaves of Georgia descended from Christopher Hargreaves of Colne in the County of Lancaster, England. While temporarily living in Maryland, he met the charming and brilliant widow of James Ward and after a romantic courtship they were married. Priscilla Gibbs Ward's former husband died, leaving her with three sons, James Preston Ward, Joab Ward, and Abram Ward. Priscilla Gibbs belonged to one of the best families of Maryland, her kins-man of Georgia was William Gibbs McAdoo, Sr., who was named for her father, Abram Gibbs.

Christopher Hargreaves was not only happy—having lovely Priscilla to grace his home but accepted with a generous heart the three Ward boys also. However, these boys were not dependent on his patrimony, for they had their own inheritance from their father's estate.

Mr. and Mrs. Hargreaves left Maryland and made their home in South Carolina, where Sept. 23, 1794 their eldest son, Abraham, was born, their next children were twins, John, and Tom Hargreaves. The Hargreaves were living happily in the home of their adoption with no thought of an approaching cataclysm but changes often come with a destructive hand, and this family passed through a real Gethsemane.

Letters came to Mr. Hargreaves from England that for important business reasons, his presence was desired in Colne. Mrs. Hargreaves was obdurate and refused in no uncertain terms to cross the water with her husband, but Mr. Hargreaves (man-like) went forward in a determined way making plans to take this important business trip to England. Never doubting for a moment that his wife and children would not accompany him.

When his plans were fully matured and he was ready to take his wife and children to Charleston, S. C. and take passage to England, much to his surprise and chagrin, Mrs. Hargreaves had made up her mind fully not to accompany him on his ocean voyage. As a last resort he insisted that she let him take his three boys with him for a visit to his old home. This she refused to do. Mr. Hargreaves, being fully determined to return to England, and if possible, to take his children with him, sought legal advice as to how he might get possession of the children and take them with him. So he left on a trip to Charleston for the purpose of converting his American currency into that of English coin.

After Mr. Hargreaves' departure for Charleston, Mrs. Hargreaves, knowing that many people seeking cheap lands in southern Georgia, were passing daily through her home town in South Carolina, came to a definite conclusion that she could take her six boys and fall in line with the southbound travelers and find obscurity in the pioneer lands of South Georgia. In changing her residence, Mrs. Hargreaves also changed her name to Mrs. Jones, but never did she falter in her determination to remain in America. She proved herself to be a woman who could not be "convinced against her will".

There are many descendants of the Hargreaves family living in Ware and Coffee Counties and for their information the following is copied from the diary of the lawyer, Mr. James Haworth of Lancaster, England, who had the Hargreaves estate in charge.

"Mar. 18th & 19th, 1816—Journey to Colne to see Mr. Christopher Hargreaves on his arrival from America, respecting the claims of his children under the will of the Testator, Mr. Abraham Hargreaves, his late brother, when an affidavit of Mr. Christopher Hargreaves, marriage, the birth of his children, etc., was prepared on these two days.

"Aug. 30th—Engaged the services of Mr. Owens of Savannah, Ga. to procure the necessary evidence, of papers, and to get in communication with the young men, and advance them 300 pounds in case they stand in need of assistance in money.

"Jan. 1817.—Rec'd letter from Mr. Owens of Sav. informing us that he has not yet heard of Christopher Hargreaves' sons.

"Feb.—Advertisement was published in the American newspapers for information of the young sons of Christopher Hargreaves.

"Jan. 1818.—Mr. Owens of Sav. informs us that he has not yet heard of the young men.

"Feb.—A letter from Mr. Owens informing me that he has heard of the Hargreaves heirs, but not yet seen them.

"Mar.—Mr. Owens informs me that he has seen the eldest son, Abraham Hargreaves, but all the young men are unwilling to come to England.

"May.—Mr. Owens writes that Mrs. Hargreaves is determined not to come ever, and she does not wish her sons to come.

"May 15th, 1818.—Rec'd letter from Mr. Owens informing me that the young men intend to leave America for this country about the middle of June.

"July 26th, 1818.—Mr. Owens of Savannah, Ga., America, has arrived in England accompanied by the eldest son, Abraham Hargreaves."

Abraham Hargreaves, eldest son of Christopher Hargreaves and Priscilla Gibbs Ward Hargreaves, joined his father in England the 26th of July, 1818 for the purpose of establishing his claim to the estate, inherited under the will made in 1799 by his Uncle Abraham Hargreaves for whom he was named. Young Abraham was with his father

(Christopher Hargreaves) when he died May 17, 1820, at his old estate in Colne, England. He was detained in the settling up of his father's business until 1823 when he returned to his home in Georgia. In 1824 Abraham Hargreaves married Miss Rhoda Carver, a daughter of Samson Carver. They had four boys, John, Abraham, Christopher, and Sydney. They also had six girls, Mary, Teresa, Lennie, Lucinda, Susan, Feraby. Mary married William M. Denton; Feraby married Major John N. Spence of Ware County, Lennie married George Moody; Lucinda married Thomas Sweat of Ware County; Susan married Jonathan L. Morgan; Teresa married Captain Cuyler W. Hilliard of Ware County.

During the War Between the States, Mr. Abraham Hargreaves' two sons and his sons-in-law were in the War. In 1864 he was notified that the remainder of his inheritance in England was awaiting instructions from him. War had put the South in a chaotic state, and Mr. Hargreaves made no special effort to obtain the rest of the inheritance of his father and Uncle's property until in 1866 when he appointed his son-in-law (Captain Cuyler W. Hilliard) and his son, Abraham Hargreaves, Jr., to go to England to complete the winding up of the Hargreaves inheritance. When these men returned from England they brought to Mr. Abraham, Sr., $70,000.00 in gold. Abraham Hargreaves liberally divided his fortune with his relatives. His will is recorded in the Ware County Court House and shows that he was a man of wealth when he died. He passed from earth April 24, 1872, and is buried at a spot he selected on his old plantation home in Coffee County in a grove of beautiful trees.

Priscilla Ward Hargreaves (Mother Jones) died about 1846. This wonderful Georgia woman sleeps not far from the home where she first settled after coming to this section, and is acknowledged in southern Georgia as one of the most notable, brave, and intrepid pioneer women.

Christopher Hargreaves' Will, Recorded in England

"I, Christopher Hargreaves, late of North America but now of Ing., near Colne, in the county of Lancaster, old England, do make, publish, and declare, this my last Will and Testament, in manner and form following. That is to say, after the payment of my debts, burial expenses, and charges of the probate hereof, with all the expenses incident to the execution hereof, I give and bequeath, all the residue and remainder of my personal estate of what kind or nature whatsoever and wheresoever and of which I have the power of disposal, unto my sons Abraham, John, and Thomas, by my wife, Priscilla, and all born in America, to be equally divided amongst them, and I appoint my said son Abraham and Edmund Cookshut, the younger of Ballgrase in the township of Colne, in the said County of Lancaster, gentleman, Executors of this my will,—hereby revoking all former wills, by me made. In witness whereof I have hereunto set my hand and seal, the ninth day of the tenth month, called October, in the year of our Lord, one thousand eight hundred and nineteen.

          Christopher Hargreaves

Signed, sealed, published and declared by the said Testator as, and for his last will and testament in the presence of
  Joseph Parkinson, D.D.
  James Haworth."

HARDY BROTHERS

The members who composed this firm were brothers, J. W. S. and C. S. Hardy. There are few families living in Waycross who were not at some time in their lives patrons of this popular firm.

Each of these men are intelligent and enterprising and have held high rank among the merchants of Waycross, and have long been identified with the best interests of the community. Mr. J. W. S. Hardy has one of the most up-to-date grocery stores in Waycross, while his brother, Mr. Clem S. Hardy has retired from the mercantile business.

The parents of these gentlemen were John L. and Nannie (nee. Becton) Hardy were natives of Stantonburg, Wilson, North Carolina. Mr. and Mrs. Hardy later removed to Mosley Hall, Lenoir, North Carolina where John and Clem were born.

The Hardy brothers came to Waycross in 1889, and in 1893 they started a small grocery in that portion of Waycross known as "Old Waycross" with a cash capital of less than a hundred dollars.

Mr. J. W. S. and C. S. Hardy are members of the Methodist Episcopal Church and J. W. S. Hardy is a K. P. and a member of the local lodge of Odd Fellows.

J. W. S. Hardy married Miss Hollon U. Scott, of La Grange, Lenoir County, North Carolina, and Rose and Alma are the children of that union. His first wife died in August, 1905 and in June, 1906, he married Mrs. Fannie E. McVeigh, who was a widow, and whose husband was clerk of the Superior Court here for a long time.

C. S. Hardy married Miss Lida Kennedy, of LaGrange, North Carolina. They have six children, Letha, Harold, Ruth, Glenn, C. S., Jr., and Lucy.

CAPTAIN CUYLER W. HILLIARD

One of the pioneers of Ware County and one of the founders of Waycross was the intelligent and far-seeing Captain Cuyler Hilliard. He assisted materially in the development of the natural resources of this locality, when almost the entire county was a wilderness. He was identified with the public as well as the industrial and civic affairs of this community and was one of the safe and reliable business men whose name deserved a permanent record in the history of the county of his nativity.

Captain Hilliard, like other pioneers, acquired a large

body of land, some of which had on it forests of pine trees. These trees surpassed in beauty, quality, and symmetry any of their kind in southern Georgia and until cut, thirty years ago, for saw mill purposes, this tract of land of slash pine, was a real "show place" to many who passed this way.

When war was declared between the states Cuyler Hilliard was one of the first to enlist for services. His first official services was as First Lieutenant, and when the War ended he was serving as Captain of Company "K", 26th Georgia Infantry. He led his company in many hard-fought battles of the Confederate War.

After peace was declared, Captain Hilliard returned to Ware where, in 1871, he, Dr. Daniel Lott, Dr. Benjamin Williams and Mr. Bailey bought the land where Waycross is now located and plans were made by these four men for the building up of a town in this forest of southern Georgia; how well they succeeded, Waycross speaks for itself.

Captain Hilliard was born November 25, 1825, died April 12, 1903. He married Theresa Hargreaves, the daughter of Mr. Abraham Hargreaves, who descended from John Hargreaves, Hair's House, Colne, Lancaster, England. From the estate of his father he inherited $70,000, and it was his son-in-law, Captain Cuyler Hilliard, who made two trips to England in the interest of the Hargreaves legacy. Captain Hilliard finally secured the $70,000 in gold left to Abraham Hargreaves, and in a most careful way turned over to Mr. Hargreaves a bag of gold. This $70,000 reached Mr. Hargreaves during the troubled days of 1865, and many homes of his relatives were brightened by substantial gifts from him.

Captain and Mrs. Hilliard are buried at Kettle Creek Cemetery.

GENERAL THOMAS HILLIARD

Thomas Hilliard was born in what is now Ware County (formerly a part of Appling), June 5th, 1805. In 1828 he was made Clerk of the Superior Court of this County. He served as Representative from Ware County from 1828 to 1830 and served as one of the first Justices of the Inferior Court in 1837. He was again elected as Representative to the Legislature in 1840 and re-elected to the same office in 1844 and again in 1846. He also served as Ordinary of the County from 1842 to 1845.

Thomas Hilliard was Commissioned Major and assigned to the 158th Battalion December 23rd, 1829, on May 21st, 1838 he was advanced to the rank of Colonel, assigned to the 76th Regiment and November 13th, 1836 was commissioned Brigadier General and commanded the 2nd Brigade.

General Hilliard's first wife was Barbara Miller, who was born in Bullock County and was the daughter of William Miller and Amy (Barker) Miller. Her father was born in North Carolina on the 8th day of March, 1759, dying in Ware County the 27th of November, 1837. Amy Barker Miller was born ____, died 1831. She and William Miller were married in 1785. William Miller drew 490 acres of land in the Kettle Creek settlement for his services in the Revolutionary War, and he came with his family to this settlement in Ware County during the year of 1837.

General Thomas Hilliard also drew 490 acres of land in the Cherokee Land Lottery for his services in the Indian Wars. This 490 acres of land was in the Kettle Creek settlement.

Barbara Hilliard died when quite a young woman and during her illness and subsequent death an instance of loyalty and affection was displayed by her servant, who had been her house maid since she was a young girl. The mistress entertained a deep affection for the little slave girl and after Mrs. Hilliard's death the maid, grief-stricken, soon commenced to show signs of illness and developed typhoid fever, which so often in those primitive days proved fatal. The girl from the early stages of her sickness was considered critically ill, and every time that her master, General Hilliard, entered her room she implored him to promise her that he would allow her body to be buried at the feet of "Miss Barbara", when she died. He told her that the negroes and white people were never buried in the same church yard, but no amount of explanation on the subject would satisfy her. It was apparent that the girl could not get well, and it seemed that she could not even die unless her mind was relieved with the promise that she should sleep near her beloved mistress. Finally, Mr. John Cason, one of General Hilliard's friends, and the one who told this story to Mr. Manning Thigpen, advised General Hilliard to comply with the girl's request by burying her where she wished, and in doing so he felt sure there would be no objection in allowing the faithful servant to find a resting place in the Kettle Creek Cemetery. General Hilliard, feeling that it would be a comfort to the girl to know that her request had been granted, told her if he were living when she died he would see that she should be buried in the place she desired. A radiant smile came into the face of the dying girl and an unalloyed peace seemed to settle in her soul. Almost immediately she sank into a sleep that lasted about two hours, when her spirit entered into rest Eternal. True to his promise, General Hilliard, had the faithful little maid interred by his wife in Kettle Creek Cemetery.

General Hilliard was married a second time to Miss Sarah N. E. Wade of Waresboro, who was born November 10, 1840, and was married 1860, and General and Mrs. Hilliard had two children, Dixie (deceased) and Thomas. General Hilliard died March 26, 1866.

SIMON WOOD HITCH

Mr Hitch was a lawyer by profession and for years was successfully engaged in the practice of law in Waycross. He was a son of Sylvanus Hitch, who was born in Clinton, Jones County, Georgia, and was descended from English ancestry. Sylvanus Hitch was born in New Bedford, Massachusetts, and was left an orphan in childhood, was brought up in the home of his grandparents.

While yet a lad he located at Clinton, in Jones County, Georgia, which was then, although without railroad facilities of any kind, a place of considerable commercial importance, being at that time a large cotton market. He opened a merchant tailor's establishment, and carried on this business until 1855, when he migrated to South Georgia, and purchased a tract of land, known as Coleraine. This land is quite historic and borders on the St. Marys River in Camden (now Charlton County). He remained there ten years, removing to Clinch County, Georgia, and retired from active business, living there until his death, which occurred in 1880, he being seventy-two years of age at that time.

Sylvanus Hitch married Ann A. Nichols, who died in 1898, leaving six children, whose names were: Sylvanus, Simon Wood, Margaret Ann, Charles, Radford, and Nanie. Mrs. Hitch's father, Simon Wood Nichols, was born in South Carolina, coming from there to Savannah in early manhood; he was for several years in general mercantile business in that city. He later bought extensive tracts of lands in Appling, Ware, and Clinch Counties, settling at Dupont in Clinch County, where he died when quite an aged man. Mr. Nichols married Margaret Waver, who was born on one of the West India Islands of French parents. She had one brother, John J. Waver. During one of the insurrections in the West Indies, she was carried by her parents to Savannah where she was brought up and educated. She survived her husband a few years.

Simon Wood Hitch, was educated in Professor Landrum's school in Oglethorpe County, and later taught school in Clinch County. Desirous of entering upon a professional career, he subsequently studied law with his uncle, John C. Nichols, and after his admission to the bar at the age of eighteen, located first in Clinch County, and later opened an office in Blackshear, Pierce County, where he practiced law for ten years. In 1887 he settled in Waycross and in the practice of his profession, he achieved well-merited success, his legal patronage being an extensive and remunerative one. Mr. Hitch was a member of the Democratic party, and served in various official positions. He was appointed by Governor Bullock a member of the election board at the time of the three-day election. Just following his admission to the bar he was appointed as solicitor-general of the Brunswick judicial district, and served in that capacity for ten consecutive years. He rendered appreciative service as a member of the Waycross Board of Education, having been a member when the present system of graded schools was adopted, and when the present school buildings were erected.

Mr. Hitch was married in Macon, Georgia, to Miss Frances Myers, who was born in Augusta, Georgia. Her father, Dr. Edward Myers, was born in Orange County, New York, and was the son of Selim and Mary (Howell) Myers. Becoming a minister in the Methodist Episcopal Church, he was for awhile a member of the Florida Conference, and also preached in different parts of Georgia, and South Carolina. He served for a short while as one of the professors of the Wesleyan Female Seminary in Macon, later serving as president of that college, an office of which he was the incumbent at the time of Miss "Fannie" Myers' marriage to Mr. Hitch, which took place in the drawing room of the institution.

Giving up that position, Dr. Myers became pastor of the Trinity Episcopal Church in Savannah, Georgia When in 1876, yellow fever became epidemic in Savannah, he was at Cape May, attending a joint meeting of the Methodist Episcopal Church, South, looking to a national union. Returning to the stricken city to care for his flock, he was himself taken ill with the disease, and lived but a short time, having given up his own life in his attempt to save others. His wife was Mary Mackie, born of Scotch ancestry, and her native home was Augusta.

Mr. and Mrs. Hitch had four children and their names are: Mary, (Mrs. E. P. Peabody), Frank, who lived but twenty-two years, James, a missionary of the Methodist Episcopal Church, South, to Korea; he married Miss Reubee Lillie; Edward S., married Miss Louise Daniel. The wife and mother departed this life on November 6, 1912, after having reared to honorable manhood and womanhood her four children. In the foreign missionary work of the Methodist Church, South, she was most active, holding at the time of her death the position of conference secretary of the foreign department of the South Georgia Conference Missionary Society. Mrs. Hitch inherited her father's fine business ability and a deep religious experience made her a notable character, as a wife, mother, and a leader in all church work.

WARREN LEE HINSON

Warren Lee Hinson was born at Hazlehurst and came to Waycross in 1894 to attend high school, and after completing school here attended the University of Kentucky, returning to Waycross in 1899, accepting position with the Excelsior Medicine Co., wholesale druggist, and was, within a few months made Secretary and Treasurer. After the Jacksonville fire, the Excelsior Medicine Co. moved to Jacksonville, Florida, and a firm was organized here known as The Seals Drug Co., wholesale and manufacturing druggist and he was Secretary-Treasurer of this Company until he went into the furniture business operating the Waycross Furniture Co. for 18 years, and in 1899 (Sept. 1st) he also opened a modern undertaking establishment which is still in operation.

W. L. HINSON

In 1915 Mr. Hinson opened an automobile business which he operated for 15 years—closing it out to give his entire attention to the undertaking business. In 1928 he built one of the most modern undertaking establishments in the state. Mr. Hinson claims the distinction of having the only business in Waycross operated for more than a quarter of a century without a single change in management and ownership—this includes the railroad and telephone companies.

His father, the late James Hinson, was one of four brothers who came to this country from England (London), two settling in Georgia, one in North Carolina, and one in Florida. His father died in 1897.

Mr. Hinson was married in 1909 to Mrs. Alice Wilson. They have three children, Warren Lee, Alice, and Fulwood.

FAMILY RECORD OF MRS. ALICE HINSON

Claims of original Huguenot Emigres to South Carolina accepted on application of Elizabeth Frances Hopkins of Thomasville, Ga., for membership in the Huguenot Society of South Carolina.

Jean Francois de Gignilliat, April 13, 1922.
Jacques Le Serrurier, November 16, 1927.
Jacques de Bordeaux, November 16, 1927.
Josias Du Pre', November 16, 1927.
Corne' Lius Du Pre', November 16, 1927.
Daniel Brabant, November 16, 1927.

James Gignilliat, b. July 30, 1746; d. Mar. 12, 1794; married Charlotte Pepper May 8, 1766, b. Nov. 17, 1748; d. Sept. 7, 1803.

John Gignilliat, d. May 25, 1750; married Mary Magdalene Du Pre' 1729, b. 1711, d. aft. 1776.

Abraham Gignilliat married Smith.

Jean Francois de Gignilliat, d. Nov. 1699; married Susanne Le Serrurier ca. 1689; d. bef. Sept. 26, 1721.

Jacques Le Serrurier b. 1635, married Elizabeth Le Ger, d. 1725.

Will proved Oct. 4, 1706.

Alice Kelly Wilson Hinson, gt. gd. dau. of John May Gignilliat is entitled to these claims; her gt. gd. mother, Sarah Evelyn Gignilliat Hall, (Henry Tudor Hall-House of Tudor, England) and her grandmother Jane Elizabeth Gignilliat Hopkins were sisters, daughters of John May Gignilliat.

Mary Magdalene Du Pre' b. 1711; married John Gignilliat.

Corne'lius du Pré married 1708 Jeane Brabant d. aft. 1723.

Josias Du Pre' married Martha ———, d. aft. 1711.
Jeane Brabant married Corne'lius Du Pré 1708.
Daniel Barbant married Magdalene De Bordeaux.
Jeane Brabant married Corne'lius Du Pre.
Magdalene De Bordeaux married Daniel Brabant, d. aft. 1733.
James De Bordeaux, b. 1808-9, married Magdalene Garillond.
Evremond De Bordeaux married Catherine Fresne'.

Mrs. Warren Lee Hinson, great, great, great granddaughter of Charlotte White Pepper and James Gignilliat. James Gignilliat appointed Justice in the Commission of the Peace, March 30th, 1776, when the S. C. Provincial Congress was dissolved and reorganized as the General Assembly of S. C., preparatory to active participation in the American Revolution. His plantation in the Beaufort District was exposed to the ravages of war, so that he had to remove his family to a safer place, "Tickton Hall," on the Broad River; but he remained in his own district for service.

Journal of the Gen. Assembly of S. C., Mar. 26-Apr. 11, 1776; p. 17. Sat. the 30th day of March, 1776;

And the said list being immediately taken into consideration—Resolved that the following persons are proper to put into the Commission of the Peace in the different Districts of the Colony, viz: Justices for Beaufort District; James Gignilliat and others.

Extracts from notes on the Gignilliat family dictated by Dr. Thomas Spalding Hopkins, husband of Jane Elizabeth Gignilliat, daughter of John May Gignilliat and Jane Mary Pepper.

John May and Jane Mary Gignilliat had nine children, Sarah, who married Henry Tudor Hall, an Englishman who claimed relations with The House of Tudor.

DR. ROBERT P. IZLAR

Dr. Izlar was born at Orangeburg, S. C., Sept. 27, 1866, and was a son of James F. and Frances (Lovell) Izlar, the former of whom was born in Orangeburg in 1833, and the latter in Charleston, S. C., in 1845.

Dr. Izlar was one of the prominent physicians and surgeons of Georgia, and was located in Waycross where he did not only a large practice in his home town, but in the surrounding counties. He held the unequivocal confidence of the entire community in which he so faithfully labored.

He served with distinction in the Spanish-American War, having enlisted on April 25, 1898, in the first Florida Volunteer infantry of which he became surgeon, with the rank of Major. The regiment was held in reserve· not being called into active service, and Dr. Izlar was mustered out at Tallahassee, Florida, December 3, 1899. He was reared to maturity in his native home, after due academic literary education he entered upon the work of preparing himself for his chosen profession. He graduated in the Medical College of the State of South Carolina at Charleston in March, 1888, duly receiving his degree of Doctor of Medicine. He served during the following year as interne in the city hospital of Charleston, and in the latter part of 1889 he located in Ocala, Fla., where he established a successful practice, in which he continued until 1896, when he located in Waycross. From 1896 to 1898 he served as attending physician and surgeon to the general hospital of the Plant system of railroads in Waycross. He later gave his attention to general professional work, having attained to a very high prestige as a surgeon. He was an honorary member of the Florida Medical Association, of which he was president in 1898, and in the same year, served as president of the Florida State Association of Railway Surgeons. In 1904 he was president of the Atlantic Coast Line railway surgeons' Association, and in 1902-3 he was president of the Plant System Railway Surgeons' Association. He was also identified with the Association of Military Surgeons of the United States; was first Vice-President, 1905, of the Georgia State Medical Association, and an appreciative member of the American Medical Association. He was affiliated with the lodge, chapter, council and Knights Templars of the Masonic fraternity, the Benevolent and Protective Order of Elks, the Knights of Pythias, and the Improved Order of Red Men. His political allegiance is given to the Democracy, and he and Mrs. Izlar are communicants of Grace Church, Protestant Episcopal, in Waycross.

On Sept. 26, 1890, at Orangeburg, S. C., Doctor Izlar was united in marriage to Miss Fernanda A. Oliveros, daughter of John B. Oliveros, of Savannah, Ga., and she died at Ocala, Fla., August 24, 1894, being survived by two children—Robert P., and Magdalena. On Oct. 27, 1897, Dr. Izlar married Miss Frances G. Wright, daughter of Abner B. and Eunice (Durham) Wright of Greenville, S. C., and of this union they had three children, Abbie James, who died in 1901, at the age of three years; William, and Wright.

Dr. Izlar died in 1917 and is buried in Lott Cemetery, Waycross.

JAMES FAMILY

The James family had not only Revolutionary ancestry but many of them fought in the Indian wars and also represented the south most valiantly in the War Between the States. The James family originally came to Georgia from North Carolina, while one family, that of John James, stopped in South Carolina. Benjamin James of North Carolina, who married Kesiah James, November 1, 1788 in Bertie County, N. C. were in all probability the progenitors of the Ware County James family. Benjamin James was a soldier in the Revolution.

Benjamin James, who married Sarah Riggins of Pierce County, came to Georgia about 1825 from South Carolina and settled on lands that later were incorporated into the county of Pierce. Mr. and Mrs. James had ten children of their own and reared sixteen orphan children, making twenty-seven children for whose guardianship they assumed the sacred responsibility.

Robert Gideon James was the youngest of Benjamin and Sarah James' children and at the age of twenty-two years was married to Miss Lavina Sweat and they made their home near Mock's Bridge, about two miles from Waycross. Mrs. James was a sister of the late Judge J. L. Sweat of Ware County. To this union were born eight children. Of this large family only four are living. Allen, Mitchell, and Ida (Mrs. Ulmer), and Bradford, who lives with his daughter, Mrs. Effie Wilcox. Mitchell James lives in Bainbridge and Ida (Mrs. Ulmer) lives in Valdosta.

MR. AND MRS. ALLEN JAMES

Mr. Allen James was born March 17, 1870 and married Miss Winnie Elnora Harper in 1892. Mrs. James was the daughter of the late Rev. William L. Harper, a Baptist minister. Mr. and Mrs. James have one son, Samuel Harper James, who is a prominent young man of Waycross.

WARE COUNTY
RECORDS COLLECTED BY MRS. ALLEN JAMES

William Thomas James, Sr., was born in Pierce County, March 3rd, 1827, and married Sarah Bennett, born Apr. 13th, 1833. This couple married quite young and moved to Ware County near Morror at this place there were born 14 children and their names are:

Lettie James, wife of D. C. Carmichael.
Tabitha James, wife of Dave Silas.
Sarah James, wife of James Mullis.
Fannie James.
Lavina James, wife of George Corbett.
Nancy James, wife of Daniels.
Jane James, unmarried.
Benjamin James, farmer.
Richard, called Dick, Primitive Baptist preacher.
Robert James, farmer now living in Ware.

John James.
Ervin James, farmer, deceased.
William James.

Thomas M. James, merchant at Morror until he died.

Uncle Tom, as he was known to the whole county, fought through the war but was spared to get home and finish the rearing of his children.

Late one afternoon, 1896, he saddled his horse and went out to drive up his cows, but didn't return when his wife expected him. She sent people out to find him. His horse came home and late that night they found him dead not far from home near what is now known as Camp Branch Church. His children erected a monument on the spot where he was found and he was buried in his field near the house where he and Aunt Sarah had reared all of the children and on May 3rd, 1908 she died and was buried by the side of him in the same field.

Uncle Tom was a son of Benjamin James and a brother of Robert Gideon James of Ware County,

JAMES BIBLE RECORD

William Thomas James was born March 13th, 1857, in Ware County and Lucilla Temple James wife of W. L. James was born Sept. 3, 1856, they were married Nov. 3, 1876. There were 12 children. M. J. James, born Aug. 16, 1877; J. A. James, born April 21, 1879; A. H. James, born April 3, 1881; Leila D. James, born March 9th, 1883; L. M. James, born June 1, 1885; S. P. James, born August 19, 1887; Mamie James, born October 19, 1889; Sarah Lavinia, born Dec. 26, 1891; Nicie James, born Jan. 21, 1894; C. R. James, born Aug. 19, 1896; Two infant daughters, born and died May 13, 1899.

MRS. LUCIUS JENKINS

Mrs. Maggie Parker (L. G.) Jenkins was born in Savannah, Georgia, Sept. 1, 1866 and came to Waycross when only two years of age with her parents, Captain and Mrs. Wm. Foster Parker, who were among the first four pioneer citizens of Waycross.

MRS. LUCIUS JENKINS

Miss Maggie Parker was married to Lucius G. Jenkins in 1883. Mr. Jenkins was one of Ware County's most progressive citizens, and was recognized as a man of fine business ability, having filled many important places of trust in this community.

Mrs. Jenkins descended from Rev. John Waldhauer Remshart, whose ancestry represented some of the oldest families in Georgia. He was born in Savannah in 1801; died 1829; and was the son of Elizabeth (Waldhauer) and Daniel Remshart. John Remshart, father of Daniel, and Jacob Casper Waldhauer, father of Elizabeth (Waldhauer) Remshart, were members of German families who came to Georgia with Oglethorpe at the time of his second voyage to his newly founded colony. The parents of these two pioneers were German Lutherans and were members of the Saltzburger Colony at Ebenezer. The Rev. John W. Remshart was united in marriage to Miss Jane Bryan, daughter of James and Elizabeth (Langley) Bryan of Savannah.

Mr. and Mrs. Jenkins have been blessed with an interesting family composed of five children, whose names are: Clyde (Mrs. W. P. Sims), Maud (Mrs. R. H. Charles), Orville Parker, H. Ponsell, and Lucius Green.

Mrs. Jenkins is a loyal communicant of the Methodist Episcopal Church and an honored member of the following organizations: Johnathan Bryan Chapter, Daughters of the American Revolution, The Daughters of the Confederacy, The Kings Daughters, The "Georgians," Woman's Federated Club, and the American Legion Auxiliary. During the World War Mrs. Jenkins was a faithful and untiring Red Cross worker. She completed the standard course in surgical dressing. She was First Lieutenant in the American Red Cross Canteen Service, and assisted with the Red Cross Garment Supply. She received two certificates of Award and War Service Badge.

HON. LEMUEL JOHNSON

Lemuel Johnson was born in Appling County, May 5, 1844, and was the son of Duncan and Lujoyce (Sellers) Johnson, both natives of Georgia, their parents having come to this state from North Carolina in the early days when settlers were few and the Indians were numerous. Duncan Johnson was a farmer, and represented his country in the general assembly two terms; was justice of the inferior court many years, and served in the Indian Wars. He was a man of unswerving integrity and was among the leading men of his county. He died June 27, 1857, age sixty years; his wife died June 17, 1867, age fifty-four years. They were the parents of eleven children, of whom nine grew to maturity.

Lemuel Johnson enlisted August 12, 1861, in Company F., Twenty-sixth Georgia Regiment, Col. E. N. Atkinson. (Commander.) He volunteered for the seven days' fight around Richmond and continued to serve throughout the War Between the States. His parole is still in possession of his family, dated at the surrender, April 9, 1865. In

1867 he began business in the town of Sellers, Appling County, twenty-five miles from the railroad, carrying a mercantile business in connection with his farm with marked success. Three years later he moved to Pierce County, and carried on the same business for a like period of time. He added the lumber business to his trade in general merchandise, and in 1880 he moved to Appling County and later to Ware.

He was a member of the firm of Stillwell, Millen & Co., Savannah; L. R. Millen & Co., New York, and Bewick Lumber Co., Hazlehurst. He was also general manager of the Waycross Lumber Co., president of the Augusta Lumber Co., general manager of Waycross Air-Line Railroad Co.; first owner of Millen & Sons' railroad from Millen to Stillmore, Georgia, a stockholder in the Satilla Manufacturing Co.,—electric light, ice factory, and planing mill; a stockholder in one of the largest dry goods stores in Waycross, the C. C. Grace Co., which did an immense wholesale and retail business.

Captain Johnson had too much public spirit to confine his efforts entirely to the accumulation of wealth, and became publicly known throughout his native state for his active interests in every good and noble cause. He represented the Eleventh district (now the Eighth) in the Georgia Senate, from 1880 to 1884, and his record was a most excellent one. He later refused further legislative honors, and concentrated constructive interests in the upbuilding of his home city. He became a member of the school board, also a trustee of school property, and a member of the sanitary and waterworks commission. He was for four years one of the trustees of Emory College, Oxford, at that time a well equipped educational institution under the auspices of the Methodist Church. Although a very busy man, he still found time to keep up his standing in the orders of Knights of Pythias and Knights of Honor, of which he was past dictator, and of the masonic fraternity, he held one of the highest offices in the gift of the chapter.

Captain Johnson was married to Miss Ann J. Youmans, daughter of Charles and Eliza (Lagg) Youmans of Pierce County, February 3, 1869. Captain and Mrs. Johnson were the parents of the following children: Marie, who married William S. Branham, of Oxford; Hershel V., who was a student at Emory College when he died in his sophomore year, January 22, 1888, at the age of sixteen; Leola, married Frank Hawkins; Alven (May Murphy); Kate (William Wadley), who died and she later was married to Thomas Linton; Clifford, and George, who died in 1930.

Captain Johnson died April 5, 1918, and Mrs. Johnson died October 16, 1930.

JAMES JONES

One of the old pioneers of Ware County was James Jones. He is today represented by several thousand descendants, and the Jones name is well and favorably known over Southeast Georgia. We could not learn where he was born but we are informed he was a native of North Carolina and that he came to Georgia about 1820. He settled about seven miles from Burnt Church in Charlton County, then in Ware County.

He was born in North Carolina about 1780. His wife, Nancy Delk, was also a native of N. C. We do not know her parent's name. James Jones and his family lived in Ware County for many years, but for several years before his death they lived in Florida, probably in Nassau County. James Jones was a member of the Primitive Baptist Church. He died in 1855 of Bright's Disease, and was buried probably at High Bluff Church.

The records show that James Jones was commissioned ensign of the militia in the 598th district of Ware County, Nov. 22, 1825, serving until 1827 when he was commissioned ensign in the 586th district May 2, 1827. He served until 1832 when he was elected second lieutenant of the 590th district May 16, 1832, serving until 1834.

The children of James and Nancy Jones were as follows:

1. Nathaniel Jones, born about 1805 probably in N. C. married Keziah Johnson. He died at the age of 80 in Alachua County, Fla.

2. Harley Jones, born 1807; married Louisa Cason of Ware County. Died in March, 1867.

3. James Jones, Jr., born about 1810. Married Sarah Mizell. He was murdered by a negro slave when about 45 years of age. Lived in what is now Pierce County. Mrs. Jones was a daughter of James Mizell.

4. Burrell Jones, born in N. C. July 29, 1803. Died June, 1877. Married Margaret, daughter of Jesse Mizell, Feb. 9, 1829. She was born August 9, 1809, and joined the Primitive Baptist Church, July, 1843.

Their children's names are: Lt. H. Jones, 26th Georgia Volunteers; Joseph Jones of Chattanooga, Tenn.; B. P. Jones, Valdosta; J. B. Jones, Waycross; Dr. J. H. Jones, N. J. Jones, Starke, Fla.; Mrs. J. H. Highsmith, Nahunta, Mrs. Margaret Blount, Lulaton, Ga.

MR. AND MRS. W. N. JONES

Wiley Newton Jones' mother was Mary Highsmith, born June 11, 1842 and James Barrell Jones, the father was born May 16, 1842, their marriage taking place September 9, 1858. Mr. James Jones died in 1932.

He served during the War Between the States as corporal in Longstreet's brigade.

Mr. W. N. Jones was born February 16, 1872, and in early life assisted his father on their farm and later settled in Waycross, entering the mercantile business. During his entire career he has stood behind every movement put forward for the good of the town, and has manifested an intense loyalty to the traditions of his native county.

His nature has ever been kind, generous, and considerate. Mr. and Mrs. Jones are members of the First Baptist

Church. Mrs. Jones, a wonderful Bible student, has been helpful as a teacher of the scripture in the Church.

They have had a long and honorable career. This would be unusual without some sorrow and disappointments, but if any shadow ever entered their lives, it never obscured the sunshine of their personality nor affected their happy relationship with their friends and family.

Minnie Margaret Brinson Jones married Wiley Newton Jones, February 6, 1872.

Maternal: John Wright Brinson, born November 30, 1832, died April 24, 1896 (Stellaville, Jefferson County, Georgia); married July 17, 1858, Sarah Wicker, born April 4, 1843.

Moses Brinson, Jr., born September 30, 1776; married Celia Tarver (second wife, Zilphia Shine), died September 3, 1859. Thomas Wicker, born 1803, died 1884. Paternal: Burrell Jones, Sr., born 1804, died 1877; married Mary Margaret Mizell, born 1810, died February 25, 1886.

Moses Brinson, Sr., born February 3, 1765, died January 7, 1850· married Agnes Wright, January 5, 1784, died 1844; married Jacob Tarver, 1804, born 1777, died 1830. Nathaniel Wicker, married Margaret McNair (or McNeir). Paternal: Allen Highsmith, married Elizabeth Knox, 1830.

Sterring (or Stiring or Sterling) Brinson, died 1778; had four brothers in Revolutionary War. Adam Brinson, in Colonial militia; lived in North Carolina. Isaac Brinson, lived in Lynne, Connecticut. Jacob Brinson, of royal Welch lineage. Richard Brinson, first settled in America from England in 1628. Absalom Tarver, born 1757, died August 27, 1831; married Ursula Smith, 1776, born 1759, died June 3, 1827.

Other names in family were Polly (or Poley) Stallings, Keziah Folke (Wicker line), Robert Holly and June Holly, Hannah Moore (Cribb).

Revolutionary ancestors: Absalom Tarver, Archibald McNeil, James Jones, Adam Brinson. The name Brinson was formerly Bronson and Brounson. Motto of Brinson line: "While I live, I hope".

The names of Mr. and Mrs. W. N. Jones' children are: Cathleen (Mrs. Joe Sawyer), Tullu (Mrs. Edward Fish) Mary Wiley (Mrs. Edwin McCarty), and Cecile (Mrs. Carey Sutlif).

ZIBER KING

Before Ware County was cut from Appling, Ziber King was born in the home located on lands that later became Ware, where his father William King owned many acres of land. Mr. King was born Nov. 29, 1818, six years before the organization of Ware, and his parents were truly pioneers of this County, their home being near the Kettle Creek settlement.

After the creating of Clinch County he made his home for awhile there. He was elected Justice of the Peace of the 970th District and commissioned Aug. 24, 1860, and served four years. On May 10, 1866, he was commissioned Judge of the first County Court of Clinch County, and served a few years, when he resigned and removed to Florida. Judge King first settled in Manatee County later in DeSoto County, Florida, where he accumulated a fortune in the cattle business and was known in the surrounding country as the "Cattle King."

On May 28, 1868 he was married to Miss Fannie A. Tanley. He later married Miss Florida Brewer, July 24, 1870 and seven children blessed this union. His death occurred March 7, 1901; he was survived by his wife and children; his remains were buried in the cemetery at Fort Ogden, Fla.

A daughter of Judge King married the Honorable J. E. T. Bowden, who was an outstanding citizen of Waycross. Mr. Bowden has since died and his wife is one of Waycross' most beloved women.

MOSES KIRKLAND

Moses Kirkland married Mrs. Margaret Carver Thigpen, the widow of Calvin Thigpen, son of James Thigpen of North Carolina. They moved to Telfare County, but when Coffee was cut from Telfare, his home was left in Coffee County. They had a large family and their children's names are: Moses, Josh, Zeno, Timothy, James, Manning, Margaret, Roxey· and Betty who married Major John Spence of Waresboro.

RUFUS CARLTON KING

It is probable that few of the colonial families of Georgia through the different generations have given more worthy and honored members to the varied professional, business, and civic life of the state than the King and Bachlott families of St. Marys, Camden County. Mr. Rufus Carlton King, the subject of this sketch came to Waycross, in 1888. The town was small, but gave promise of one day being important in commercial and civic affairs. He has never lost faith in the town of his adoption.

Rufus King, the statesman, who upheld the very highest ideals of government and who represented Massachusetts in the Federal Convention of 1787 that drafted the United States Constitution, is a member of this distinguished Georgia family.

Mr. King was born in Charlton County, where his parents had refugeed during the War Between the States to avoid an unpleasant encounter with the obtrusive Mr. Sherman, the unforgotten Yankee General, who slighted few settlements on his march through Georgia.

The father and mother of Mr. King were Rufus Lemuel King, and Eleanor Ann Bachlott, who were married at Blount's Ferry, Columbia County· Florida, March 4, 1847. Eleanor Bachlott's mother was a Miss Pritchard, whose family was among the first settlers of Jacksonville, Fla.

James King and Margaret O'Neal were the grandparents of Mr. Carl King. Margaret O'Neal was born September 26, 1787 and she and James King were married at Morehead, North Carolina, and were the great-grand parents of Mr. Carl King.

Joseph Blachlott, his great-great-grandfather, was born in Amos County, Virginia, May 11, 1792, died at St. Marys, Georgia, Aug. 16, 1822. He married Mary Francis Rudolph, born 1805. She was the daughter of Thomas Rudolph, born Dec. 15, 1760, and his wife Elizabeth. All are buried in the cemetery at St. Marys. Thomas Randolph was a Revolutionary soldier and his wife drew a pension as his widow.

Mr. King's great-great-great-grandfather, John Bachlott, and Miss Mary Conrad of Richmond, Va., were married by Rev. Buchanan in 1785. They lived for a time in Amos, Va., and in 1796 moved to South Carolina, near the hills of Sante, 1797 to Charleston, 1799 to Amelia Island, Fla., 1800 to St. Marys, Georgia.

John Bachlott came to America to fight with Lafayette and his name appears in the list of certified soldiers of the Revolution. He drew in the land lottery of 1827 land in Camden County for his services in the Revolution. John Bachlott fought in the battle of Yorktown, Va., and the epitaph on the marble headpiece above his grave gives the record of service that he rendered to America and revealing the fact that Yorktown was once known as Little York.

The inscription that appears on his tombstone that rests under the beautiful trees in the cemetery at St. Marys is as follows:

Sacred to The Memory of John Bachlott, Seur a Native of Saint Milo France, who departed this life on the 6th of June, 1833, aged 73 years. He was a soldier in the memorable Battle of Little York which Terminated the War.

The Sesqui-Centennial of the Battle of Yorktown was held in Yorktown, Va., from Oct. 16th to 20th, 1931, and the descendants of John Bachlott were invited to take part in the celebration.

Mr. Carl King was married to Miss Della Jones of Calahan, Florida, in 1890, and they have two daughters, Della (Mrs. Joseph Pettibone), Carl, (Mrs. Carrol Varnedore).

MR. AND MRS. ARTHUR MERRILL KNIGHT

Few citizens settling in a newly organized town, ever held the public interest at heart more than Mr. A. M. Knight. He came to Waycross from Jacksonville, Florida, when quite a young man, and in an able way took a prominent part in civic work; giving generously of his time and experience. He made constructive plans for the advancement of the city's interest and carried them out in an able way. His superior ability left the impress of his active life in and around Waycross.

It was during his administration as Mayor of this city that the land on Mary street was purchased for a city park. This land was formerly owned by Dr. Frank Folks, who sold it to the city for a nominal sum and in view of this fact, the park was named by the Tree and Park Commission, in honor of Dr. Frank Folks.

It was largely through the untiring efforts of Mr. and Mrs. Knight, that the first Episcopal Church was replaced by a new one of Spanish architecture, in which they placed beautiful memorial to their beloved dead.

It has been justly said of Mr. and Mrs. Knight that they did their full duty by their friends and by their community.

Mr. Knight was of New England ancestry, on the paternal side, being the grandson of Peter M. Knight, a man of letters, who possessed much literary taste and ability, as is attested by a unique volume, Gems of Poetry, beautifully illustrated with a pen by his own hand, written in 1832. Allison Williamson Knight, the son of the poet, was born in Brunswick, Maine, Jan. 5, 1825. He was a prominent physician of White Sulphur Springs, Florida. He moved to Live Oak, Fla., in 1871, and later to Jacksonville, where he remained until his death which occurred Sept. 6, 1889. Dr. Knight's wife was Miss Caroline Demere, a descendant of one of two brothers of that name who came over with Oglethorpe and were officers in his army. They settled at Frederica, on St. Simons Island, where Mrs. Knight was born. Her brothers were in the southern army during the War Between the States. Arthur Merrell Knight was the fifth son of Dr. and Mrs. Knight, and was born at White Sulphur Spring, Fla., Nov. 16, 1859.

May 6, 1884, Mr. Knight was married to Miss Susan Fatio Daniel, daughter of Col. James Jacquelin and Emily (L Engle) Daniel, of Jacksonville, Fla. Col. Daniel, who was widely known for his large-hearted benevolence, died in 1888 of yellow fever, a sacrifice to his care and sympathy for the suffering, to whom he devoted himself. The mother of Mrs. Daniel, Mrs. Susan Fatio L'Engle, died in Jacksonville, Fla., March 5, 1895, in the eighty-ninth year of her age. Mr. and Mrs. A. M. Knight were blessed with three sons who reached the age of maturity, Dr. Jacquelin Emile (deceased), Arthur Merrill, and Gerald B.

KIRTON FAMILY RECORD
Marriages

Philip Kirton and Olive Gasque were married on the 18th of July, A. D., 1787.

Samuel Kirton and Elizabeth Gasque were married on the 22nd of Dec., A. D., 1825.

William W. Kirton and Mary E. Collins on 30th November, A. D., 1865.

Remarks:—Philip Kirton was a local minister of the M. E. Church, and continued to preach until his death.

Births

Philip Kirton, born 16th day of July A. D., 1765.

Olive Kirton, the wife of Philip Kirton was born the 7th day of Dec., 1767.

Samuel Kirton, born 13th March, A. D., 1803. Elizabeth Kirton, wife of Samuel Kirton born on the 11th day of Feb., A. D., 1805.

William Philip Kirton, was born 22nd day of Sept. A. D., 1828. Mary E. Kirton, born on the 30th day of June, A. D., 1833.

Jane Kirton was born 20th day of Oct., A. D., 1837.

Samuel P. Kirton, born 27th day of July, A. D., 1839.

William W. Kirton· born 26th day of Sept., A. D., 1843.

Mary Elizabeth Kirton, the wife of William W. Kirton was born 18th day of Oct., A. D., 1847.

Samuel Robert Kirton, son of William W. Kirton, born on the 25th day, July, A. D., 1867.

Mary Elizabeth Kirton, daughter of William W. and Mary Elizabeth Kirton, born 7th day of Dec., A. D., 1860.

Deaths

Olive Kirton, wife of Philip Kirton, departed this life the 15th of April, A. D., 1834, age 64 years, 4 months and 9 days.

Philip Kirton· departed this life, 22nd day of March, A. D., 1837, age 69 years, 8 months and 6 days.

William Philip Kirton, departed this life Nov., A. D., 1828, age about two months.

Jane Kirton, departed this life, 28th Oct., A. D., 1838; age one year and 8 days.

Samuel P. Kirton, departed this life on 4th of Jan., A. D., 1855, age 15 years, 5 months and 9 days.

Samuel Kirton, departed this life the 15th day of Feb., A. D., 1867· age 63 years and 11 months.

Elizabeth Kirton, departed this life, 1st day of Jan., A. D., 1869, age 63 years, 10 months and 11 days.

W. W. Kirton, departed this life on the 24th day of Jan., A. D., 1869.

CAPTAIN JAMES KNOX

James Knox was born in Wayne County (now Brantley) Georgia, Oct. 12th, 1831. He was the son of Reddick Knox who was born in Pitt County, North Carolina, where his parents, who were of Welsh and Scotch ancestry, settled on coming to America. Brought up in his native state, he migrated to Georgia in 1826, he and his wife and three children making the removal with teams.

At the end of two years of frontier life, he and his family went back to their old home and after two years stay they returned to Georgia in 1830 settling on the site they had chosen on their first trip. Buying a tract of wild land, he established a farm and there spent the remainder of his life.

He married Ruhama Taylor, who was born in North Carolina, and lived to the ripe old age of 83 years, and died on the home farm in Wayne County in 1850.

Capt. James Knox grew to manhood beneath the parental roof and upon the breaking out of the War Between the States offered his services to the Confederacy. Being commissioned captain of Company D, Twenty-sixth Georgia Volunteer Infantry he went with his regiment to Virginia, and as a part of the "army of Northern Virginia" he was under the command of "Stonewall" Jackson. After the death of Gen. Jackson his regiment was put under the command of Gen. Robert E. Lee, where he served until the surrender at Appomattox Court House when he received his parole. During his service in Virginia, which lasted about three and one-half years, he was at the front in many engagements of importance, and only suffered once from a shell wound. After receiving his parole at the close of the war, Capt. Knox turned his face homeward, and walked, barefooted, the greater part of the distance. He resumed his former occupation, that of farming and timber business with Burnt Fort as the market for timber. He also carried on a large mercantile business at Lulaton, Wayne County, which was the only business of the kind in a large area of that county.

In 1879 Capt. Knox, with his family, came to Waycross, which was then a quiet village of about five hundred souls, and, having opened a general store, the second of its kind in the town, was here a resident until his death Aug. 6th, 1899.

Capt. Knox married Mary Jane Jones, who was born in what is now Pierce County, near Big Creek, not far from the birthplace of her father, James Jones. Her paternal grandfather was born in North Carolina of Welsh ancestry, and came to what is now Pierce County, Georgia, in pioneer times, when the Indians made such frequent raids upon the newcomers that it was necessary to have in each county one or more large log forts to which the settlers might flee for safety when the red men became too troublesome. Securing title to extensive tracts of land, he carried on farming with slave labor until his death. James Jones, the father of Captain Knox's wife became owner of a large plantation near the east end of the Okefinokee swamp, and was profitably engaged in farming and stock-raising the remainder of his life, passing away in 1850, being murdered by a slave belonging to one of his neighbors. The maiden name of Mrs. Knox's mother was Sarah Mizell, daughter of Jesse Mizell. She spent her brief life in this immediate section of Georgia, dying in early womanhood. Mrs. Knox survived her husband several years, her death occurring May 20th, 1907 at the advanced age of 75. Mrs. Knox was a member of the Methodist Episcopal Church.

Capt. and Mrs. Knox reared nine children as follows: Sarah, who married Rev. John Strickland; Kate, deceased, was the wife of J. L. Courson; J. Franklin Knox, deceased, married Mollie Wainright; Mary, died at the age of twenty-five years; Dora, wife of Andrew J. Miller; Belle C., wife of Dr. Gustavus P. Folks; William L., married Mrs. Beulah O'Hara; Edward W., deceased, married Rebecca Wilcox; James, Jr., deceased, married Nettie Chastain.

DR. DANIEL LOTT
ONE OF THE FOUNDERS OF WAYCROSS

The first Lotts to come to this country were of Danish descent· the family having been founded by three brothers of the name who came to America during the eighteenth century, one settling in South Carolina, and the other two in Georgia, some of whom became merchants and planters. Dr. Lott descended from Joel Lott, who married Rhoda Davis,

WALTER LOTT

MRS. WALTER LOTT

and was the son of either Daniel or Arthur Lott, who settled, after reaching Georgia, in Bulloch county.

Dr. Daniel Lott was born not far from Waresboro, March 9, 1828, four years after the county of Ware was organized. Susan (Mobley) Lott was the wife of Dr. Lott, and her father and mother's names were Solomon and Elizabeth Mobley. Susan (Mobley) Lott was born June 3, 1829 in Appling County, now a part of Ware.

Dr. Daniel Lott was educated in the schools of his native county, and after farming a short while took up the study of dentistry under an able preceptor, becoming skilled in his profession, to which he devoted his attention for a number of years at Waresboro, G e o r g i a where he remained until November, 1871, when he retired from practice and moved to what is now Waycross, although at that time it was a wilderness of pine trees. He became owner of the land, where the city of Waycross is now located and his was the first family to locate here, after he laid out the town.

He not only was the first dentist to practice dentistry in Ware but opened the first real estate office in Waycross. He owned several sawmills, which he put into operation and sold the plants. In 1852 he was elected to represent his county in the state legislature, served one year, and was then elected to the state senate, of which he was a member one term. He was a man of sterling character, prominent and influential in local affairs. At the inception of the War between the States, he went forth as a loyal soldier of the Confederacy as a private in the Fourth Georgia Cavalry. Soon after his enlistment, however, he was elected Judge of the inferior court, and through assuming the duties of this office he was exempt from military service.

It was largely through his efforts that the county seat

MRS. FANNIE LOTT SHARP

of Ware was transferred from Waresboro to Waycross of which town he was one of the founders. Dr. Lott gave to Ware County her first Court House, this being a small donation to this town compared to his other liberal gifts of land upon which to put many of the city and county buildings. Dr. Lott has many living memorials to his credit, that will have life and being as long as Waycross exists. He died in Waycross June 24, 1880 and his wife died July 16, 1892. Dr. and Mrs. Lott were the parents of six children whose names were: Mrs. J. S. Lightsey, John A., Warren, Mrs. Fannie Sharp, Walter, and Joel. This entire family now sleeps in the cemetery, named for Dr. Lott, of which he gave the larger part of the land for this Silent City. It was his wish that it be used for the interment of the members of all denominations.

The Descendents

Children of Daniel and Susan Mobley Lott:

(1). Elizabeth married Steven Lightsey. Children, Linton, Custis, Jake Julius, Frances, Tom.

(2). John Augustus, married Josephine Bailey. Issue, Oscar, Dan, Elmer.

(3). Warren, married Hattie Williams. Issue, Warren, Edith, Clyde, Arthur, John Henry.

(4). Walter, married Georgia Hilliard. Issue, Dan Joel, Miller, Walter, Carolyne.

(5). Frances, married (1) Josiah Simmons. Issue, Cora, Eustace. (2) John Sharp Issue, Susie John, Turner, Walker, Wadley. (6) Joel married Kate Gray. Issue, Katie, Glenn and Joel.

WARREN LOTT

Judge Warren Lott was born in Ware County eight miles north of Waresboro, October 20, 1853. He secured his early education in the schools of his native county, and for a short time attended an academy at Valdosta.

JUDGE AND MRS. WARREN LOTT

In 1873, in partnership with his brother John A. Lott, he engaged in the general merchandise business in Waycross, their store being located on the corner where the Merson Hotel is now located.

Upon the incorporation of the town in 1872, he was elected its first city clerk and treasurer, and he also served three terms as clerk of the county, having been first elected in 1877. In 1882-3 he represented the county in the state legislature, having been elected on the local prohibition issue. He introduced and carried to enactment the bill for prohibition, and also introduced and carried to enactment the local bill prohibiting the sale of intoxicating liquors in Ware County. In 1889, Judge Lott was elected Judge of the Court of Ordinary, and he served in this office until removed by death. He was a prominent leader in the Democratic party, and served as Chairman of the County Democratic Executive Committee for over ten years. He was Vice-President of the First Bank established in Waycross which was in 1889—"South Georgia," which was afterwards changed to the First National Bank.

He was a Knight Templar in the Masonic fraternity and was a charter member and past chancellor of the lodge of Knights of Pythias. He frequently served during different times as a member of the city board of education. On June 29, 1881, Judge Lott was united in marriage to Miss Harriott J. Williams, daughter of Dr. Benjamin F. and Sarah (Hicks) Williams of Waycross. Judge and Mrs. Lott became the parents of seven children: Warren, Mabel (died at the age of four years), Edith, Clyde, Benjamin (died at the age of three years), Arthur, and John Henry. Judge Lott died December 20, 1907.

JOHN AUGUSTUS LOTT

John Lott was born in Ware County, about ten miles above Waresboro, at a place known as Coleman's Still. He was the son of Dr. Daniel and Susan Lott. His mother was the daughter of Soloman and Elizabeth Mobley. His father, Daniel Lott, was a large landowner and one of the founders of Waycross. Dr. Lott was in the Confederate service in

MR. JOHN LOTT

MRS. JOHN LOTT

the Fourth Georgia Cavalry about one year. Joel and Rhoda (nee Davis) were the parents of Dr. Lott.

Mr. Lott was educated in schools at Blackshear, Valdosta, and Waycross. He acquired a keen business capacity that made him one of the leading financiers of his native county. His religious affiliation was with the Methodist church, and from his early youth was actively identified with the work of that denomination. He was a Mason, often holding important offices in the Masonic Order. He was also a K. P. He married Miss Josephine Bailey, daughter of William S. and Mary Bailey; the children living are Oscar, Daniel, and Elmer. Mr. Lott died Feb. 26, 1930.

MRS. THOMAS RUFUS LYON
(Clara Welch Sutton)

Mrs. T. F. Lyon was born in Albany, Ga., March 28th, 1854, the ninth child of Lewis Green Sutton, Esq., and his wife Elizabeth Rebecca Welch. She descended from Richard Sutton of Westmoreland County Virginia, and James Welch, one of the earliest settlers of St. George's Parrish, now Burk County, Georgia. She received her education from governesses and private teachers, finishing at "Prof. Mallory's School for Young Ladies." She was especially gifted in music, and received her training from Mrs. Tab Warren in Albany. After the death of her husband, she attended the Conservatory of Music in St. Louis, Missouri. She served as organist in the First Methodist Church of Albany, St. Pauls Episcopal Church, Albany, and the First Methodist Church of Waycross. She removed to Waycross to become a member of the faculty of the Public Schools, where she taught until her death, Nov. 18th, 1900. Clara Sutton Lyon was a careful student of books from her earliest years, and few women had a more thorough appreciation of the beauties of literature. She was strongly endowed with the thought that to be a good teacher was to know the subject that she desired to impart to her pupils and each day during the years that she taught in the public school of Waycross, she was found to be daily prepared to do efficient work in behalf of the children whom she felt were vitally under her guidance.

Mrs. Lyon was a devout and active member of Grace Episcopal Church, and the first sum raised for the erection of the present building was made during her presidency of the Woman's Guild. Mrs. Lyon had a benignity of nature which made friends of all who approached her.

She disarmed all enmity, softened all asperity. She mitigated every rudeness. She carried to its highest perfection the noble art of friendship.

Of her four daughters, two are residents of Waycross: Clara Welch, now Mrs. Henry Storey Redding and Mary Sutton, Mrs. Harrison Davenport Watts. Elizabeth Anne, Mrs. William Hale Ham, resides in Bridgeport, Conn., and Virginia Place, Mrs. Jeptha Harris Rucker, lives in Athens, Ga.

Mrs. Lyon sleeps beside her loved ones in the cemetery at Albany, Georgia. Close to her last resting place are many of the friends of her youth, the same green coverlid is over them all and the same mourners softly come and lingering go, it is as she would have it, back in her beautiful home of long ago.

Mc OR MacDONALD CLAN

"Not for to hide it in a hedge,
Not for a train attendant
But for the glorious privilege
Of being independent."

In the land of Bruce, Wallace and Burns, the McDonald's of Scotland took their place among the galaxy of heroes and literary men whose names are still the synonyms of daring and chivalry.

Scotch history shows that the McDonald clan was divided into four great branches; Clans, Ranald-Glengarry-Sleat and Staffa. There is some little doubt as to which was the parent family of these great divisions of the clan but the weight of evidence seems to be in favor of the MacDonalds of the Isles and Sleat, for they can be traced back to the year 1135 and the clan is known to have existed even prior to that. It is one of the most interesting histories of all the clans of Scotland and there is no more interesting history in the world than that of these Scottish clans. From 1135 down to the present time the MacDonalds have been conspicuous both in war and in peace, wherever Scottish or British people have penetrated.

In 1745 they adhered to the Stuarts and were able to put two thousand fighting men in the field. After the destruction of the Stuart cause an enormous number of the MacDonald Clan immigrated to North Carolina and there as a condition of being allowed to take up lands they were compelled to take the oath of allegiance to the British Crown. They had fought the House of Hanover until fighting was hopeless. Their loyalty to a pledged word may be judged by the fact that having taken the oath of allegiance to the House of Hanover in order to secure their lands when the Revolutionary War came although in full sympathy with the Colonists a large number of them took up arms for the Royal cause on the ground that they could not break their plighted word. Deserted in the first year of the war by the Royal leaders the majority of them returned to their homes and remained quiet during the war, while a minority feeling that they had sufficient provocation to renounce their allegiance, joined themselves to the Colonists and some of them made notable records as soldiers; and it is from this strong stock that the McDonalds of Ware County descended.

DR. RANDALL McDONALD
The First Medical Doctor to Come to Ware County

Ranald or Randall McDonald was born on the Isle of Skye, Scotland, April 24th, 1797. He was the son of Donald McDonald (Dahl Mach Abhuir), son of the Sheriff, Donald McDonald.

He descended from the great Scottish Clan, who for hundreds of years disputed the place of supremacy among the Scottish Clans with the Campbells.

Donald McDonald leaving his native home in Scotland in 1805 immigrated to America and settled in Moore County, N. C., where lived his relative General Donald McDonald; and later removed to Bullock County, Georgia, where his name is listed among the early settlers.

General Donald McDonald espoused the cause of Royalty at the opening of the Revolution and was made State

General, and was defeated at the battle of Moore's Creek by the Whigs under Colonel's Coxwell, Lillington and Moore. Gen. McDonald was granted parole after the battle and does not seem to have taken further part in the Revolutionary struggles although other kindsmen did.

Donald McDonald, father of Randall, after coming to Bullock County, Georgia, purchased large tracts of land and began its improvement but a few years later a tragic ending of his life occurred, he was bitten by a rattlesnake which proved fatal. He was survived by his wife, young Ranald or Randall and a daughter. His wife, then middle aged, married Thomas Brown, a Scottish adventurer from North Carolina. He and his wife died leaving the two McDonald children, Randall and his sister.

Randall McDonald, being a kind, sociable, just and industrous boy, soon became a favorite with the white settlers and the Indians. His versatile nature enabled him to turn his time and opportunities to great advantage and he soon acquired ample means to educate himself and he became a practical scholar, acquiring also a good practicing knowledge of medicine and surgery.

April 18th, 1816, he was married to Catherine Miller, a native of Bullock County, Georgia. He moved to Ware County soon after the County was organized and settled near Waresboro where he engaged in extensive farming, operating with slave labor. He was a popular and successful political leader and represented his County in the legislature many times. He was a Georgia Senator in 1835-36 and fought in two Indian Wars. His diploma shows that he graduated from the Oglethorpe Medical College in 1858 at Savannah, Georgia. He died at the age of 67, December 21st, 1864.

Catherine Miller McDonald was the daughter of Henry Miller, grand-daughter of William Miller and great-grand daughter of David Jesse Miller. Catherine was born in Bullock County, December 25, 1799, she died July 14, 1877. Dr. and Mrs. McDonald are buried in Kettle Creek Cemetery in Ware County.

COL. WILLIAM ANGUS McDONALD

William A. McDonald was born in Bullock County, Georgia, 1817, and was the son of Dr. Randall McDonald. Colonel McDonald was a small boy when his parents removed from Bullock County to Waresboro in Ware County.

COL. WILLIAM McDONALD

After he began his independent career he purchased large tracts of land near Waresboro where he farmed successfully with slave labor. Indians were numerous and during those days the early settlers were in constant warfare. William McDonald enlisted in the State Militia and served four years in the Indian Wars. He represented his County six terms in the legislature and served in the State Senate and House for over forty years.

When the Secession Convention convened in Milledgeville, Wednesday, 16, 1861, Colonel McDonald and C. W. Styles represented Ware at this convention, and when the counties were called, upon the presentation of their certificates of election, they were duly enrolled as members of the Convention, and they had the honor of signing the Ordinance of Secession.

He attained great success as a business man, politician and Minister of the Gospel. He was founder of the village of McDonald in Coffee County, it being named for him.

Upon the breaking out of War Between the States, William McDonald enlisted in the Confederate Service and was commissioned Captain of Company "H" of the 26th Regiment of Georgia Volunteers, which was organized with Cary W. Styles as Colonel and W. A. Lane as Lieutenant Colonel. This regiment was for a time on the Georgia Coast under Lawton and Captain McDonald accompanied that officer to Richmond, Virginia, in time to share in seven battles; thence forward serving in the army of Northern Virginia until reaching Appomattox, where in the Division commanded by General Clement A. Evans and the Corps of John B. Gordon, it served in the last charge of that illustrous army. During this long and honorable service E. N. Atkinson succeeded Col. Styles in Command of the regiment and William A. McDonald was a brave and able successor of Lieutenant Colonel Lane. Colonel McDonald remained in the service until the close of the war. His slaves were faithful and cultivated his land until his return from the war. His estate three miles from Waresboro, Ware County, remained his home until his death in his eightieth year. He was married three times; his first wife was Tabitha Sweat, a native of Ware County, and a daughter of James A. and Elizabeth (Newburn) Sweat, and to their union were born ten children. His second marriage was to Mary Ann Deen, who bore him seven children; the maiden name of his third wife was Rebecca Thompson and five more children were reared from this marriage. Colonel McDonald left his descendants the record of a brave soldier, a loyal son of the South and a Citizen of worth, integrity and unbounded respect. He certainly was one whom nature framed to bear "The grand old name of Gentleman."

Children of Colonel William A. McDonald
Grand Children and Great Grand Children
By First Wife:

Dr. James McDonald   Mary McDonald
Randall McDonald   Martha McDonald

William A. McDonald, Jr.
Col. John C. McDonald
Thomas McDonald
Tobitha McDonald
Serene McDonald
Bobie McDonald

By Second Wife:

Edward McDonald
Rev. George McDonald
Robert McDonald
Charlie McDonald
Miller McDonald
Mollie McDonald

Kathrine McDonald

By Third Wife:

Frank B. McDonald
Ida Rebecca McDonald
Millie T. McDonald
Susan Emily McDonald

Frances T. McDonald

Children of Dr. James McDonald

Joseph McDonald
Edward McDonald
Hugh McDonald
Henry McDonald
Minnie McDonald
Lilla McDonald
Annie McDonald
Mollie McDonald
Mattie McDonald
Amy McDonald

Children of Randall McDonald

Lizzie McDonald
Tobitha McDonald

Children of John McDonald

Cuyler McDonald

Children of Thomas McDonald

Rev. John McDonald

Children of William A. McDonald, Jr.

Harry McDonald
Donald McDonald
William A. McDonald III
Barnett McDonald
Ebb McDonald
Eva McDonald
Mattie McDonald
Ola McDonald

Children of Mary McDonald Hargraves

Bartoe Hargraves

Children of Martha McDonald Crawley
Col. J. Lee Crawley

Edward H. Crawley
Col. William Crawley
Randal Crawley
Thomas Crawley

David Crawley
John Crawley
Margaret Crawley Davis
Dollie Crawley

One Infant girl—Can't recall name.

Serene McDonald
Not married

Tobitha McDonald
Not married

Bobbie McDonald Tyson's Children

Lula Tyson
Mattie Tyson
Mamie Tyson

Era Tyson
Charlie Tyson
Edward Tyson

Edward McDonald
No children.

Miller McDonald
No children.

Children of Robert McDonald

Mamie McDonald
Edith McDonald
Catherine McDonald

James McDonald
Edward McDonald
Bryant McDonald

Children of Rev. George McDonald

Vella McDonald

Eula McDonald

Children of Charlie McDonald

Ethel McDonald Bullard
Pearl McDonald
Ruby McDonald
Aline McDonald
Maggie McDonald

Roy J. McDonald
Oscar McDonald
Herbert McDonald
Rev. Eustace McDonald
Julius McDonald

Children of Kathrine McDonald-Durham

Dillard A. Durham
Morma Durham Levy
Frankie Durham
Infant, not named, died.

Children of Mollie McDonald-Sweat

J. Lester Sweat
Vera Estelle Sweat Parker
Ora Kate Sweat
Infant, not named, died

Children of Susan E. McDonald-Sweat

Thelma Lucille Sweat-Miller
Lillian Marie Sweat-Cowart
Carey McDonald Sweat
Ralph Franklin Sweat
Juanita Rebecca Sweat-Odum
Norman Ancel Sweat
Susan Emily Sweat-Fason
Fred Carlton Sweat

Children of Frank B. McDonald

Frank B. McDonald, Jr.
Mary McDonald
Martha Burnum McDonald

Children of Millie McDonald-Parker

Cecil Parker

Ida McDonald-Parker-Cone

No children

Frances McDonald

Not married.

Child of J. Lester Sweat

Marguerite Sweat

Children of Vera Estelle Sweat-Parker

Vera Estelle Parker
Lee Parker, Jr.
Jack Parker

Ora Sweat

Died when two and a half years old.

Infant Son

Died when just a few days old.

Thelma Sweat-Miller
No children

Marie Sweat-Cowart's Children
Robert Lee Cowart, Jr.   Dorothy Marie Cowart

Carey McDonald Sweat, Jr.
Married, no children.

Juanita Sweat-Odum
No children.

Susan Sweat-Fason
No children.

Ralph Franklin Sweat
Not married

Norman Sweat
Not married

Fred Carlton Sweat
Not married

Children of Joseph McDonald
Willie McDonald-Stewart   Edna McDonald-Gunters

Children of Edward McDonald
Eddie McDonald   Mary Lou McDonald

Children of Hugh McDonald
James McDonald   One son died when infant.

Henry McDonald
No children, died when a boy.

Children of Minnie McDonald-Parker
Frank L. Parker   Gordon Parker, Jr.
Milton Parker   Maud Parker
Louise Parker

Children of Lilla McDonald-Brooker
Lillian Brooker Mary Brooker

Children of Annie McDonald-McCrary
Eva Clough McCrary Alton McCrary
Thurston McCrary Ann Lenora McCrary
Mary Dale McCrary

Children of Mollie McDonald-Lamkin
Kathrine Lamkin Elizabeth Lamkin

Mattie
No children, died when young.

Children of Lizzie McDonald-Becton
Lee Becton One son died at infancy

Tobitha McDonald
Married, do not remember who to.
One Son, whose name I do not know.

Harry McDonald's Children
Two girls, but do not know their names.

Child of Donald McDonald
Vera McDonald

Children of William A. McDonald III
Murphy McDonald Alice McDonald
One other daughter whose name I do not know.

Children of Barnett McDonald
Alice McDonald Barnett McDonald, Jr.

Children of Ebb McDonald
Three children whose names I do not know.

Children of Mattie McDonald-Moore
Harry Moore
Wardlaw Moore Arthur Moore, Jr.
Evelyn Moore Dorothy Moore
One son dead. Do not know name.

Eva McDonald
Never married.

Ola McDonald
Died when a baby.

Children of Bartoe Hargraves
Abe Hargraves
Leon Hargraves Mabel Hargraves
Sidney Hargraves Ruth Hargraves
Others whose names I do not know.

Children of J. Lee Crawley
Edward Crawley George Crawley
Donald Crawley Margaret Crawley

Children of Mamie McDonald-Enfinger
Robert Enfinger Mamie Enfinger

Children of Edith McDonald-Corbett
Mary Edith Corbett Hazel Corbett
Lavinia Corbett

Children of James McDonald
Two children whose names I do not know.

Children of Bryan McDonald
Three children whose names I do not know.

Children of Vella McDonald
Six children whose names I do not know.

Child of Eula McDonald
One child whose name I do not know.

Children of Ethel McDonald-Bullard

Elizabeth Bullard   Ethel Maude Bullard
Edna Bullard   Muzette Bullard

Children of Pearl McDonald-Miles

Charles Miles   Joyce Miles

Children of Ruby McDonald-Herrington

Jessie Herrington   Gene Herrington
Mary Herrington   George Herrington
     One baby son whose name I do not know.

Children of Aline McDonald-Christian

Mary Addie Christian   Clifford Christian

Children of Maggie McDonald-Johnson

Charles Malcom Johnson   One baby dead

Children of Roy J. McDonald

Margaret McDonald   Carey Eugene McDonald
Vada May McDonald   Fred McDonald
Charles McDonald   William McDonald

Children of Oscar McDonald

Lista McDonald   Fay McDonald
Ella Margaret McDonald   Madge McDonald
Myrtis McDonald   Carylon McDonald
          Oscar J. McDonald, Jr.

Children of Herbert McDonald

Frances McDonald-Tanner   Ina Lou McDonald
Blanche McDonald   Herbert McDonald, Jr.
          Mary Addie McDonald

Children of Eustuce McDonald

          Addie May Eufaula McDonald
Dorothy McDonald   Nerl Deen McDonald
          Infant, do not know name

JULIUS MCDONALD
Not married.

CHILDREN OF NORA DURHAM-LEVY
Kathrine Levy

DILLARD A. DURHAM
No children.

FRANKIE DURHAM
Not married.

REV. JOHN M. MARSHALL

Rev. John M. Marshall was born in Augusta, Georgia, Feb. 22, 1822. He was of English descent and, while his parents were not among the Colonists, his father had the honor of serving his country in the War of 1812. He was the youngest of six children. His father was an Episcopalian and his mother was a Methodist, both deeply pious, looking closely after the moral and religious training of their children.

During the forty-one years of his ministry, he served faithfully and lovingly, many charges both in north and south Georgia, and was returned after a lapse of years to a number of pastorates formerly served, finding always a most cordial welcome.

In 1849, he was married to Miss Margaret Amanda Wade of Marshallville. Eight children were born to them, only two of whom are living, Dr. Walter Marshall of Cordele and Frank Marshall of Atlanta. In 1869 this wife died, and he was later married to Mrs. Malvina Houston Simms. From this union six children were born of whom three survive, S. A. Marshall of Jacksonville, Fla., F. A. Marshall of Meridian, Miss., and the writer of this sketch, Mrs. W. A. Kennon of Monroe, La.

After my father's superannuation, he made Waycross his home. For four years as presiding elder he had resided there, and the warm welcome he received upon his settling permanently in Waycross never wore out or grew cold. He looked upon citizenship as a sacred duty and was always in sympathy with any movement for civic improvement or betterment and his advice and opinion on municipal affairs were sought and valued by those in authority in the community in which he lived. Possessed of a broad culture, both religious and secular, he was deeply interested in education, and was a moving spirit in placing the public school system of Waycross on an enduring foundation. He was a member of the city board of education from its creation and at his death was its honored president, ever foremost in speaking of the schools and for the schools. Just here it is fitting to say that to the zeal and courage of my father and of Dr. J. L. Walker, Judge Warren Lott, H. W. Reed, H. Murphy and a few others the public school system of Waycross is today a monument more enduring than brass.

On May 14, 1895, my father went home to that God to whom he had so constantly lifted his soul in prayer. Truly his life is a noble sermon teaching faithfulness in duty both to God and our fellow man.

The above was written by Pearl Marshall Kennon in 1900.

CAPTAIN DAVID A. McGEE

Captain David A. McGee moved to Tebeauville, Ga., in 1866. He was a typical example of the early builders of this section, who sought to serve in a sense of duty, their state and community as good citizens, rather than to seek the glory of public favor.

He was born in Screven County, May 2nd, 1837. He married Miss Martha J. Wilson of the same County on January 12th, 1859. Mrs. McGee was a woman of rare Christian character, a woman who loved her home and family and a faithful member of the Baptist church to which she belonged. Nine children were born of this union, Henry A., James T., David B., Ida J., John W., William J., Mrs. E. D. Carswell, Dr. Paul K. McGee and Mrs. W. F. Eaton.

Mr. McGee was first employed by the Central of Georgia R.R. in Feb. '61. When there was a call to arms, Jefferson Davis, President of the Southern Confederacy commissioned Mr. McGee to remain at his post on the railroad. Following the devastating march of Gen. Sherman through Georgia the railroads were torn up, tracks destroyed and rails bent into impossible use. Mr. McGee was stationed in Augusta and was called to serve the South by using his experience in road building to straighten and rebuild these tracks.

When he moved to Tebeauville he was employed by the Atlantic and Gulf R.R., afterwards known as the Savannah, Florida and Western, Plant System and Atlantic Coast Line.

That he faithfully performed every duty is shown by his long connection with the railroad, having been pensioned by the Plant System at the age of seventy-one. He died at the age of eighty-one.

In 1889 he was permanently located at Waycross and made Manager Instructor for the Apprentice School for railroad track work. His headquarters were located on the lot where the R.R. Y. M. C. A. now stands. The beautiful evergreen oaks now shading the grounds were set out by his own hands and will be a living monument to his love of beauty for years to come.

For forty-eight years Mr. McGee or as he was familiarly known as "Uncle Dave" served the railroad, holding the responsible positions of Conductor, Supervisor and Road Master.

He was a conscientious member and a deacon of the Central Baptist Church. Also a member of the I. O. O. F., K. of P. and Masonic Fraternities. He served as a member of the City Council for several terms.

It was said of him that he had as his life motto, "Do it now and when you do it, do it right."

"Well done thou good and faithful servant" would not be inappropriate for a life like his. A man who loved his home, his country and his God.

JESSE MIZELL

Jesse Mizell was another old pioneer of original Ware County, living in what is now Charlton County. He was a native of North Carolina, coming to Georgia, living for awhile in Emanuel County, then moving to Camden County and in a few years locating in what is now Charlton.

He died at the age of 60 and his wife, whose name we have not learned, died at the age of about 80. They had the following children:

1. Noah Mizell, who married Lovey Nobles.

2. James Harvey Mizell, born 1804 in N. C. Married Rebecca Tomlinson, daughter of William and Nancy (Register) Tomlinson of Clinch County. They lived in Clinch County, later removing to Hillsboro Co., Fla.

3. Owen K. Mizell, married (1) Nancy Wright, (2) Nancy Griffin. Served as representative from Charlton County.

4. Perry S. Mizell, married Lottie Albritton. Lived and died in Charlton County.

5. Sarah Mizell, married James Jones, Jr. Lived in Pierce Co.

6. Mary Margaret Mizell, born 1809, married Burrell Jones; died 1886.

MR. AND MRS. HERBERT MURPHY

Mr. and Mrs. H. Murphy's names are inseparably linked with the early history of Waycross, and they were always known as truly progressive citizens. They came here from New Jersey in 1879, when Waycross was but a crossing of the railroads and only a small hamlet. However, from the very day of their arrival Mr. Murphy began to clear away the virgin pine from the lot of land where his house was to stand. Dr. Lott gave him an acre of ground, provided that he build on it a good house "with glass windows in it." For over a year Mr. Murphy kept the blinds closed so that the passers-by would not observe that the house, although a good one, was for a time minus the glass windows. He later complied with all stipulations required by Dr. Lott and his home became known as one of the most attractive places along Plant Avenue.

MR. AND MRS. HERBERT MURPHY

Their long life in Waycross was one of enterprise and industry. They manifested a wonderful amount of interest in the material welfare of the town. Their lives, their precepts, and example in this community were worth more to the people in establishing order, law, good citizenship and civic righteousness than all the policemen and all the sheriffs that could be summoned to enforce respect for law and order. Their connection with the First Methodist Church was a long and useful one. Mr. Murphy for a number of years was chairman of the Methodist Board of Stewards, and neither he nor Mrs. Murphy were ever absent from their place of worship unless detained by providential causes.

Mr. Murphy was born January 18, 1836, and died April 18, 1922. Mrs. Murphy was born August 25, 1839, died February 17, 1922. Their children are numbered among some of Waycross' most useful and honored citizens, viz: Robert (who married Pauline Wilson), Kate (who married Dr. George Roach), Carrie (married Col. Leon Wilson), Charles (married Lollie Cook), Hattie (Judge Lee Crawley), May (Alvin Johnson).

DAVID JESSE MILLER

Mr. Miller was born November 11th, 1847, near Waresboro, Georgia; he was the son of Captain David J. Miller of Indian War fame who was born on a farm in Bullock County, Georgia. He joined the militia when a young man and was made Captain of a company which he led against the Indians. There were two forts at that time in this vicinity, one being located at Waresboro and the other on the present site of Waycross. Whenever the Indians were on the war-path the women and children took refuge in these forts, while the men with their trusty rifles pursued the invading foe. During the entire life of Captain Miller there were no railroads in the state and he had to market his cotton and his surplus farm products in Centerville and St. Mary's fifty miles away, journeying there and back with teams. On his return trips he would load his wagons with useful things for his family in exchange for his cotton and other produce carried there.

He was married to Loanza Dyer, who was born in his homestead until his death, at the age of seventy-two years.

He was married to Loanza Dyer, who was born in Tattnall County, and died in Bullock County, when sixty-seven years old. The union of Captain and Mrs. Miller was blessed by the birth of twelve children: William, Henry, Thomas, James, David, Jr., Stephen F., Nancy, Mary, Caroline, Susan, Serena and Anna.

Leaving home at the age of twenty-one years, David Jesse Miller purchased land in Ware County near Waycross and for a few years carried on a successful general farming business. Mr. Miller united with the Methodist Church as a youth and in 1879 was licensed as a local preacher and has since that time preached in various places in Ware County and nearby towns of other counties and has been recognized as a faithful minister of the Gospel.

Rev. Miller married in 1869, Miss Serena C. Sweat, who was born in October, 1847. She was a daughter of James and Mary (Blackburn) Sweat. Mrs. Miller passed to the life beyond in 1910, leaving five children whose names are: Mollie (Mrs. J. L. Stephens), Cora (Mrs. A. J. Williams), Lovina (Mrs. J. P. Lide), Della (Mrs. W. W. Webster), and James T. who married Minnie Davidson.

The children of Captain Miller, the great-grandfather of Mr. Jesse Miller, are: William Miller, father of Capt. David Miller, Martin and Ezekiel Miller, Catherine (Miller) McDonald, Susan (Miller) Jones, Mary Ann (Miller) Blackburn, Barbara (Miller) Hilliard, wife of Thomas Hilliard.

THOMAS MORTON

Thomas H. Morton was one of the early settlers of Waycross coming to this county and establishing his home near Waresboro in 1858. He was the son of David and Naomi Rebecca (Phillips) Morton and was born April 27, 1831 in Screven County, Georgia, but when he was quite young his parents moved to Effingham County, where he spent his childhood days. After coming to Ware County, he entered into all progressive activities for the upbuilding of the county and was one of the first to build a home in New Waycross. He bought from Mr. Banner J. Waldren a tract of 490 acres of land which Mr. Waldren had purchased from Dr. Daniel Lott when the timber on it was primeval, for the sum of $1,000.00. Mr. Waldren sold this property (after the timber was cut from the front of it) for $600.00. This 490 acres of land commenced near the arch that spans Reynolds street, and included the land for several blocks down Gilmore Street, extending back some distance beyond Morton Avenue School house. The land deeds show that when the deed was first made to Mr. Waldren the land was situated in the 8th district, Appling County and distinguished by lot number 203. When the War Between the States came on in 1861 Mr. Morton entered the service of the Confederate army, becoming a member of Company K, 26th Georgia Infantry, Gordon's Brigade. He served with distinction the Confederate Cause.

After his return from the War he was made tax collector for a period of 16 years. He also served on the first organized Board of Education, serving in that capacity for six years. He was a member of the committee who secured the site from the S. F. & W. railway company for the erecting of a school building, to be known as the "Plant Institute." This school, for lack of funds, was not built until 1887, which later became Central High School.

Mr. Morton was also a member of the board of Aldermen for several years. He donated to the city the original lot upon which the Morton Avenue School is built.

Mr. Morton was married March 13, 1859, to Miss Luvicy Sweat, who was the daughter of Captain James A. Sweat and his wife Elizabeth (Newburn) Sweat of Ware County. Mrs. Morton was a woman of fine intelligence, strong in character and exalted in high ideals.

Mrs. Morton was burned and her death was the result of the accident which happened in a very peculiar manner. It seems that she had lain down on her bed in the afternoon for a rest. A smoke had been made in the room to drive away mosquitos. The pan containing the fire, was immediately under the edge of the bed and Mrs. Morton's skirt hung over the side of the bed and rested on the fire. It soon caught and blazed up and before she could be rescued by parties in the house she was so seriously burned that she at once began to decline and death relieved her of her suffering. Mrs. Morton died September 7, 1905.

Mr. Morton later was married a second time to Mrs. Elizabeth Grovenstine Sweat, who was reared in St. Marys, Georgia. Mr. Morton died January 6, 1909. He left the following children:

Allen Strickland Morton, born March 23, 1860.

David Oliver Morton, born Sept. 22, 1861, died Nov., 1909.

Farley A. Morton, born April 19, 1865, died Jan., 1925.

Screven Morton, born Feb. 21, 1867.
George Newbern Morton, born Jan. 22, 1869.
Emma Charlotte Morton Yearby, born July 18, 1871.
Naomi Rebecca Morton Hall, born Nov. 21, 1873.
Thomas H. Morton, Jr., born Oct. 25, 1875, died 1913.
James A. Morton, born July 26, 1877.
Silas Virgil Morton, born Nov. 14, 1879.
Colquitt Morton, born Aug. 21, 1881, died 1884.

JONATHAN L. MORGAN

Jonathan Morgan was the son of Thomas C. Morgan who married Jane Moody. Jonathan Morgan was born in 1832. He married Susan Hargreaves, and they had three children, viz: Abraham, Rosa (Mrs. Frank Folks) and Mrs. Linnie Taylor. Mr. Jonathan Morgan died in Waycross May 5, 1907. Mrs. Morgan died June 28, 1916, at the age of eighty-two.

Mr. Abraham Morgan was born in that part of Appling, now Ware County, October 8, 1856. Jonathan Morgan, his father, moved to Clinch County in 1860.

ABRAHAM MORGAN

Mr. Morgan was born in Appling County, October 18, 1856. He was the son of Jonathan L. Morgan, and was reared on his father's farm about ten miles from Homerville. When a boy he was employed by Mr. Josiah Sirmans at Homerville to assist in his store, express office, and post office. After the death of Mr. Sirmans in 1881, Mr. Morgan was elected Clerk of the Superior Court of Clinch County, and commissioned January 13, 1881 for two years. After his term of office expired he moved to Waycross, where he was appointed postmaster by President Cleveland, May 5, 1885. When this office was raised to the third class in 1887, he was re-appointed and continued as postmaster until the Republicans went into power. He was appointed postmaster at Haylow, Georgia, in 1895, but in 1899, resigned and returned to Waycross, where he was employed as a clerk in the post office. In 1903 he was appointed assistant postmaster by W. A. McNeil, and reappointed in 1905 by Mr. C. E. Murphy and in 1913 by Mr. H. C. Bunn. He was assistant postmaster before resigning in 1928.

He married Miss Julia Wideman of Waycross, June 30, 1886, and they have one son, James Morgan.

The Headlight, published July 7, 1886, has this to say of Mr. and Mrs. Morgan on their wedding day:

"Miss Julia is a young lady of accomplishments of mind and art that make her a fit companion for the man whom she has chosen for a husband, and Mr. Morgan is a gentleman of honor, good business habits and an adornment to any town that claims his citizenship. Buoyant with hope, and basking in the sunshine of loves young dream we wish for them a safe passage down the valleys and over the mountains of life's road, and with the exception of short stops near the fountains of happiness that shall be found on the route we wish them a journey of pleasure without a pause."

JUHU JACKSON STYLES MURRAY

Mr. Jack Murray, as he is familiarly known, in his home town, was born and reared about eight miles from Waresboro. His parents were J. J. S. and Amanda (Fulwood) Murray. His grandfather's parents were J. J. S. and Sebra (Dyess) Murray. The Murray and Dyess families drew land in Ware County through the Cherokee Land Lottery in 1827. Mr. Murray's grandfather on his mother's side was Wilkins Fulwood, who was born in North Carolina in 1773, and settled in Appling County in 1840, later moving to Ware to be near his brother, James Fulwood, who was one of the early settlers of Ware, and afterward represented this county, not only in the Legislature, but was a Senator from here during the years of 1827-1834-41-43.

Mr. Murray, the subject of this sketch, having descended from sturdy pioneer parentage, has inherited a strong character and a determined spirit. He was educated in the public schools of Ware, and through the passing years had acquired an intimate knowledge of books and is recognized as one of the capable and outstanding citizens of the county of his nativity. He is a successful and enterprising farmer and is engaged in an extensive turpentine business.

Mr. Murray was married in Putnam County, Georgia, to Miss Mary Eugenia Harbin. The Harbins were an old and honored family of that county and Mrs. Murray has a right to value her lineage. Mr. and Mrs. Murray's children's names are: Maud, LeForest, Orian, Harry, Bernadine, Downing, Jack, Marizelle, and Earl.

WAYCROSS ONCE THE HABITAT OF WOLVES

The late Jackson S. Murray, father of Mr. Jack Murray, while on his way to the trading post at Centerville, Camden County, had the experience of meeting a pack of wolves not far from the land where Waycross now stands. He had just stopped for the night at Double

Branches not far from Dubuss Bay and tied his horse to a sapling close by, when in a short space of time he noticed that his horse was in a state of terror, showing this disturbed condition by continuously walking 'round and 'round the tree. Mr. Murray fully realizing that there was a cause for the agitation displayed by his horse, took his rifle from his cart, and waited for the coming of the denizens of the forest, for he really thought that he soon would be in mortal combat with the Indians. Suddenly he heard a noise in the air that was imminently the howl of wolves, and soon a pack of these carnivorous animals were in the path that ran by his camp. He climbed a tree, and shot into the drove of wild animals, which dispursed them and at daylight Mr. Murray proceeded safely on his journey to do his trading at Centerville, sixty miles away.

MRS. ALICE NIXON

Mrs. Nixon was the daughter of Benjamin H. and Alice (Boleyn) Russell. Col. Benjamin H. Russell, her father, was born in Wilkes County, Georgia, but moved to Florida in 1845. He was assassinated in 1861. He was a son of Benjamin Russell, a native of Georgia, and one of the early settlers of Bibb County. Mrs. Alice Russell, was born in Tallahassee, Fla., and was a daughter of Edwin Boleyn, a native of Loudoun County, Virginia. She died in Bainbridge in 1878, Mrs. Russell was a close relative of John Rolf and was a direct descendant of Robert Boleyn of Virginia, whose line of ancestry extended to the early settling of that state by the Boleyns of noted English ancestry.

Mrs. Nixon's husband, Mr. James Nixon, died while both were young, and she was left with two small children, totally dependent upon her for support. Few women ever faced the serious problems of life with a braver heart, and a more resolute spirit than Mrs. Nixon. She was frequently heard to say that the stumbling blocks that often arose to confront her, became stepping stones to her undaunted desire to surmount them, which she usually did. She was a woman of strong mentality, her brilliant mind was an inheritance from a long line of intellectual ancestry. She was a woman of singular nobility of character, enjoying the unqualified respect and confidence of all.

She came to Waycross from Bainbridge in the early part of 1885, and her name can almost be listed among the early settlers of Waycross. There were few people living in the town at that time who did not know Mrs. Nixon and those who were fortunate to claim her friendship then never lost it as long as she lived. She fully grasped the inspiring thought that "One cannot go far in life without entering upon partnership either in business or politics or friendship." She fully demonstrated her loyalty to those with whom she was daily associated that,

"Friendship is love with understanding."

She sleeps in Lott Cemetery beneath a marble slab, recently placed above her grave by her son, Frank Nixon, who is a progressive citizen of Greenville, S. C. Her daughter, Mrs. Lillian Brown's grave, is close beside that of her husband, James Brown and the wonderful Alice Russell Nixon.

MRS. MATILDA O'NEAL

That tigers were quite common in Ware about the year 1835-45 is shown by a series of "tiger stories" as related by Mrs. Matilda O'Neal, 92 year-old Ware Countian, who is now residing at the home of her son, W. J. Booth, near Waycross.

Mrs. O'Neal's full name is Matilda Jane Inman Booth O'Neal. Her maternal grandfather, Dr. Randall MacDonald was one of the first settlers of Ware County, coming here about the time the first settlements were made in Georgia, from the highlands of Scotland.

Her paternal grandfather, John Inman, was also an

early settler of this section. He was a local preacher in the M. E. Church, being one of the first ministers to preach in Kettle Creek Church, Ware County's oldest place of worship. He and all his immediate connections are buried at Kettle Creek.

Serene MacDonald Inman was Mrs. O'Neal's mother. She was married to James I. Inman (born 1812, died, 1897) Mrs. O'Neal was first married to Jesse G. Booth, who died while home on a furlough during the Civil War. He was serving at the time, in Virginia with the 26th Georgia Regiment.

Mrs. O'Neal, who, despite her advanced age still has a good memory, and can be induced at times to tell interesting occurrences of Ware County's past, relates the following:

About the year 1840, her mother, Mrs. James I. Inman, was walking one day, to the plantation home from a vacated tenant house, where she had been weaving cloth, when she saw what she thought was a large yellow dog. She told her husband of the strange dog, and he immediately suspected that it was a tiger. Next day Mr. Inman went to the house in which she had been weaving, and found where the tiger had torn up the ground around the door in an effort to get in. Feeling certain that the tiger would come back a neighboring planter, Mr. James, concealed himself in a Mulberry tree that grew near the door, armed with a gun. Some time later the tiger came back and Mr. James killed him. He was full grown, measuring over ten feet in length.

Mrs. O'Neal tells another interesting tale of a mother who saved her child's life by chopping off a tiger's paw with a hoe. This lady, a neighbor of the Inman's, was living, at the time, in a house with a "stick" chimney. At the foot of this chimney was a small scuttle hole through the wall. On this occasion the child was sleeping on an old-fashioned pallet with its head near this opening. A tiger crept up to this scuttle-hole on the outside, and when the mother's attention was first attracted was in the act of poking one of his front paws through to the child's head. The woman grabbed a hoe that happened to be inside the house, and chopped the paw off. A hunt was started by neighbors and tiger, minus a paw was found and killed.

The Inmans and Booths came to Georgia from the Carolinas and Virginia. They were among the early settlers of Ware County, along with the Corbitts, Lees, Millers and others. Both the Inmans and MacDonalds were cotton planters and slave-holders.

ALEXANDER O'QUINN

Alexander O'Quinn was born in North Carolina, Apr. 17th, 1819, and was moved by his father, Silas Peter O'Quinn, to Wayne County about the year 1821. This County included what is now Appling, Wayne and Pierce, and Ware, and was raised to full manhood with seven brothers and one sister, and married Susannah Dent, Feb. 9th, 1848, and there was born to them nine children, eight of which lived to be grown and married, the names of which was T. A. O'Quinn, Rebecca O'Quinn, Susannah T. O'Quinn, S. P. O'Quinn, A. H. O'Quinn, Nancy J. O'Quinn, John H. O'Quinn and William Duncan O'Quinn. His first wife died and he was married to Miss Mary Shaw of Liberty County.

He moved to Waycross in the Fall of 1882, bringing only two boys with him, John H. and William Duncan, having moved to Waycross to get nearer better schools, but not finding much school opportunities in Waycross and Ware County at that time, but barrooms running wide open on every corner.

One of his first acts on reaching Waycross and finding liquor sold everywhere was to help drive it out of Waycross and Ware County. His next act was to build bigger and better schools for Waycross, having served on the first School Board with Dr. Frank Folks, W. J. Carswell and others for several years, and retired as an honorary member of the Board.

He was always a great church worker, having helped to build and organize the first Baptist Church in Waycross, which was then in old Waycross on Albany Avenue. Afterwards this church was moved or rebuilt on the location which is now the First Baptist Church. He never failed to do what he could in the building of good schools and churches wherever he was located.

Mr. O'Quinn's son, William D. O'Quinn, has been eminently successful in his large business enterprises and his financial affairs have been well managed. His tireless energies were always exerted in behalf of any forward movement and he has been a particularly effective force in the development of Waycross. His business, the W. D. O'Quinn Clothing Co., is one of the oldest establishments in Waycross and is rounding out a stretch of thirty-five years of active existence.

MR. AND MRS. WILLIAM FOSTER PARKER

Mary Ewen Remshart, daughter of Rev. John W. and Jane Bryan Remshart was born in Savannah, Georgia, June 29, 1933.

William Foster Parker, son of Rev. Asa Hattey and Martha Foster Parker, was born in Sparta, Georgia, Sept. 27, 1824. His stepmother was Lucy Foster Breedlove.

MRS. W. F. PARKER

William Foster Parker and Mary Ewen Remshart were married by Rev. W. M. Crumby, December 13, 1853 in Trinity Methodist Church, Savannah, Ga.

In 1868 Mrs. William Foster Parker was confirmed in St. Johns Episcopal Church, Savannah, Georgia, by Rev. John W. Beckwith, D. D., Bishop of the Diocese of Georgia on Easter Day. Rev. Samuel Benedict, Rector. William Foster Parker was confirmed in Grace Episcopal Church, Waycross, Ga., Sunday, March 6, 1892, by Bishop Cleland K. Nelson, Bishop of Georgia, Rev. J. Richards Bicknell, Rector.

Mrs. Parker was one of the first members of Grace Episcopal Church and was lovingly called the Mother of the Church. She was Secretary and Treasurer of the Guild until she passed away.

When Mr. and Mrs. Parker and children moved from Savannah to Tebeauville there was no Episcopal Church here so Mrs. Parker, Mrs. U. J. Williams, and Mrs.

Oleman, decided to try and build one and they began by having bazaar festival suppers, and cake and candy sales and with the assistance of the gentlemen, the material that was given such as lumber, nails, and other building supplies—it did not take them very long to finish a place in which to hold their meetings.

Before the Church was built the ministers would come to Waycross and have services. The first Episcopal services held in Waycross were at the courthouse. The following was copied from a little clipping of Mrs. Parkers':

"There will be divine services of the Episcopal Church at the courthouse in Waycross the second Sunday in Lent morning and afternoon, the morning services the Ri. Rev. Bishop Beckworth will preach; Rev. Mr. Boon of Savannah will preach the afternoon services. At the morning services there will be Holy Communion—the afternoon services,—3 o'clock P. M."

Those who attended the Episcopal services at the courthouse were: Mr. and Mrs. William Foster Parker, Mr. and Mrs. U. J. Williams, Mr. and Mrs. Vincent Starr and daughter Annie, Mr. Orville D. Parker, Mrs. Nixon and daughter Lilla, Mrs. Oleman and daughter Haddie, Maggie M. Parker (late Mr. L. G. Jenkins), Mr. William Wright, Sr., his sons William, Robert, Alex, and Vincent.

Mrs. Parker worked untiringly for the upbuilding of the church of her faith and many children were trained in the Episcopal Sunday School under her devout Christian teaching. Her beautiful face was often lighted by the great love that she infused into her work of carrying the message to the young people of her community.

Mr. Parker was Captain in the Confederate War and served through the entire War and was with General Lee at Appomattox when he surrendered.

The children of Mr. and Mrs. Parker, are: Lucy M. (later Mrs. J. G. Lipscomb) Maggie (Mrs. Lucius Jenkins) Orville, Foster, Sumter.

PHILIP COLEMAN PENDLETON

One of the first settlers of Tebeauville was Mr. Philip Coleman Pendleton. This well-known newspaper man was born in Putnam County, Georgia, in 1812. His father, Coleman Pendleton, came to Georgia about the year 1807 from Culpepper County, Virginia, and settled in the then new county of Putnam. Mr. Pendleton married Catherine Tebeau, of Savannah, whose father was the grand-nephew of John Adam Trentland (first Governor of Georgia) and whose mother was Hulda Lewis of New York, into whose family Betty, the sister of George Washington, married and whose descendants now own Washington's two swords.

For several years Mr. Pendleton practised law in Macon but later embarked in the newspaper business, and for awhile published The Southern Post.

In the year 1836 the Seminole War in Florida broke out and the young editor, seized with a patriotic fire to serve his country, he either suspended the Post, or merged it into one of the other papers of the city of that day, and volunteered for the war, enlisting with the Macon Volunteers. They had several months of hard service and at one time besieged in a blockhouse and came near being starved. When relief came they were planning to kill and eat the Major's horse, the only animal they had.

Captain Pendleton drew a tract of land on Lake George, St. John's river, Florida, from the government as a bounty for his service in the Seminole War. On this tract he planted an orange grove and wished to move his family to it, but his wife remembered the war in her childhood and still had a fear of the Indians.

He then plunged into the pine woods of South Georgia and got as near to Florida as he could. The location he selected was the spot where Waycross now stands. Here he was planting and selling his large timber acreage to Aaron Reppard when the War came on. Although fifty years old, he responded again to the call of his State and enlisted for the War. He raised a company of volunteers in Ware County and upon its organization became the Major of the Fiftieth Georgia Regiment. He participated in several Virginia campaigns, and did valiant service at the second battle of Manassas.

Major Pendleton never wholly recovered from a spell of sickness while he was in the war. In January, 1864, he removed from Ware to Lowndes County and engaged in planting.

The close of the war found him broken in health and fortune. But with renewed hope and courage he began at Valdosta in 1867 the publication of the South Georgia Times, (now Valdosta Times), which he continued to publish till his death.

LOUIS BOUREGARD PENDLETON

Louis Pendleton, son of Philip Coleman Pendleton, was born at Tebeauville (Now a part of Waycross, Georgia) April 21, 1861. His father was a well-known Georgia editor, who established "A Southern Lady's Book" in Macon, in 1840. He is the great-grand-nephew of Edmund Pendleton and the brother of Charles Pendleton (late editor of the Macon Telegraph) he was a former citizen of Ware County during his youthful days.

After completing his education in the North, he contributed to "The Sunny South" under the pseudonym of "Richard Penfield" an imaginative serial entitled "Louelle", which was written when he was only nineteen. It opened wide the gates of authorship and he has since written a number of successful volumes of fiction, among them "Bewitched", a novel of South Georgia life; "In the Wire Grass" (New York, D. Appleton and Co.), "King Tom and the Runaways", a story of adventure in the Georgia Swamp, 1890, "The Sons of Ham", a study of the race problem in narrative form, 1895, "The Wedding Garment", 1894, "In the Okefinokee", "Curita", a Cuban romance, "Corona of the Nanlahalas", a tale of the North Carolina mountains, "Lost King Ammon", "In Assyrian Tents", "A Forest Drama", and "In the Camp of the Creeks", a story of the Indian uprising in Georgia in 1836. The latest production of his pen is "The Life of Alexander H. Stephens", an excellent portrayal of the great commoner and sage of Liberty Hall. For several years he has resided at Bryn Athyn, Pa.

EDWARD ALDINE POUND

For seventeen years Professor Pound was the efficient Superintendent of the Waycross Public Schools and the people with one accord keenly realized that his going away, to take up other work, was an irreparable loss to the entire community. The departure of Professor Pound from Waycross was regretted not only by those who personally knew the graciousness of his life and friendship but also by the people of the entire community. His name was linked with a cause that has blessed the Waycross people; men, women and particularly little children and his fine influence will continually bless them through the coming years. Waycross schools and the people learned to lean on the brain and the strong personality of this man and when the hour of his departure arrived each were face to face with saying good-bye. It was then that the heart-strings were wrenched asunder and Waycross saw its loved and esteemed one through a mist of tears. It could not have been otherwise. The man who daily for seventeen years played upon the heart-strings of a people without striking a minor cord could not have gone from among them without an expression of sadness veiling the face of the people. Out of the confusion and medley of the social jargon this unique educator's words often dispelled clouds and cares. An expressive thing he once said to a graduating class in the city schools was: "Life is ever a series of contrasts: First the night and then the day, the shadow and then the sunshine, the gloom and then the joy, the trial and then the triumph.

"If life be set in God-arranged grooves and in accordance with His will this is always the natural order for however dark the night, the brightness of the day comes after the darkness of the spiritual night and the greater the trial, the greater the triumph."

After leaving Waycross he often came back to see his friends whose hearts were ever brightened by his presence. He now comes no more. The great Arcane hour of death found him ready and now he is satisfied in the Great City not made with hands. He is there no doubt still carrying on in a greater and grander way, the beautiful life that had its beginning on earth.

MR. WILLIAM PARKER

Mr. William Parker was born in that part of Appling that is now a part of Ware, January 24, 1843, and was fifty-four years of age when death came to him July 28, 1897. He was so quiet and unassuming that his acts of kindness, and not his light was hidden. In sickness and sorrow he could be counted upon, his sympathy and pockets were always respon-

WILLIAM PARKER

sive. Those who did not know him were his only critics, and he has been heard to say that if he ever harmed anyone he was sorry for it, and that if anyone felt unkindly toward him he was sorry he had given them cause.

MRS. WILLIAM PARKER

William Parker was the son of a well-known physician, Dr. C. G. B. W. Parker. Dr. Parker moved from Appling County to Baker County, Florida when William Parker was thirteen years old, and he was living there when the tocsin of War Between the States was sounded. Like the true man he always proved to be, he volunteered and went to the front with the Fifth Florida Volunteers. He was in the fights around Richmond, Manassas, Bull Run, Petersburg, and many others of less importance, but was never wounded. In the latter part of 1864, he was with a scouting party, who surrendered in the mountains of North Tennessee, where they were captured but not until his Captain and the larger part of his comrades were wounded or dead. When the War closed in 1865, he was a prisoner in the state of New York, and having made friends with some of the soldiers who guarded him during his captivity, when he was paroled he went home with some of the "Boys in Blue" when they were mustered out of service. Mr. Parker located in Palmyra, N. Y., where he worked for wages, and spent his earnings in going to school, for nearly three years. In the latter part of 1868 he returned South to visit his father who had moved from Florida to Coffee County, Georgia. There he met Miss Charlotte Ricketson and after a brief courtship they were married on the 17th of June, 1869.

They made their home in Clinch County, subsequently returned to Coffee County, where they resided until they moved to Waycross in 1886.

In politics Mr. Parker was a Democrat, but the last few years of his life, he joined the Prohibition Party and voted exclusively in the interest of that cause.

He was a newspaper man, he published the Pioneer at Pearson in 1870, sold it out, and then started and published the Coffee County Gazette. He later moved to Waycross, selling out his paper interest in Coffee, and bought The Waycross Headlight. He afterward sold this, and at the time of his death, was in no active business.

Mr. Parker's wife, Mrs. Charlotte Parker and three daughters survive him. His eldest daughter, Annabelle, is Mrs. Jefferson Wilcox, wife of Dr. Wilcox of Willacoochee; his second daughter, Arloa, married Mr. Alonzo Strickland of Blackshear, Georgia, his third daughter, Agnes, is Mrs. Samuels of Florida.

ALEXANDER PARIS PERHAM

Perham, Alexander Paris, soldier, publisher, was born at Farminton, Maine, Jan. 21, 1838, son of B. F. and Carolyn Ann (Bryant) Perham, who in that year removed to Thomasville, Ga. His father was a civil engineer.

JUDGE ALEXANDER P. PERHAM

Alexander P. Perham received his education in the schools of Thomasville. At the outbreak of the Civil War he enlisted in the Thomasville Guards, which were mustered into the Confederate service as a part of the 29th Regiment, Georgia Infantry. He was elected First Lieutenant of his Company. Later served under Johnston and Hood. Was on Gen. Stevens and Gen. Johnston's staff with rank of Captain for nearly two years and served until the end of the war, displaying much gallantry.

He then took up his residence at Quitman, Ga., where he was elected ordinary of Brooks County, and repeatedly re-elected, remaining sixteen (16) years in that relation. During a part of this period he was editor and owner of the Quitman "Free Press." In 1893 he settled at Waycross, Ga., and shortly thereafter established the "Waycross Evening Herald," of which he was editor and publisher until 1912, when he sold his interests and retired from active business cares.

Gov. Joseph M. Terrell (q. v.) appointed him trustee of the Confederate Veterans Home of Georgia, in

1905, and Gov. Joseph M. Brown (q. v.) reappointed him in 1911. In 1910 he was appointed Census Supervisor of the 11th Congressional District of Georgia.

He was Commander of his camp, United Confederate Veterans, and a member also of the Masonic Fraternity. He was a communicant of the Central Baptist Tabernacle, Waycross, Ga. He found his chief recreation in truck farming and fishing.

In the columns of his newspaper he daily advocated those things that tend to make a community better and more prosperous. In him was found the perfect type and model of good citizenship. In his editorial columns he led in many reform movements for the better government of the city and community, and he was likewise a leader in many undertakings for the commercial development of Waycross and of Georgia and the South.

He analyzed with agreeable frankness the personal qualities of great and good men, even when they sat in high places, and as an unmasker of political and social intrigue and humbug he was surpassed by but few country editors. He was a brave soldier, a sound newspaper man, a thorough student of many momentous questions that arose in his time.

He, although born in the North, imbibed, cherished, upheld and illustrated the best traditions of the South. He was a staunch friend of many of the celebrated old line newspaper editors of Georgia, and his own journal wielded a powerful influence in moulding public opinion in a district far beyond its legitimate field of circulation.

Judge Perham was married at Quitman, Ga., 1869, to Alice, daughter of D. W. McNeil of Quitman. Alice McNeil was a woman of rare charms, in brilliancy of conversation and in graciousness of manner, she was excelled by none. In all relationship of her, as wife, mother, friend, and Christian, love dominated. Her qualities of mind and heart fitted her to adorn any society; sweetness and gentleness were prominent traits in her character, naturally endearing her to her friends and acquaintances. Nor did she lack firmness, one of the most important elements in one's personality. Superior in intellectual attainments and possessing the sweet amenities of the heart, she was a typical representative of the noble women of the Old South.

Judge and Mrs. Perham had a deep sorrow to accidently come to them in the death of their only son, Alexander Paris Perham, who was killed in 1909 by a live electric wire that had fallen on the sidewalk during a storm.

Judge Perham died April 18th, 1915, and Mrs. Perham soon followed him to their eternal home, her death occurring during the year of 1918. They left in Waycross two strong representatives of their name in their two daughters, Daisy and Carrie Perham, who live in the old home, established by one of Georgia's most brilliant editors and his accomplished wife.

The late Judge A. P. Perham, editor of The Waycross Herald, writing of the Atlanta Journal, said, "The Journal covers Dixie like the Dew."

The Atlanta paper immediately expressed thanks for the good words of Editor Perham and in a few days those same words became the slogan which is so familiar to readers of The Atlanta Journal.

TRAVIS PITTMAN

Travis Pittman was the son of Linsey Pittman, who was born in Robinson County, North Carolina, and when attaining his majority, he boldly struck out for himself, coming to Georgia and settling in Ware County, which was then a frontier region. Indians still inhabited the woods, far outnumbering the whites and frequently terrorized the new settlers. He first purchased a tract of wild land on Kettle Creek and later bought land including the present site of the Congregational Church. After improving a part of his land, he moved to the southern part of the county, and on the farm which he there bought and improved, spent the remainder of his long life, passing away at the age of seventy-four years.

Travis Pittman was born in Ware County and assisted

his father in the pioneer labor of redeeming a farm from the wilderness, and well remembers through his life many of the thrilling incidents of those early days. As a boy he heard the report of the guns when the Wilds family was massacred, and saw the soldiers rushing madly by in their pursuit of the fleeing savages, that having been one of the worst crimes committed by the Indians within his memory. On reaching man's estate, he bought land near the old homestead and by dint of heroic labor cleared and improved a farm. In his early days, there being no railroads in this section of the country he was forced to haul all of his surplus farm productions to Centerville and Traders Hill, over fifty miles away, that being the nearest market or trading post. Selling his farm in 1886, he explored Florida, looking for a more progressive location. After a thorough search in the more fertile parts of that state, he became convinced that Georgia had much greater advantages and resources, and returned to his native county. Purchasing land near Waresboro he subsequently resided there until his death in 1906.

Converted in his youth, Travis Pittman joined the Methodist Episcopal Church, and having been licensed, preached for some years in Ware and adjoining counties. He later united with the Congregational Church and continued a preacher in that denomination, continuing for many years an earnest and zealous worker in the Master's vineyard.

Rev. Travis Pittman married Miss Kate Mills, who was born in Milledgeville, a daughter of Mr. and Mrs. George Mills. She and Mr. Pittman were the parents of seventeen children. Their home is on a wonderfully equipped farm near Waresboro, where Mrs. Pittman has lived since the death of her husband.

THOMAS SPALDING PAINE

Dr. Spalding Paine was the youngest son of Charles Joshua Paine, the former a prominent physician of Georgia, and for a number of years dean of the physicians of the state, whose duty it was to examine all physicians before license to practice could be given. Dr. Paine died in 1859. His son, Thomas Spalding, who was born in Milledgeville, April 17, 1839, was educated in the public schools of his native city and in the military school at Marietta. Immediately after his father's death he left the city of his birth and went to Thomasville, where for two years he engaged in a clerical position, which he resigned in July, 1861 to enter the Confederate Army. He received the commission of first Lieutenant of Company B, Twenty-ninth Georgia regiment, which was sent to the coast. The following April he was transferred to Brevard's battalion of Florida as ordinance sergeant, under Gen. Finnegan, stationed near Jacksonville, whose force had an engagement Nov. 9, 1862 with gun-boats on the St. John's River. In January, 1863, Captain Paine organized a cavalry company, Company E, of the Twentieth Georgia Battalion, and was stationed on the coast that year. In April, 1864, the battalion was ordered to Virginia where, in an engagement with the Federal forces advancing upon Cold Harbor, Trevilian Station, Captain Paine received a slight wound. The next January, they were transferred to Gen. Joseph Johnston's command and sent to Charleston, S. C., from which time, until the surrender they were almost constantly engaged in skirmishes. After his discharge and return home, Captain Paine at once went into the drug business.

During the war, Dec. 24, 1862, Captain Paine was happily married to Miss Lena Mary Serxas of Thomasville, a grand-daughter of Jacob Serxas, a refugee from the island of San Domingo, during the insurrection.

Captain Paine and family removed to Waycross in 1892. Mrs. Paine dying April 15, 1912, and Captain Paine following her to their home eternal Sept. 14, 1914. Captain and Mrs. Paine have three children living: Annie (Mrs. Ernest Mann), Lena (Mrs. Jelks) and Charles Paine, a prominent druggist of Waycross.

REV. JOHN WAY QUARTERMAN
MRS. LAURA YOUNG (McCOLLOUGH) QUARTERMAN

John Way Quarterman was born in Jonesville, McIntosh County, Georgia, March 18th, 1841.

His ancestry, on both sides, can be traced back to the Colony that crossed the ocean, settling first in Massachusetts, then in South Carolina, then in St. John's Parish, Georgia.

REV. AND MRS. JOHN WAY QUARTERMAN

His father was Edward William Quarterman. His paternal grandparents were Rev. Robert and Rebecca (Quarterman) married September 1st, 1807.

His (1) great grandparents were Thomas and Rebecca (Baker) Quarterman, married in 1779.

His (2) great grand parents were John and Elizabeth (Baker) Quarterman. His mother was Adaline Way.

His maternal grand parents were John and Rebecca (Jones) Way, married September 17th, 1807.

His (1) great grand parents were John and Sarah (Goulding) Way, married Feb. 15th, 1790.

His (2) great grand parents were Moses and Lydia (Mitchell) Way, married Feb. 9th, 1776.

His (3) great grand parents were Parmenas and Elizabeth (Andrews) Way, married 1756.

His (4) great grand parents were Moses and Sarah Way.

His (5) great grand parents were Aaron and Joanna (Sumner) Way.

His (6) great grand parents were Henry and Elizabeth Way who came from Bristol, England in 1631.

Much of his boyhood life was spent at the plantation home at Riceboro in Liberty County. The greater part of his common school education was received under the teaching of Mr. Samuel Varnedoe.

Blessed with pious parents he grew up under the influence of a strict home religion and was a regular attendant at, and life-long member of old Midway Church His father was a deacon in this Church for thirteen years up to the time of his death in 1864. His grandfather, Robert Quarterman, was deacon for twelve years and pastor for twenty-five years until his death.

Following this ministerial influence young John early decided to become a minister himself, and then began the struggle to secure college and seminary training. At the age of eighteen he secured his first school to teach in Irwin County. In October, 1859, he entered Oglethorpe College as a Sophomore. In the spring of 1861 he completed his Junior work but an interruption came in the breaking out of the War Between the States. Duty called to the defense of the Southland and the entire Junior class at Oglethorpe College responded. In 1861 John Quarterman went into the army as a member of the Liberty Independent Troop, of Liberty County, which was soon mustered out for picket service on the Georgia coast. After six months a change was made, and the young soldier became a member of Company B, 20th Battalion of Ga. Cavalry, and was stationed on James Island, S. C. A heavy picket from Co. B was placed on Stone river where the Federal gun-boat "Isaac Smith" was captured with all on board. In 1863 Co. B was returned to the Command in Georgia and did picket duty on the coast from Savannah to Darien. Early in 1864 the Command was ordered to report for service to Gen. R. E. Lee, then above Richmond, Va. A forced march took them to Richmond about May 25th. On May 28th in a desperate battle at Hawe's Shop the Georgia Command lost heavily, the Colonel and Major and many of the officers of Co. B were killed. In all of the bloody struggles in the vicinity of Petersburg Co. B bore its full part in killed and wounded. Though greatly needed, new officers were not given to this Battalion, instead the Command was disbanded and the Companies set off in other regiments. Co. B was made Co. G in "Jeff Davis' Legion" in Young's Brigade of Hampton's Cavalry commanded by Col. Fred Waring. In January of 1865 the whole Command was transferred to the army then under command of Gen. Jose. E. Johnston and met the forces of Gen. Sherman at Orangeburg, S. C. There followed a period of almost constant engagements in the states of North and South Carolina, but in all of this desperate fighting, when comrades, even a loved brother also, fell beside him, God seemed to cover and protect the head of the young soldier, John Way Quarterman. He was never wounded, never made a prisoner. In April, 1865, when Gen. Johnston surrendered to Gen. Sherman at Greensboro, N. C., John Quarterman, with one dollar in his pocket, and a mule on which to ride, returned to Georgia and entered upon the task of gathering up the threads of life in a devastated South Georgia home.

On Feb. 21st, 1864, while his Command was stationed in Georgia, John Way Quarterman married Laura Young McCollough of Walthourville, Liberty County. She was born October 7th, 1843, and reared in the same Dorchester Colony. Her mother came of the Quarterman family and her father was a native Scot, coming to America at about the age of seventeen years. The plantation home of the McColloughs was named "Pleasant Valley" and here the children grew up, going to school in Walthourville under the teaching of Dr. Farmer, a noted educator of his time. Hers was a typical Puritan home and her church connection was with old Midway Church.

Leaving his young bride, John Quarterman marched

with his Command to Richmond and for three months there was no word of communication between the lovers. She knew of the terrible battles in which the soldiers were engaged. He knew that all he held most dear lay in the path of Sherman's march to the sea. What else may have befallen neither knew.

With what rejoicing John Quarterman found his young wife with her parents in Montgomery County whither they had refugeed. Work on the farm and in the school room afforded a meager living and all thought of preparation for the ministry was abandoned. But God was calling this young man and with the coming of his uncle, Rev. R. Q. Way, as pastor of the Mt. Vernon church, young John arranged to study Theology under his direction.

The student was taken under the care of Savannah Presbytery in 1867, licensed to preach at Thomasville in 1868 and ordained to the full ministry at Brunswick in 1871 with Rev. I. S. K. Axson, D.D., as moderator of the meeting of Presbytery. A call from the Darien church was placed in the hands of the young minister and was accepted by him.

Rev. and Mrs. Quarterman with several small children, came to live in Waycross in the year 1880, moving to this town from Blackshear where, for five years Rev. Quarterman was pastor of the Presbyterian church and also in charge of the Academy. Upon moving to Waycross he again took this double responsibility of preaching and teaching. In those days the old Academy stood on the corner where Col. L. A. Wilson's home now stands. The one house of worship occupied the middle of what was then Pond, now State St. at the intersection of Church St. This church was built by the money and efforts of all the Christian people of Waycross as a Union Meeting House. It was used by all denominations under a most harmonious arrangement, each taking a Sunday in turn. As Waycross grew the Methodists planned for a full-time preacher and the other denominations used the court house until they could erect their own buildings.

For about five years Rev. Quarterman had charge of the Waycross Academy, and during that time he had two assistant teachers, Miss Virginia Williams, now Mrs. S. C. Houk; and Dr. George Corbett of South Carolina. The names and the personalities of these three teachers linger still in the minds of the pupils who may be living today.

In 1881 the Quartermans purchased a lot and built a home in which, as Rev. Quarterman himself states "we spent fifteen years—perhaps the happiest years of our life."

Even in those early days Waycross was a railroad center and from his home town this earnest man of God went forth to preach, many churches feeling the influence of his ministry. A true pioneer missionary he was, going into the far corners of Savannah Presbytery, often in his buggy, sewing the seed of the Word of God. There were few churches in the Presbytery which were self-supporting and to care for his family of eight children supplementary work was necessary—so he preached and taught and plowed his fields. Asked once when he thought out his sermons he replied, "my sermons unfold to me as I watch the earth break beneath my plow." Twice Rev. Quarterman was chosen to represent Savannah Presbytery at the meeting of the highest court of the Presbyterian church, the General Assembly. One meeting was in St. Louis, Mo. and the other in Richmond, Va. As a visitor he attended the Calvin General Assembly meeting in Savannah.

In the year 1895 Rev. Quarterman was called to a group of churches of which Marlow was the center, so the family moved to that town. From that time until 1909 Rev. Quarterman continued to live with the churches which he served as pastor, not living in Waycross but keeping in close touch through his children who had settled there. About this time a little home was bought in Beach, only twenty miles from Waycross, in preparation for the time when he would be retired from the active ministry. In this modest home Rev. and Mrs. Quarterman celebrated the golden anniversary of their marriage on Feb. 21st, 1914. The children, with their families and a few close friends gathered for the occasion and the day, bitterly cold, passed happily. Many remembrances from absent friends were received, among them a personal letter from President Woodrow Wilson who was a friend of long standing.

In the fall of 1914 Rev. Quarterman was retired from the active ministry after nearly fifty years of service as a soldier of the Cross. In the summer of 1915 Rev. and Mrs. Quarterman spent several weeks in beautiful Montreat where he was entertained as a guest of the Southern Presbyterian Church.

Rev. John Way Quarterman passed into the great beyond on April 4th, 1916 when he was 76 years of age.

After his death Mrs. Quarterman moved back to Waycross, making her home with her daughter, Mrs. L. O. Futch and her eldest son, Mr. Leland Quarterman. For nearly ten years Mrs. Quarterman dwelt among her children, alert and interested in all of their affairs and also the affairs of the whole town, religious and civic.

On December the 3rd, 1925, she joined the loved companion who had gone on before.

Four of their daughters still live in Waycross, Mrs. L. O. Futch, Mrs. J. R. Whitman, Miss Winifred Quarterman and Mrs. R. W. Walker. Their only living son, Mr. J. B. Quarterman, lives in Valdosta with a family of four children.

REV. JOHN WALDHAUER REMSHART

Rev. John Waldhauer Remshart was a representative of two of the earliest pioneer families of Georgia, and he labored faithfully for a score of years as a clergyman of the Methodist Episcopal church, his life being one of signal consecration and nobility. He died July 3, 1878, at Tebeauville, now Waycross, Ga. He was born in the city of Savannah, Ga., Jan. 7, 1801, a son of Daniel and

Elizabeth (Waldhauer) Remshart, both of whom were likewise natives of Savannah, where the former was born Oct. 20, 1767, and the latter June 20, 1773.

John Remshart, father of Daniel, and Jacob Casper Waldhauer, father of Elizabeth (Waldhauer) Remshart, were members of German families who came to Georgia with Oglethorpe, at the time of his second voyage to his newly founded colony. The parents of these two sterling pioneers were German Lutherans and joined the Salzberger colony, at Ebenezer in February, 1736. Both John Remshart and Jacob C. Waldhauer were educated under the tutorship of John Martin Bolzius, the finest scholar of his time in Georgia. John Remshart's name appears in various historical collections as among those citizens of Georgia who protested against the action of the colonies in taking up arms against the British crown, their animus being the result of the fact that England had afforded them freedom to worship God according to their convictions and ideas, and this prompted a spirit of loyalty. After the conflict and bloodshed in North Carolina, however, Mr. Remshart warmly espoused the cause of the colonists. Rev. John W. Remshart was in active service as a minister of the Methodist Episcopal church for a score of years, his retirement resulting from the loss of his voice, which rendered it impossible for him to continue public speaking as a vocation.

On Nov. 11, 1822, Rev. John W. Remshart was united in marriage to Miss Jane Bryan, daughter of James and Elizabeth (Langley) Bryan, of Savannah, and she died in 1881. Concerning the children of this union the following is a brief record: Ann Elizabeth became the wife of John May; Amanda Jane married Saul S. Box and after his death became the wife of Elliott C. Johnson; Pamelia Nowlan became the wife of Edward O. Withington; Mary Ewen married William F. Parker; Margaret Eliza died at the age of twenty years, and Daniel at the age of eighteen. William Capers was a soldier in the Confederate army during the War Between the States, and died on

March 3, 1878; and Isabella Cornelia became the wife of Dr. Joseph H. Redding, on April 28, 1892.

MRS. ISABELLA REDDING

Mrs. Isabella Redding was born in Savannah, and spent a part of her childhood days there. Her parents, Rev. John Waldhauer Remshart and Jane Bryan Remshart, were refugees to Waycross from Savannah when Sherman captured that city. They settled at Tebeauville, where they lived until their death. Isabella Remshart later lived in a home of her own in "New Waycross."

In 1887 "Miss Isa." organized a literary society in Waycross, a W. C. T. U., and the Francis S. Bartow Chapter, United Daughters of the Confederacy. She was president of both of the latter named societies for over ten years. In 1888 she organized the first circle of the Kings Daughters in Waycross, and one of the seven circles is named in her honor. The Kings Daughters for over twenty-five years have maintained the King's Daughters Hospital, and she served for 14 years as secretary of the hospital board.

In 1892 "Miss Isa." was married to Dr. Joseph H. Redding, a prominent physician of Waycross, who passed into eternity July 7, 1914.

Mrs. Redding organized the Jonathan Bryan Chapter, Daughters of American Revolution and served as regent of that chapter for over twenty-eight years. In 1914 she was elected honorary state regent of Georgia, having served four years as state chairman of the historic program committee. She was twenty-four years president of The Georgians, and remained an active member as long as she lived.

Since childhood Mrs. Redding took deep interest in Christian welfare activities. She served for many years as chairman of the Woman's Missionary Society of the Methodist Episcopal Church, and when the First Methodist Church was built in New Waycross, she was active in doing her part in the furnishings of that church. She put her best work into that of the Sunday School of which she was a beloved teacher. Her last years were given to Bible study, and she acquired a great knowledge of that "Book of Books."

She was long an active member of the Methodist Episcopal Church, South, and her heart was always in its interests.

She was a woman of fine literary attainments and was the author of the "Life and Times of Jonathan Bryan," "The League of Nations," and "My Beloved Country." She gave three hundred copies to the Army Y. M. C. A. She was often a contributor of articles on current topics to the newspapers.

Mrs. Redding was a member of the City Library Board, that she helped to organize, was a member of the Colonial Dames of America and a Girl's Scout Councilor.

After serving well her generation, by the will of God, she fell asleep on the way and the weary pilgrim's journey ended in peace, May 13, 1929.

DR. J. HENRY REDDING

Dr. Redding was born in Monroe County, Georgia, Nov. 26, 1848, a son of James Tarpley and Ann (Dickson) Redding, the former born in Monroe County, and the latter in Crawford County, Georgia. James Tarpley Redding was the son of William Chambliss and Margaret (Flewellyn) Redding, the former was a son of Anderson Redding, who was a valiant soldier in the Continental line during the war of the Revolution, and was present at the surrender of Lord Cornwallis at Yorktown. Dr. Redding's parents moved to Louisiana in December, 1858, and were refugees to Texas in 1863. In April, 1865, Dr. Redding, who was then sixteen years old, donned the Confederate uniform and rode on horseback, a distance of forty miles in Texas to visit the nearest postoffice to learn where he could join the Confederate

Army. Great was his dismay and disappointment when he received the information concerning the surrender of General Lee.

Dr. Redding secured his literary education in Emory College, Oxford, Georgia, the family having returned to this state after the close of the War. In 1878-9 he attended medical lectures in Louisville, Ky., and in 1881 he was graduated in the College of Physicians and Surgeons of Atlanta, receiving his degree of Doctor of Medicine and being valedictorian of his class. His standing as a student may be comprehended when it is stated, that he took every prize offered by the faculty. He was engaged in practice in the city of Macon until 1884 when he took up his residence in Waycross, where he controlled a large and important professional business and was held in high regard as a citizen and physician.

He was a member of various medical associations, was a Democrat in his political adherency and both he and his wife held membership in the Methodist Episcopal Church South.

On Feb. 2, 1873, he was married to Miss Lucy C. Story, daughter of Col. Richard L. and Jane (Dickson) Story of Hancock County, Georgia. She was summoned to the life eternal on August 1, 1882, survived by two sons—Henry Story, born May 25, 1875, and Charles Leonides, born July 31, 1879. Dr. Redding was later married to Mrs. Lula Edwards Tomblinson of Macon, Georgia, who died in Waycross, June 21, 1889. On April 28, 1892 was solemnized the marriage of Dr. Redding to Miss Isabella C. Remshart, daughter of Mr. John Remshart, who was one of the early settlers of old Tebeauville.

AARON REPPERD

Mr. and Mrs. Repperd and their three children once lived in Tebeauville. Mr. Repperd owned and operated a large saw mill on the site where the Murson Hotel is now located. This was one of the most extensive mills in

Southern Georgia. It was Mr. Repperd's organized forces who cut the primeval forest in this section and it was from his saw mill that millions of feet of lumber were daily shipped to Savannah and other ports.

Aaron Repperd built and operated the first circular-saw mill ever established in the state of Georgia, the mill was located near Thomson, in McDuffie County. He was the inventor of the Repperd Roller Gauge, one of the most valuable inventions of the sort ever made. Mr. Repperd was a millwright by trade, and erected hundreds of saw mills in different parts of the State.

After coming to Tebeauville, he built a comfortable home for himself and family. This was later owned by Mr. William Parker, but the land on which once stood this old home is now covered by the A. C. L. Shops.

Mr. Aaron Repperd and family moved to Tebeauville sometime before Waycross came into existence, and due to the fact that he and Mrs. Repperd came from north of the Mason and Dixon line, the place where the saw mill was located was called Yankee Town. Mr. Repperd was born in New Berlin, Pa., April 9, 1824, and Flavia Merrill Repperd, his wife, was born in South-Lee, Mass., Sept. 4, 1826.

The names of Mr. and Mrs. Repperd's children were: Augusta, Robert, and Harry. Mr. Robert Repperd was one of the most celebrated Sunday School men of his day. Frequently during revivals in Trinity Church, he would bring a large number of orphan children from Bethesda Orphan House to attend the meetings, and while in this little town they would be entertained in the different homes. Robert Repperd was filled with the spirit of love for his fellowman and carried sunshine into many lives. He was one of the State's most beloved men.

JAMES CARLISLE RIPPARD

Dr. Rippard was a Pennsylvanian by birth, having been born Nov. 30, 1857 in Wilkesbarre. His parents were Josiah Alexander and Catherine Pauline Rippard, the former a well-known and esteemed bank cashier of Wilkesbarre. The son, James C., having received a good education in the public schools of his native city, continued with a course in the College of Physicians and Surgeons at Baltimore, Md., graduating in 1881. Returning to Wilkesbarre, the young physician opened an office during March of the same year, and for nearly ten years remained there in practice, in which his skill and diligence achieved success.

Early in 1891 Dr. Rippard came south and after brief stops in Savannah, and Fort Valley, he finally located in Waycross, where through his personal kindliness, and his rare understanding, he drew patients from various walks of life. Although he has passed away, his memory still lives in the grateful hearts of many Waycross citizens, whom he served. The work that he put forward in the interest of Waycross is still going on.

He was one of the prime movers in formulating plans and regulations for the first Medical Health Board in the county of Ware, and the city of Waycross. In 1898 he was appointed by the Plant System Railway (A. C. L.) as chief surgeon to have charge of all their Hospitals in Georgia and Florida.

He was married June 28, 1893 to Miss Jennie May Barnes, daughter of Mr. Henry V. and Sarah Elizabeth Barnes (of sainted memory) whose former home was Urbana, Ohio.

In 1900 Dr. Rippard resigned from Plant System R. R. and resumed his regular practice of Medicine in Waycross; he continued until his death, which occurred July 4, 1914. His wife and two children survive him, Lucile Elizabeth (Mrs. J. H. Brewton) and James Carlisle Rippard.

HENRY WADSWORTH REED

Mr. Reed was the second son of Harrison and Ann Louisa (Turner) Reed, whose native home was Neenah, Wis., where he was born March 12, 1856.

Mr. Reed's father was a man of outstanding influence in public affairs, both west and south. He was the first editor of the "Milwaukee Sentinel;" in December, 1847 he was made a member of the Constitutional Convention from Marquette and Winnebage Counties, Wis. From 1868 to 1872 he was Governor of the State of Florida. Both he and his wife were lineal descendants of Pilgrim stock, each having had an ancestor among the passengers on the historic Mayflower. Mr. Reed's grandfather, Joseph Turner, an officer in the Revolutionary War, was a direct descendant of Jonathan Turner of the Mayflower. Several members of the Turner family, who are near relatives of Mr. Reed, are prominent in the affairs of Wisconsin. William P. Turner was President of the Board of Education of Milwaukee; two other uncles were members of the First Constitutional Convention of the State.

When Henry W. Reed was four years old his mother died and he was sent to live with relatives in Flint, Mich., where he was trained in the public schools until he was twelve years old. His father had made his home in Florida, and the youth, for the benefit to be derived from its excellent curriculum, entered the John S. C. Abbott Academy at Farmington, Me., where he remained for over two years, studying for the two years following at Syracuse University, Syracuse, N. Y. Thence Mr. Reed returned to Jacksonville to engage in various surveying and engineering enterprises, toward which his natural bent was strong and for which he had been fitting himself by private study and preparation. So marked were his progress and ability that at the early age of twenty-two years he was placed in charge of the Peninsular Railroad, from Waldo to Tampa, Fla., as Superintendent of Construction. Within two years he was promoted to the responsible position of locating engineer on the Waycross and Jacksonville line, having as one of his functions the locating, planning and laying out of the present City of Waycross, whose citizens thoroughly appreciate his enterprise and public spirit. Within a year Mr. Reed was advanced from his intermediate position to that of Master of Roadways for the Savannah, Florida and Western Railroad, which place he filled for fourteen years.

An enumeration of the enterprises in which Mr. Reed's efficient support has been felt would be incomplete without reference to the Cherokee Farm and Nursery Company, of which he was one of the originators. This was established on the large sub-division now known as "Cherokee Heights," and had its beginning during the year 1883. This great enterprise was one of the most successful of the kind in the South. It shipped produce to all parts of the United States and even to foreign countries; had large orders from the North, which kept twenty agents at work in the Southern States. This farm did a valuable and useful work in experimenting with foreign fruits, especially Dafon and Russian cherries, pears, plums, etc. Of these the Dafon varieties seem especially adapted to this locality.

Mr. Reed was married at Waldo, Fla., to Miss Emma Livingston, on May 4, 1880. Mrs. Reed was a lineal descendant of Philip Livingston, signer of the Declaration of Independence, and a member of the noted family of that name which settled in the beautiful valley of the Hudson River in Colonial times.

Mr. and Mrs. Reed spent their latter days in California where they died in 1914.

JOHN SALISBURY

Noteworthy among the prominent business men and the active and enterprising citizens of Waycross was John Henry Salisbury who came to this city when there were not over five hundred people living here. His home was formerly at Richmondville, N. Y., where he was born March 24, 1836. He married Miss Ursula Bates, Oct. 5, 1858, whose birth took place March 8, 1836 at Richmondville, N. Y. Mr. and Mrs. Salisbury were living in

Worchester, N. Y., where their two children were born, Genevra and Delavan. Ursula Salisbury died in New York, August 12, 1868.

Mr. Salisbury was married to Miss Sarah Evelyn Crippen Oct. 31, 1869. Mr. and Mrs. Salisbury and their two children, Genevra and Delavan, came to Waycross during the year of 1879. They built for themselves a very attractive home on Parallel, now Oak Street and were here only a short time before they were closely identified as valued and useful members of Trinity Church.

Mr. Salisbury had a long line of English ancestry. Descending from the Salisbury's of Salisbury, England. He was of the same line of descent as that of Lord Robert Cecil Salisbury, the great English statesman. Mr. Salisbury was a gentleman of high and honorable principles, and left an unblemished name as a valuable inheritance to his children. He died Feb. 6, 1911.

Mrs. Salisbury had no children of her own, but loved the two Salisbury children, Genevra and Delavan, as if they were her own. She was in every way a true mother to her husband's children, and they never for a moment realized that she was not their very own. Mrs. Salisbury was a woman "nobly planned," and filled her place not only in the church but in the social life of Waycross. She died July 27, 1903.

Genevra married Allen Morton in 1880 and their children's names are: Mary, Hattie, Nellie, Cleo, and Sarah, and Allen. Mrs. Morton died in 1895.

Delavan Salisbury married Sallie Lanier, Nov. 9, 1887. She was the daughter of Thomas and Sarah (Strickland) Lanier. They had one daughter, Sarah, who married A. E. Smith. After the death of Mrs. Salisbury, Mr. Salisbury married Miss Stella Walker of Madison, Georgia, daughter of Dr. Thomas J. and Emma Louise (West) Walker of Madison. Mr. and Mrs. Salisbury have one daughter, Stella Delavan.

REV. WILLIAM H. SCRUGGS

The First Baptist Church was only a few years old when the especially gifted young minister, William Scruggs, was called to the pastorate. He preached his first sermon in Waycross the 5th Sunday in August, 1886, after which he became Pastor of the little unfinished church on Albany Avenue with less than twenty-four members. He served the First Baptist Church from Sept. 1st, 1886 to October 7th, 1908, a total of twenty-two years. When he retired as pastor of that church its membership roll revealed over four hundred names on the church register.

Reverend Scruggs was born in Brooks County near Blue Springs, July 15th, 1849. He was married April 15th, 1875 to Miss Sarah Hendry at Marvan, Brooks County, Georgia.

Mr. Scruggs was one of those men who almost seemed to have been born to piety and good works. He is eminently a pious man and is especially distinguished for his benevolence, ever using his influence and his means to advance the various worthy objects connected with his church, his denomination and the community at large. His service to his church and to his city can not be over-estimated.

It was largely through his efforts that the Central Baptist Church was built. Mr. Scruggs with his daughter, Mrs. J. Walter Bennett, through untiring efforts, visiting nearly every white citizen's home in the city asking for a free-will offering of one dollar from the ladies of the homes, to assist in finishing the brick work on the Tabernacle. They were six weeks making the canvass, there were few homes that refused to give the sum asked for, and history reveals that the Tabernacle roof garden originated with Mrs. J. Walter Bennett.

Mr. Scruggs was pastor of the Central Baptist Church from May 30th, 1909 until July 1st, 1913 and since that time Pastor Emeritus.

MR. AND MRS. W. W. SHARPE

William Walter Sharpe is of English lineage, his grandfather having come from England in 1820 and settled in Winnsboro, S. C., moving later to Jefferson County, Florida, where he engaged in the tannery business, and where he spent the remainder of his life. His son, James Edward Sharpe, served in the Mexican War, and came near losing his eyesight from an attack of measles while in Mexico. He married Angeline, daughter of Daniel Ulysses McNeal, who settled in Lowndes County, and later moved to Quitman, where he held office of Sheriff twenty-five years; he was also treasurer of the county for eight years and was a prominent and influential man in his community. His only son, William W., was born August 22, 1857 at Long's Mill, Brooks County; he acquired his education in the city schools of Quitman.

After some six months experience as a clerk, he opened a general store in Boston, Georgia, in Sept., 1873, with W. A. McNeal and sold out to A. H. McCardel. He formed a partnership with Mr. B. C. Pollard but later moved to Valdosta and opened a general furniture store and undertaking business in his own name, with D. W. Roundtree as silent partner. This he gave up in 1881, to enter the employment of the railroad company as foreman of department work in Savannah, having charge of the wharfs and terminal repairs of the Savannah, Florida and Western Railway Company. In 1886 Mr. Sharpe was promoted to the division superintendency, which position he held for many years. Great responsibility developed upon him while holding this position, he having the care and maintenance of all the buildings, wharfs, tracks, bridges, telegraph lines, and structures of all kinds, with the custody of all the property, within his division limits. The standing and ability of Mr. Sharpe as a railroad man had been widely recognized. He has served as secretary of the Roadmasters Association of America, and before the convention, which was held in

Chicago Sept., 1893, he read a valuable paper entitled, "How to Maintain the Best Track at Least Cost," for it he was awarded the premium.

Mr. Sharpe is a prominent mason and has been a representative to the Grand Lodge and has served ably on committees of jurisprudence. March 2, 1880 Mr. Sharpe married Miss Inez Estelle Ashcraft, daughter of Augustus Bruce and Carolina (Williams) Ashcraft of Newnan. Her father was a private in the Confederate Army, and her grandfather was a Presbyterian Minister of the State of Connecticut. Mrs. Sharpe has been one of the outstanding women of her community, and if all of her activities were recorded, many pages of this book would be filled. She is a charter member of The Kings Daughters and a leader of the Inez Sharpe Kings Daughters Circle, a U. D. C., a D. A. R. Colonial Dames, a member of the May Flower Association, and has served one term on the School Board of Education, twenty years as President of the Kings Daughters Hospital Board, and President of the Library Board. Mr. and Mrs. Sharpe have one daughter, Mrs. P. A. Hay, and one son, William.

PROF. STERLING P. SETTLE

Prof. Settle had a fine part in the Educational upbuilding of Waycross. He moved here from Pierce County in 1885, having formerly taught in the academy at Blackshear. He was only in Waycross but a short time when he proved himself to be an efficient teacher, an accomplished gentleman, and one capable of training young people for useful lives, in all branches of learning.

He organized a high school for boys and girls, and taught in Oleman Hall on Albany Avenue, and for several terms conducted this school. Young men and women attended it from several counties surrounding Waycross. Prof. Settle afterward organized the Waresboro High School and this school became famous in the great uplift it gave many young men, in fact it may be said that Waresboro furnished, through the instrumentality of Prof. Settle's School at that place, more young men to the business and professional life of Ware County, and the counties contiguous than perhaps any town in the state.

The Hon. Randall Walker, an outstanding Ex-Congressman from this district, was one of Prof. Settle's students, and was always a warm and appreciative friend of the professor. There are still a number of men in the business life of this and other states that received their schooling under Prof. Settle. He was a mathematician of the kind that are called "experts", thus showing the order of his intellect.

In the history of Ware County no man should be accredited with the results of a constructive service in character and intellectual building more than Prof. Settle. In point of merit a monument should be erected by the young men and women who received instructions from this fine educator for his untiring interest in their future welfare, for he truly labored for the betterment of the people among whom he lived, and his work was one of unselfish devotion to duty.

Chronology of the Life of Prof. Settle:

Prof. Sterling Preston Settle was born Sept. 15, 1851 at Lynchburg, Va. Educated at the University of Virginia. Admitted to the Bar to practice law in the State of Virginia at the age of 19. Came to Georgia in 1879 and settled in Pierce County near the Forks of the Big Hurricane Creek. Married Miss Martha Long of Pierce County in 1883. Moved to Waycross in 1885, moved to Waresboro in 1887 and again moved to Waycross in 1898. Taught school in practically all of south Georgia, principally in Ware, Clinch, Pierce, and Lowndes counties. Died in Savannah October 17, 1915, buried in Lott cemetery in Waycross.

He left his wife and the following children who are living in Waycross:

Linton, Walker, Bernice, Martha, Marie, Preston (died 1931), Lloyd, Mary and Frankie died in early childhood, and are sleeping in Lott's cemetery in Waycross.

NOTE:—Excerpts from a tribute in memory of Prof. Settle by V. L. Stanton that appeared in the Evening Herald, 1915.

JOSIAH SIRMANS

Josiah Sirmans was the son of David J. Sirmans, who was born March 1, 1819 and married Eliza Wilkerson, daughter of John Wilkerson of South Carolina. To this couple were born: Lewis, who married Rachel Lightsey, Alice, Tully, Lucius, who married Eliza Fiveash, and Josiah, who married Fannie L. Lott, of Waycross, Ezekiel who married Martha Register and Benjamin, who married Ida Crumm. Josiah was postmaster at Homerville for several years and died in 1881. His wife, Fannie Lott, and her three small children moved to Waycross after the death of Mr. Sirmans, this being the former home of Mrs. Sirmans. Fannie (Lott) Sirmans was reared under genial auspices, and kindly influences, her home was the abode of boundless hospitality, whose law was simple kindness, and Christian charity, and whose beneficence extended far, especially into homes of the poor and lowly. No sufferer or seeker for aid was ever turned empty handed from her door, and the old time Southern life was shared by guest and stranger. She led the vicarious life forgetful of self, striving always to put happiness into the hearts of others.

Mr. Sirmans descended from a long line of ancestry, his great-grandfather was Benjamin Sirmans, who was born in Emanuel County, Feb. 6, 1792, was the son of Josiah Sirmans and his wife, Artie Hardeman, who also has a long lineage of Georgia ancestors. Benjamin became a man of great wealth, owning many slaves, and large possessions. He married Martha Johnson, a sister of General David Johnson.

Mr. and Mrs. Josiah Sirmans left the following children, Cora, Eustace, and Bessie (deceased). Mrs. Sirmans married Mr. John Sharpe some years after the death of Mr. Sirmans and the following are the names of their children: Susie, John, Walker Wadley (deceased) and Turner (deceased).

WILLIAM J. SMITH

W. J. Smith was the son of Nathaniel and Louise Frances Smith and was born in Lowndes County, April 10, 1851. During his infancy, his parents moved to Hamilton County, Florida and after the War Between the States, to Jasper, Florida, where his father engaged in the mercantile business. In 1862 his father enlisted in the Confederate Service and served through the War. His grandfather was an officer in the Revolutionary War, entering the service from the state of South Carolina. William Smith, besides making use of such school privileges as his own neighborhood afforded, also attended school in Jacksonville, Florida, for a short time. Later he clerked for his father until 1870 and then engaged in business in Smithville for about two years.

In January, 1880 he moved to Waycross and opened a livery and sales stable, the first in the city. Two years later he discontinued this, and engaged in a general merchandise business, and in 1886 he took John Adams, a progressive young business man (a native of Florida) into partnership. Mr. Smith also had an interest in various other firms in Waycross, he starting several friends in business. He handled considerable real estate, building a block of stores on Plant Avenue, which was occupied by himself and his business associates. His interest was never wholly selfish, for he took an active part in the public affairs of Waycross, having been a member of the council several years, and Mayor one year. He was a member of the board of Education, and of the committee for building the first brick school edifice in Waycross, and was prominent in his efforts for the exclusion of the whisky traffic, and most active in the promotion of morality and sobriety.

Mr. Smith associated with himself and his former partner, Mr. Adams, Mr. William Parker, under the corporate name of Smith, Adams and Parker Company. This business was one of the most prominent business houses in the city.

Mr. and Mrs. Smith were valued members of the Methodist Church, Mr. Smith serving through several years as a faithful steward of this denomination. He was a prominent Mason and Odd Fellow, having been through all the chairs of the last named fraternity, being deputy district grand master, and a member of the Grand Lodge of Masons.

Jan. 6, 1876, Mr. Smith was married to Miss Margaret Theresa Staton, of Clinch County. They were blessed with five girls and two boys. Miss Nora Lee and Miss Isabella are accomplished musicians and have established a Conservatory of Music in Waycross, the first and only one that has ever existed here, supplying a much needed school in the musical world.

Mrs. Smith died July 27, 1912 and Mr. Smith died Feb. 27, 1927.

DR. J. E. W. SMITH

Job Elbert Wilder Smith stood eminent among the professional men of Waycross. He was the eldest son of James David and Edith (Folsom) Smith, and was born Nov. 24, 1854, in Hamilton County, Florida, but soon after his birth his parents moved to Echols County, Georgia.

His father represented his senatorial district in the General Assembly two years, and was a member of that body in 1876, when called to the Constitutional Convention of 1877. His son, after receiving a good common school education, attended the University of Georgia two years, and then attended medical lectures at the Georgia Medical College at Augusta, during the winters of 1879-80, concluding with a course at Vanderbilt Medical College, Nashville, Tenn., from which he graduated March 1, 1882. In Dec., 1888 he moved from Jasper, Florida to Waycross, where he built up a fine medical practice and being a public spirited citizen did all in his power for the welfare of the city of his adoption. Ambitious to stand in the front of his profession, to which he was devoted, Dr. Smith took a post-graduate course at the Post Graduate Medical School and Hospital in New York City in 1892.

He was surgeon for the Savannah, Florida and Western Railway. He was an active member of the Board of Education, a faithful member and a deacon in the Presbyterian Church; was Worshipful Master in the Masonic Lodge, he was an Odd Fellow, in which order he served as Past Grand Master.

March 23, 1880, Dr. Smith was married to Miss Cordelia Carter, daughter of John A. and Mahala (Walker) Carter of Echols County, Georgia, and to them were born the following children: Darwin Ray, Vesta, Irene, Juno, Hoke Victor, Warren Lott, Rossa Elbert, and LaFayette.

JOSEPH DEDGE SMITH

Mr. J. D. Smith was born in Appling County (now a part of Ware) April 23, 1837. His father was named Austin and his mother, Mary Smith. Austin Smith was a large land and slave owner; his grandfather was John G. Smith, and had extensive lands which he cultivated with slave labor. Mr. J. D. Smith was a Confederate Veteran and was a member of the Home Guard of Confederate Veteran's Camp. He was for many years County School Commissioner of Ware and served in this office in a most efficient way. He was a Mason, a member of the Knights of Pythias, and a loyal member of the Methodist Episcopal Church. He married Miss Jane, daughter of Ephriam Knowles of Burke county. Their children's names are: Joseph Lee, Edward, Jr., Mrs. Ella Bibb, and Mrs. Mary Mallon (deceased).

MOSES W. SPENCE

Mr. Spence was comparatively a young man during the early part of the War Between the States. He enlisted in the beginning of hostilities for service and it was his privilege to serve the southern cause, and to engage in some of the hardest fought battles of the great conflict.

He was the son of Joshua and Miss ———— (Middleton) Spence of Appling County. Moses Spence was born in Appling County, December 26, 1829. He married Susie McCall, daughter of George and Nancy (Tillman) McCall. Moses and Susie Spence had twenty-one children, of whom Allen B. Spence is one, who is an honored citizen of Waycross.

Allen Spence is now serving as Solicitor-General, Waycross Judicial Circuit, and was born Feb. 1, 1875; graduated Mercer University, B. L. degree, Aug. 27, 1902; Methodist, Mason; Shriner; K. of P.; Solicitor City Court, Waycross, Nov. 27, 1908-Jan. 1, 1918; County Attorney Ware County, 1912, 1914, 1915, 1916; Appointed Judge of the Waycross Circuit Dec. 10, 1924 by Governor Clifford Walker to fill unexpired term and declined the appointment. Awarded the A. G. Miller medal in 1926 for rendering most distinguished service to Waycross during the year.

Allen Spence married April, 1900 in Waresboro, Ware County, Mina Darling Furlong (died Feb. 11, 1915) daughter of Benjamin Furlong (born Jan. 15, 1852, died Sept. 8, 1886). Their children's names are: Clyde W., Earl A., Allen B., Gertrude Mina, Sarah Vivian.

Moses Spence's first wife, Susie (McCall) Spence, died, he then married Mrs. Sue Harris of Pierce County, and later married Mrs. Prendergast whose former husband was a prominent Plant System railroad employee. Mr. Spence died in Ware County, Sept. 6, 1895.

JAMES W. STRICKLAND

James Wentworth Strickland was born in Ware county June 7, 1847. His parents were Allen C. and Cassie (Sweat) Strickland. His mother was the daughter of Captain James A. Sweat. Mr. Sweat was a successful farmer, and during the War Between the States, joined the Southern Army, and was Captain of Company G., Fourth Georgia Cavalry, and died from natural causes after serving two years in the War. Mr. Strickland's grandparents were James and Nellie Strickland. He was educated in the public schools and also was a pupil in the Blackshear Academy in Pierce County.

Mr. Strickland enlisted in the Confederate service at the age of seventeen, entering as a private in Company G., Fourth Georgia Cavalry, and served during the last year of the war under Captain Alexander McMillan. He was at Scriven, Georgia with his company at the close of the war.

Several years after the war he was married to the beautiful and accomplished Miss Annie Hendry, daughter of Captain E. D. and Caroline Hendry. Each of the members of this family have passed from earth, leaving an only daughter, Miss Carrie E. Strickland, who is deeply loved in Waycross for her spiritual zeal and magnetic personality.

Mr. Strickland was a Mason, Knight Templar and Past Chancellor of the Knights of Pythias, an Odd Fellow and a member of the First Methodist Church.

VALENTINE LEGARE STANTON

Valentine Legare Stanton was born at Charleston, South Carolina May 26, 1859, and was an honored representative of an old and prominent southern family. He was a son of Valentine and Catherine Rebecca (Parry) Stanton, and his mother's parents were Peter and Harriett Emily Parry. His father's parents were George Henry Stanton, who settled in Baracoa, Cuba, and there married Nicholas Prientzer, daughter of Nicholas Prientzer, who was killed at the battle of Dresden, August 26-7, 1813, while serving under Napoleon Bonaparte.

VALENTINE STANTON

Napoleon Bonaparte sent Nicholas Prientzer (Prouter) with the Ninetieth French Regiment to Saint Domingne, and it was there he met Mlle. Raingeard, whom he married and who is in lineal descent to Valentine Stanton. Through this line comes the connection by marriage with the Cappee (pronounced Capay) and David Byrdie Mitchell, who was governor of Georgia 1811-1815, and in line with William Bacon Stevens of Savannah, Georgia and William Stevens, Bishop of Pennsylvania. The famous French poet, Francois Cappee, is also in lineal descent with this family.

Valentine Stanton, Sr., is descended from Jacques de L'Homaca who was born in Austria in the eighteenth century and came to the French Colony of St. Domingne.

Jacques married Elizabeth de Lorma, the eldest daughter of her parents who came from France. After their marriage they lived on their plantation a few miles from Aux Cayes on the South Coast. She lived in Savannah, Georgia. They were the parents of thirteen children. Of these, Niccoletta Pauline first married in 1790 Jean Francoise Raingeard de Lavillate, who was born in 1763, the son of a lawyer of Nantes, France. In 1799 they settled in San Domingo on a coffee plantation near the river La Cue, seven leagues from Aux Cayes, and where he died in 1802.

Thus about the close of the eighteenth century the members of this prominent European stock were transplanted to the shores of America. Valentine Stanton, Sr., was born October 10, 1830. He died at Savannah, Georgia, January 29, 1865, and was buried at Laurel Grove Cemetery under direct orders from General Sherman who was present at the funeral services and who had recently occupied that city with the Federal troops.

Valentine Stanton, Sr., during the War was a coast guard in the Confederate army stationed at Savannah. In earlier years he was engaged in the printing and lithographing business and lived in Charleston, South Carolina, being in business with Walker-Evans-Cogswell of that city. He afterward removed from Charleston to Savannah.

Valentine Stanton and Catherine Rebecca Parry had the following named children: Valentine, born October 8, 1855, died October 10, 1855, Franklin Lebby, the Poet Laureate of Georgia, born February 22, 1857, died in Atlanta, Jan. 7, 1927, Valentine Legare, born May 26, 1859, Henry Stokes, born in April, 1861, and Burrell Sanders, born in 1863 and died January 30, 1865.

Valentine Stanton received his early education partly in South Carolina and partly at Savannah, Georgia. He had a very receptive mind, and was a master of words, he was possessed of a rare store of historical knowledge, which caused him to be often sought to substantiate important facts.

On first coming to Waycross Mr. Stanton was engaged in the railroad business, and he established an agency for the handling of general insurance, one of the largest offices of the kind in southeast Georgia.

On June 20, 1883 at Baltimore, Md., Mr. Stanton was married to Miss Margaret Clark, a woman of brilliant intellect and a charming personality. She was the daughter of Richard and Margaret Clark of Philadelphia. Mr. and Mrs. Stanton were parents of the following children: Cecil V., Mary M., Catherine, Margaret, Frances, Walter, and Valentine.

It was characteristic of Mr Stanton that the angel of death found him prepared. His business affairs were in order and his loved ones had little trouble in carrying out every detail of his will.

So closed the earthly career of one who left his indelible mark upon the State of his adoption, the church to whose services he had dedicated his life, and to the people of his home town for whom he labored so lovingly and so well.

Like the setting sun, which seems larger as it descends to the West, he sank down into the grave with unclouded disk, leaving the rays of his twilight glory gilding the memories of the past.

THE FRIEND AFAR
(Dedicated to V. L. Stanton by his brother, Frank L. Stanton)

How have I sighed to wake, and see
The face—once all the world to me;
The friend of youth—all friends above—
The one dear brother of my love.

From travelled land
And sea-white foam
Ever love led
His footsteps Home.

But now he comes not ... In the night
Had Home no windows shining bright?
Did he not know they waited there
With eyes he dimmed not with a tear?

He could not lose
  The loved home-way
Who made Love's starlight
  And its Day.

But I shall go to him, for he
Shall never more return to me;
For all that sow, and all that reap,
Shall fall on sleep—shall fall on Sleep.

No more the dim
  Life-way to roam,
    We'll Sleep and sleeping,
  Dream of Home.

THE STANTON BROTHERS

By Isabella Remshart Redding

The passing from earth of Franklin Lebby Stanton, the beloved Poet Laureate of Georgia, sent a wail of sorrow throughout the wide world, because poems that he wrote found a responsive chord in the hearts of men everywhere.

The passing into Eternity of his brother, Valentine Legare Stanton, was a great loss to South Georgia, and especially to Waycross where he lived from his youth. His tender heart was in sympathy with every age and class. He had been many years superintendent of First Methodist church Sunday school. The children on our city streets called him Brother Stanton, and tenderly loved him.

Handsome in person with a rich melodious voice he

loved to lead the Sunday school in music. Keenly alive to every public interest of his city and country, it was such men as he who were the founders of Waycross, men who brought hope and confidence to the people, and made it a happy, prosperous city of 12,000 people at the time he was at the head of the water commission. It was through his efforts that the plant was moved from Beauty Park to its present site, and those who knew him best, recollect how happy he was, when the building was made large enough not only to house the machinery for water, but also large enough for an equipment to supply electric lights for our city.

He felt that with these factors owned by the city, it had a permanent asset that would greatly reduce taxation.

It is impossible to compute the value to a community of men of such character.

Mr. Stanton is missed in every walk of life, in the business world, in social life, in the highway department, on the Board of Education and among the lowly who found in him a friend, and especially in his church which he loved with an ardor that only those can know who love the Lord. His name will not be so widely known as his brother's, the poet, but,

> "There are heroes without the laurel,
> And conquerors without the triumph."

The grandfather of these men, George Henry Stanton, was an Englishman who having business interests in Baracoa, Cuba, lived there with his wife Nicolette, and there, their son Valentine Stanton the first was born Oct. 10, 1830. He married in Charleston, S. C. Dec. 21, 1854 Catherine Rebecca Parry, whose father Peter Parry was born in Wales, but her mother was Miss Legare, and she was born on Kiawah Island, South Carolina. In those days the sea islands of Georgia and South Carolina were an earthly paradise, but soon after the War Between the States began, they were devastated, homes laid waste and the inhabitants fled to the interior of the state. The family has a picture of Valentine Stanton, the first, in Confederate uniform, but his health failed and they went from Charleston to Savannah with their two sons, Frank age 7 and Valentine age 5, hoping to find a blockade runner to take them to England. Soon after Savannah was evacuated by a small band of Confederate troops in Dec., 1864. On December 21, 1865, the largest army in modern times captured Savannah and Valentine Stanton I died Jan. 29, 1865. Soon after her husband's death Mrs. Stanton moved to Homerville, Georgia, where a number of refugees from South Carolina had located, but her boys aged 6 and 8 years became henceforth loyal Georgians.

Years after she married an elegant gentleman, Dr. Malone, and they moved to St. Matthews, South Carolina where she died Easter Sunday, 1880. Her refined, cultured character and earnest Christian faith made a deep impression on her children and sustained them through the vicissitudes of life.

Franklin Lebby Stanton, born Feb. 22, 1857, married Leona Jossy April, 1892, died in Atlanta Jan. 7, 1927.

Valentine Legare Stanton, born in Charleston May 26, 1859, married Margaret C. Clarke June 20, 1880 and entered Eternity June 15, 1923.

War had left the South desolate; Sherman's torch had destroyed everything in its path which was from 12 to 40 miles wide, extending from Chattanooga to Savannah, and thence to Columbia, S. C. Homes, public buildings, churches and schools were destroyed and it was eight years after the war before that army was removed from the South, although Gen. Grant advised that it be removed soon after the surrender. For this reason thousands of southern children attended poorly equipped country schools. Many of these were taught by men and women of the highest culture, and the Stanton boys were taught to work the garden and attend these schools.

Frank Stanton went to Savannah and learned the printer's trade and Valentine learned telegraphy and located at Waycross. Frank afterwards went to Atlanta. Later he became editor of the Smithville News and made a unique venture in journalism. His locals and personals were purely imaginary.

Smithville was overgrown with freak vegetables no garden ever knew; the town thronged with visitors that never drew breath, and fetes and festivals recorded that were only dreams.

When he accepted a position with the Atlanta Constitution and his "Up From Georgia and Songs from Dixie" reached the ears and hearts of readers throughout the land, the Billville Banner seemed to have been a descendant of that paper, and although it never had a subscription list, there were frequent applications for it.

Those of us who recollect Waycross when Frank Stanton wrote "The Love Feast at Waycross," recall the fact that there were not over 2000 in our town then that the little church described stood on the spot where Trinity Methodist church is now, and it was the boast of the community that every grown man and woman in Waycross belonged to some church and all the children of both races went to Sunday school.

Frank Stanton's mind was deeply imbued with the poetic principle and like all poets whose works have been filled with pathos, there was a deep underlying sense of humor that made his delineation of character real.

Our native countrymen he depicted true to life, and in the dialect of the Georgia negro of his era that is fast passing away, he has preserved the type of the happy, carefree race as it emerged from slavery—that puts to silence the slanderers of the South.

But the deepest and holiest sentiments of his soul are expressed in the tender thoughts, love and devotion to his wife.

Amused, cheered, thrilled and comforted were thousands who for many years daily read his column in the Atlanta Constitution and few men have lived for whom so many tears were shed as when these lines were published, having been scribbled and left on his office desk a few days before he passed away January 7, 1927.

> *"Adieu, Sweet Friends—I have waited long,*
> *To hear the message that calls me home,*
> *And now it comes like a low, sweet song*
> *Of welcome over the river's foam.*
> *And my heart shall ache and my feet shall roam*
> *No more—no more; I am going home!*
> *Home where no storm—where no tempest raves.*
> *In the light of the calm, eternal day;*
> *Where no willows weep over lonely graves*
> *And the tears from our eyelids are kissed away.*
> *And my soul shall sigh, and my feet shall roam*
> *No more—no more; I am going home."*

JAMES ISAIAH SUMMERALL

James Summerall, jurist and agriculturist, was born at Baxley, Appling County, Georgia, May 24, 1864, son of William and Matilda (Hurst) Summerall. Left an orphan at an early age he was self-educated and underwent great hardships and privations to fit himself for his chosen profession. He was educated in the public schools at Blackshear, Ga., and at South Georgia College, Thomasville. After teaching school for a period in Pierce County, he studied law under Capt. John C. Nicholls at Blackshear, was admitted to the Georgia bar in 1894 and began practice at Blackshear. From the outset he became a factor in civic and public life and politics. He served as tax receiver for the county during 1890-96, and as ordinary from 1896-1914. For several years he practiced law alone but later was associated successively with E. Lawton Walker, Andrew B. Estes and S. Forster Memory, these firms taking rank with the leading legal partnerships in this section of Georgia. In 1914 Mr. Summerall was elected judge of the superior courts of the

Waycross judicial circuit, embracing the counties of Ware, Pierce, Coffee, Charlton, Bacon and Brantley, and remained on the bench until his death. He tried many criminal and civil cases of wide interest.

Aside from professional activities he was extensively interested in farming in Pierce county, having large land holdings. He was a trustee of the Piedmont Institute, a Baptist preparatory school at Waycross, was chairman of the board of deacons of the First Baptist Church of Waycross, and was active in the work of the Men's Evangelistic Club, Waycross. He was a member of the Georgia State Bar Association, the Waycross Bar Association, the Masonic fraternity, the Knights of Pythias, in which he was a past chancellor, the Junior Order United American Mechanics, the Independent Order of Odd Fellows, and the Kiwanis Club, Waycross. Politically he was a Democrat.

He was a man of unimpeachable character, strong intellectual endowments and judicial temperament, with a thorough understanding of the law; was possessed of great patience, industry and urbanity, and he took with him to the bench the highest qualifications for the office. His record as a judge was in complete harmony with his record as a lawyer. His every official act was characterized by patience, sympathy, love of his fellow men, devotion to right and respect for law. Throughout his entire career he exemplified the highest virtues of true manhood and citizenship. He was married at Blackshear, May 6, 1891, to Zoe Estelle, daughter of James Brown, a farmer. They had three children: Leila Estelle, Lois Virginia, and William James Summerall. He died at Telmore, Ga., Nov. 30, 1924.

CAPTAIN BURRELL SWEAT

Captain Sweat was the son of a pioneer settler of Ware County and was born October 17, 1825. He was a soldier in two of the Indian Wars and his last enlistment in the service occurred July 5th, 1844 where he served until all of the Indians were driven out of this section of Georgia. He entered into Indian warfare under Captain James Sweat and next under Captain David Miller. During his youth Indians were numerous and at times troublesome. Each settlement had a fort and often the women and children were left at the settlement fortress for safety while the men worked in the fields. When quite a young man Captain Sweat served as a guard for the homes in the settlement and was regarded as a "minute man." He often told blood curdling stories of the dangers that lurked in the close proximity of the homes of the early settlers of Ware. He knew Billy Bowlegs and remembered seeing him peddling hides, beeswax and tallow on the streets of Waresboro.

Captain Sweat was elected Senator from his district in 1859 where he served until the beginning of the War Between the States. He joined the Confederate Army in 1861 and served as a private throughout the entire four years of the war and was discharged from the army with an honorable and brave record.

In 1879 Mr. Sweat was elected Justice of the Peace for the 1131st District and held that office until his death, which occurred September 12, 1905.

In his youth he was married to Miss Lucretia Sweat, born April 20, 1828 and for a great many years resided in their little cottage on Thomas Street in Waycross. He had long passed his allotted span of life when the Angel of death bore his spirit into the "Land o' the Leal." He passed from this life just three hours before "The old, old fashion death" claimed the spirit of his beloved companion, who had so long shared his sorrows and his joys and who was always a source of comfort to this real gentleman of the old south. These two pioneer citizens dying the same night truly "In death were not divided."

JUDGE J. L. SWEAT

For over forty years Judge Sweat held a secure and substantial position as a member of the Georgia bar. During the greater part of his time his home was in Waycross. His career was not only one of unusual length, but of variety of experience. He was a Confederate soldier, and served his country and state in many ways aside from his work as a lawyer.

BRIG. GENERAL J. L. SWEAT

He was born September 21, 1847, in the Northeastern portion of Ware Afterwards included in the formation of Pierce county. He was still a youth when his parents died and he lived with his Grandmother Strickland on the old plantation immediately north of where the Town of Blackshear was built up and which later became the county seat of the new county of Pierce.

Joel Sweat attended the Blackshear Academy until April, 1862, when at the age of about fourteen years he enlisted in the Confederate army. He served three years until the surrender in April, 1865; a portion of the time he served with Wheeler's Cavalry. Judge Sweat took a deep interest in the United Confederate Veterans Association, having organized a camp in Waycross of which he frequently became commander and was for several years commander of the South Georgia Brigade.

In 1869 Judge Sweat was married to Miss Maggie M. Hitch. There were two children, Lee L., and Lula M., the latter dying in her early womanhood.

With the exception of the time he was on the bench, Judge Sweat had from his admission to the bar been actively engaged in the practice of law throughout South Georgia, and was regarded as one of the most competent and successful members of the legal profession. He was also successful in business affairs, having been attorney for the First National Bank of Waycross and the Waycross Saving & Trust Company, and attorney at Waycross for the A. B. & A. Railway Company. In 1912 he was elected senator from the fifth district, serving in the Georgia Senate during 1913-1914. Having previously been connected with the clerical department of the Legislature and for a part of the year 1871, a clerk in the executive department under Governor James M. Smith, he was elected and served as chief clerk of the House of Representatives in 1875 and 1876. In April, 1892, he was appointed Judge of the Brunswick Judicial Circuit, then composed of nine counties including Ware, in which his home town of Waycross was located. He succeeded in that office, Judge Spencer Atkinson, who had resigned. After having been twice elected by the General Assembly and serving together about seven years on the bench, Judge Sweat retired, his administration of public justice having met with strong approval by the bar and people.

Always a Democrat, Judge Sweat took a prominent part in political affairs, being a member of the Georgia delegation to the National Democratic Convention that first nominated Grover Cleveland for President at Chicago; and after at St. Louis, and was frequently a member of congressional and state conventions, and a leader in their work and deliberations. Judge Sweat was a member of the Methodist Church and of the Masonic Order. He died in Waycross, and was buried in Lott Cemetery.

DANIEL B. SWEAT

Daniel Sweat, city editor and publisher, and later owner of the Waycross Reporter, was born in Ware County,

June 30, 1864. His father, Thomas M., was born in Ware County, Nov. 8, 1831, following farming until 1880, when he removed to Waycross and engaged in the mercantile business. His wife, Eliza (Phillips) Sweat, was born in Emanuel County, Georgia, January 10, 1826, and was the mother of nine children, of whom Daniel B. is the eighth. He was reared in Ware County, on a farm and received an academic education. At the age of sixteen he entered the Reporter office as an apprentice, where he won the confidence and esteem of his employer, and before the completion of his apprenticeship, he was promoted to the position of foreman, which place he filled, giving entire satisfaction. In the early part of 1886 Mr. Sweat purchased the printing outfit and commenced the publication of the Reporter in his own name.

November 16, 1887 he was married to Miss Hattie Lanier, daughter of Rev. R. F. Lanier, a prominent minister of the Christian Church. She died June 27, 1890 and on May 16, 1894 he married Miss Minnie Lee Buchanan, youngest daughter of Mr. and Mrs. C. C. Buchanan of Waycross.

Mr. Sweat has acquired considerable literary ability, and his reputation as a newspaperman has been ably sustained along with his other achievements.

CAPTAIN JAMES SWEAT

Captain James A. Sweat came to Georgia when quite young, and located in what is now Pierce county. The settlements were few and far apart and in those hectic times the farmers had to go armed to work in their fields and often the women and children, while the men were away, took refuge in forts built as a place of refuge against the invasions of the Indians. Military companies were organized for the protection of the white settlers, and James Sweat became a Captain of one of these brave bands of pioneer soldiers. In 1858 Captain Sweat moved to Ware County, Georgia, and having purchased a tract of wild land five miles south of Waresboro, erected first a log house, and later replaced the orginal structure with a substantial frame house. With the assistance of slaves, he cleared and improved a homestead, and later as his means increased, bought large tracts of land in Ware and adjacent counties, becoming an extensive and prosperous landholder. He continued his agricultural operation until his death, at which time he was sixty-one years old.

Captain Sweat was married three times. His first wife was Elizabeth Newburn. She died in 1853, leaving eleven children, whose names were: Thomas, Martin, Bryan, Farley Elias, Ancil, Charlott, Cassie, Marcia, Tabitha, and Mary. His second wife was Mary Newburn, a sister of his first wife. His third wife was Mrs. Serena (Miller) Clough, who by her union with her first husband Jonathan True Clough, had four children: Jonathan J. Clough (deceased), Mary, Emma and Lilla, dying in their early youth. Mrs. Sweat was born in Ware County, Georgia, a daughter of Martin and Nancy (Brewton) Miller, and a grand-daughter of William Miller, a pioneer of Bulloch County, and a soldier of the Revolutionary War (page 425, Georgia Roster of The Revolution).

Captain and Mrs. Sweat had two sons, Carey M. and Frank L. Sweat (deceased).

CAREY M. SWEAT

Having lived in the county of Ware all of his life, Mr. Sweat possesses a broad interest in general welfare of this section and is identified with various enterprises of magnitude and importance.

CAREY M. SWEAT

His activities have extended along the lines of commercial, civic, and industrial development, and his connection with different activities, has broadened his views in public progression.

He is a son of a soldier of the Indian Wars of Southern Georgia and Florida, Captain James Sweat. Carey Sweat was born December 9, 1861 in Ware County, Georgia, on a farm located five miles south of Waresboro, at that time the county seat of Ware.

Mr. Sweat is a stockholder in the Consolidated Naval Stores Company, a stockholder in the State Life Insurance Company, a stockholder and Vice-President of the New Willard Naval Stores of Texas.

Politically he is a staunch Democrat, but has been too much absorbed in his personal affairs to engage in politics, although he has served as a member of the City Council.

Fraternally he belongs in Waycross Lodge, Number 305, Ancient Free and Accepted Order of Masons.

Religiously both he and his wife are consistent members of the Methodist Episcopal Church.

Mr. Sweat has been twice married. On April 27, 1887, he was married to Miss Mollie McDonald, who was born in Ware County, a daughter of Col. William A. and Mary Ann (Deen) McDonald. She died December 7, 1892 leaving two children, James Lester and Vera E.

Mr. Sweat married second, May 14, 1901, Susan E. McDonald, a daughter of Col. William A. and Rebecca (Thomson) McDonald. Of this marriage their children's names are: Thelma, Lucile, Lillian, Marie, Carey M., Ralph F., Juanita Rebecca, and Norman Ancil, Susan, Emily and Fred C.

Since this sketch was written, Mr. Sweat has passed on to his home eternal. He died August 15, 1933 and sleeps in the Kettle Creek Churchyard where his forefathers have slept for over a hundred years.

THIGPEN FAMILY OF WARE

Calvin Thigpen was the first of that name to come to Ware County. The home of his nativity was North Carolina. His wife was Margaret Carver, who was also a native of North Carolina. When coming to Georgia they settled in Emanuel County near Swainsboro. They had only one child, a son, Travis Thigpen, born in Emanuel County, and when young Travis was about one year old, his father died.

Travis Thigpen, the son, and his mother moved to Coffee County, (Later to Ware), where he grew to manhood and was married to Mary Davis of that county. She was a daughter of Stafford Davis and Penny (Lott) Davis. Penny (Lott) Davis was a sister of Joel Lott of Bulloch County, and whose son, Dr. Daniel Lott, was one of the founders of Waycross. Stafford Davis found when coming to Ware that there were more Indians than white settlers here, and that the greater portion of the settlement was gathered 'round the caldrons and the blazing fires, than was found in houses. He also found here huge straight trees, all covered with veils of moss, and their trunks rose proudly like columns in this primeval forest. The startled hares, deer, and even wolves, and other wild denizens of the woods often bounded away from his path. Mr. Davis was truly one of the first settlers of the county of Ware, but when Coffee was cut from Ware, his home was left in the New County. Stafford Davis lived to be one hundred and ten years old and died after a long and useful life with an unclouded mind, and with divine faith of an entrance into a wondrous life Beyond.

TRAVIS THIGPEN

Travis Thigpen and Mary Davis had the following children: Stafford, who was killed in the War Between the States, Barbara, married Cuyler Kirkland, Mary (never married) Calvin L., married Miss Eliza Bailey, daughter of William Bailey, one of the founders of Waycross, Susan, born Dec. 24, 1849, married Alfred B. Finley, Delilah, mrrried Alfred Sweat, Maggie Thigpen, ———, Manning Thigpen, born Jan. 12th, 1859. He first married Miriam Miller, Feb. 24, 1876. She was the daughter of Ezekiel Miller and Ellen Dyas Miller. Ezekiel Miller was a son of William Miller, who is buried with his entire family at Kettle Creek Cemetery, and grave of William reveals that he was a Revolutionary soldier. After her death, Mr. Thigpen married Miss Maggie Jones, who died, and his last wife is Mrs. Rosa Aldridge Woodcock, an early settler of Ware County.

Travis, born July 31, 1863, married Martha L. Blackburn, Feb. 18, 1885. Martha Blackburn was the daughter of Martin E. L. Blackburn and Mary Cason Blackburn, who was the daughter of Frederick Cason and Elizabeth Williams Cason.

Rev. Joseph Thigpen married Matilda Mullis. Dr. Gaines R. Thigpen married Miss Minnie Jeffords. Barton Thigpen married Miss Nancy Barber, daughter of James I. and Mary Ann Blackburn, Margaret Carver Thigpen married a Kirkland and is buried in the Old Kirkland cemetery in Charlton County.

MRS. AMANDA DAVIS THOMAS

Mrs. Thomas' father and mother were old settlers of McIntosh County, Georgia, and reared a family of several sons and daughters of which Amanda Ocala Davis was one.

She was married September 9, 1873 at Darien, Georgia, to William Ryley Thomas. After living in Darien for several years they moved in 1882 to Waycross, then a town of about five hundred people. Mr. Thomas was ordained a Baptist Minister in 1889 at the First Baptist Church, and the Rev. W. H. Scruggs acted as ordaining minister. Mr. Thomas only served a year as a minister of the gospel, when becoming ill, died Feb. 5, 1890, leaving his wife and five small children alone to battle with the world.

Their children's names are: Cassie Ocala Thomas (Mrs. A. C. Blythe), Amy Amelia Thomas (Mrs. Charles Dunn), Leffler McArthur Thomas, William Joseph Thomas, Jefferson Davis Thomas, and the grandchildren of Mrs. Thomas are:

Helen Dunn McGowan, Waycross, Ga., Hilda Dunn Miller, Waycross, Ga., Tessie Lee Dunn, Waycross, Ga., Charles Dunn, Waycross, Ga., Albert C. Blythe, Jr., Waycross, Ga., Dorothy W. Blythe, Waycross, Ga., The following children are of Jacksonville, Fla.: Newnan Thomas, Richard Thomas, Joseph Thomas, Fannie K. Thomas, Edgar Thomas.

Amanda Davis Thomas's earthly voyage was filled with activities. These activities were the outstanding works of her life and it was in her home that she was known and loved best. Her unselfish heart and her rare Christian character were often revealed to those near and dear to her. She died at the home of her daughter, Mrs. A. C. Blythe, December 28, 1918, fully assured of an entrance into the "Beautiful home not made with hands."

BANNER H. THOMAS

Banner H. Thomas was born September 24, 1857. Spent his boyhood around the present site of Waycross.

Married Katie Byrd June 27, 1882. She was the daughter of William Byrd who fought in the War Between the States with the Fourth Georgia regiment and was killed in action.

HON. BANNER H. THOMAS

Two children are living, W. R. Thomas and Beulah Kate Thomas (Mrs. W. N. Smith).

Bought his first home in old Waycross in 1889. A few years later he bought a block, facing Pendleton, from the corner of Carswell to the canal.

At this time was Clerk of the Superior Court, which office he held until the term expired. Was elected Clerk of City Court. Was then elected Ordinary, which office he held until he retired. Was Chairman of the County Commission when the present jail was built. He was never defeated in an election.

Was associated with his son-in-law, W. N. Smith, in the vehicle business for several years.

His grand-children are: Kate Marie Smith (Mrs. Buell Kennady), Dorothy Will Smith (Mrs. Arthur Flanders), Beulah Frances Smith, Billie Katherine Smith, Katherine Thomas, Banner Thomas, the third, and Dorsey Thomas.

Active steward in Trinity Methodist Church.

His wife died February 21, 1918. He died September 17, 1924.

WILLIAM GUY THOMAS

A man who has been useful in the community in which he has lived since his youth is William G. Thomas. He has, in an able way, promoted the agricultural activities in his community, and nearly all of his life has been a merchant and tiller of the soil and in this wonderful independent occupation still finds interesting pleasures.

He was born Feb. 12, 1851 and soon after redeeming his farm from a wilderness, he, on January 4, 1872, made a home for himself and the interesting and bright Miss Vicy Warren by getting married on that date and settling in Ware County.

The following are the names of their children: William Guy, Vicy Warren, Welthie, John Banner, Willie Leon, Lilla, Rosa Lee, and Clinton.

After Mrs. Thomas' death Mr. Thomas was, on June 6, 1889, married to Miss Virginia E. Woodward and the following children have blessed this union: Ethel, Thomas, Letha, Dewey, and Edgar.

William Thomas' father was Banner Thomas, one of the pioneers who served for many years as Justice of Peace of Ware County. He also served in several Indian skirmishes in this county. The wife of Banner Thomas (William's grandmother) was Miss Lovie Denmark.

REV. W. H. THOMAS

"Uncle Thomas," as he was lovingly called, was an old fashioned Methodist minister, who with saddle bags preached and sang from the mountains of North Georgia to the marshes of the Southern Atlantic. "When the World's on Fire, Hallelujah!" was composed by him and was ever his favorite song.

REV. W. H. (Uncle) THOMAS

He was among the first to blaze the way for the coming city in the pine forest of southeast Georgia. In fact, he was so closely identified with Waycross and its interests since the laying of its first foundation stone, that he was known everywhere as the father of Waycross. His voice was ever heard in defense of right and his life was a benediction to all who came in contact with him. This faithful patriarch was always among the first in efforts made for the upbuilding of Christ's Kingdom in the town, and was an active worker in the building of churches and in providing for the support of the missions and ministers of the Gospel.

He served on committees to build three churches and two parsonages in Waycross, and was equally active in the cause of education. He preached one of the first sermons ever delivered in Waycross, and in every good work he was always in the front ranks.

Uncle Thomas was born on Thursday, Jan. 11, 1810,

in old Franklin county, Georgia. He was a son of William Thomas, a farmer and "horse-drover." In his infancy, with his mother and father, they moved to Kentucky. Mr. Thomas was married at the age of nineteen years to Miss Sarah Allcom. Five sons and five daughters were the result of this union. His wife died in 1860, while he was pastor of the Waresboro Circuit.

In 1866 he married Miss Laura Baker, the daughter of Judge Richard M. Baker, and of this marriage their son, Charles C. Thomas, was the first white child born in Ware county.

It was always interesting to hear Uncle Thomas tell of the primitive days when railroads were few and far between and when most of his traveling was done on horseback. He studied his Bible as he traveled and when he opened his mouth the Lord filled it with His Holy words.

On one occasion, at a place in Georgia, he held a class meeting in an old academy. The house was crowded, lawyers doctors, and all classes of citizens being out in force. Before beginning the service, he walked deliberately to the door and closing it, fastened it securely on the inside, remarking as he did so, "Now, I've got you!" And sure enough, before the "prisoners" were released from the old school house many of them had been released from the bondage of sin and were new creatures. The old school house has long since passed out of existence; still for many years men and women lived nearby who often thanked God for blessings that came to them from that class meeting held behind locked doors.

While Uncle Thomas was on the Circuit of Ware, he took the census of the county, State, and the United States. He prayed at all the homes he visited, and won the title of "praying census taker."

For over ninety years this faithful man lived upon the earth, always a blessing to the community in which he lived.

ELIAS D. WALDRON, SR.

Elias Waldron was born June 7, 1811, in that part of Ware that later became Appling County. His wife, Nancy Thomas, was born in 1811, and was the daughter of Captain Banner Thomas, who served in the Indian War of 1837. Captain Thomas was an early settler of Ware County. Mr. Waldron enlisted in the Indian War of July, 1831, and was made second lieutenant. Mr. and Mrs. Waldron's children were named: Elias D., David J., Henry J., Eliza (Mrs. Thomas Hilliard), Isabella (Mrs. Newburn), Mary Elizabeth (Mrs. Steinhelper), Georgia (Mrs. Bryan), and Thomas E.

DR. JOHN LOTT WALKER

The Waycross Journal of Wednesday, May 15, 1929, contains the following account of Dr. Walker's death and a sketch of his life and service, along with a resolution of the same date by the City Commission of Waycross:

Dr John Lott Walker, 74, eminent Georgian, who for years has been regarded as one of the first citizens of Waycross and Ware county, died at his home here last night following an extended illness, removing from Waycross a character who has taken a leading part in the building of Waycross and Ware county, and who has been, for years, one of the most universally loved men of this entire section of the state.

Doctor Walker's personal history is one of service and one which shows a marvelous degree of success. His loss to Waycross is inestimable, and the city is bowed in the deepest sorrow. Although retired for several years, his influence has not ceased to be felt in the city and state he served.

Native Georgian

He was born Aug. 27, 1854, in Washington county, Georgia, the son of Martha Webb Walker and Elisha

Walker. He graduated in medicine from the Atlanta College of Physicians and Surgeons in 1878 and from the Kentucky School of Medicine in the year 1880. He later took post graduate work in the New York Polyclinic Medical School and also the Chicago Polyclinic Medical School.

He engaged in the active practice of medicine for 47 years, his career being marked by philanthropy and generous service to mankind. He came to Waycross in 1886, after practicing at Wrightsville, Ga., in Johnson county for eight years. He was married in the year 1883 to Miss Laura Singleton of Eatonton, Ga.

Physician

As a Georgia physician, Doctor Walker probably is one of the best known in the past half century of the state's history. He was a member of the Ware County Medical Society, the Georgia State Medical Association and also the American Medical Association. He was a member of the State Board of Medical Examiners, appointed first by Governor Candler, and re-appointed by Governor Terrell. He was appointed to the State Board of Health by Governor Hoke Smith, and was re-appointed by Governor Hugh Dorsey and succeeding governors, being a member of that Board probably longer than any other member in the history of the state. He also was a member of Governor Terrell's staff.

Civic Leader

As an educator his career has been a proud one. He was a trustee of the Eleventh District Agricultural and Mechanical College at Douglas and also of the College for the Deaf and Dumb, at Cave Springs, Ga.

He served three times as president of the Waycross Board of Education, being a member of the board for more than a quarter of a century.

In his public life as a citizen of Waycross and Ware county he has served as alderman, commissioner and as mayor. He was the first president of the Waycross Chamber of Commerce organized here in the year 1907. He served as city physician and as county physician, and was at one time chairman of the Ware County Bond Commission.

Banker and Capitalist

As a banker and capitalist he gained widespread recognition. For more than a quarter century he was director of the First National Bank of Waycross, serving for several years, until his retirement, as president of the bank. At the time of his death he held the position of Chairman of the Board, being the first to hold this office in connection with the bank.

He has been regarded as one of the largest real estate holders in this section of the state, and has been prominently identified in extensive developments in Waycross and Ware County.

He was a trustee of the First Methodist Church of this city when the present church was built many years ago, and has been an active officer of this church.

He was a Mason, and a Shriner, also a member of the Odd Fellows, the Knights of Pythias and the Elks, having gained wide distinction as a fraternal leader.

RESOLUTION ON DEATH OF DR. J. L. WALKER

A Resolution Deploring the Death of Dr. J. L. Walker as Offered to the City Commission by Commissioner S. T. Wright

Whereas, the All-wise and merciful Father has called our beloved and respected fellow citizen, Dr. J. L. Walker, and,

Whereas the golden gateway to the Eternal City has opened to welcome him home, and

WHEREAS he has completed his work in the ministering to the wants of the afflicted, in shedding light into darkened souls and bringing joy into places of misery, and

WHEREAS the City Commission of Waycross deplores and regrets his passing and feels that in his death the city, the state and the county has lost one of its most beloved and valuable citizens,

THEREFORE, BE IT RESOLVED that the City Commission of Waycross, in testimony of its loss, tender to the family of the deceased our sincere condolence in this deep affliction.

BE IT FURTHER RESOLVED that the flag on the City Hall be lowered to half mast on this date and the Mayor and City Commission attend the funeral in a body, and that these expressions of sympathy be placed on the minutes of the City Commission, a copy sent to the Waycross Journal-Herald for publication, and a copy sent to the family.

DONE AT THE MUNICIPAL BUILDING in the City of Waycross, this the 15th day of May, 1929.

H. S. REDDING, Mayor

Attest: W. E. LEE, City Clerk.

JOHN VANDY AMBROSE WARREN

The life of Mr. Warren has been intimately connected with the growth and development of the farming interests of Ware county. When he came here in 1874 Waycross was only two years old and his years were less than twenty. He soon manifested an active interest in the prosperity of his adopted home, and took a hand in some of the most beneficial enterprises. Mr. Warren was ever in full sympathy and accord with every movement that tended to encouragement and foster agricultural advancement, which he considered the most important vocation under the sun and the only safe and sure vocation that would keep the nation alive and prosperous.

He was born in Emanuel county in the year of 1855. He married in 1877 Miss Matilda Thomas, daughter of Mr. Banner Thomas of Ware county. They settled eight miles east of Waycross on the Old Brunswick road, where they built their home. Mrs. Warren died November 14, 1892.

She was a woman of great force of character, and was devoted to her family, never losing sight of their comfort and happiness. She died while her children were quite young, but Mr. Warren, with true devotion to her memory, filled his place and hers in the home and their children were well reared and are now honored citizens of Waycross.

Mr. Warren died in Waycross May 13, 1931. The names of Mr. and Mrs. Warren's children are: Bennett Dawson, William Lawson, A. Ambrose, Mattie Pauline (Mrs. J. W. Freeman), Lloyd Carswell, Effie Mae (Mrs. J. D. Driggers), Birdie (Mrs. O. M. Hiers).

JACK WILLIAMS

Mr. Williams, in his chosen profession, has had ample opportunity for achieving success. His ability and personal popularity have found many testimonials for he has been called upon to serve in offices of trust, not only in the city in which he maintains his home, but the State at large. He holds secure prestige as one of the leading newspapermen of Georgia and in his political policies, he retains a clean slate, always being on the right side of every question. He has ever held aloft the banner of true Democracy with his sound resourcefulness and versatility as the Editor and Publisher, Waycross Journal-Herald. Born at Castle Hayne, N. C. Educational preparation, Cape Fear Academy, Wilmington, N. C.; Graduate Oak Ridge Institute (N. C.) 1904; Married Ethel Katharine Woodard of Martin, Tenn., 1912; four children.

JACK WILLIAMS

In purchasing Department, A. C. L., Wilmington and Waycross, 1899-1902; same position with A. B. & C. R. R., Waycross, 1905-1906; general storekeeper with same railroad, Fitzgerald, 1906-1907; manager publishing company, Boston, Mass., 1909-1911.

Editor and Publisher, Waycross Journal-Herald, since 1915; also publisher Blackshear Times, 1924-1926; Hogansville News, 1925-1926; LaGrange Reporter, 1924-1927.

Director Merchants and Mechanics Loan & Savings Company Waycross· Building and Loan Company, Waycross Hotel Company, Morgan Plan Bank.

President Eleventh District Press Association, 1926-1931; Vice-President Georgia Press Association 1929-1931; president Georgia Press Association 1931-1933; Vice-President National Editorial Association 1931-1933.

Awarded the Baynard Knight Cup, 1923, as being the Kiwanian who rendered the greatest service to the community during that year. Awarded the Miller Medal, 1932, as being the citizen of Waycross who had rendered the greatest service to the community during that year.

The Waycross Journal-Herald was awarded the Sutlive Trophy in 1925 for having rendered the greatest service to its community of any paper in the state. It was also awarded the Biltmore Thophy in 1931 for having rendered the greatest service to health of any paper in the state.

It was awarded the Sutlive Trophy again in 1932.

WILLIAM WILSON

William Wilson, was the eldest son of Soloman and Pidian Wilson, who was born April 16th, 1826, in the Province of Posen, Poland, where he received his early education and served for nine years as an apprentice tanner. In the fall of 1848 he left his homeland for the United States, making a short stay in England on his way. His first two years in America were spent in Philadelphia after which he was engaged for a period of four years in the mercantile business at Columbus, Georgia, at the end of which time he sold out and removed to Philadelphia. The Sunny South, however, had woven a spell around him and after two or three months he returned to Georgia and settled in Waresboro as a merchant. At the beginning of the War Between the States, Mr. Wilson entered the army, having joined Company

E of a regiment which was assigned to General Joseph E. Johnston's Division and afterward under the command of General Hood. Mr. Wilson served in the various engagements in and around Atlanta and in numerous skirmishes but was neither wounded nor captured and at the end of the struggle received an honorable discharge. He then returned to Ware county and engaged in the sawmill business. In 1884 he left Waresboro, which up to that time had been his home, and settled in the growing town of Waycross with the same activities and interests of which he was ever identified. He carried on a large and thriving business and in 1890 erected an elegant new block of stores which did credit to his enterprise and taste. The corner block, known as the Wilson corner, has been torn down and the Murson Hotel now occupies the site which was once the most prominent business section of Waycross. Mr. Wilson was an outstanding Mason in this section and held various positions of honor in that fraternity. In 1858 he was married to Miss Martha Smith and the following children composed their family: Col. Leon A. Wilson, William M. Wilson, Mrs. Geo. O. Turner, Mrs. Robert H. Murphy, and Mrs. John Strickland.

Mr. and Mrs. Wilson were a fine example of an upright people and were among the valued pioneer citizens of Ware county. Mr. Wilson died Nov. 17th, 1911.

LEON WILSON

The law has no finer man in that profession than the honorable Leon Wilson. As a jurist, he measures up favorably along with some of the most able and reliable members of the bench and bar, and is recognized as a man of ability, energy, and uncompromising integrity.

He was born in Waresboro, Ware county, Nov. 14, 1859. His parents were William and Martha J. (Smith) Wilson. His education was acquired in the common schools and in part under a private tutor. He read law with Messrs. Jackson, Lawton & Besinger, Savannah, and June 9, 1880, was admitted to practice in superior court, and in February, 1891, to the supreme court.

From Mr. Wilson's earliest entrance into public life his outstanding ability has been recognized by appointments and elections to positions of trust and responsibility. In 1883 he was appointed by Governor Alexander Stephens Judge of the County Court, which office he resigned at the end of two years. The ensuing year he was elected Mayor of Waycross. In 1892-93 he represented Ware county in the General Assembly, and was placed upon several of the most important committees, general judiciary, corporations, etc., and was appointed chairman of that on temperance. In 1894 he was elected to represent the fifth senatorial district in the General Assembly. Mr. Wilson has ever been one of the standard-bearers of the temperance cause in Georgia, and at one time was a member of the prohibition executive committee of his district.

Mr. Wilson was married Sept. 23, 1882, to Miss Carrie Murphy of Waycross, formerly of Dunnellon, N. J., a union which has been blessed with three children, Irean (deceased), Kate, and Hurbert.

J. J. WILKINSON

Mr. Wilkinson was born January 10, 1842, at Tebeauville, later known as Old Nine. He was reared on a farm in Ware county, and was a successful tiller of the soil. In Feb., 1862, he enlisted in the 13th Georgia Regiment, which was organized as the 26th Regiment. His regiment was assigned to Lee's Army of Northern Virginia, in General Gordon's Brigade, with Stonewall Jackson as corps commander. Mr. Wilkinson served with distinction as private all through the war, receiving a slight wound at the battle of Bull Run.

On Sept. 18, 1868, he was married to Miss Mary J. Sands, daughter of Mr. and Mrs. J. N. Sands, prominent residents of Ware county. Five girls and six boys have been born to them, all of whom are living except one boy. Their names are: John Gordon, Cicero, James Martin, Amanda, Katie, Eliza, Sallie, George, Tom, and Elizabeth.

Mr. Wilkinson's first offices were constable and justice of the peace. In 1872 he was appointed by Governor Bulloch to fill a vacancy as tax collector. He was elected to the office two successive terms, serving five years. In 1877 he was elected ordinary of Ware county, serving four years, when he voluntarily retired to private life. While working on the farm, Mr. Wilkinson was called again into public life by being elected receiver of tax returns for Ware county, which office he held for several terms. He most faithfully discharged every duty imposed upon him, and was conceded to be one of the best officials the county ever had. He was, on several accasions, complimented very highly by the comptroller general for the excellent returns he had sent in.

He did his work well and the people recognized in him a faithful servant, and were pleased to compliment him with the office he desired to hold. Mr. Wilkinson died in 1909 and Mrs. Wilkinson died in June, 1912.

MILLEDGE WOODARD

Mr. Milledge Woodard, a son of William and Nancy Martin Woodard, was born in Emanuel county, October 22, 1846. He moved to Pierce county in 1874 and the following year came to Ware county where he built his home in what is known as the Woodard Settlement, about three miles south of what is now Waycross, and has lived there ever since. At the time Mr. Woodard came to live in Ware county there were only four families between his home and Big Creek, some ten miles distant. In 1864 he married Miss Priscilla Stone, a daughter of Henry and Sophia Dowling Stone. Mrs. Woodard died in 1914. The following children were born to them: Missouri (Mrs. John Strickland), Lenon (married Nancy Strickland), Aaron (married Mary Williams), Henry (married Lottie Jones), Hulce (married Cecil Ake), Vandie (married Sadie Fox) and Malinda (Mrs. R. E. Kennedy).

Mr. Woodards early education was limited, owing to the meagre school facilities that were available during and just following the war. A greater part of his education was self-acquired. Beginning life for himself in the settlement that was named for his father, the "Woodard Settlement," he has always maintained a well established house, and was listed among Ware county's most progressive farmers, keeping free from debt, and leading the independent life of owing no man. Long before the slogan, "The cow, the hen, and the hog," was adopted by the Farmers Association, the cow, the hen, and the hog were the most important factors on the Woodard estate. He had the first real chicken farm in Ware, and supplied many families in this place with butter, chickens, eggs, mutton, and beef. He was truly a progressive farmer and he handled his produce in a successful and profitable way.

Mr. Woodard has passed the years allotted to man as a sojourner upon the earth, but he possess all of his mental faculties, and is especially interesting when talking about the times when a home could be liberally supplied with commodities that were raised on the farm— the place where all the family should have duties that were carried out in an orderly way.

DR. BENJAMIN F. WILLIAMS

Dr. Benjamin F. Williams was born in Green county, North Carolina, September 2, 1820. His father, Joseph Williams, was a successful planter, who lived and died in North Carolina. His mother, Avey (Murphy) Williams, was also a native of North Carolina. Joseph and Avey Williams had ten children, the youngest of whom is the subject of this sketch, Dr. Williams. He was reared and partially educated in the state of his nativity and afterward attended Madison University in New York. In 1843 he commenced to read medicine with Dr. Robbins of Troy, New York, subsequently attending the medical college at Albany, New York, and was a student in the office of Prof. James McNaughton of that city.

In 1847 he returned to his home in North Carolina, and practiced medicine. He was elected to the house of representatives of North Carolina from his county in 1850. In 1853 he married Miss Sarah F., daughter of Samuel and Sarah Hicks of New Hartford, New York. To this union were born seven children, viz: Sarah V., Henry C., Harriet J., Joseph Samuel, Martha F., Benjamin H., and William P.

Dr. Williams moved in 1857 to Burnt Fort, at that time Camden county, and from there removed to Sunny Side, Ware county. He served a short time in the Confederate Army, and after the War closed he retired from his medical profession. He was a member of the first constitutional convention of Georgia after peace was restored. In 1873 he moved to Waycross and became one of the founders of the town, he being one af the first two settlers. He was one of the first turpentine workers in this section. His still was located on the old Atlantic and Gulf railroad near the Satilla river. Dr. Williams was one of the largest land owners in the county. He was the second mayor that served in Waycross. Dr. Williams did a large medical practice in a wide scope of the surrounding county, and was a man who did much good in a quiet and unassuming way. He died May 7, 1892, in Waycross.

MRS. SARAH HICKS WILLIAMS

Sarah Francis Hicks was born in New Hartford, New York, on March 7, 1827. She graduated at the Albany Academy in Albany, N. Y. in 1844. There were forty members in her class—she outlived them all by several years. Mrs. Williams was the daughter of Samuel Hicks, who was born in 1783 in Long Island, N. Y. He married Sarah Parmlee, October 8, 1821. Sarah Parmlee (Mrs. Williams' mother) was born August 19, 1794 in the state of Connecticut. Samuel Hicks died April 8, 1876, at New Hartford and Sarah, his wife, died in 1880 in Utica, New York.

While in Albany, New York, Sarah Hicks met Dr. Benjamin F. Williams, who was studying medicine there, and later was married to him September 20, 1853. They lived for a while in North Carolina and then moved to Burnt Fort, Camden county, Georgia, becoming owners of extensive virgin forest lands both in Camden and Ware counties. In 1860 Dr. and Mrs. Williams moved to Ware county and settled in a beautiful section of Ware not far from the Satilla river. Mrs. Williams named their home Sunny Side. In 1872 Dr. and Mrs. Williams came to Waycross to live. The home they built was on the corner of Screven and Knight Avenue. This was the second house built in Waycross.

The first school and the first Sunday school was organized in Mrs. Williams' home, and out of this Christian inspiration there grew into being the Old Union Church, which stood near the present site of Trinity church. She was often called the mother of the Presbyterian house of worship on Williams street, she being one of the founders. Her undaunted spirit made her a leader among women. She elevated the standards of her community, and neglected no opportunity that promised advancement for her town. Her life was one of service, and those who knew and loved Mrs. Williams best, were those who were often with her in her own charming home. Hicks street, one of the prominent streets of Waycross, was named for her.

GEORGE R. YOUMANS

Mr. Youmans is truly a pioneer citizen of Ware county, locating in Waycross when quite a young man, he saw busy years come and go. His native home was Pierce county where he was born in 1858. His parents, James and Elizabeth Cleland Youmans, were among the first settlers of Pierce county, where they located after leaving their native home near Barnwell, S. C. Mr. and Mrs. James Youmans witnessed the advent of the first locomotive carrying passengers through Blackshear. The railroad was known as the Atlantic & Gulf, later as the Plant System and now as the Atlantic Coast Line. This noted event occurred in 1859 and on the day that the "Railroad Train" appeared, great excitement prevailed. Free rides were granted to all those who desired to be passengers on the train. It only went as far as "Old Nine" or Tebeauville and returned to Blackshear some time during the afternoon. A great fear came over some of the spectators when they looked down the road recently built from Savannah, and beheld the great "Iron Horse" advancing through steam and smoke to this quiet little town in the Wiregrass. Some fainted and others took to the woods.

Mr. Youmans was married to Miss Janie Mallon in Blackshear in 1881 and in 1885 they located in Waycross. Mrs. Youmans lived only a few years after coming here. In 1891 Mr. Youmans was married to Mrs. Frances Carswell.

Mr. Youmans' sound judgment in matters of business and his absolute integrity in his relations with others has won for him the highest confidence and admiration of a large circle of friends and business associates.

During his long and useful life he has given generously of his time, talents and means to his city, county, and his state. While his public life has been long and honorable, it is, perhaps, in his home life that the sincerity of his character and personal charms are more truly expressed. He has ever entertained a loyal devotion to his family, of whom some are still left to cheer his home. The Angel of Death entered its portals November 17th, 1927, and bore away to her eternal rest, the sweet spirit of Frances Carswell Youmans. Mr. Youmans is greatly blessed in having three step-daughters whom he has loved as if they were his own, and it is through the presence of one of the daughters and two grand-daughters, since the passing of Mrs. Youmans, that his home has been kept cheerful and with such life as often radiates from having young people around.

INDEX

Land grants, rosters of soldiers, crosses of honor to Confederate soldiers, county officers, and cemeteries are paged but not indexed.

A

	Page
Advisory Committee	195
Albany	92
Albany, Atlantic and Gulf	92
Albertson, M.	151
Allen, B. F.	93, 171
Allen's, B. F., Memories of Long Ago	102
Allen, W. A.	107
America's Answer	285, 286
American Legion Auxiliary	291, 292, 293, 294, 295, 296
Andrews, C. Fort	170, 171
Appling, John	20
Appling, Rebecca Carter	20
Archibald, P. C.	154
Ashmore, Hon. Otis	85
Atkinson, Lieutenant Colonel	106
Atkinson, Judge Davis	192
Atkinson, Mamie	250, 251, 252
Atkinson, Sam	106
Atkinson, Spencer	106
Atwell, Mrs. Tululah Brinson	177, 178

B

Bailey, Isaac	71
Bailey, William S.	5, 90, 97
Bailey, Mrs. William	90
Baldwin, Abraham	81
Barnard, Timpoochee	62
Barnard, Timothy	73
Barnard, William	73
Bartram, Brinton	5
Bartow, Frances S. Chapter, Daughters of the Confederacy	183
Baschlot, John	146
Beard's Bluff	74
Beaton, Mayor Scott T.	85
Beaton, Wilbur	148
Beck, Miss Willie	185
Bedford, Peter	82, 98, 99, 106
Bennett, A. R.	130
Bergman, A. F.	154
Bird, R. P.	151, 152, 186, 256, 257
Blackburn, Daniel I.	129
Blackshear	93, 107
Blackshear, Belle	182
Blackshear, General David	68, 69, 70, 71, 72, 78
Blackshear, Capt. Elijah	62

(533)

	Page
Blackshear, Zoe	346
Blanchard, John	170
Blythe, Dorothy	7
Boifeullet, John T.	184
Bottome, Mrs. Margaret	182
Bowlegs, Billy	5, 6
Bradley, B. D.	98, 99
Brantley, W. G.	103
Brewer, H. P.	130, 131, 151, 169
Brewer, Joe	130
Brewer, Turner	145
Brewton, E. G.	98, 99
Bridges, R. M.	130
Brinson, G. W.	154
Brown, Blondel	170
Brunswick	92
Bryan, Jonathan Chapter, D. A. R.	189, 190
Bryan, Philemon	147
Burgess, William	66
Burnt Fort	84, 89
Byrd, Thomas	98, 99

C

	Page
Camden County	66, 71, 78
Camp Pinckney	63
Cannon in Phoenix Park	262
Capital Road	82
Carldwell, Dr. Frank H.	157
Carr, Jim	14
Carswell, Dr. Alexander	151, 154
Carswell, W. J.	131
Cason, J. B.	98, 99
Cason, Rand	97
Cason, W. A.	151, 153
Caswell, James	96
Cavender, R. C.	179
Cemeteries:	
Kettle Creek Cemetery	37, 38, 39, 40, 41
Mount Pleasant Cemetery	42, 43
Providence Church Yard	41
Census, Federal	148, 149
Centerville	66, 72, 73, 95
Children of the Confederacy, Listed	189
Churches, Some of Oldest in Ware:	
Camp Branch Church	109
Catholic Church	123
Central Baptist Tabernacle	124
Grace Episcopal Church, The	121
First Baptist Church	119
First Christian Church	126
First Methodist Church	117
First Presbyterian Church	118
Trinity Methodist Church	111
Civil Courts and Their Officers	309, 310
Clark, Gen. John	81, 82

INDEX

	Page
Clary, John Lucius	147
Clerks, Court of Ordinary	306, 307
Clerks of the Inferior Court	303, 304
Clough, Jonothan	92
Club Department of Work	194
Clymer, George	191
Coleraine	66, 69, 73
Collins, Benjamin	8
Colquitt's Brigade	82
Confederate Graves in War	243, 244
Confederate Hero	255
Congressional	310, 311
Congressional Districts	311, 312, 313, 314
Cook, Rev. Osgood	192
Cooper, L. J.	166, 170
Coroners	304, 305
Cottingham, Edward	97
County Commissioners	195
County Senators	308, 309
Cowart, Dan	179
Cowsewatte Town	81
Cox, John M.	61
Crawley, Capt. Edward	101, 130, 147
Crawley, Judge Lee	195
Crawley, Jerome	195
Crawley, Tom	154
Cross Keys	81
Crosses of Honor to the Confederate Veterans	186
Cushing, Elijah	154

D

Darien	70, 74
Davis, Early	98, 99
Davis, Pres. Jefferson	186, 263
Davis, Mrs. Jefferson	186
Davis, O. E.	179
Davis, Stafford	14
Davidson, David	98, 99
Deen, G. W.	154
DeLoach, J. D.	107
DeSoto, Hernando	2
Devine, Bill	98, 99, 148
Dixon, Capt. N.	105, 129
Douglas, James	99

E

Eagle Tavern	81
Early Settlers of Appling County Before Ware was Cut From That County	19
Early Settlers of Ware	22, 23
Eatonton	5, 81
Elkins, J. S.	179
Elkins, Liston	7
Ellicott Mounds	75

INDEX

	Page
Enchanted Island, The	55, 56
English, William	151
Eunice (Nunez), Alexander	17
Everett, T. L.	179

F

Fence, Pond	66
Finn, D. B.	152
First Merchants of Waycross	159
Floyd, General Charles	7, 13, 75
Floyd, General John	17, 68, 73, 75
Folks, Dr. Augustus	103
Folks, Dr. Frank	103, 151
Folks, William B.	98, 99, 102, 103, 129, 130, 144, 167, 168
Folks, William B. II	154
Folsom, Mrs. F. B.	7, 136, 195
Forsythe, John	22
Forts and Indian Trading Houses:	
Coleraine	11
Detroit, Ark	11
Fort Dearborn	75, 78
Fort Floyd	78
Fort Gilmer	2, 17
Fort Mitchell	74
Fort Mudge	78
Fort St. Stephen	11
Jellico	11
Foster, Stephen	49
Founders of Waycross:	
Bailey, William	88
Hilliard, Capt. Cuyler	88
Lott, Dr. Daniel	88
Williams, Dr. Benjamin	88
Freeman, James	167, 168
Fulwood, James	163

G

Georgia Land Lottery, Register No. 1	25
Georgia Land Lottery, Register No. 3	26, 27
Georgia Land Lottery Showing Some of the Early Settlers of Ware	24
Geotte, George	98, 99
Gerber, F. W.	154
Gibson, C. E.	179
Giddins, O.	96
Gillette, George	66
Going Away (Article)	263
Gordon, Gov. John B.	151, 155, 184, 257
Grace, C. C.	257
Grand Central Hotel	145
Grant, George	90
Green, William	97
Greer, John	7, 170, 171
Grey, Anne	66

INDEX

	Page
Groff, J. D.	130
Grovenstine, Farley	146
Grovenstine, Joe	146
Grovenstine, John	146
Grovenstine, Kate	146
Grovenstine, Lizzie	146
Grovenstine, Mrs. M. M.	145, 146
Grovenstine, Rosa	146

H

4-H Clubs of Ware County	176
Hayden, Charles J.	48, 49
Haines, Major Harry	93, 103, 144
Hall, Lyman Chapter of D. A. R.	87, 190
Hamilton, G. P.	154
Happenings in Waycross	144
Harbin, W. M.	257
Hargraves, John	173
Harley, Mrs. P. N.	181, 182
Harper, J. A.	98, 99
Harris, H. D.	257
Harrison, W. H.	253
Hartford	70
Hartridge, Julian	104
Hatfield, G. R.	179
Hawkins, Benjamin	191
Hawks, C. R.	170
Hawks, Mrs. C. R.	170
Henderson, William G.	71
Herrin, Lee	171, 173
Herrin, Mary	173
Herrin, William	173
Heyde, Dr. R. D.	176, 179
Hilliard, Capt. Cuyler W.	5, 91
Hilliard, Mrs. Cuyler	91
Hilliard, Thomas	14, 99, 101
Hillman, Joseph	98, 99
Hitch, Mary	130
Hitch, Simon W.	144
Holmes, C. T.	257
Horse Path	144
Hospital, A. C. L.	74
Hospital Association	181
Hospital, Plant System	157
How Waycross Got Its Name	93
Hundredth Anniversary of Ware County	325, 326, 327, 328
Hunter, Colonel, R. L.	75
Hurricane Creek	74
Huxford, Folks	7, 97

I

Indian Wars ....199, 200, 201, 202, 203, 204, 205, 206, 207, 208, 209, 210, 211, 212, 213, 214, 215, 216, 217, 218, 219, 220, 221, 222, 223, 224, 225, 226, 227, 228, 229, 230, 231, 232, 233, 234, 235, 236, 237, 238, 239, 240.

	Page
Ingram, L. M.	130
Inman, James	98, 99
Izlar, Dr. R. P.	157, 181

J

Jackson, Gen. James	192
Janes, Dr. Thomas	101
Jarrett, Captain	81
Jeffords, Ed.	96
Jeffords, Martin	96
Jeffords, Mrs. S. P.	96
Jenkins, Prof. Charles J.	104, 108, 129, 163
Jenkins, Mrs. L. G. Chronology	145
Johnson, J.	257
Johnson, L.	131, 151, 153
Jones, Mrs. W. N.	177
Justice of Inferior Court	301, 302, 303

K

Kennard, Jack	68
Kennon, Dr. B. N.	70
Kettle Creek, The Naming of	36
King, William	108
King Daughter's Golden Rule Circle No. 2, Members	183
Kings Daughter's Sunshine Circle No. 1, Members	183
Kings Road	79
Kingsbury, Capt. S. T.	184
Knight, A. M.	131, 151, 182
Knight, Minnie	130
Knoff, Lula	130
Knowles, Daniel	98, 99
Knox, Ed.	154
Knox, Henry	9
Knox, James	102, 103, 104, 108
Kuhn, Ruth (Mrs. C. M. Stephens)	157

L

Lafayette Hall	81
Lamar, John	82
Land Lots of Ware	27, 28, 29, 30
Lang, David	67
Lanier, T. E.	147, 167
Lawson, Hugh	81
Lee, John	98, 99
Lee, Gen. Robert E.	85
Le Moyne	44
Lester, Rufus E.	104
Lewis, J. B., Sr.	192
Little, Talbot	99
Lott Cemetery	186
Lott, Dr. Daniel	5, 88, 91, 92, 93, 97, 98, 99, 101, 102, 108, 144, 167, 168
Lott, John	7, 82, 97, 100
Lott Mrs. J. A.	7, 87

INDEX

	Page
Lott, Oscar	182
Lott, Mrs. Susan	91
Lott, Major Warren	97, 103, 131, 145, 147, 151, 182
Love Feast at Waycross—Held at Trinity Church	114
Lumpkin, Governor William	71
Lyon, Virginia	185

M

Merchon, Judge	105
Madison, Georgia	81
Mattox, Charles	59, 60, 61
Mattox, John H.	98, 99
Mattox, Dr. L. C.	98, 99
McClure, William	97
McCullough, Dr. Kenneth	157
McDonald, Charles	21
McDonald, D. J.	98, 99
McDonald, Mrs. J. G.	182
McDonald, Capt. James	101
McDonald, John C.	104
McDonald's Mill	155
McDonald, Randall	98, 99
McDonald, Roy	179
McDonald, Colonel William	101
McFarr, Capt. J. P.	154
McGee, Major	90
McIntosh County	78
McLendon, W. B.	98, 99
McQuaig, Joseph	98, 99, 144
Memorial Bridge	289, 290, 291
Merriam, Prof. C. L.	154
Military	197
Militia Districts	33, 34, 35
Milledge, John	81
Miller, A. G.	85
Miller, A. J.	98, 99
Miller, Capt. David	36
Miller, David, Jr.	36
Miller, David J.	127, 129
Miller, Capt. Jesse	14
Milwood Advance	169
Minchew, Dr. B. H.	7
Mitchell, Governor	70, 78
Mitchell, Joseph	59, 60, 61
Mizel, David	67
Mizell, Joseph	192
Mock, Jack	97
Mock, Miriam	97
Moore, Mrs. Lee Sheldon	185
Moran, A. J.	179
Morgan County	82
Morton, T. H.	129, 130
Mount Pleasant Cemetery, Records of	42, 43
Mullis, Mr.	96
Murphy, Charles E.	145, 182

INDEX

	Page
Murphy, Herbert	102, 103, 104, 129, 130, 145, 151, 152, 164
Murphy, R. H.	145
Myers, Judge John T.	192
Myers, W. H.	99

N

Negroes of Ware	320
Newspapers, Waycross	167
Newton, Ralph	7
Nichols, John C.	98, 99, 105, 106
Norcross	93
Norman, J. M.	179

O

Officer's Bonds	305, 306
Oglethorpe, General	9
Okefinokee Swamp	51, 52, 53, 54, 66, 67, 75, 78
Islands in Okefinokee Swamp	75, 76
Oleman, Mrs. Elizabeth	123, 129
Oneekachumpa	5
O'Quinn, Alexander	130
O'Quinn, John	96
O'Quinn, W. D.	179
Ordinaries of Ware County	299
Osceola	3
O'Steen, John A.	67

P

Pafford, E. M.	104
Pafford, Hon. Rowan	104
Paine, Annie Willis	185, 188, 257
Paine, Edna Lee	186
Paine, Capt. Spalding	186
Paine, Dr. T. Spalding	253
Parker, George Foster	146
Parker, Lucy M.	146
Parker, Maggie M.	146
Parker, Mrs. Mary	87
Parker, Oville D.	92, 146
Parker, Sumter B.	146
Parker, Judge T. A.	192
Parker, Capt. William Foster	146
Parker, William, Jr.	92, 167
Parks, B. G.	179, 186
Peeples, Eddie	170
Pendleton	87, 107, 169
Pendleton, Lewis Beauregard	83
Pendleton, Major Philip Coleman	83
Perham, Judge A. P.	169, 257
Perham, A. P., Jr.	154
Phoenix Hotel	145
Pickens, Andrew	191
Pierce County	78

INDEX

	Page
Pierce, Franklin	163
Pinckney, Camp	96
Pittman, C. R.	154
Pittman, L. W. H.	98, 99
Pittman, S. D.	154
Plant, H. B.	30, 179, 180
Politics	162
Ponce de Leon	1
Pound, E. A.	184
Pound, Mrs. E. A.	185, 188
Powell, Dr. R. H.	49
Powell, William	4
Price, W. A.	170
Putnam County	82

Q

Quarterman Street School	92

R

Racepond	31
Recollections of the Confederacy	261
Redding, Dr. J. H.	151, 153
Redding, Mrs. J. H.	182, 188
Reed, E. H.	151, 153
Reed, Mrs. E. H.	181, 182
Reed, H. W.	129, 130, 151
Reminiscences of a Confederate Soldier	248, 249
Reminiscences of War Life	244, 245, 246, 247, 248
Remshart, Isabella	146
Remshart, Mrs. James	146
Remshart, Rev. M.	146
Remshart, Mary E.	146
Rennie, William	98, 99
Rentz, Daniel	99
Representatives	308
Revolutionary Soldiers, List of	197
Rifles, Charter Members of Waycross	156
Riley, Colonel Peter	155
Rippard, Dr. J. C.	181
Rippard, Mrs. J. C.	182
Rivers, W. J.	98, 99
Roach, George S.	129
Rocky Mount	157
Rock Mountain	82
Rollings, George	146
Roster of World War Soldiers	264
Russell, Hon. Ben E.	169, 257

S

Saint, Illa, Capt.	44, 45, 46, 47
Saint Marys	71, 72, 82, 108
Saint Marys River	63, 74, 191
Saint Simons Island	145

	Page
Salisbury, Dell	154
Sanders, J. B.	192
Sassnet, H. H.	257
Satilla House	108, 148
Satilla River	44, 84, 89, 90, 146
Schomber, Aug.	154
Schools, Ware County:	
First Schools of Waycross	129
Piedmont Institute	142, 143
School Administration	132, 133, 134
School Board Officers	136
School Chronology	136, 137, 138, 139, 140, 141
School Members of the City—Board of Education	135
School Records	135
School Superintendents and Principals	132, 133, 134
Waresboro	127
Wildesville and Kettle Creek Schools	128
Screven, John	84
Scruggs, Rev. W. H.	181
Seabring, W. H.	257
Seagrove, Robert	66
Secoffee	5
Senatorial Districts	315
Settle, S. P., Sr.	96, 129
Sharp, Fannie	169
Sharpe, W. W.	164
Sheldon, Mrs. C. A.	185
Sheldon, Capt. Charles A.	186
Sheriffs of Ware County	299, 300
Shine, Mrs.	108
Shine, Miss Emma	129
Shine, Miss Mamie	129, 130, 159
Sirmans, Benjamin	130, 154
Sirmans, Walter Eustace	192
Slocum, Dr. Robert	157
Smith, Austin	101
Smith, J. D.	96, 98, 99
Smith, Dr. J. E. W.	154
Smith, William D.	98, 99
Smith, W. J.	130
Smith, William W.	98, 99
Spear, D. D.	256
Spence, Major	101
Spence, Miriam	96
Spence, Hilly (Hilliard)	96
Spratt, Dr.	157
Stafford, D. N.	179
Stanton, Cecil V.	195
Stanton, Frank	93
Stanton, Valentine	95, 104, 107, 148, 151, 153, 164, 166
Stark, John	102
Steffis, J. G.	103
Stephens, Alexander	84
Stephens, J. W.	99
Stewart, Rev. James	98, 99
Stewart, John L.	148
Stewart, John S.	21

INDEX

	Page
Stewart, W. G.	99
Stiger, J. M.	103
Story of a Tragic Death	316, 317, 318
Strickland, Allen	99
Strickland, William	96
Styles, Colonel Cary	92, 168
Summerall, Ernest	170
Superior Court Transfers	314
Suwanee River	47
Sweat, Captain Burrell	6
Sweat, D. B.	145, 154, 169, 170
Sweat, J. L.	257
Sweat, R. G.	170
Sweat, Samuel	129

T

	Page
Tallassee Chief	191
Tanner, B. H.	98, 99
Tebeau, Charlie	146
Tebeau Creek	92
Tebeau, Edward	146
Tebeau, Emma	146
Tebeau, Capt. F. E.	84
Tebeau, Minnie	146
Tebeau, Rev. Lewis C.	146
Tebeauville	82, 107, 145, 146
The Old Country Road	58
Thigpen, Gaines	96
Thigpen, Manning	14
Thomas, Dr. G. G.	157
Thomas, Jim (James)	96
Thomas, Rev. W. H.	93, 100, 104, 130
Thompson, John A.	99
Thompson, L. R.	98, 99
Tillman, Judge Joseph	167
Tillman, Joseph	107
Tippins, John	67
Tompkins Inn	81
Tompson, General	4
Toomer, Hon. W. M.	131, 184
Trader's Hill	66, 72, 73, 82, 95
Trails and Roads:	59
Barnard Trail	72, 73, 74, 75
Blackshear Trail	69, 70, 71
Columbus or Market Road	71, 72
Floyd's Trail	75
Hunter's Trail	75
Indian Trails and Mounds in the Okefinokee Swamp	75, 76
Kennard Settlement and Trail	68
Old Train Road	64, 65, 66, 67, 68
Trails in the Okefinokee	75
Train Wreck	148
Travelers Rest	81
Treasurers of Ware County	300, 301
Twiggs, John	81
Troupville	82

U

	Page
United Confederate Veterans, List of	258
Utilities of Waycross	150

V

Varn's Still	155

W

Wadley, Mrs. J. E.	185
Wagner, D. J.	179
Walker, Charles	98, 99
Walker, Freeman	22
Walker, Dr. J. L.	151
Walker, Mrs. J. L.	5, 164, 166
Walton, George	81
War Between the States	240, 241, 242
Ware County Officers	297, 298, 299
Ware's First Board of Health	151
Ware, Nicholas	21
Ware's Unknown Soldier	197, 198, 199
Waresboro	74, 82, 91, 92, 95, 104
Waresboro Masonic Lodge	98
Washington, George	80, 81, 82
Waycross	107
Waycross, A Religious Town	93
Waycross, Canteen	286, 287, 288, 289
Waycross Clubs	181
Waycross Georgian	169
Waycross Headlight	168
Waycross Journal Herald	169
Waycross Reporter	169
Waycross Woman's Club	192
Webb, William	97
Webster, Daniel	163
Weise, Leopold	147
Wells, J. M.	131
Wesley, A. G.	170
Wesley, Charles	170
Wesley, John E.	170
Wesley, Willie	170
Wheeler, Gen. Joseph	186
Wilds, J. L.	8
Wildes Massacre	6
Williams, Dr. Benjamin	5, 89, 97, 102, 103, 129
Williams, Mrs. Benjamin	89, 129, 146
Williams, B. H., Jr.	151
Williams, Dan	7
Williams, H. A.	154
Williams, Jack	7, 171, 179, 195
Williams, Judge J. S.	103, 154
Williams, Mattie	7, 182, 185
Williams, Micajah	81
Williams, U. J.	154
Williams, Volney	171

INDEX

	Page
Williamson, Judge W. B.	102, 103
Wirz, Major Henry	186
Wilson, C.	96
Wilson, Leon A.	104, 129, 147, 164, 195
Wilson, William	145, 151, 153
Woman's Club, Officers and Board Members	194
Woodard, D. A.	59, 60, 61
World War Navy	283, 284, 285
World War Officers	282, 283
World War Veterans (Alphabetical)	265, 266, 267, 268, 269, 270, 271, 272, 273, 274, 275, 276, 277, 278, 279, 280, 281.
Wright, Dr. A. H.	7

Y

Yankee Town	90
York, B. M.	154
Youmans, C. F.	99
Youmans, George	167
Youmans, Mrs. George R.	182
Young, John	170

BIOGRAPHIES—1824-1890

Andrews, Charles Haynes	330
Ansley, William Wesley	334
Bagley, Dr. James	336
Barber, Obediah	343
Barley, James Stacy	338
Barnes, George	342
Barnes, Mrs. George	342
Bates, Francis Asher	367
Bates, Maud Monroe	367
Beaton, James T.	335
Bennett, David Hopps	349
Bennett, John W.	341
Blackburn, Daniel	347
Blackburn Family	348
Blackshear Family	345
Brewer, Judge H. P.	350
Bridges, P. M.	351
Buchanan, C. C.	353
Buchanan, Mrs. C. C.	353
Bunn Family	354
Burnett, John	356
Cason, William	360
Carswell, Alexander	357
Carswell, Dr. Thomas James	358
Carswell, William	357
Clough, Jonathan Gilman	361
Cottingham, Robert	362
Cox, John Madison	363
Crawley, Capt. Edward	366
Crews, Bryan	369
Croom, Capt. George	370
Darling, Thomas Jefferson	371

INDEX

	Page
Denton, W. M.	373
Dunn, Charles E.	374
Elliston, George M.	375
Folks, Frank C.	376
Folks, William Barden	375
Fulwood, Thomas	383
Fulwood, Wilkins	381
Goodrich Family	387
Greer, John W.	385
Hardy Brothers	393
Hargreaves Family	389
Hilliard, Cuyler	394
Hilliard, General Thomas	395
Hinson, Alice	402
Hinson, Warren L.	401
Hitch, Simon W.	397
Izler, Dr. Robert P.	403
James Family	405
Jenkins, Mrs. Lucius	408
Johnson, Lemuel	409
Jones, James	411
Jones, W. N.	413
Jones, Mrs. W. N.	413
King, Rufus C.	415
King, Ziber	414
Kirkland, Moses	415
Kirton Family	418
Knight, Arthur M.	417
Knight, Mrs. Arthur M.	417
Knox, Capt. James	420
Lott, Dr. Daniel	422
Lott, John A.	427
Lott, Warren	425
Marshall, John M.	441
Mc or MacDonald Clan	429
McDonald, Randall	430
McDonald, William A.	432
McGee, David	442
Miller, David Jesse	446
Mizell, Messe	444
Morgan, Abraham	450
Morgan, Jonathan L.	449
Morton, Thomas	447
Murphy, Herbert	445
Murphy, Mrs. Herbert	445
Murray, Jackson S.	451
Nixon, Mrs. Alice	452
O'Neal, Mrs. Matilda	453
O'Quinn, Alexander	455
Paine, Thomas S.	468
Parker, Mrs. Mary E.	457
Parker, William	463
Parker, William F.	457
Pendleton, Louis B.	460
Pendleton, Philip C.	459
Perham, A. P.	465
Pittman, Travis	467

INDEX

	Page
Pound, Edward A.	461
Quarterman, Rev. John Way	470
Quarterman, Mrs. Laura M.	470
Redding, Mrs. Isabella	477
Redding, Dr. J. H.	478
Reed, Henry Wadsworth	481
Remshart, Rev. John W.	475
Repperd, Aaron	479
Rippard, James C.	480
Salisbury, John	483
Scruggs, Rev. William H.	485
Settle, Prof. Sterling P.	487
Sharpe, W. W.	486
Sharpe, Mrs. W. W.	486
Sirmans, Josiah	489
Smith, Joseph Dedge	492
Smith, Dr. J. E. W.	491
Smith, William D.	491
Spence, Moses W.	493
Stanton Brothers	498
Stanton, Valentine L.	495
Strickland, James W.	494
Summerall, James	502
Sweat, Capt. Burrell	503
Sweat, Cary M.	509
Sweat, Daniel	506
Sweat, Capt. James	507
Sweat, Judge J. L.	505
Thigpen Family	506
Thigpen, Travis	511
Thomas, Mrs. Amanda D.	512
Thomas, Banner H.	513
Thomas, William G.	514
Thomas, Rev. W. H.	515
Waldron, Elias S.	517
Walker, Dr. John L.	517
Warren, John Vandy	520
Wilkerson, J. J.	525
Williams, Benjamin F.	527
Williams, Jack	522
Williams, Sarah Hicks	528
Wilson, Leon	524
Wilson, William	523
Woodard, Milledge	526
Youmans, George	529

www.ingramcontent.com/pod-product-compliance
Lightning Source LLC
Chambersburg PA
CBHW020632300426
44112CB00007B/89